The History of Linguistics in Europe

Authoritative and wide-ranging, this book examines the history of western linguistics over a 2,000-year timespan, from its origins in ancient Greece up to the crucial moment of change in the Renaissance that laid the foundations of modern linguistics.

Some of today's burning questions about language date back a long way: in 400 BC Plato was asking how words relate to reality, and medieval philosophers put forward one hypothesis after another to explain the interaction of language and mind. Other questions go back just a few generations, such as our interest in the mechanisms of language change, or in the social factors that shape the way we speak. Vivien Law explores how ideas about language over the centuries have changed to reflect changing modes of thinking. A survey chapter brings the coverage of the book up to the present day.

Classified bibliographies and chapters on research resources and the qualities the historian of linguistics needs to develop provide the reader with the tools to go further.

The late VIVIEN LAW was Reader in the History of Linguistic Thought at the University of Cambridge, and Fellow of Trinity College. Her books include *The Insular Latin Grammarians* (1982), *History of Linguistic Thought in the Early Middle Ages* (1993), *Wisdom, Authority and Grammar in the Seventh Century* (1995) and *Grammar and Grammarians in the Early Middle Ages* (1997).

Vivien Law

The History of Linguistics in Europe
From Plato to 1600

CAMBRIDGE
UNIVERSITY PRESS

PUBLISHED BY THE PRESS SYNDICATE OF THE UNIVERSITY OF CAMBRIDGE
The Pitt Building, Trumpington Street, Cambridge, United Kingdom

CAMBRIDGE UNIVERSITY PRESS
The Edinburgh Building, Cambridge CB2 2RU, UK
40 West 20th Street, New York, NY 10011-4211, USA
477 Williamstown Road, Port Melbourne, VIC 3207, Australia
Ruiz de Alarcón 13, 28014 Madrid, Spain
Dock House, The Waterfront, Cape Town 8001, South Africa

http://www.cambridge.org

© Cambridge University Press 2003

This book is in copyright. Subject to statutory exception
and to the provisions of relevant collective licensing agreements,
no reproduction of any part may take place without
the written permission of Cambridge University Press.

First published 2003

Printed in the United Kingdom at the University Press, Cambridge

Typefaces Quadraat Regular 9.5/13 pt and Quadraat Sans   System $\LaTeX 2_\varepsilon$ [TB]

A catalogue record for this book is available from the British Library

Library of Congress Cataloguing in Publication data

Law, Vivien.
The history of linguistics in Europe from Plato to 1600 / Vivien Law.
  p. cm.
ISBN 0 521 56315 1 – ISBN 0 521 56532 4 (pbk)
1. Linguistics – Europe – History. I. Title. II. Series.
P81.E9 L39   2002
410'.94–dc21   2002017400

ISBN 0 521 56315 1 hardback
ISBN 0 521 56532 4 paperback

To my parents
and to the memory of Bobby Robins,
who waited a long time for this book

Contents

	List of illustrations	page x
	List of maps	xii
	List of boxes	xiii
	Preface	xv

1	**Getting ready to study the history of linguistics**	1
	1.1 What does this book cover?	1
	1.2 Getting ready	1
	1.3 What is the history of linguistics?	2
	1.4 What background knowledge do you need in order to study the history of linguistics?	2
	1.5 What do historians of linguistics do?	4
	1.6 Why study the history of linguistics?	7
	1.7 Being aware of language and doing linguistics: are they the same?	8
	Further reading	11

2	**Greek philosophy and the origins of western linguistics**	13
	2.1 Introduction	13
	2.2 Before the Greeks: the world-view of the ancient Near East	13
	2.3 The Greek discovery of the independent human intellect	15
	2.4 Plato: language as a route to reality	17
	2.5 Aristotle: language in use	23
	Further reading	33

3	**Towards a discipline of grammar: the transition from philosophy**	38
	3.1 The Stoics	38
	3.2 Varro: linguistic analysis from first principles	42
	Further reading	49

4	**From literacy to grammar: describing language structure in the ancient world**	52
	4.1 From literacy to grammar	52
	4.2 The Hellenistic world and the scholarship of Alexandria	52
	4.3 The first grammars in the West	55
	4.4 Grammar in the Roman world	58
	4.5 Quintilian and the ideal education	60
	4.6 Donatus and the *Schulgrammatik* genre	65
	4.7 After Donatus: the commentators	81
	4.8 *Regulae* grammars: foreigners and form	83
	4.9 Integrating meaning and form	86
	4.10 Priscian	86
	Further reading	91
5	**Christianity and language**	94
	5.1 The arrival of Christianity	94
	5.2 The Bible on language	99
	5.3 Medieval priorities: focus on the spiritual	108
	5.4 Form or meaning? Which branch of linguistics?	109
	Further reading	110
6	**The early Middle Ages**	112
	6.1 Linguistic thought in the Middle Ages	112
	6.2 Language as a pointer to higher things: medieval *littera* theory and correlative thinking	115
	6.3 The language policy of the Church: a push towards linguistic materialism?	124
	6.4 The linguistic conversion: creating descriptive grammars of Latin	125
	6.5 Developing an awareness of word structure: morphological metalanguage and visual representation	131
	Further reading	136
7	**The Carolingian Renaissance**	139
	7.1 The notion of 'renaissance'	139
	7.2 The Carolingian Renaissance	140
	7.3 The rediscovery of Priscian's *Institutiones grammaticae*	143
	7.4 Linking grammar with the laws of thought: the Carolingian discovery of Aristotelian logic	147
	Further reading	155
8	**Scholasticism: linking language and reality**	158
	8.1 Universities and universals	158
	8.2 Aristotle's *Physics*: from motion to phonetics and syntax	165

	8.3	Aristotle's *Metaphysics*: distinguishing the essential from the arbitrary	171
	8.4	Practical grammar	179
	8.5	A new development: making the invisible visible	182
		Further reading	185
9	**Medieval vernacular grammars**	190
	9.1	What is a vernacular grammar?	190
	9.2	Why write a vernacular grammar?	192
	9.3	Vernacular grammar in England	193
	9.4	Reforming the orthography: the Old Icelandic *First Grammatical Treatise*	199
	9.5	Thinking about the vernacular: the Occitan *Leys d'Amors*	201
		Further reading	204
10	**The Renaissance: discovery of the outer world**	210
	10.1	Turning-points in the history of linguistics	210
	10.2	Focus on the material world: training the faculty of observation	212
	10.3	The scientific mentality: collectors and dissectors	220
	10.4	The rediscovery of Classical Latin	223
	10.5	Latin: a language like any other?	230
	10.6	Ennobling the vernaculars	232
	10.7	New ways of thinking about linguistic form: Christians meet Hebrew	241
		Further reading	250
11	**A brief overview of linguistics since 1600**	258
	11.1	Introduction	258
	11.2	Looking back: main themes	258
	11.3	The process continues: observation and linguistics after 1600	260
	11.4	Linguistics in the twentieth century	272
12	**Becoming a historian of linguistics**	276
	12.1	Going further	276
	12.2	Cultivating the faculties a historian needs	276
	12.3	Ethics and the historian of linguistics: the impact of your work	279
	12.4	Ethics in working methods	281
	Research resources in the history of linguistics	284
	Notes	290
	Index	299

Illustrations

1	Raphael, *The School of Athens* (1508), Vatican	page 23
2	A Greek youth sits reading a papyrus roll (ca 470 BC), vase painting	68
3	Image from a twelfth-century copy of Martianus Capella's allegory. Florence, Biblioteca Mediceo-Laurenziana, Cod. S. Marco 190, f. 15v	103
4	Diagram of the human being as the microcosm. (Regensburg, ca 1150). Munich, Bayerische Staatsbibliothek, Clm 13002	123
5	Hereford Cathedral Library (Photo: Clive Friend, Woodmansterne)	129
6	Extract from an early medieval copy of the *Ars Ambianensis*. St Gall, Stiftsbibliothek, 877 (Switzerland, s. ix in.), p. 178 (278)	133
7	Transcription of *haec porticus* from the Bobbio manuscript. Naples, Biblioteca Nazionale, lat. 1 (Bobbio, s. vii), f. 28vb	134
8	Transcription of *haec uirtus* from the Corbie manuscript. Paris, Bibliothèque Nationale, lat. 13025 (Corbie, s. ix in.), f. 41vb	135
9	Transcription of *haec cogitatio* from the Corbie manuscript. Paris, Bibliothèque Nationale, lat. 13025 (Corbie, s. ix in.), f. 41va	135
10	Paradigms from the *Ars Bonifacii* copied out in a fine Caroline minuscule hand. Vatican City, Bibliotheca Apostolica Vaticana, Vat. Pal. Lat. 1746 (Lorsch, s. ix^1), f. 169v	141
11	Sculpture of Grammatica, one of the Seven Liberal Arts. Chartres cathedral, west portal	160
12	Representation of grammar, from Gregorius Reisch's *Margarita philosophica nova* 'New pearl of philosophy', published in Strasbourg in 1515.	161
13	Diagram from the margin of a twelfth-century English copy of Priscian's *Institutiones grammaticae* setting out the implicit structure of Priscian's discussion of pronouns (Cambridge University Library, Ii. 2. 1, f. 134r)	182
14	Diagram showing the divisions of the noun according to Priscian which was added in the twelfth century to a copy of the *Institutiones grammaticae*. Leiden, Universiteitsbibliotheek, BPL 91 (s. xii^1), f. 85r	183

xi List of illustrations

15	Paradigm from a deluxe grammar ca 1487. Reproduced from *Die 'Seligenstädter Lateinpädagogik'*, ed. M. Asztalos et al. (Stockholm: Almqvist & Wiksell International 1989), vol. 2	184
16	The opening of a Middle English syntactic treatise from Trinity College, O.5.4 (s. xv), f. 4v	198
17	Luca della Robbia's portrayal of Grammar on the bell tower of the Duomo in Florence (1437)	212
18	Artists drawing from life to prepare the illustrations for a book on plants, Leonhard Fuchs's *De historia stirpium* (Basel, 1542)	213
19	Scene from a French manuscript, ca 1300. Montpellier, Bibliothèque de la Faculté de Médecine, MS 196 (French, s. xiii ex)	216
20	Sandro Botticelli, *Annunciation* (Photo: Alinari Picture Collection)	217
21	The title page of Claude Duret's *Thresor*. Cambridge University Library	221
22	Cutaway diagram showing the organs of the vocal tract from Aquapendente's *De locutione* (1603). Cambridge University Library	224
23	The opening of Chrysoloras's *Erotemata*, his beginners' grammar of Greek in question-and-answer form (printed at Ferrara in 1509)	226
24	The beginning of William Bullokar's discussion of the verb, including his list of modal auxiliaries, reproduced in his reformed orthography from the facsimile of his *Pamphlet for Grammar* (1586) published by J. R. Turner (Leeds: The University of Leeds School of English 1980)	240
25	Diagram from Agathius Guidacerius's *Grammatica hebraicae linguae* (Rome, 1514?). Cambridge University Library	244
26	Lucas van Valckenborch, *The Tower of Babel* (1594). Musée du Louvre, Paris	262

Maps

1	Major centres of learning in Europe in Antiquity	*page* 84
2	Major centres of learning in Europe in the early Middle Ages	113
3	Major centres of learning in Europe in the later Middle Ages	159
4	Major centres of learning in Europe after the Renaissance	211
5	Early European grammars of non-European languages	222

Boxes

2.1	Language learning in the ancient Near East	page 14
2.2	Prometheus and the gift of fire	16
2.3	Nature vs convention	21
2.4	Neoplatonism	27
2.5	Early use of metalinguistic terms	30
3.1	What is a Golden Age?	39
3.2	Can we trust our sources? Diogenes Laertius on Stoic grammar	40
3.3	Pythagoras and the Pythagoreans	42
4.1	Alexander the Great, the Hellenistic world and their Byzantine heirs	53
4.2	Who wrote the *Tekhnē grammatikē*?	56
4.3	The parts of speech (word classes)	59
4.4	Terminology 1: *littera*	61
4.5	Ancient education	63
4.6	Studying under the rhetoricians: the *ars rhetorica*	64
4.7	Latin grammars wholly or partly of the *Schulgrammatik* genre	66
4.8	The ancient book	67
4.9	The virtues and vices of speech	69
4.10	Latin inflectional morphology	77
4.11	Late Latin commentators on Donatus's grammars	81
4.12	The changing Latin language	82
4.13	*Regulae* grammars	85
4.14	Apollonius Dyscolus	89
4.15	Becoming aware of transitivity	90
5.1	The Bible	95
5.2	The Church and its members	97
5.3	The Fathers of the Church	98
5.4	Interpreting the Bible: the techniques of exegesis	99
5.5	St Augustine (354–430)	100
5.6	The Seven Liberal Arts	101
5.7	Augustine's early theory of the sign	102

6.1	The Church and culture	114
6.2	The Venerable Bede: interpreting the figurative language of the Scriptures	116
6.3	The first linguistic parody	120
6.4	Macrocosm and microcosm	122
6.5	Memory and learning	127
6.6	What price grammar?	128
6.7	Terminology 2: describing the parts of a word	132
7.1	Text and manuscript	142
7.2	What's happened to all the medieval manuscripts?	144
7.3	Alcuin of York (ca 735–804)	146
7.4	Learning by asking: the parsing grammar	148
7.5	The transmission of Aristotle's writings	149
7.6	Early theories of the sign	151
8.1	From the parts to the Arts	162
8.2	Distinguishing between signification and reference	163
8.3	The twelfth-century rediscovery of Aristotle	164
8.4	Applying Aristotle's four causes to grammar	165
8.5	The first use of *subject* and *predicate*	168
8.6	Anonymous, pseudonymous – or female?	170
8.7	The Modists	174
8.8	The *modi significandi*	176
9.1	Why 'First' *Grammatical Treatise*?	200
10.1	Opening windows onto the world	214
10.2	Observation and the artist: Claude Lorrain (1600–82)	215
10.3	Becoming aware of non-verbal communication: an explorer describes a sign-language encounter	218
10.4	Early European grammars of non-European languages	219
10.5	How did the West learn Greek?	225
10.6	Linguists and printing	228
10.7	The first grammars of the vernacular	234
10.8	From Donatus's *Ars minor* to Kennedy's *Shorter Latin Primer*: the *Shorte Introduction of Grammar* by Lily and Colet	238
10.9	Grammar in the Arab world	242
10.10	Medieval grammarians of Hebrew	246
10.11	How did Jewish scholars explain the notion of root?	249
10.12	Terminology 3: root and affix	250
12.1	What do you see?	277

Preface

'You're writing a textbook on the history of linguistics? That's impossible: only a team can do it now.' That was the reaction of a French colleague when, back in 1990, I told her I was writing this book. On a practical level she was right. As the German scholar Peter Schmitter pointed out a year later,[1] the history of linguistics was then growing faster than any other subdiscipline of linguistics. Even in the late 1980s, over five hundred publications were appearing annually in the history of linguistics, more than twice as many as in syntax, semantics or phonetics, its nearest competitors. No one person can claim to have read all the literature, or even a large percentage of it, much less all the primary literature – all the writings which touch upon language, whether by philosophers, theologians, grammarians, psychologists, anatomists, educationalists or indeed linguists – from every era and every corner of Europe. We are necessarily specialists. All the same, however, most historians of linguistics have to teach. When we pluck up the courage to do so, we overcome our private panic at the torrent of secondary literature and the daunting jungle of sources, in order to guide our students to the overviews from which they can get some sense of the overall shape of the subject. Naturally we linger in our own favourite spots, hurrying past those of our colleagues with scarcely a glance. What we lose by being selective, though, we gain by becoming alive to the grand themes and recurring patterns of the 2,500 years of European intellectual history. This sense of perspective (albeit a personal one) is what disappears between the cracks in a multi-authored history, for the writers of the separate chapters are inevitably sensitive to some issues and themes and blind to others. Continuity is hard to maintain, no matter how rigorous the editor. The panoramic view enforced by teaching gives such sweeping themes a chance to emerge. Not that meticulous detailed research doesn't have a place, though: without it the generalisations would lose their authority.

So, far more than is the case with a research monograph, I must acknowledge my debt to the (usually) responsive students and colleagues who, wittingly or unwittingly, have helped to shape this book since I started to teach a course in the history of linguistics in 1981, and far more directly since 1989, when Peter Matthews suggested that I write this textbook. More particularly, the comments since 1996 of undergraduates on drafts of several chapters have helped to illuminate a number of obscurities.

Andrew Wolpert's 'Spirit of English' classes at Emerson College, East Grinstead, where I taught for two week-long blocks in 1997 and 1998, responded very differently (but no less helpfully), challenging me to explain *why* these issues mattered – something which exam-conscious Cambridge students are more prepared to take on trust. Several people have generously commented on drafts of portions of the book – Ildi Halstead, Andrew Linn, Peter Matthews, Judith Olszowy-Schlanger, R. H. Robins, Irène Rosier, Nick Shackleton and Chris Stray. Ildi, as well as spotting several infelicities of one sort or another, pointed out parallels with present-day linguistics which, by and large, I'm afraid I've left the reader to supply. Bobby Robins threw himself with gusto into the challenge of improving 'the book that is to replace me', as he put it (time will tell!). Indeed, his and Ildi's delighted response, and that of several other advance readers (not least the anonymous American reader for the publisher), is what has kept me – a researcher rather than a textbook-writer by temperament – going, for the going has been hard. Even though such recondite points as precisely which planets were in conjunction in the third week of December 1991 could (thanks in this case to Adam Perkins at the Cambridge University Library) be checked, in very many other cases the line between the verifiable (and verified) fact and the commonplace taken over from other writers had to be drawn far earlier than this pedantic perfectionist finds acceptable. Writing the history of European linguistic thought is a task of no less magnitude than a history of European literature would be. Many people have helped to make it possible: my students, who, ever since I gave my first lectures, in 1976, gently taught me to favour accessibility over erudition; fellow historians of linguistics, whose warm regard and measured judgements in encounters at conferences and over e-mail has supported me more than I can tell; the staff at the Cambridge University Library, a magnificent working environment without which this book, and the two and a half decades of research on which it is based, would have been, if not impossible, at least very much more difficult; and, last but not least, the tolerant staff at Heffers, Cambridge, who never uttered a word of complaint on seeing their bookshop used as a bibliographical resource. Many individuals have helped with points ranging from checking a reference to supplying me with relevant offprints or lending books too obscure for even the Cambridge University Library; among them are Anders Ahlqvist, Wolfram Ax, Mildred Budny, Henry Chadwick, David Cram, András Cser, Gillian Evans, Russell Evans, Suzanne Evans, Karin Margareta Fredborg, Jonathan Harrison, Louis Holtz, Ann Hutchison, Jee Yeon Jang, Simon Keynes, Tony Klijnsmit, Anneli Luhtala, John Marenbon, Ann Matonis, Brian Merrilees, Christos Nifadopoulos, Nicholas Orme, Marina Passalacqua, Fabrizio Raschellà, Irène Rosier, Vivian Salmon, John Saunders, Marion Saunders, Peter Schmitter, Pierre Swiggers, Kees Versteegh, Alfons Wouters. My thanks to them and to the numerous others who have helped and supported me, directly or indirectly, in the twelve years that this book has taken to write. The staff at the libraries whose materials have contributed directly to this book deserve thanks – the St John's College Library and the Wren Library, Trinity College, Cambridge; the British Library, London; the Bodleian Library, Oxford; Worcester Cathedral Library; the Bibliotheek der Rijksuniversiteit, Leiden; the Bayerische Staatsbibliothek, Munich; the Stiftsbibliothek, St Gallen; the Bibliothèque Nationale, Paris; the

Bibliothèque Nationale et Universitaire, Strasbourg; the Biblioteca Nazionale, Naples; the Arxiu de la Corona d'Aragò, Barcelona. Despite all the efforts of these people and institutions mistakes will no doubt remain: my fault rather than theirs. What I wanted above all was to write a book that would at once be readable and stimulate *you* to think about the implications of thinking about language. Thinking about thinking is, after all, one of the most human things we can do.

1 Getting ready to study the history of linguistics

1.1 What does this book cover?

This book is about the history of linguistics in the West from its beginnings in the fifth century BC up until 1600. Although linguistics in many cultures outside Europe – in India, the Judeo-Arab world and China, to name only three – is at least as complex and as developed as linguistics in Europe and its American cultural offshoot, this book concentrates on Europe alone. There are now a number of good introductions to the non-European linguistic traditions by specialists, and it is misleading to treat these rich traditions as if they were merely an appendage to Europe. As for the chronological coverage, you'll find that up to the Renaissance, the intellectual history of western Europe can be discussed as a fairly coherent whole (if only because of the perspective which our distant vantage-point lends us). The Renaissance constitutes a major turning-point in western history, a turning-point marked by a new-found awareness of the outer, material, world, and consequently of external differences between nations, races, languages, customs, artefacts and so on. The markers of national differences, once perceived, contributed to the ever sharper definition of distinct national ways of experiencing the world, as much in intellectual life as in any other sphere. So from about 1600 on it becomes increasingly difficult to survey the history of linguistics in Europe as a whole; rather, you really need to focus separately on England, France, Germany, the Low Countries, Sweden, Bohemia, Italy and Spain, and their mutual interaction. So that you won't be left completely up in the air in 1600, chapter 11 summarises the main developments in linguistics since then – but I hope you won't rely on that alone!

1.2 Getting ready

Because this subject is different from anything you are likely to have studied before, and uses different methodology and even different habits of thought, it will be worthwhile to make explicit some of the assumptions we shall be building on. They can be summed up in three questions:

1. What is meant by 'the history of linguistics'?
2. What background knowledge do you need in order to study the history of linguistics?
3. What do we actually do when we study the history of linguistics?

1.3 What is the history of linguistics?

Let's first get clear what it is that we are studying: what is the history of linguistics? It is *not* the history of a language, nor is it historical linguistics, the discipline which deals with the principles underlying language change; rather, the history of linguistics is the discipline which investigates what people thought about language long before we were born. It is concerned with the various forms which the discipline we call 'linguistics' took in the past, with the diverse ideas that past thinkers had about language, and with the texts in which they recorded their ideas. The history of linguistics is a branch of intellectual history, for it deals with the history of *ideas* – ideas about language – and not directly with language itself. One could argue that the natural academic home of a historian of linguistics would be a department of intellectual history; however, since intellectual historians are usually interested in the history of politics and philosophy, on the one hand, or in the history of science and medicine on the other, nearly all historians of linguistics work within departments of linguistics or languages. Like other intellectual historians, historians of linguistics work at one remove from real-world phenomena: they consider language as filtered through human cognition. Just as a historian of science isn't interested in fossils in their own right, but wants to know how scientists interpreted them in days gone by, so historians of linguistics are not directly concerned with problems like the relationship between language and reality, or how many linguistic levels there are, or the nature of ergativity; rather, they want to know how people have tackled such problems in the past. Did they ask the same questions as we do? If not, why not? What kinds of answers did they find satisfying? Do we find their answers acceptable today? Why – or why not? Essentially, then, we are dealing with *people* and their ideas about a uniquely human phenomenon.

1.4 What background knowledge do you need in order to study the history of linguistics?

Any kind of intellectual history makes considerable demands of its practitioners. Forget all those stories about history being 'easy'! To start with, you need a fair amount of historical knowledge, notably the intellectual history of the period you are studying – the trends and fashions, the buzzwords and slogans, the ideas in the air, and of course mainstream thinking in science, philosophy and religion, three areas which have played a crucial role in shaping other disciplines, linguistics included. Other kinds of history may also be helpful: political history might, for instance, account for a sudden shift in the intellectual affiliations of a particular region as the result of a military conquest. Social and economic history can help us to understand events such as the spread of literacy, the growth of print culture, and changes in the availability of education, all of which have consequences for the history of linguistics. And of course an awareness of the changing linguistic map of Europe is vitally important: how can you hope to understand what Dante said about the Romance languages if you have no idea of the linguistic situation in his day? The first requirement of the historian of linguistics is thus a basic knowledge of all relevant branches of history. For our purposes, however, relatively little historical knowledge is assumed in this book. To fill in possible historical gaps, boxes signalled here and there in the text will introduce the background knowledge needed to place the history of linguistics in context, from Pythagoras and the Seven Liberal Arts to printing and the price of grammar books. There are also boxes that explain the history of certain terms and concepts, and boxes that explain who first came up with a particular idea.

The second fundamental requirement of a historian of linguistics is a knowledge of some form of contemporary linguistics. If you know nothing at all about modern ideas about language, whether in the form of traditional grammar or comparative philology, or in the guise of the latest syntactic or phonological theories, then you will probably find it difficult to make sense of what people were saying about language even two hundred years ago, let alone twelve hundred years back. Given the diversity of people's backgrounds, technical terminology will be kept to a minimum in this book, but some awareness of the language of traditional grammar will be assumed. (If any of the technical terms puzzle you, a basic dictionary of linguistics such as those listed in the bibliography to this chapter (pp. 11–12 below) will help to demystify the jargon.)

Thirdly, it helps to have a reading knowledge of the language or languages relevant to the themes and periods you are studying. Even a linguist of world renown like Noam Chomsky laid himself open to criticism when he made his first foray into the history of linguistics (*Cartesian Linguistics: A Chapter in the History of Rationalist Thought* (1966)) because of his apparent failure to realise that many of the seventeenth-century thinkers he was studying – and some he overlooked – published some of their most important works in Latin. Consequently, the picture he painted of the linguistic thinking of the period was inadvertently distorted, drawing as it did only upon French-language texts. You are about to embark upon a programme of study which will introduce you to texts written in a number of European languages: Ancient Greek and Latin, Old English, Old Icelandic, Occitan, French, German, Italian, Spanish, Hebrew and others besides. Because few people can read all these languages, you'll find passages from relevant texts quoted in translation in this book to give you an idea of their flavour, and references to published translations are to be found in the bibliographies. Many of the most important linguistic texts from ancient Greece and Rome have been translated into English. By contrast, linguistic literature from the Middle Ages and the Renaissance has tended to be overlooked by translators. As for secondary literature, where the professional historian of linguistics should be able to read articles in the five 'conference languages' at least – English, French, German, Spanish and Italian – you will find references in the bibliographies to materials in these and occasionally other languages. No one expects you, as a student, to read them all! By and large, you'll find you can get a long way with English alone, but to go more deeply into certain areas, you may well need to branch out into foreign-language materials. I've sometimes supplemented references to English-language materials in the bibliographies with references to articles in other languages which overlap to a greater or lesser extent with English-language materials, to maximise your chances of finding relevant material. Occasionally, where there are few or no relevant publications in English, foreign-language materials predominate.

The basic prerequisites for a historian of linguistics are thus a grasp of the main historical and cultural developments in the period under study; a basic knowledge of at least one model of linguistics; and a command of the relevant languages. Does this sound like a tall order? Compare it with what one distinguished scholar, the late Yakov Malkiel (well known for his work in Romance philology), considered necessary:

Perhaps the four most desirable conditions for developing satisfactory working habits as a historian of linguistics are to have personally witnessed the rise and decline of one or more fashions; to have lived in several countries long enough to have absorbed their disparate intellectual climates, from grammar school to university seminar; to have cultivated, with a certain alacrity, more than one major genre of linguistic investigation; and to have focused attention, at least during one's years of apprenticeship, on a period definitely closed, with whose chief protagonists the writer has not been so closely involved, in terms of personal relations, as to have developed any bias, be it animus or subservience.[1]

Rather few historians of linguistics (apart from Malkiel himself) measure up to this demanding list! In practice historians of linguistics come from a wide range of backgrounds, and the subject is all the richer for the diversity of knowledge, questions, assumptions and approaches that they bring with them.

1.5 What do historians of linguistics do?

History – any kind of history – isn't just a matter of chronicling what happened when: that is only the beginning. The interesting part comes when you start asking *why*. Only when you ask why something happened at a particular time, in a particular place, involving those particular people, do you start to see patterns and to make connections; it is only then that history begins to make sense. What kind of answer do you give to a 'Why?' question? It's not like asking 'Who?' or 'What?' or 'Where?' or 'When?', which invite very limited answers. 'How?' allows rather more scope, but 'Why?' is the freest of all. If you ask, 'Why did the Soviet Union collapse?', you are free to give all kinds of answers. You might, for instance, invoke economic or political factors such as the breakdown of the command economy and increasing pressure from zones of interethnic conflict. An earlier generation of historians would have attached greater importance to the personalities involved, and might have tried to explain it in terms of the conflicting ambitions of individuals such as Mikhail Gorbachev, Eduard Shevardnadze and Boris Yeltsin. Still another historian might see it as the inevitable consequence of the artificial imposition of an unworkable totalitarian ideology. But no contemporary academic historian would say, 'Because Mercury was in conjunction with Mars.' That is not a valid answer according to present-day academic habits of thought. Yet such an answer would have been acceptable in some scholarly circles as late as the end of the seventeenth century. So the kind of answer that one gives to a 'Why?' question depends very much on the intellectual climate of the time. It is coloured by the cargo of assumptions and prejudices that we all carry around with us. To become a good historian it is essential to become aware of these assumptions, or of as many of them as possible. Only if you are aware of at least a few of your own assumptions can you begin to understand someone else's way of thought – a way of thought which might be based upon quite different assumptions. This does not mean that you have to drop your present-day assumptions when studying the history of linguistics, and still less that you should adopt those of another age. What matters is that you should be able to imagine what it would feel like to hold a different view. (The White Queen's comment in *Through the Looking Glass* would be good training for any intellectual historian: 'Why, sometimes I've believed as many as six impossible things before breakfast.' Just make sure that you know they are impossible!) Very many people believed that the world would come to an end in the year 1000: how would you behave if you *knew* for sure, as surely as you know the sun will rise tomorrow, that the world will self-destruct on the first of January? If you can live with that idea for a few minutes, you will be better placed to understand the mass panic that gripped people as the year 1000 approached.

Of course, it's not just a matter of empathising with the period you are studying, although it is important to do so if you are to arrive at any understanding of it. Another very real problem is that our prejudices and prior knowledge to a large extent determine what we notice – and overlook. Einstein once remarked, 'It is the theory which decides what we can observe.' Of course, if that were always true, we would not be able to see anything unexpected; but in order to notice things which don't fit in with our preconceived notions we have to wake up to what these notions are and what they exclude. Ideally, we will adopt an approach closer to the working methods of an anthropologist. Anthropologists go to a foreign environment and join in the life of people there, trying to figure out the inner logic behind the way in which they organise and justify their way of life. Since the best way of learning how something works is to try it out oneself, anthropologists relearn how to think, using the logic and assumptions of the people under study. They 'try on' these unfamiliar habits of thought and live with them for a while, before returning home to analyse them. Ideally that is how we should behave as historians; but we have a problem the anthropologist does not have to face: we can't buy ourselves a ticket to Renaissance Italy or Anglo-Saxon England. Instead, we have to proceed by cultivating the anthropologist's attitude to the written texts which are our informants: we need to learn to listen to what they say with openness and acceptance. That doesn't mean that we have to accept every statement as true in our world, for much of what we read will be quite unacceptable – wrong – in the context of today's linguistics. Nonetheless, by asking what it was like to hold that 'wrong' belief we may well achieve a deeper understanding of the past than we will by sneering at it. Let's take an example. Throughout the Middle Ages and well into the sixteenth century, Jews, Muslims and Christians, scholars and lay people alike, believed – *knew* – that there were precisely seventy-two languages in the world – no more and no fewer. As historians, we can respond to this in two ways. We can say (as did many historians of an earlier generation): 'Oh, how stupid! It's obvious that there are more than seventy-two languages. Couldn't they just count up all the languages they knew about?' In reacting like this you create a barrier within yourself out of your superiority and your preconceptions, and in so doing you cut yourself off from the possibility of understanding why people held that view, and what its consequences were. Alternatively, you can try to suspend judgement for a moment and ask yourself what assumptions about the world you need to hold in order to believe that there are, always have been and always will be seventy-two languages. You will probably have a different view of time and of processes of change from ours. Your ideas about how languages originate and diversify will not be those held by linguistics professionals today. In short, your mental universe will be quite different from that of a person living in present-day Europe or the English-speaking world. How might your ideas come to change? Imagine that you are living in the sixteenth century, with the fact that the world contains seventy-two languages a secure part of your knowledge about the world. As you grow up, one explorer after another returns from expeditions with reports of yet more totally unexpected languages. After a while, it dawns on you that the tally of languages must surely exceed seventy-two. You count them up, and sure enough, the total is well over the time-hallowed number. What do you do now that the empirical data conflict with inherited knowledge? It's not easy to set aside a fact passed down for many centuries with the weight of authority behind it. (How do you feel when you are told that something you were taught at school is wrong?) You might begin to think more critically about the issues surrounding linguistic diversity. Where have all these languages come from? Are they really languages in the full sense of the word, or could some of them be dismissed as mere dialects? Could one 'save the appearances' by giving more careful attention to the distinction between 'language' and 'dialect'? Could some of these languages be explained away as transformed versions of older or newer ones? But help! That would imply that languages change through time. As sixteenth- and seventeenth-century thinkers grappled with these questions they gradually arrived at many of the concepts and ways of thought which underlie today's historical linguistics. That belief in seventy-two languages, so easy for us to deride, was in fact enormously stimulating and creative: today's historical linguistics would not be the same without it.

We, as historians, would miss all that if we simply dismissed such a notion as 'wrong-headed' and 'naive' and hurried on to something more 'scientific' (i.e. closer to what we ourselves believe). By projecting our own beliefs and our own criteria of scientificity onto the past we miss much more than we see. If we are to learn anything in the course of our reading, we should approach each text with an attitude something like this: 'This text made sense when it was written. How should I read it in order to appreciate what it meant to its author and the people it was written for?'

In order to enter into any text from the past intelligently, you need two qualities, empathy and knowledge. Empathy you cultivate within yourself; knowledge is what this textbook is meant to bring you. The more background knowledge you can acquire about each period you study, the better: exhibitions, visits to historical sites and exhibitions, museums and galleries, books about cultural and intellectual history, other works written during the era under study – all these help you to develop a sense of how people thought and felt and related to the world in the epochs that we shall be considering. How people thought about language in any era is closely paralleled by their way of thinking about the world at large. So from time to time in this book you will find comments about the world-view of a particular age. Without that sort of background knowledge, the history of linguistics runs the risk of turning into a listing of theories and 'discoveries', the intellectual historian's equivalent of the much-derided 'battles and dates' of the traditional historian.

1.6 Why study the history of linguistics?

Justifying the history of linguistics in an age concerned above all with relevance and cost-effectiveness isn't easy. How can one claim that the past is 'relevant' to the present when countless people are getting on perfectly well without knowing about it? Historians like to trot out the old saying, 'Those who forget their history are doomed to relive it'; at one level, this may be true, but are present-day phoneticians or syntacticians really going to make the same mistakes as their fourteenth-century predecessors? Even if their conclusions look superficially similar, they will have been reached by very different routes. Other historians claim that studying history will give you new ways of solving contemporary problems. It's an attractive idea, but I have yet to come across a single present-day linguist who admits to having found the answer to a current problem in old books. Today's linguists, like scholars in every other discipline, pride themselves on their ingenuity and originality. Only when they have worked out a solution themselves do they begin to wonder whether anyone else ever had the same idea. So knowing about the history of linguistics is likely to be of *direct* use to the practising linguist only marginally, if at all. The real reasons for studying the subject lie deeper than that.

Each of us assumes that our experience of the world is uniquely well-rounded; other people are one-sided and a bit blinkered. As we get older, we realise that everyone secretly holds the same view: even your best friend perceives you as one-sided. Just as it is easier to see someone else's one-sidedness than one's own, so whole generations assume that their particular way of looking at the world is the only right one. We lose a great deal by going along with this collective one-sidedness. We sleep through many areas of experience, dismissing them with easy put-downs: 'Unscientific!' 'Materialistic!' 'Just so much religious fantasising!' 'Leftist hogwash!' 'It's all psychological!' And that all-purpose label drawn like a heavy dusty curtain across one thing after another, blocking out a ray of light just waiting to fall upon some neglected corner of experience: '*Boring!*' If we become aware of how one generation is utterly convinced of the centrality of its priorities, only to see their children plunge with equal intensity into a totally different approach to life, we learn to beware of complacently accepting – or worse still, parading – our one-sidedness in a world which confronts us with ever more subtle issues. By 'trying on' the ideas of a great range of people from the past we cultivate an ability to see things from another person's point of view, a skill which we can carry over into everyday life.

And that sense of perspective should help us to find our right place in time too. Of course we see the whole of history as conspiring to bring about the present, and in a sense this is true. At the same time, though, we are part of a present which is conspiring to bring about a whole series of futures; we are in transition, just as much as every past era was part of a process of transition and change leading ultimately to us. If in studying the history of linguistics we avoid the temptation to focus only on the bits that foreshadow our own preoccupations, but look too at the ideas which didn't live on to the present, we will develop a much stronger sense of the ebb and flow of ideas, an ebb and flow of which we are part, just as our predecessors were.

All this applies equally well to any branch of intellectual history. What does the history of linguistics have to offer that one could not find just as well in the history of philosophy, or the history of science, or the history of anything else? As our academic disciplines are organised at present, there is a gap right at their heart. What discipline deals with the human being? Anatomy, biochemistry and molecular biology deal with the physical structure and substance of the body; physiology, biology and genetics with life processes; psychology with the mind and emotions; anthropology and sociology with human interaction and organisation; philosophy with man's place in the universe; and theology with man's relationship to the spiritual; but no single discipline brings all these together. If we were to study the history of all these disciplines, we would be able to grasp how our view of the human being has changed through time. We would be better able to understand why our picture of the human being is so disjointed, and to take the first steps towards restoring its lost wholeness. In practice, though, who is in a position to understand the development of disciplines as diverse as anatomy, psychology and theology? Despite its fragmentation into subdisciplines, linguistics offers us a short cut, for language (as linguists are fond of saying) mirrors the nature of man. From its physical basis in the vocal tract and sound waves to its life in human interaction and its potential for awakening knowledge of the invisible and the unspoken, language encapsulates the diversity which characterises the human being. Consequently, views about language are a guide to views of man; by studying the history of linguistics, we can form a pretty good idea of how people saw the human being in any given epoch. The one-sidedness that we perceive in the past warns us to be alert to the one-sidedness of the present: where is our understanding lacking? Can this be remedied? Can we heal the disjointedness? It is here that the history of linguistics has something to offer which no other branch of intellectual history can.

1.7 Being aware of language and doing linguistics: are they the same?

Linguistics entails a way of thinking which is abstract, analytical and systematic. To think about language in this manner we have to stand back from it and reify it, making it into an object 'out there'. That is a paradox, for language cannot exist without us. Yet to carry out all those analytical procedures that we take for granted – to think of language as a system independent of the speaker, or to divide a word into morphemes, or to represent a sentence diagrammatically – is to take a step away from the reality of our daily experience. This process of distancing ourselves from the phenomena is so much a part of our modern way of thinking that we do so unquestioningly, totally accepting the inherent paradox.

But there are still some places in the world where this is regarded as a strange thing to do. And if you go back far enough in history, you come to a time when no one thought in this way. And yet, even in the most ancient times from which records have come down to us, people were very much aware of language. This stanza from a hymn in the *Rig Veda*, one of the collections of hymns for use in the Brahmin rituals of ancient India early in the first millennium BC, gives us a glimpse of a totally different experience of language:

Speech was divided into four parts that the inspired priests know. Three parts, hidden in deep secret, humans do not stir into action; the fourth part of Speech is what men speak.[2]

Our modern intellectuality can make very little of this. What are the four parts of speech? Why can we not activate three of them? What is meant by 'stirring into action'?

The association of speech and action is central to very ancient texts. Compare this passage from an Egyptian creation myth:

Thus all the gods were formed . . . Indeed, all the divine order really came into being through what the heart thought and the tongue commanded. Thus the *ka*-spirits were made and the *hemsut*-spirits were appointed, they who make all provisions and all nourishment, by this speech . . . Thus life was given to him who has peace and death was given to him who has sin. Thus were made all work and all crafts, the action of the arms, the movement of the legs, and the activity of every member, in conformance with this command which the heart thought, which came forth through the tongue, and which gives value to everything.[3]

It is the performative aspect of speech, its ability to bring about an effect in the world, which is celebrated in these very ancient writings. The power of speech – not, of course, the debased words of everyday speech, but the divine creative Word – to bring the world itself into existence is the example *par excellence*; but even in later literature, such as the epics of Homer, it is the performative function of speech which is stressed. (Curiously, this is an aspect of language which has only recently been taken up into modern linguistics via the subdiscipline of pragmatics, although it was studied for many centuries as an aspect of rhetoric.) In texts such as these it is clear that we are not dealing with linguistics. Speech is here being *experienced*; the self-conscious *distancing* from it which makes intellectual study possible has not yet taken place. The experience of the mysterious creative power of speech is universal; not so the distancing which leads to linguistics. Virtually all peoples have myths in which the Word creates, and most peoples have myths about the origin of human speech. But that does not lead to the development of linguistics. Nor does it follow that contact with speakers of foreign languages necessarily brings about the appearance of linguistics, any more than literacy inevitably leads to it. Granted, the analysis required to create a phonemic writing system is a very sophisticated kind of analysis; yet it seems to take place at a partly conscious level. There is not a single case of the invention of a writing system leading directly to the more detailed investigation of phonetics, phonology or linguistics in general; rather, literate peoples tend to ascribe the origins of their writing system to a mythical demigod, as if to underscore the small part played by the consciously reasoning mind.

Let us take two examples:

1. The ancient Egyptians were able to write before 3000 BC, but in the course of the first 2,500 years of their civilisation they wrote nothing that has come down to us

about the structure of their language or other linguistic issues. Only when they came into contact with the Greeks, who by the end of the first millennium BC had developed a lively tradition of language-consciousness, did the Egyptians begin to think and write about their language.

2. The Jews were able to write from early in the first millennium BC, and their culture was a highly literate one, with not only the Torah and other religious texts being recorded in writing from very early times, but also extensive law codes, commentaries upon religious and legal texts, edifying tales and many other works. Yet they wrote almost nothing that one could regard as linguistics until the tenth century AD, after they had come into contact with the Arabs and their flourishing tradition of philosophical and grammatical thinking. But the Jews were well able to solve practical problems of a linguistic nature. Early in the Christian era, for instance, Jewish scholars realised that the lack of vowel signs in the Hebrew alphabet was a great inconvenience, for Hebrew, the language of the Scriptures and of religious ritual, was no longer anyone's native language, and young people were increasingly uncertain about which vowel went where. They therefore devised a quite complex system of vowel signs which they described in detailed treatises. But this did not immediately lead to anything more. The practical problem which confronted that generation of scholars had found a solution: an appropriate linguistic 'technology' had been devised without recourse to linguistic 'science', so to speak. So dealing with a practical linguistic problem does not necessarily lead to the development of linguistics.

Nor can we say that possessing the terminology needed to talk about language – *metalanguage* – is necessarily a sign of a nascent linguistics. It has been said that all speech communities have the basic terminology needed for everyday metalinguistic discourse. This basic terminology includes words for:

> sentence/saying/utterance
> word/name
> sound/letter
> vowel
> consonant

To take the further step required to develop a technical language which can cope with all the peculiarities of a natural language entails a very substantial conceptual leap – the leap from using language instinctively to thinking about it consciously and systematically. Language is so much a part of ourselves that this act of distancing oneself from it in order to study it is often experienced as something quite painful: how many children *enjoy* learning grammar, no matter how imaginatively they are taught it? The desire to abstract and generalise, and thereby to construct a systematic description of a language, is not necessarily connected with a practical need (although it may be). There are millions of people around the world today who have learnt to speak a second language fluently and grammatically without ever having opened a grammar book; untold millions in the past accomplished the same feat. So what is it that makes people take the step of standing back and distancing themselves from language in order to think about it?

Further reading

Surveys of the history of linguistics

Vivien Law, 'Language and its students: the history of linguistics', in N. E. Collinge, ed., *An Encyclopaedia of Linguistics* (London: Routledge 1990), pp. 784–842.

R. H. Robins, *A Short History of Linguistics*, 4th edn (London and New York: Longman 1997).

Giulio C. Lepschy, ed., *History of Linguistics*, 4 vols. so far published in English and one more forthcoming (London and New York: Longman 1994–); Italian original *Storia della Linguistica*, 3 vols. (Bologna: il Mulino 1990–4).

Sylvain Auroux, ed., *Histoire des idées linguistiques*, 2 vols. so far published (Liège and Brussels: Mardaga 1989–).

Peter Schmitter, ed., *Geschichte der Sprachtheorie*, various vols. so far published (Tübingen: Narr 1987–).

E. F. K. Koerner and R. E. Asher, eds., *Concise History of the Language Sciences From the Sumerians to the Cognitivists* (Oxford and New York: Pergamon 1995).

P. Seuren, *Western Linguistics: An Historical Introduction* (Oxford: Blackwell 1998). [Relatively brief on eras before the twentieth century; provocatively critical on twentieth-century developments.]

Sylvain Auroux et al., eds., *History of the Language Sciences: An International Handbook on the Evolution of the Study of Language from the Beginnings to the Present* (Berlin and New York: de Gruyter 2000). [Articles in English, French and German.]

Dictionaries and encyclopedias of linguistics

Hadumod Bussmann, ed., *Routledge Dictionary of Language and Linguistics* (London: Routledge 1996).

David Crystal, *A Dictionary of Linguistics and Phonetics*, 4th edn (Oxford: Blackwell 1997).

David Crystal, *The Penguin Dictionary of Language*, 2nd edn (London: Penguin 1999).

Geoffrey Finch, *Linguistic Terms and Concepts* (London: Palgrave 2000).

P. H. Matthews, *The Concise Oxford Dictionary of Linguistics* (Oxford and New York: Oxford University Press 1997).

R. L. Trask, *A Student's Dictionary of Language and Linguistics* (London: Arnold 1997).

R. L. Trask, *Key Concepts in Language and Linguistics* (London and New York: Routledge 1999).

R. E. Asher and J. M. Y. Simpson, eds., *Encyclopedia of Language and Linguistics*, 10 vols. (Oxford: Pergamon 1994).

N. E. Collinge, ed., *An Encyclopaedia of Language* (London and New York: Routledge 1990).

David Crystal, ed., *The Cambridge Encyclopedia of Language*, 2nd edn (Cambridge University Press 1997).

Kirsten Malmkjaer, ed., *The Linguistics Encyclopedia* (London: Routledge 1991).

Linguistics outside Europe

Giulio C. Lepschy, ed., *History of Linguistics I: The Eastern Traditions of Linguistics* (London and New York: Longman 1994); Italian original *Storia della Linguistica*, vol. 1 (Bologna: il Mulino 1990), pp. 29–185.

Sylvain Auroux, ed., *Histoire des idées linguistiques 1: La naissance des métalangages en Orient et en Occident* (Liège and Brussels: Mardaga 1989).

Kees Versteegh, *Landmarks in Linguistic Thought 3: The Arabic Linguistic Tradition* (London and New York: Routledge 1997).

Georges Bohas, Jean-Patrick Guillaume and Djemal E. Kouloughli, *The Arabic Linguistic Tradition* (New York and London: Routledge 1990).

Hartmut Scharfe, *A History of Indian Literature 5.2: Grammatical Literature* (Wiesbaden: Harrassowitz 1977).

R. A. Miller, 'The Far East', in Thomas A. Sebeok, ed., *Current Trends in Linguistics 13.2: Historiography of Linguistics* (The Hague: Mouton 1975), pp. 1213–64.

Ancient myths about language

The Rig Veda: An Anthology, transl. W. D. O'Flaherty (Harmondsworth: Penguin 1981), hymns 10.71; 10.125; 1.164.

Arno Borst, *Der Turmbau von Babel: Geschichte der Meinungen über Ursprung und Vielfalt der Sprachen und Völker*, 4 vols. (Stuttgart: Hiersemann 1957–63), vol. 1.

2 Greek philosophy and the origins of western linguistics

2.1 Introduction

Without the Greeks of the fifth and fourth centuries BC western civilisation as we know it today would be unimaginable. It was the Greeks who laid the foundations of virtually all the scholarly disciplines cultivated up to the Renaissance – grammar, rhetoric, dialectic, arithmetic, geometry, music and astronomy, not to mention philosophy, literary criticism and medicine – as well as of almost all the literary genres practised to this day. The Greeks were the first Europeans to study language systematically, and not only that: they identified many of the issues which have occupied linguists down to the present day – the origin of language, the nature of the linguistic sign, the relationship between language, thought, and reality, and that between sound and meaning, the causes of language change, and the analysis and description of linguistic structure. It is extraordinary that in the space of three generations a small group of people could set the agenda for much of the subsequent intellectual history of the West, and of western linguistics in particular. How did this come about? Why were the Greeks so different from their predecessors? The Greek way of looking at language follows naturally from their newly emerging world outlook, and that outlook was very different from anything that had previously existed.

2.2 Before the Greeks: the world-view of the ancient Near East

Great civilisations had come and gone in the ancient Near East long before the rise of the Greeks: in the third millennium BC, the Sumerians and Akkadians; in the second millennium, the Hurrians and Hittites; extending on into the first millennium, the Babylonians, Assyrians, Elamites and Egyptians; and in the first millennium BC, the Persians. The Greeks saw themselves as differing in fundamental ways from these ancient eastern civilisations. Apart from the cruelty and licentious living with which the Greeks regularly charged them, oriental peoples seemed to relate very differently to their environment. They regarded their rulers as embodiments of their gods, and in such

> **Box 2.1 Language learning in the ancient Near East**
>
> In the third millennium BC the Sumerian language, a non-Indo-European language typologically similar to some present-day Caucasian languages, was used as the medium of diplomacy and record throughout the powerful kingdom of Sumer, which was situated between Baghdad and the Persian Gulf in what is now Iraq, and far beyond its frontiers as well. Long after Sumer had given way to the empires of Babylonia and Assyria and its language had died out as a mother tongue, Sumerian continued to be used as a literary and administrative language by speakers of unrelated, mostly Semitic, languages. How did the scribes responsible for keeping records and writing letters learn it? There were no grammars; instead, glossaries were compiled, organised sometimes by subject, sometimes by sound. Occasionally lists of verb forms were drawn up, or even of bound morphemes, with parallel translation into another language: Babylonian, Assyrian, Akkadian, Elamite. Language learning was treated as a lexicological problem: each word form was listed and learnt separately with its translation. No rules – generalisations from a specific data set to other analogous cases – were formulated. It was the Greeks who first made generalisations about language.
>
> *Reading*
>
> E. Reiner and others, 'Linguistics in the ancient Near East', in Giulio Lepschy, ed., *History of Linguistics 1: The Eastern Traditions of Linguistics* (London and New York: Longman 1994), ch. 3 (pp. 61–96).
>
> K. Van Lerberghe, 'Language in Sumer and Akkad', in Pierre Swiggers and Alfons Wouters, eds., *Le langage dans l'Antiquité* (Leuven and Paris: Peeters 1990), pp. 47–55.
>
> Antoine Cavigneaux, 'L'écriture et la réflexion linguistique en Mésopotamie', in Sylvain Auroux, ed., *Histoire des idées linguistiques 1. La naissance des métalangages en Orient et en Occident* (Liège and Brussels: Mardaga 1989), pp. 99–118.

theocracies human reason played but a minor role. Natural phenomena were perceived as the result of divine activity, arbitrary, unfathomable and overwhelming. In these circumstances, neither science nor even intellectual inquiry as we now understand them could arise, for they are based upon the premise that the world is inherently intelligible. Babylonian and Egyptian advances in practical domains such as irrigation, surveying, architecture, astronomy and even grammar (see box 2.1) demonstrate how expertly these peoples could solve the immediate problems before them; but to proceed from the particular data before them to abstract generalisations applicable to many different situations is a step they did not take. After all, if each event depended upon the will of an apparently capricious and unpredictable deity, how could one hope to learn anything worthwhile by studying the phenomena, which were by definition arbitrary? Far better to concentrate on the practical task of propitiating the gods. Because of this preoccupation with immediate practical problems, the intellectual activity of the ancient Near East comes closer to what we understand by technology than to science in the modern sense. Craftsmen of the ancient Near East often employed techniques which in our culture presuppose an extensive body of scientific knowledge; yet the medical procedure of trepanning, and the complex skills required for the orientation and construction of the Great Pyramid at Gizeh, were developed and applied without any such theoretical underpinning. Nor did the exercise of these practical skills and techniques create a desire for theoretical knowledge for its own sake.

Some Greeks, such as the famous historian Herodotus and the philosopher-initiate Pythagoras, travelled to the great centres of Egypt and the Near East to imbibe the ancient wisdom guarded there; but for a great many Greeks, their only knowledge of these civilisations came from trade and travellers' tales. In the early years of the fifth century BC a new form of contact came: war. The Persian empire was then the greatest state in the Near East. In the second half of the sixth century it had incorporated all of Asia Minor (modern Turkey), including the Greek colonies on the Aegean coast, and in the 490s and 480s the Persians and their allies made repeated attacks on Greece. All the troops of that vast empire could not withstand the defence offered by a relatively small number of determined Greeks, and in 480 BC the Persians were driven back into Asia.

2.3 The Greek discovery of the independent human intellect

The Greek victory over the might of the Persians signals the onset of a change in the way in which people perceived and related to the world around them, inner and outer. Up to the time of the Persian wars, the Greeks had lived in a mental world very remote from our own, and not dissimilar to that of their eastern neighbours – a world peopled by gods and demigods. Consequently, they perceived external phenomena like the weather quite differently. If you heard thunder, you didn't explain it in terms of hot and cold fronts and electrical charges; rather, you said to yourself, 'Zeus is thundering.' Or if you saw a rainbow, you knew that Iris, the messenger of the gods, was tripping down her bridge to earth on a divine errand. Where we think of an invisible natural force – gravity, magnetism, instinct – the early Greeks, like their eastern neighbours, saw divine activity.

But even in the earliest texts that have survived from Greece, the Homeric epics (the *Iliad* and the *Odyssey*) of the eighth century BC, the Greek gods are never as inexorable and overpowering as those of the Persians and Egyptians; they may recommend a particular course of action and punish an individual who disobeys them, but they do not compel human beings to do their will. In the *Iliad*, the goddess Athena announces to Achilles: 'I have come down from heaven to put a stop to your wrath – if you consent.'[1] Humans have free will; the gods are no longer all-powerful. Greek literature from the eighth to the fourth century BC depicts a gradual awakening to independence and freedom of action. Guided rather than commanded by the gods in the *Iliad*, counselled by friends in the *Odyssey*, sometimes advised and sometimes reproached by the chorus in the tragedies of Aeschylus, Euripides and Sophocles, in the end human beings are left to their own resources, deep in thought. This withdrawal of divine guidance – for so it seemed to them – could have been perceived as a shattering loss, but in general it was not. The Greeks did not accuse the gods of having left them helpless and without protection;

> **Box 2.2 Prometheus and the gift of fire**
>
> As the story is told in Hesiod's *Theogony* (seventh century BC), and in the drama *Prometheus Bound*, traditionally ascribed to Aeschylus (fifth century BC), Prometheus was one of the great benefactors of mankind. He taught human beings to build houses and make tools, to plant crops and tame animals, to write and to observe the stars, to make medicines and mine metals. But one thing was still missing: fire. Without fire there could be no cooking, no heating and no working of metals. To bring fire to mankind was a risky undertaking, however, for Zeus, king of the gods, had decreed that anyone who dared to do so would be severely punished. Nonetheless, Prometheus, with the help of Athena, goddess of wisdom, managed to catch a spark from the sungod's chariot and brought it down to Earth. His punishment was indeed terrible: he was chained to a mountain in the Caucasus to await the eagle which arrived every day to tear out his liver. Every night his liver regrew, ready for attack the next day, until after many ages had passed, Prometheus was finally rescued by Heracles (Hercules is the Latin form of his name), son of Zeus.
>
> Ancient myths and legends have many layers of meaning which later generations discovered as they lived with them. One interpretation of this story is this. Prometheus (whose name means 'forethought') was reputed to possess a kind of clairvoyance through which he could predict the future. The fire that he gave mankind, however, was a quite different kind of capacity: the power of rational thought. For rational thought to develop fully, traditional clairvoyance had to be suppressed, and indeed, although it has lingered on down to the present day in such places as the Scottish Isles, in most of Europe and those parts of the world dominated by European culture it vanished centuries ago. The beginnings of this process took place in ancient Greece.
>
> *Reading*
> Peter Kingsley, *In the Dark Places of Wisdom* (Inverness, CA: The Golden Sufi Center 1999). [This unusual book evokes a very vivid picture of what it might have been like to experience the prerational consciousness that prevailed in Greece and elsewhere before the fifth century BC.]

instead, the myth of Prometheus and the story of Odysseus point to a compensatory factor, the development of the intellect (see box 2.2). The 'fire' of the intellect (fire is traditionally associated with the intellect in many cultures worldwide), stolen from heaven by the demigod Prometheus for man's benefit, is the quality which the Greeks developed above all others.

From around 600 BC the old certainty that the gods were responsible for everything in the universe gave way to intensive questioning. If the gods were not directly, 'personally', responsible for all events on earth, how did things happen? What forces were responsible? If reality was no longer simply the actions of the gods in the world, what was it? Surely not the material objects we see around us, for those are subject to decay and destruction. Today's daisy will not exist in a week's time; if we wait long enough, today's mountains will become plains and today's plains mountains. What is reality? Is there any absolute reality? Or is everything arbitrary, random and subject to chance?

The Greeks threw themselves into this problem, so new in western history, with all the enthusiasm and keenness they could muster. It was discussed at every level of society and from every conceivable point of view. In Ionia, a zone of Greek settlements on the Aegean coast of what is now Turkey, and in the Greek colonies in southern Italy, a series of natural philosophers (as people who studied the natural world used to be called; the word 'scientist' only appeared in 1840, coined by the Cambridge mathematician William Whewell) began to apply their lively intellects to the question. These individuals, the so-called *pre-Socratic philosophers*, sought to identify the essential principles which underlie all earthly phenomena. What was actually stable and eternal when everything seemed subject to change? As they pondered this problem, a new phenomenon emerged: intellectual disagreement. As long as everyone was aware of the activity of the gods, they shared the same knowledge, but once they began to unfold their own thinking, different people could – and did – arrive at different conclusions. As the generations passed, one thinker after another put forward his view of the universe. Pythagoras and his followers, in southern Italy, sought to grasp the proportions and harmonies inherent in the universe in terms of numerical relations. In Ionia, Heraclitus regarded change as fundamental, while Parmenides emphasised stability. Empedocles stressed the interplay of four primary elemental substances, fire, air, water and earth. Leucippus and Democritus posited the materialistic theory of atomism: only two things exist – the void and atoms, infinitely numerous indivisible particles. The proliferation of so many apparently conflicting hypotheses, each of them energetically defended, drew attention to a fundamental philosophical question: it is all very well to speculate about the nature of reality, but how can we claim to *know* anything about it? What does it mean to know something, and how do we acquire knowledge? Far from sweeping this awkward question aside, the Greeks brought all their intellectual skills to its solution in the decades around 400 BC. Ultimately every teacher might feel himself to be threatened by the implications of this debate; in practice, those most deeply involved were teachers of rhetoric and argumentation, the Sophists. At their best perspicuous thinkers, at their worst purveyors of empty verbal trickery (hence our disparaging term 'sophistry'), the Sophists found their confident claim to impart knowledge challenged by an able opponent, Socrates (ca 469–399 BC). This unprepossessing man, a snub-nosed midwife's son with protruding eyes, is one of those remarkable figures who wrote nothing himself, but was vastly more influential than all but a tiny handful of all the writers who have lived since. He was depicted in action by his pupil Plato.

2.4 Plato: language as a route to reality

It was Plato, one of the greatest thinkers who has ever lived, who linked the problem of knowledge with language. Plato (429–347 BC) was a citizen of the Greek city-state of Athens and a follower of Socrates until the latter's execution in 399 BC. Plato then went into self-imposed exile in the Greek city of Syracuse, in Sicily, for a number of years. When he returned to Athens pupils clustered around him, and in due course he founded an institute, the Academy (the first establishment to bear that name).

Throughout his life, Plato was deeply concerned with the question of knowledge. If we can no longer take it for granted that we all have access to the same ultimate reality, then how can I be sure that when you talk about important issues like freedom and responsibility and prejudice, you mean the same realities that I do? We need to find new ways of guaranteeing the truth of what we think we know. This problem occupied Plato, Socrates and their associates throughout their lives, and has continued to occupy philosophers and seekers after truth ever since. In a series of dialogues Plato depicts Socrates deep in debate, showing how, through a careful process of questioning, it is possible to elicit knowledge that a person has never been taught. In the dialogue known as the *Meno* (most of Plato's dialogues are named after one of their protagonists), for instance, Socrates gets a slave boy with no prior knowledge of geometry to arrive at some not immediately obvious geometrical concepts. That, says Socrates, shows that this knowledge is already there, latent within us, acquired before we were in human form. Confronted with an apparently insoluble problem, we should pluck up courage and try to discover – or recollect – what we don't know (or have forgotten). Socrates concludes: 'We shall be better, braver and less idle if we believe it is right to search for what we don't know than if we believe there is no point looking because we can never discover what we don't know' (*Meno* 86C).[2]

This fearless quest, not only for knowledge itself, but also for effective routes to it, runs through all of Plato's writings. The implications of the loss of the old certainties, the old modes of perception, were very clear to him. And intellectual knowledge was by no means the only domain of existence affected. If, to take another example, we no longer feel obliged to behave ourselves (because we no longer fear the punishment the gods will send if we don't) then what basis is there for morality? Are we free to go around stealing, trespassing, cheating, as much as we like, constrained only by how cleverly we can cover our tracks, or is there in fact some good reason why we should live an upright life? You can see why the question of knowledge was so urgent. In his dialogues, Plato repeatedly portrays Socrates guiding his friends to the point where they 'recollect' their latent prebirth knowledge for themselves; or, as Plato puts it elsewhere, they catch a glimpse of the spiritual realities, the Archetypes or Forms or Ideas (modern scholars use all three terms) which are the blueprint for everything around us. If you imagine a perfect triangle and then try to draw one, or try to imagine the archetypal dog as distinct from any particular dog, you'll get an inkling of the relationship between the Archetype and any visible instantiation of it.

But there was a problem, and Plato knew it: by no means everyone was going to be able to learn by themselves how to see the Archetypes. That ability was fading very fast, especially in Mediterranean Europe. So in order to ensure that you and I mean the same reality, you need to describe what you see and experience to me, using words as your tool. Words thus become extraordinarily important, acting as they do as a bridge between us and other human beings, but also as a means to knowledge. Through words you can teach me what you know about anything from rollerblading to aspidistras, clarinets to algebra. But are words in some sense 'right'? Do they have some necessary inner connection with what they denote, or are they arbitrary and conventional? Although the orthodoxy in present-day linguistics is to regard them as arbitrary (with the exception of a small class of onomatopoeic words), scholars and readers in other areas – rhetoric, cultural anthropology, literary criticism – see them differently. The native speakers of any language tend to experience a fairly large proportion of the vocabulary of their language as 'right': most of us feel a certain sympathy with the English speaker who exclaims: 'Isn't "cow" a wonderfully cow-like word!' Clusters of words in which sound is consistently coordinated with sense reinforce our instinctive feeling of the 'rightness' of words, as in the vaguely unpleasant English *sn-* words: snide, snooty, snoop, sneak, sneer, snigger, snarl etc., or the flowing, fluid, floating, flickering, flighty nature of *fl-*.

What happens if we suspend judgement and step outside linguistic orthodoxy for a moment? What if the vocabulary of our language is not arbitrary and conventional? If you had never heard the word 'cow' before, the very sounds of the word might contain a hint as to the meaning – something pointed, like the horns of a cow, and rounded, like its heavy underbelly. If language is non-arbitrary, as this approach assumes, then words could be a route to knowledge of reality. Since we all have ready access to words, this could solve the problem of how to learn about reality in a world of constant change.

The Greeks – the Sophists, Socrates and Plato too – were deeply immersed in this problem. Even the techniques of argumentation, formalised in the discipline of dialectic (see section 2.5 below), depended upon language for their very existence. To the basic problems of the nature of reality and the nature of knowledge was thus added a third: the nature of language. Was it a reliable tool in the search for knowledge? Could you cut short the quest by showing that if you know the words, you already know the things?

These problems concerned Plato very deeply, and he devoted most of his career to pondering them. Was reality constantly in flux, as the philosopher Heraclitus claimed, changing from one moment to the next, so that nothing could be grasped as a thing-in-itself, but only in relation to other things which were themselves constantly changing? Or was there some sense in which things do have a fixed unchanging reality of their own? And what of the human relationship to reality? Can we escape from total subjectivity? In one of his dialogues, the *Theaetetus*, Plato shows that the extreme position of the philosopher Protagoras, 'Man is the measure of all things', results in an untenable theory of total relativism: knowledge becomes impossible. Plato's own position, alluded to briefly, as we shall see, in his dialogue *Cratylus* and described more fully in his *Phaedo*, was the opposite: there is an absolute reality independent of the observer and not dependent upon sense-impressions for its intellection – the reality of the Forms, or Ideas. Any particular thing here on earth, whether a cat or an act of kindness or a comb, is an imperfect reflection of a perfect transcendental reality which we knew before birth and come to recollect gradually during our life on earth. The knowledge for which we are striving is knowledge of these archetypal Forms. Ultimately, empiricism and materialism, relying as they do upon the messages our senses send us about the visible phenomena around us, lead to relativism and the denial of knowledge. Plato spent his life reasoning his way to true knowledge of the world, a kind of knowledge as absolute and inevitable as mathematics.

If, like Plato, we accept that there is such a thing as a reality independent of the human being which we can cognise, there are two possibilities for language. Either language 'reflects' reality in the same way a mirror does, changing as reality changes; or else it is arbitrary, lacking any intrinsic link with reality. If language reflects reality directly, then we need look no further: knowing language will be enough. But if it turns out to be arbitrary, then language will be of no use at all in apprehending reality, and we will need to find other ways of getting to know the real world. Either position has huge implications for human existence. If language turns out to mirror reality faithfully and inevitably, then we have no freedom to use it as we choose – elegantly or awkwardly, appropriately or inappropriately, truthfully or lying; we must unavoidably speak in accordance with the truth inherent in the world. If, on the other hand, language is arbitrary, we are cut off from reality – but at the same time we are free: free to speak and act in accordance with the truth of reality, or not.

This is the problem to which Plato dedicated one of his dialogues, the *Cratylus*. Named after one of its protagonists, its subtitle – *The Rightness of Names* – gives a better indication of its content. The untenability of Protagoras's relativist position ('Man is the measure of all things') is made clear from the beginning, with frequent references to Heraclitus's teaching ('Everything is constantly changing'). Either position would, if accepted, make the search for knowledge through language pointless: if Protagoras were right, we would have to agree, with Humpty Dumpty, that words mean what I want them to mean; while Heraclitus's position would ultimately make reference impossible, with both word and referent constantly changing. The existence of an unchanging reality – the Forms – is a vital postulate for the dialogue, for otherwise there would be no debate: the nature of language would be a foregone conclusion.

Instead of presenting his arguments in the form of theoretical reasoning couched in discursive prose, like most later philosophers, Plato prefers dialogue form, as he does in the majority of his writings. Dramatising an argument, putting the arguments for a case into the mouth of one speaker and those against into the mouth of another, with a third to act as moderator, suited the Greek perception of reasoning. Instead of imagining the search for truth as a straight path with occasional detours along false tracks, the Greeks experienced it as a zigzag lurching between extremes. They saw the world as a series of antitheses – foolhardiness and cowardice, prodigality and stinginess, nature and convention (see box 2.3). The truth was the middle way. As Aristotle, Plato's pupil, put it: 'In all our conduct it is the mean that is to be commended. But one should incline sometimes towards excess and sometimes towards deficiency, because in this way we shall most easily hit upon the mean, that is, the right course.'[3] In the *Cratylus*, Socrates, playing the role of a midwife helping to bring ideas to birth, holds the balance between the extremes represented by Hermogenes and Cratylus. (Socrates is generally held to voice Plato's own opinion in these dialogues.) The spineless Hermogenes represents the view that language is arbitrary and conventional, serving simply as a means of communication, while Cratylus puts up an energetic defence of the opposite view. Socrates proceeds in his accustomed manner, showing first Hermogenes and then Cratylus how absurd their positions are if taken to their logical extremes. Hermogenes's conventionalist view emphasises the communicative function of speech,

2.4 Plato: language as a route to reality

> **Box 2.3 Nature vs convention**
>
> The antithesis between nature and convention was a theme which ran right through Greek experience in Plato's generation. In trying to find some kind of basis for order in what looked like an increasingly chaotic world, as the old certainties faded into tradition, Plato and his contemporaries examined every aspect of life in a search for order. Order, they realised, was of two kinds: one kind is innate, inevitable, and intrinsic to the things or beings to which it applies; while the other kind is externally imposed by arbitrary human decision. The first type the Greeks called *phusis*, a word that is often translated as 'nature', for it denotes what is intrinsic to things, their inner 'nature'. The second type was called *nomos* 'law' or *thesis* 'convention', something arbitrarily imposed. The opposition between *phusis* and *nomos/thesis* was pursued by the Greeks through all spheres of life. In politics, they puzzled over whether states came into being by natural necessity, by *phusis*, or whether their existence was arbitrary, conventional and probably temporary. In ethics, they pondered the question of moral laws: were they natural, universal and inexorable, or were they likewise arbitrary and conventional? (This problem was expressed very profoundly in the great tragedies by Aeschylus, Euripides and Sophocles, as well as in Herodotus's *Histories* and Aristotle's *Ethics*.) Most tellingly, the Greeks found themselves asking whether the gods existed by *phusis*, or whether they were merely agreed to exist by human convention. Gone were the old days of inner certainty, of direct communion with the gods.
>
> Reading
>
> G. E. R. Lloyd, *Polarity and Analogy: Two Types of Argumentation in Early Greek Thought* (Cambridge: Cambridge University Press 1966, repr. Bristol: Bristol Classical Press 1987).

but it is just this which breaks down if arbitrariness is pushed too far: people are not free to use words in whatever way they like if they are to communicate successfully. Convention has a certain normative force. Contrariwise, if we assume with Cratylus that words have been formed in perfect accord with what they denote, then, Socrates argues, they must actually at some point be indistinguishable from what they denote. When I say 'Cratylus', if the word is a perfect copy of Cratylus, shouldn't I see Cratylus himself standing in front of me? If words *are* what they represent, then we have a logical impasse: it should not be possible to lie.

Crucial to Socrates's argument are words themselves. Do they in fact mirror reality or not? Ideally, we would study the words used by the gods, but they are too lofty for human understanding; so Socrates begins with the names of heroes from the distant past. The Homeric *Astyanax* was the son of Hector, defender of the city of Troy: the name – from *astu* 'city' and *anax* 'lord' – accords with the essence of the person who bears it. Similarly, *Atreus*, notorious for his cruelty and murderous nature, bears a name which reveals him as stubborn (*ateirēs*), daring (*atrestos*) and destructive (*atēros*). Words to do with human existence follow, including the famous explanation of *anthrōpos* 'human being' as the being who 'looks up (*anathrei*) at what he has seen (*ha opōpe*)'. Because the

Greeks regarded the ability to walk upright and look at the stars overhead as one of the important features of human nature, distinguishing man from the animals, they found it appropriate that this quality should be built into the word for 'human being'. The word for 'body', *sōma*, likewise reflects what it denotes: it is simultaneously the tomb (*sēma*) of the soul, and the sign (*sēma*) that a soul is present, and also a safe (*sōma*) where the soul is kept. A great many words seem to have motion encoded in them, Socrates says, as if to confirm Heraclitus's pronouncement, 'Everything is constantly changing' (*panta rhei*, literally 'everything is flowing'), ranging from wisdom, *phronēsis* (so called from cognisance (*noēsis*) of flowing (*rhou*)), to erotic love, *erōs* (so called because it flows in (*esrei*) to our eyes from outside). But as he explores one word after another, Socrates points out that many words are opaque to his reasoning: some are foreign in origin, and so not susceptible to explanation through Greek; some have changed with the passing of time; and some require explanations so far-fetched as to be ludicrous. What about a different way of matching word to reality? If the earliest words were really intended to be imitations of what they denoted, then surely they must imitate by means of the sounds of which they are composed. Thus, r expresses motion in words indicating various types of motion: *trekhein* 'run', *rhumbein* 'whirl', *kermatizein* 'crumble', *tromos* 'tremble', *rhoē* 'current' and so on; n, an internal sound, appropriately appears in *entos* 'within' and *endon* 'inside'. Socrates works his way through most of the Greek alphabet in this way.

However powerful the affective role of such unconscious associations in the mind of the native speaker, only part of the vocabulary of any language lends itself to explanation in these terms. Counter-examples are not far to seek, as Socrates points out: if r indicates motion, how are we to explain the anomalous word *sklērotēs*, meaning 'rigidity'?[4] In short, neither approach yields a comprehensive solution: working solely with the semantic content produces increasingly implausible results on the formal level, while taking the sounds as the starting-point and positing a pervasive kind of sound-symbolism reveals all kinds of semantic anomalies. Thus, although one can demonstrate that words possess a good deal of intrinsic 'rightness', one ultimately has to concede that convention – arbitrariness – plays a significant part in their makeup. That conceded, we still have an important epistemological question to contend with: how did it come about that some words do seem to reflect reality? Socrates invokes the traditional Greek view that legendary figures – demigods or especially inspired men – were responsible for inaugurating various beneficial institutions. Each city-state had its own law-giver, for instance, revered for bringing social order to the community. Analogously, Socrates posits a name-giver ('nomothete') for each language, an individual who was able to perceive absolute reality directly. The names the name-giver bestowed mirrored what they denoted more or less closely, according to the accuracy of his perception and his skill in translating his percepts into speech sounds. This hypothesis accounts for the existence of different languages: different communities had different name-givers with diverging insights into reality. Furthermore, it allows for deviations from reality both in the original imposition of names and in subsequent changes brought about by the passage of time and by processes such as laziness and the desire for euphony. By the same token, however, it shows that language is at best a very imperfect mirror of reality: corruption can creep in at many points. The name-giver was fallible, like ourselves, and, like everything else in the world, language is subject to change. However, the fact that some words do appear to reflect reality accurately has an important implication: it suggests that it is possible to gain accurate knowledge of reality without using words. So we should not despair! Since the name-giver was able to perceive reality directly, reasons Socrates, so can we. Therefore we should concentrate on getting to know reality directly, without bothering with inferior imitations – words.

The dialogue is thus fundamentally about an epistemological problem and only secondarily about a linguistic one. 'How do we reach the truth?' is the basic question which runs through much of Plato's thought. In the *Cratylus* he investigates the claim that language has truth encoded in its very words. Having dismissed that claim as only partially true, Plato goes on to search for other sources of knowledge. Language no longer interests him.

2.5 Aristotle: language in use

In 1508 Raphael painted a fresco called *The School of Athens* in the papal apartments in the Vatican. In the centre, amidst all kinds of busy intellectual activity, stand two men deep in conversation. The older, Plato, points upward, to the Forms which for him were the only route to certain knowledge; but the younger gestures downwards, as if to call our attention to the earth. That younger man is Aristotle, Plato's pupil. His gesture indicates the central feature of his thought: empirical research and step-by-step logical thinking as the route to knowledge. Everything in his thinking flows from his insistence upon the physical world as the starting-point for knowledge.

Aristotle (384–322 BC) was born in Stagira, Macedonia (northern Greece). He studied under Plato in Athens from 367 until Plato's death in 347, and then left Athens, travelling for several years to various towns along the Greek-colonised western coast of Asia Minor and Macedonia. For a time he was tutor to the young prince of Macedonia, Alexander, later known as Alexander the Great. When Alexander became king, in 336 BC, Aristotle returned to Athens and opened a school of his own, the Lyceum, where he taught until shortly before his death.

1   Raphael, *The School of Athens* (1508), Vatican

Aristotle wrote voluminously on a vast range of subjects: ethics, politics, economics, logic, rhetoric and natural history (including works on what we now call psychology, biology and physics). Although over thirty of his writings have survived, many more have not come down to us. Of those extant, some are long and densely argued books, like the *Ethics* and the *Metaphysics*, while others are brief and succinct – little more than chapter headings or notes for a lecture. Reconstructing Aristotle's teaching is thus by no means always straightforward, both because we are lacking some of the texts in which his ideas were more fully expounded, and because some of the surviving works are brief to the point of obscurity. And there is the additional problem which confronts us when studying any ancient or medieval author: the state in which the text of his works has reached us is not always the same as the state in which it left his hands. The transmission of Aristotle's works to the Middle Ages and beyond is a problem which was to reemerge several times in the history of linguistics (see boxes 7.5, pp. 149–150, and 8.3, p. 164, below).

One crucial element in Aristotle's intellectual makeup is foreshadowed in his father's profession: medicine. Although the practice of medicine and the thinking behind it were in many respects very different in ancient Greece from today, doctors were involved in a certain amount of empirical work. Indeed, because prognosis was considered the central medical skill, far more highly regarded than diagnosis, it was vitally important to observe the patient's symptoms and progress accurately. Aristotle learnt to prize careful observation, and spent much of his time while he was in Asia Minor studying coastal wildlife. This interest in observation, unusual in his time (for it was only at the Renaissance that observation became the cornerstone of western scholarship), is symptomatic of his particular turn of mind – to prefer inductive reasoning to deductive. And yet Aristotle insisted on matching methodology to content:

It is a mark of the trained mind never to expect more precision in the treatment of any subject than the nature of that subject permits; for demanding logical demonstrations from a teacher of rhetoric is clearly about as reasonable as accepting mere plausibility from a mathematician.

(*Nicomachean Ethics* 1094b, transl. J. A. K. Thomson)[5]

Like Plato, Aristotle was deeply concerned with the problem of knowledge. What constitutes real knowledge? For Aristotle, the answer to that question lay not in the transcendental Platonic Forms, but was immanent in the things themselves. And yet material things were transient and inherently unknowable. Aristotle urged that we study elements, causes and origins. The elements (*stoikheion*, pl. *stoikheia*) – earth, water, air and fire – came into being through the action of the primordial qualities – hot and cold, wet and dry – and through that interaction all matter came into existence. Aristotle's 'causes' (*aitia*, pl. *aitiai*) are, as we shall see, the factors which underlie the existence of anything. Under 'origins' (*arkhē* pl. *arkhai*) he understood not only how a thing had come into being, but why and for what purpose, for his thinking was strongly teleological. But elements, causes and origins are almost as inaccessible to observation as the Forms. We cannot observe them directly; rather, we come to know them by observing and pondering the processes at work in the world around us. For Aristotle, processes of change were all-important: all nature, and human existence too, was caught up in a process of striving, alteration, transformation. Much of his life was dedicated to the observation of these processes, whether of generation and corruption (birth and death), or motion, or the realisation of inherent potential. Like most of his successors up to the Renaissance, he thought more naturally in terms of dynamic processes than of static entities, substances or states. Thus, although he both preached and practised observation, he did so not so much in order to get acquainted with individual animal species or physical matter as to penetrate through the observable phenomena to the processes of change manifested in them. Many things, he noticed, possess a latent power (*dunamis*) to become something else: an acorn has a force within it which, given proper conditions, will eventually result in an oak tree, even as a human embryo contains the inner forces which will lead to its growing up into a man or woman. That kind of change, a transformation through time, had its counterpart in a different type of power, *energeia*: the power to actualise a potential latent at the present time. A considerate person can only truly be said to be considerate when acting considerately; builders are only builders in the full sense when they are actually putting up a house. Happiness, or as we might say, fulfilment, exists only in activity.

How does one go about grasping the nature of things and beings themselves? Aristotle was too wide-ranging a thinker to neglect this question. He singles out four fundamental aspects of things, the four 'causes'.[6] 'Cause' is a traditional technical term which only very loosely approximates to what we understand by 'cause' in Modern English: 'circumstance', 'factor' or even 'parameter' might better convey Aristotle's meaning today. Likewise, the English terms for the individual causes have been in use for five hundred years in this specialised technical sense, which is rather different from what we understand by these words in normal everyday English:

1. The *formal* cause: the form something takes. A candle, for instance, is long and thin with a wick down the middle.
2. The *material* cause: the substance of which it is made. In the case of the candle, wax and string are its material cause.
3. The *efficient* cause: the physical agent which brought it into being – the candlestick maker, in our example.
4. The *final* cause: the purpose for which the thing came into existence, consciously or unconsciously, or as we might say, its intended function. The candle was made so that it might give light, and this was its maker's intention; but equally, the final cause of an apple is to provide food for human beings or animals, even though the apple tree had (we assume) no such intention.

Schematic as such a description may seem, to ancient and medieval thinkers it appeared flexible and comprehensive, a good framework within which to investigate any phenomenon.

Of the four causes, matter was by far the least accessible to our cognition, in Aristotle's view. Material things might lead us to recognise a general process realised in their activities, but in themselves they were inscrutable. How could one claim to 'know' the substance of an apple? Recognising the potential of its seeds to become apple trees, or seeing the force of gravitation at work in its fall, was quite another question. The more a particular discipline had to grapple with matter, the less certain its results, in Aristotle's eyes. Where matter was heavily involved, the most one could hope for was practical knowledge – knowledge based on experience that could be realised in action. But a higher sort of knowledge, theoretical knowledge, is accessible to us in those domains where the content is not bound up with matter: mathematics, physics and theology. Only in these disciplines could one hope to reach truth, unimpeded by the enigmatic opacity of matter; only these disciplines were truly theoretical.

The study of language is thus inevitably a practical rather than a theoretical discipline. Aristotle's relationship to language, puzzling at first, flows naturally from his epistemology. Although he does not say so in any of his surviving writings, it follows that language exists in man in the same way as musical ability or happiness do: as *energeia*, latent potential which is actualised in every act of speaking. That potential can be actualised only by physical means, through the vocal organs. Language is thus inextricably bound up with the world of matter, and its investigation can lead only to practical knowledge.

Language in the service of thought and feeling

Even if language was of no interest in its own right, its role as an instrument – a tool to be used in pursuing higher ends – lent it a certain degree of significance in Aristotle's eyes. Certainly, language itself was to all intents and purposes arbitrary, conventional, and in itself unable to reveal any kind of higher, lasting truth; but because it might be used to achieve some practical goal, it was important to understand how it worked. Aristotle wrote no grammar or treatise on language as such. Instead, he wrote three treatises on the use of language in the service of two fundamental activities of the soul: thinking and feeling.

Using language to think: dialectic

Do we need language to think? You've probably had the experience of realising something in a flash, without words. But when you try to explain it to someone else, or even to think about it yourself, you set it out in linear fashion, one part following another, articulated into 'before' and 'after', 'because' and 'therefore'. Inspiration is non-linguistic and non-linear, whereas reasoning is linguistic and sequential. We learn to reason as part of the process of growing up. In the English-speaking world, learning to reason is for the most part unconsciously assimilated as we argue things out with others; but in much of Europe until recently, reasoning was formally taught through lessons in logic. Formal logic is part of the training of a philosopher to this day.

That young Europeans are taught logic does not mean that they are incapable of thinking logically without those lessons, any more than the young Englishman or American's lack of them cripples his thinking for life. Plato wrote his dialogues without the benefit of formal logic, for none existed in his day; but, recognising that it was implicit in his method, he gave his pupil Aristotle the task of codifying the laws of thought. This he did in a series of treatises on dialectic (*dialectic* is the name given to logic as used in debate, but for our purposes the term is interchangeable with 'logic') which later came to be known collectively as the *Organon* ('Tool', 'Instrument' (of reasoning)):

- *Categories* (sometimes known by its Latin title, *Praedicamenta*), on the general terms that may be predicated of a subject;
- *De interpretatione* ('On Interpretation', also known by its Greek title, *Peri hermeneias*), on propositions;
- *Prior Analytics*, on syllogisms;
- *Posterior Analytics*, on demonstrations;
- *Topics*, on premises and definitions;
- *Sophistical Refutations* (also known by its Greek title, *Sophistici Elenchi*), on logical fallacies.

Later, this group of texts circulated with a preface, the *Isagoge*, by Porphyry, a Neoplatonist philosopher of the third century AD (see box 2.4). In the *Isagoge* Porphyry provided clarification of certain basic notions: genus, species, difference, property, accident.

Box 2.4 Neoplatonism

Within a couple of generations of Plato's death two new philosophical movements, Stoicism and Epicureanism, were on the rise, pushing Platonism into the background. Only around 100 AD did it resurface, metamorphosed into a system we call Middle Platonism. Whereas Plato had seldom referred to God, Middle Platonism placed a supreme principle, Mind (or God), at the summit of the hierarchy of being. The 'thoughts' of this supreme Mind were the Platonic Archetypes or Forms. The supreme Mind was also identified with Aristotle's Prime Mover, the transcendent Mind that imparts motion to the universe of being. These ideas were further developed by a philosopher from Alexandria in Egypt who taught in Rome, Plotinus (205–270), who in his *Enneads*, the fundamental text of Neoplatonism, insisted that the supreme Mind was not part of the hierarchy of being, but outside it, able to affect any part of it directly, in a position exactly analogous to that of the Christian God. Plotinus's pupil Porphyry (ca 234–ca 305), originally from Tyre but who became a member of Plotinus's school in Rome, devoted himself to integrating Aristotelian logic into Platonic teaching. He wrote commentaries on Aristotle's works on logic (of which all but that on the *Categories* are lost) and an introduction (*Isagoge*) to the *Categories* which ultimately inspired much of the later medieval discussion of universals. For Neoplatonism had a long history. Early medieval philosophers such as John Scottus Eriugena grappled with the version of Neoplatonism they found in the works of a later writer, pseudo-Dionysius (ca 500), and Neoplatonism was revived in fifteenth-century Florence, most notably by Marsilio Ficino.

Reading

E. K. Emilsson, 'Neo-Platonism', in David Furley, ed., *Routledge History of Philosophy 2. From Aristotle to Augustine* (London and New York: Routledge 1999), pp. 356–87.

A. H. Armstrong, ed., *The Cambridge History of Later Greek and Early Medieval History* (Cambridge: Cambridge University Press 1970), parts III and IV.

As a dialectician, Aristotle worked on the assumption that language was wholly conventional, for otherwise logic would be impossible. This is made very clear in the opening lines of the *De interpretatione*, as a prelude to his discussion of propositions:

Spoken signs are representations of impressions in the soul, and written signs are representations of the spoken ones. Just as letters are not the same for all men, so the sounds are not the same either. However, what these signs stand for – the impressions of the soul – are the same for everyone, and the real-world things of which they are the likeness are also the same.[7]

Aristotle here recognises four fundamental components: real-world things, impressions (percepts), spoken signs (utterances), and written signs. This theory of the sign differs in one important respect from modern theories. That written signs represent spoken ones (i.e. words) is uncontroversial, and likewise the fact that we all receive impressions of the external world through our senses.

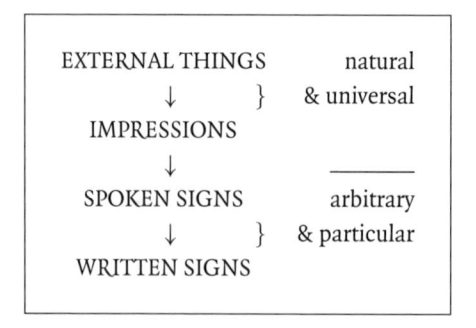

```
EXTERNAL THINGS        natural
       ↓        }     & universal
   IMPRESSIONS
       ↓               ─────────
   SPOKEN SIGNS        arbitrary
       ↓        }    & particular
   WRITTEN SIGNS
```

Between words and impressions there is something missing from Aristotle's schema, to our way of thinking: the concepts that we form based on our impressions. For Aristotle, the impressions are universal but the words differ arbitrarily; there is no intermediate level. Aristotle and his successors through Antiquity and up to the end of the Middle Ages, and indeed well beyond, experienced thought as something universal, common to all human beings. Individual error was possible, of course, as they acknowledged, but differences in the concepts acknowledged by different groups of people – national differences in part created by linguistic differences – are something to which Europeans only awakened in the second half of the eighteenth century. Up until then, Aristotle's experience of impressions *and therefore concepts* as universal apparently reflected the experience of the great majority of Europeans.

Hence too his confidence that in developing formal logic he was formulating the laws of thought in a manner that was absolute and universally valid. Indeed, Aristotelian logic took the place of the fast-fading glimpses of the Platonic Archetypes as the principal epistemological tool of European thinkers for nearly two thousand years, up until the fifteenth century; and of course we still rely very heavily upon it. Only in the seventeenth century, with the rise of empiricist philosophy in England, and of Cartesian rationalism in France, taken up and developed by the German philosopher Leibniz, were serious modifications to Aristotle's system undertaken. The notion that the Aristotelian 'laws'

2.5 Aristotle: language in use

of thought were universally valid was not challenged until the end of the nineteenth century. More recently, it has been remarked that Aristotle's logic is dependent to a high degree upon the structure of his native language, Ancient Greek. Had Aristotle spoken an incorporating language like Inuit, for instance, his formalisation might well have proceeded differently.

Aristotle identifies three components as central to the proposition: *onoma*, *rhēma* and *logos*. These terms are translated differently depending upon the context of the discussion – grammar or logic.

LOGIC	ARISTOTLE	GRAMMAR
subject	onoma	noun
predicate	rhēma	verb
proposition	logos	sentence

As we'll see in chapter 8, it was only in the twelfth century that grammarians began to think in terms of the units that we understand by *subject* and *predicate*, and to create new terminology to make this distinction clear (see box 2.5 for the beginnings of this distinction, and box 8.5, p. 168 below, for its history). Aristotle defines each of these units in a manner appropriate to its function in logical analysis. Thus, he writes: 'The *onoma* is an utterance which has meaning by convention and lacks tense/time, and no part of it has meaning by itself.'[8] The fact that the *onoma* has meaning by *convention* has to be underlined, for any attempt to demonstrate that it necessarily reflects external truth makes logic impossible: if rational thought is to take place, language has to be free of any necessary tie to external reality. The requirement that no part of *onoma* can be significant on its own is connected with the stipulation of conventionality: if every time we used the word 'Cambridge' we had to take into account the etymological possibility that we might be talking about a bridge over the river Cam, our conversation would be unbearably encumbered. As for the *rhēma*, Aristotle says: 'It consignifies time, no part of it has meaning by itself, and it is always a sign of something said about something else;[9] in other words, its necessary etymological opacity is stressed again, but in addition it possesses the property of being predicated of something else, and (along with whatever else it might signify) it indicates time (or tense, in the language of grammar). Given that logic deals in statements that are universally true, the fact that the (Greek) verb obligatorily shows time is an inconvenience which Aristotle later comments on briefly (*Prior Analytics* 34b). As for the *logos*, it too signifies *by convention*, but differs from the *onoma* and the *rhēma* in that its parts – the *onoma* and *rhēma* – have meaning in their own right. Conventionality and relationship to the *logos* as a whole are thus important constituents of these preliminary definitions.

Having established this, Aristotle goes on to discuss the structure of propositions. To do so, he makes heavy use of the notion of predication. What may be predicated of a subject? Ultimately, he says, all predicates fall into one of ten fundamental

Box 2.5 Early use of metalinguistic terms
How would you explain the difference between these propositions?

1. A student is listening
2. A student is not listening
3. Not a student is listening
4. Not a student is not listening

What metalanguage did you find yourself using? Can you imagine doing it without terms for 'subject' and 'predicate', 'noun' and 'verb'?

In order to begin to talk about statements, you need to be able to talk about their parts. Greek, like all other languages before the scholarly study of language began, originally possessed a very basic repertoire of metalinguistic terms. In Plato's day these terms were just beginning to acquire specific technical senses, and Plato himself played some part in helping to extend their meaning: just how much is uncertain. This is how he works on the terms which came to take on the sense of 'noun' or 'subject' (*onoma* in Greek), 'verb' or 'predicate' (*rhēma*) and 'sentence' or 'proposition' (*logos*). The translator uses the English terms 'noun', 'verb' and 'sentence' or 'discourse' for these three Greek words; feel free to disagree if you want!

THE STRANGER: We have two kinds of vocal indications of being.
THEAETETUS: How so?
THE STRANGER: One called nouns, the other verbs.
THEAETETUS: Define each of them.
THE STRANGER: The indication which relates to action we may call a verb.
THEAETETUS: Yes.
THE STRANGER: And the vocal sign applied to those who perform the actions in question we call a noun.
THEAETETUS: Exactly.
THE STRANGER: Hence discourse is never composed of nouns alone spoken in succession, nor of verbs spoken without nouns.
THEAETETUS: I do not understand that.
THE STRANGER: I see; you evidently had something else in mind when you assented just now; for what I wished to say was just this, that verbs and nouns do not make discourse if spoken successively in this way.
THEAETETUS: In what way?
THE STRANGER: For instance, 'walks', 'runs', 'sleeps' and the other verbs which denote actions, even if you utter all there are of them in succession, do not make discourse for all that.
THEAETETUS: No, of course not.
THE STRANGER: And again, when 'lion', 'stag', 'horse', and all the other names of those who perform these actions are uttered, such a succession of words does not yet make discourse; for in neither case do the words uttered indicate action or inaction or existence of anything that exists or does not exist, until the verbs are mingled with the nouns; then the words fit, and their first combination is a sentence, about the first and shortest form of discourse.

2.5 Aristotle: language in use

> Reading
> F. Ildefonse, 'Sujet et prédicat chez Platon, Aristote et les Stoïciens', *Archives et Documents de la Société d'Histoire et d'Epistémologie des Sciences du Langage* (SHESL), 2nd ser., 10 (1994), 3–34.

categories:

- substance, or being, e.g. man and horse;
- quantity, e.g. four-foot, five-foot;
- quality, e.g. white, grammatical;
- relative to something else, e.g. double, half, bigger;
- local, e.g. in the Lyceum, in the market;
- temporal, e.g. yesterday, last year;
- position, e.g. is lying, is sitting;
- possession e.g. shod, wearing armour;
- action, e.g. cuts, burns;
- being affected, e.g. is being cut, is being burnt.

Everything can be reduced to these ten categories, which he discusses in detail in the *Categories*.[10] Although Aristotle presents it as a list of conceptual categories corresponding to the real world, and his interpreters accepted it as such, later thinkers (including some modern commentators) were intrigued by the obvious resemblance of several of his categories to linguistic categories. We shall see their shadows here and there in the subsequent history of linguistics.

We need not follow Aristotle further into the description of propositions, for that belongs to logic rather than to grammar or linguistics. But logic has never been very far from linguistics. Linguistics has repeatedly absorbed ideas and techniques from logic, as we shall see. The subject–predicate distinction, for instance, was not taken up by grammarians in the ancient world, for their word-based (dependency) syntax made it redundant. Whenever scholars have tried to construct a sentence-based (constituency) syntax, they have borrowed the subject–predicate distinction from logic.

The *Rhetoric*: persuasion and probability

Rhetoric was vastly more important in ancient Greek and Roman society than it is in our paper-bound culture overflowing with documentation – contracts and written confirmation, voluminous directories of this and that, encyclopedias, computer databases and Web pages. Negotiation between equal partners, often behind closed doors, followed up by the signing of a document, is our preferred way of doing business; public speeches, whether in Parliament, or from a soap box in Hyde Park, or on television, look increasingly ritualised and old-fashioned. Ancient Athens was a direct democracy: all free adult males had the right, and indeed the duty, to participate in the government of their city-state, which was conducted orally in public assemblies. Consequently, the ability to reason well and express oneself cogently was highly prized. Rhetoric, like dialectic, was a means to an end, the goal of convincing one's listeners of the truth (or of the rightness of one's position). To achieve this, one needed to master both the construction of syllogisms (hence Aristotle considered rhetoric to be a branch of dialectic) and the workings of human character and emotions. Aristotle's treatise on rhetoric begins with two books devoted to these issues. Only then, in the final book, does Aristotle turn to expression – the appropriate way to present one's arguments.

The third book of his *Rhetoric* is a treatise on prose style parallel to that on poetic diction in his *Poetics*. In both works he discusses metaphor and other ornaments of diction at some length, providing a systematic analysis of the functioning of metaphor, amplified with numerous examples in the *Rhetoric*. As he points out, 'Strange words simply puzzle us; ordinary words convey only what we know already; it is from metaphor that we can best get hold of something fresh.' Both good and bad prose style are discussed, Aristotle recommending against the indiscriminate use of adjectives, compound words, neologisms, and inappropriate metaphors like the Sophist Gorgias's 'events that are green and full of sap'.[11]

The *Poetics*: language as catharsis

The purpose of poetry, in Aristotle's view, was to purge feelings of pity and fear from the soul of the listener. Poetry's concern with universal truth made it more worthy of serious attention than history, which charts particular facts, a view shared with Aristotle by a great many thinkers up to the Renaissance and beyond. But its cathartic effect could only be achieved by dint of careful planning. A well-constructed tragedy, for instance, has four vital elements: plot, character, thought and diction. Diction (*lexis*, 'word-as-form'), placed at the end of the list, occupies Aristotle only briefly, in three chapters which form an interlude between the discussions of tragedy and of epic. As in the *De interpretatione*, Aristotle is interested in language only in so far as it is relevant to his goal, understanding how poetry brings about certain effects. It is with this in mind that we should read his account of the basic constituents of speech: the minimal unit (*stoikheion*), i.e. the letter/speech sound, syllable, connective, article/relative pronoun, noun, verb, inflected forms, sentence (*logos*). If you come from a background in grammar or linguistics you might be surprised at the mix of word classes ('parts of speech') and other elements; but it is no part of Aristotle's purpose to set up a system of word classes. Speech, when one thinks of it as a formal entity, has units of various kinds, both purely formal (letters/sounds and syllables) and functional, right up to the complete meaningful utterance, the sentence or proposition (*logos*). The shift of emphasis in the definitions of the noun and verb, by comparison with those in the *De interpretatione*, underscores Aristotle's unwavering attention to the context in which language was to be used. Here, he describes the noun and the verb as 'a composite of sounds with a meaning',[12] a point relevant to the literary use and analysis of language, but he drops the element of conventionality, significant to the logician but irrelevant to the poet (or in some ways even wrong). The other elements in the definition – lacking or showing time, and having parts with no independent meaning – remain constant.

Next, Aristotle considers nouns more closely, with his literary critic's hat on. Not for him a systematic investigation of their properties; rather, he concentrates on aspects relevant to the poet: compounding, semantics, metaphor (discussed at some length here), and the letters/sounds in which nouns end and their genders.

Conclusion: the philosopher's instrumental view of language

As philosophers, Aristotle and Plato shared the view that in itself, language can tell us nothing about reality. It does not reflect the world sufficiently accurately to act as an alternative route to truth. Consequently, its only value is instrumental, in that we can use it as a tool in our search for the truth. For this reason neither Plato nor Aristotle wrote a treatise on language as such; that was left to those scholars who had renounced the search for absolute truth, contenting themselves instead with a more immediate but contingent form of knowledge: the grammarians.

Further reading

Reading on Plato

Much of the voluminous secondary literature on Plato, particularly that in English, has been written by classical philosophers for others of their kind. Their interest in Plato is of a very different nature from that of a historian of linguistics: they analyse Plato's reasoning as if he were a contemporary philosopher, seeking to show where he goes wrong. Setting him in his historical context is not, as a rule, their concern. Consequently, although some of their writings have been included in the list of secondary literature, both more and less specialised, you would be well advised to begin by reading the *Cratylus* in the light of one or more of the background works, and only then, if you are keen, move on to the English-language secondary literature.

Background

H. D. F. Kitto, *The Greeks* (London: Penguin 1957).
Kenneth Dover, *The Greeks* (Oxford: Oxford University Press 1982).
Kenneth Dover et al., *Ancient Greek Literature*, 2nd edn (Oxford: Oxford University Press 1997).
Terence Irwin, *A History of Western Philosophy 1: Classical Thought* (Oxford and New York: Oxford University Press 1989).
Bruno Snell, *The Discovery of the Mind in Greek Philosophy and Literature* (New York: Dover 1982), ch. 2. [On the changing attitude to the gods in early Greek literature.]
G. E. R. Lloyd, *Polarity and Analogy: Two Types of Argumentation in Early Greek Thought* (Cambridge: Cambridge University Press 1966, repr. Bristol Classical Press 1987), part 1 'Polarity', pp. 15–171. [Provides background to the *phusis–nomos/thesis* debate.]

Linguistic thought before Plato

Peter Schmitter, 'Vom "Mythos" zum "Logos": Erkenntniskritik und Sprachreflexion bei den Vorsokratikern', in P. Schmitter, ed., *Geschichte der Sprachtheorie 2: Sprachtheorien der abendländischen Antike* (Tübingen: Narr 1991), pp. 57–86.

Peter Schmitter, 'From Homer to Plato: language, thought, and reality in ancient Greece', in P. Schmitter, ed., *Essays towards a History of Semantics* (Münster: Nodus 1990), pp. 11–31.

Plato

Terence Irwin, *A History of Western Philosophy 1: Classical Thought* (Oxford and New York: Oxford University Press 1989), ch. 6.
R. M. Hare, *Plato* (Oxford and New York: Oxford University Press 1982).
David Melling, *Understanding Plato* (Oxford and New York: Oxford University Press 1987).

The Cratylus

There are many editions and translations of the *Cratylus* into English and other languages, on its own, or, more frequently, as part of Plato's complete works: three of the more accessible ones are listed below. If short of time, concentrate on the beginning to 400C; 409A–413C; 421C to end. (These numbers are found in all editions and translations, providing a standard way of referring to Plato's works. They are derived from the pagination in one of the early printed editions of his works.) If you don't know the Greek alphabet, try either to get hold of a translation which transliterates the Greek of the etymologies into our alphabet, or better still, find the Greek alphabet with English equivalents and do the transliteration yourself. Any Greek grammar will provide this information.

Plato: Complete Works, ed. John M. Cooper and D. S. Hutchinson (Indianapolis and Cambridge: Hackett 1997), pp. 101–56. [The etymologies are transliterated.]
Plato IV. Cratylus, Parmenides, Greater Hippias, Lesser Hippias, transl. H. N. Fowler, Loeb Classical Library no. 167 (London: Heinemann and Cambridge, MA: Harvard University Press 1977), pp. 1–191. [This edition is in a great many public and academic libraries. Greek original and English translation are on facing pages. The etymologies are left in Greek.]
Plato: The Collected Dialogues, ed. Edith Hamilton and Huntington Cairns, Bollingen Series 71 (Princeton, NJ and Oxford: Princeton University Press 1961), pp. 421–74. [The etymologies are left in Greek.]

Secondary literature

J. L. Ackrill, 'Language and reality in Plato's *Cratylus*', in J. L. Ackrill, *Essays on Plato and Aristotle* (Oxford: Clarendon 1997), pp. 33–52, repr. from Antonina Alberti, ed., *Realtà e ragione: studi di filosofia antica* (Florence: Olschki 1994), pp. 9–28.
David Bostock, 'Plato on understanding language', in Stephen Everson, ed., *Companions to Ancient Thought 3: Language* (Cambridge: Cambridge University Press 1994), pp. 10–27.
M. M. Mackenzie, 'Putting the *Cratylus* in its place', *Classical Quarterly* 36 (1986), 124–50.
R. H. Weingartner, 'Making sense of the Cratylus', *Phronesis* 15 (1970), 5–25.
Nicholas P. White, 'Plato (427–347)', in Marcelo Dascal et al., eds., *Sprachphilosophie/ Philosophy of Language/La philosophie du langage* 1 (Berlin and New York: de Gruyter 1992), pp. 234–44.

Eugenio Coseriu, *Die Geschichte der Sprachphilosophie von der Antike bis zur Gegenwart. Eine Übersicht I: Von der Antike bis Leibniz*, Tübinger Beiträge zur Linguistik 11 (Tübingen: Narr 1975), pp. 40–60.

Tilman Borsche, 'Platon', in P. Schmitter, ed., *Geschichte der Sprachtheorie 1: Sprachtheorien der abendländischen Antike* (Tübingen: Narr 1991), pp. 140–69. [In German.]

Daniele Gambarara, 'L'origine des noms et du langage dans la Grèce ancienne', in Sylvain Auroux, ed., *Histoire des idées linguistiques 1: La naissance des métalangages en Orient et en Occident* (Liège and Brussels: Mardaga 1989), pp. 79–97.

Pol Vandevelde, 'Le statut de l'étymologie dans le *Cratyle* de Platon', *Etudes Classiques* 55 (1987), 137–50.

More specialised studies

Timothy M. S. Baxter, *The 'Cratylus': Plato's Critique of Naming* (Leiden: Brill 1992).

Geneviève Clerico, 'Lectures du *Cratyle*, 1960–1990', *Historiographia Linguistica* 19 (1992), 333–59.

J. Derbolav, *Platons Sprachphilosophie im Kratylos und in den späteren Schriften* (Darmstadt: Wissenschaftliche Buchgesellschaft 1972). [Useful, if now somewhat dated, bibliography.]

Rudolf Rehn, *Der Logos der Seele: Wesen, Aufgabe und Bedeutung der Sprache in der platonischen Philosophie* (Hamburg: Felix Meiner 1982), pp. 7–40.

Jetske C. Rijlaarsdam, *Platon über die Sprache. Ein Kommentar zum Kratylos* (Utrecht: Bohn, Scheltema & Holkema 1978).

John Sallis, *Being and Logos: Reading the Platonic Dialogues*, 3rd edn (Bloomington and Indianapolis: Indiana University Press 1996), pp. 183–311.

Antonia Soulez, *La grammaire philosophique chez Platon* (Paris: Presses Universitaires de France 1991), pp. 36–110.

Reading on Aristotle

As was the case with Plato, classical philosophers have written prolifically about Aristotle's views on language, but relatively little of their output is relevant to a historian of linguistics. Amongst the more useful works (not all of them by classical philosophers!) you may find the following:

On Aristotle

Terence Irwin, *A History of Western Philosophy 1: Classical Thought* (Oxford: Oxford University Press 1989), ch. 7.

Jonathan Barnes, *Aristotle* (Oxford and New York: Oxford University Press 1982).

G. E. R. Lloyd, *Aristotle: The Growth and Structure of his Thought* (Cambridge: Cambridge University Press 1968).

J. L. Ackrill, *Aristotle the Philosopher* (Oxford: Clarendon 1981).

David Ross, *Aristotle* (London and New York: Routledge 1995).

Jonathan Barnes, ed., *The Cambridge Companion to Aristotle* (Cambridge: Cambridge University Press 1995). [Chapters by specialists survey various aspects of Aristotle's thought, including 'Logic' (pp. 27–65) and 'Rhetoric and Poetics' (pp. 259–85); an extremely useful bibliography concludes the volume (pp. 295–384).]

Aristotle's writings on language

Like many later philosophers, Aristotle refers to problems of language many times throughout his writings without ever devoting an entire treatise to language as such. The passages discussed in the text are:

Categories, chs. 1–9.
De interpretatione, chs. 1–4.
Poetics, chs. 20 and 21.
Rhetoric, book 3.

All these works are translated in editions of Aristotle's complete works such as:

The Complete Works of Aristotle, ed. Jonathan Barnes, 2 vols., Bollingen Series 71.2 (Princeton, NJ and Oxford: Princeton University Press 1984).

Some useful excerpts are to be found in:

Aristotle: Selections, transl. Terence Irwin and Gail Fine (Indianapolis and Cambridge: Hackett 1995): Categories 1–5, 12–13; De interpretatione 1–4, 7, 9, 12–13. Amongst the numerous translations of relevant individual texts are the following:
Aristotle, Categories and De interpretatione, transl. with notes and glossary by J. L. Ackrill (Oxford: Clarendon 1963).
Aristotle, Categories, On Interpretation, Prior Analytics, ed. and transl. H. P. Cooke and H. Tredennick, Loeb Classical Library no. 325 (Cambridge, MA, and London: Harvard University Press 1938).
The Poetics of Aristotle: Translation and Commentary, by Stephen Halliwell (London: Duckworth 1987).
Aristote, La Poétique, transl. with notes by Roselyne Dupont-Roc and Jean Lallot (Paris: Seuil 1980).
Aristotle, Poetics with the Tractatus Coislinianus, Reconstruction of Poetics II, and the Fragments of the On Poets, transl. with notes by Richard Janko (Indianapolis and Cambridge: Hackett 1987).
Aristotle, The Art of Rhetoric, transl. H. C. Lawson-Tancred (London: Penguin 1991).
Aristotle, On Rhetoric: A Theory of Civic Discourse, transl. with notes by George A. Kennedy (New York and Oxford: Oxford University Press 1991).
Aristotle, Art of Rhetoric, transl. J. H. Freese, Loeb Classical Library no. 193 (Cambridge, MA, and London: Harvard University Press 1926).

If you would like to get something of the flavour of Aristotle's scientific writings, try the first book of *De partibus animalium* ('The Parts of Animals').

Secondary literature

(a) Aristotle's ideas on language in general

Hermann Weidemann, 'Grundzüge der aristotelischen Sprachtheorie', in P. Schmitter, ed., *Geschichte der Sprachtheorie 2: Sprachtheorien der abendländischen Antike* (Tübingen: Narr 1991), pp. 170–92.

Richard McKeon, 'Aristotle's conception of language and the arts of language', *Classical Philology* 41 (1946), 193–206, and 42 (1947), 21–50.

Anne Cauquelin, *Aristote. Le langage* (Paris: Presses Universitaires de France 1990).

Wolfram Ax, 'Aristoteles (384–322)', in *Sprachphilosophie/Philosophy of Language/La philosophie du langage* 1, ed. Marcelo Dascal et al. (Berlin and New York: de Gruyter 1992), pp. 244–59. [In German.]

Eugenio Coseriu, *Die Geschichte der Sprachphilosophie von der Antike bis zur Gegenwart. Eine Übersicht I: Von der Antike bis Leibniz*, Tübinger Beiträge zur Linguistik 11 (Tübingen: Narr 1975), pp. 68–112.

Gianluca Sadun Bordoni, *Linguaggio e realtà in Aristotele* (Bari: Laterza 1994).

Stephen Halliwell, 'Style and sense in Aristotle's Rhetoric Bk. 3', *Revue Internationale de Philosophie* 47 (1993), 50–69. [Challenging attempt to deduce Aristotle's theory of language from the Rhetoric.]

Ronald A. Zirin, 'Aristotle's biology of language', *Transactions of the American Philological Association* 110 (1980), 325–47.

(b) *De interpretatione*

Ronald Polansky and Mark Kuczewski, 'Speech and thought, symbol and likeness: Aristotle's *De interpretatione* 16a3–9', *Apeiron* 23 (1990), 51–63.

C. W. A. Whitaker, *Aristotle's De interpretatione: Contradiction and Dialectic* (Oxford: Clarendon 1996), chs. 1–3.

Elio Montanari, *La sezione linguistica del 'Peri hermeneias' di Aristotele*, 2 vols. (Florence: Università degli Studi di Firenze, Dipartimento di Scienze dell'Antichità 'Giorgio Pasquali' 1984–8).

Hans Arens, *Aristotle's Theory of Language and its Tradition: Texts from 500 to 1750*, Studies in the History of Linguistics 29 (Amsterdam and Philadelphia: John Benjamins 1984). [Deals only with the opening chapter of the *De interpretatione*, translating many late antique and early medieval commentaries on this passage.]

3 Towards a discipline of grammar: the transition from philosophy

3.1 The Stoics

Out of the Greeks' tireless questioning of everything around them grew the discipline of *philosophia*. It is hardly right to think of it as a unitary discipline, and still less to equate it with our modern philosophy, for the *philosophia* of the Greeks subsumed many disparate areas of knowledge. In the generations after Aristotle, countless thinkers took up the task of working through the wealth of ideas inherited from the Golden Age of Athens (box 3.1). Work of two kinds lay before them: systematisation and taking stock, and elaboration of the original often concisely expressed and sketchily developed ideas. Amongst the people who participated in this activity were the members of the most famous philosophical school in the ancient world, the Stoics. Founded by Zeno of Citium in the third century BC, and based as much in Asia Minor (modern Turkey) as in Greece, the Stoics grew in numbers and reputation, even counting a Roman emperor, Marcus Aurelius (121–180 AD), amongst their later adherents. Despite the esteem in which they were held in their own time, almost none of their writings have survived; they are known to us only from the snippets quoted by other writers, and from a sort of biographical dictionary, *Lives of the Philosophers*, compiled by Diogenes Laertius in the first half of the third century AD. For the historian of linguistics this is an intensely frustrating state of affairs, for, as we shall see, there is reason to suppose that the Stoics played a part in giving shape to the discipline of grammar.

On surveying the vast domain of philosophy as they had inherited it, the Stoics recognised that it fell into three distinct areas: logic, ethics and physics. Each of these could be further subdivided; thus, logic, the domain into which problems of language fell, was subdivided into dialectic and rhetoric. Dialectic and rhetoric, but not grammar: the Stoics shared with Plato and Aristotle the philosopher's view of language as a tool for use in the search for truth rather than as a subject worthy of study in its own right. And yet their concern to fathom the nature and possibilities of language led them to bring together ideas from Aristotelian dialectic, rhetoric and natural philosophy and organise them into a structure which in some respects prefigures that of the ancient

> **Box 3.1 What is a Golden Age?**
> World history is peppered with eras which are labelled 'Golden Ages', from 'the Golden Age of Greece' up to all those cliché-ridden 'Golden Ages of jazz/blues/Hollywood...' of nostalgic retrospection. All such 'Golden Ages' have several features in common: their brevity, characteristically no more than three generations; their geographical focus, centring on just one or two communities in close proximity; and the intensity and chaotic prolificness of their intellectual life. Such periods are characteristically followed by much longer eras during which the new ideas spread far beyond their original birthplace. Few fresh ideas emerge; rather, people work through the ideas inherited from the recent 'Golden Age', digesting them, systematising them, watering them down into textbooks and encyclopedias until they become part of the school curriculum, and disseminating them to a broader public. An analogous process, greatly speeded up, took place in linguistics in the second half of the twentieth century, when Noam Chomsky's ideas about language, first disseminated amongst enthusiasts during the 1960s, the so-called 'decade of private knowledge', gradually entered mainstream linguistics textbooks, until a watered-down version found its way into popularising books about language for the general public, and even into school textbooks. Intellectual history proceeds by a kind of 'punctuated equilibrium': not by a process of gradual, linear evolution, but in sudden leaps followed by lengthy periods of consolidation. That label 'Golden Age' makes very clear how significant such brief periods seem in retrospect.

grammatical treatise as it was to emerge centuries later. Writing a grammar as such was not their intention, however. For the Stoics, dialectic was closely connected with epistemology. Whereas rhetoric dealt with the invention of arguments, their expression and delivery, dialectic had in its purview the things signified in speech and speech itself. Several Stoics wrote treatises on speech (*Peri phōnēs*), none of which have survived. If we can trust the account given by Diogenes Laertius (box 3.2), the Stoics constructed their theory of speech around three key terms:

- *phōnē* 'noise, sound, voice, vocal utterance'. Since *phōnē*, defined as 'air struck by an impetus', is a natural phenomenon (like all things that bring about a physical effect in the world), it properly speaking belongs to the domain of physics. Some sounds – those which are not mere noises – can be written down, and once such a sound has been put into writing, it is a *lexis*.
- *lexis* 'writable sound' does not necessarily convey meaning. A nonsense word or onomatopoeic formation such as /pɪŋ/ (the Greek equivalent is *blituri*) or /kəplʌŋk/ is a *lexis* just as much as /miːt/ or /ətɛmpt/. Because a *lexis* is a written utterance (like the items written in the International Phonetic Alphabet in the preceding sentence) it can be said to be made up of smaller units, in this case the twenty-four letters of the Greek alphabet.
- *logos* is a 'meaningful sound', or 'meaningful utterance', as we would be more likely to say – a word as a semantic unit, or a sentence or part-sentence. Five

classes of *logos* were identified: the proper noun, the common noun, the verb/predicate (*rhēma*), the linking-word (probably including both conjunction and preposition) and the article.[1]

Box 3.2 Can we trust our sources? Diogenes Laertius on Stoic grammar

Since no Stoic texts on language have come down to us, we have to rely upon indirect evidence – the snippets quoted by other writers and the précis of their doctrine given by people who mentioned them only in order to disagree with them. Our most important source (along with the polemical writings of Sextus Empiricus) is a sort of biographical dictionary by a writer of the third century AD, Diogenes Laertius, called *Lives of Eminent Philosophers*. In this work Diogenes surveys the main philosophical schools of Antiquity, giving a brief account of their history and development, and listing the writings of their principal representatives. Book VII is devoted to the Stoics, and in it Diogenes outlines their doctrine, mentioning various sources along the way. Having given a brief introductory summary, he says: 'I will quote verbatim what Diocles the Magnesian says in his *Synopsis of Philosophers*. These are his words: . . .' (Diocles was an important Stoic thinker of the first century BC.) What follows is our chief source for Stoic linguistic thought. The difficulty comes in establishing just how much comes from Diocles's account, for Diogenes does not tell us where the quotation finishes. Ancient manuscripts, unlike modern printed editions, had no devices such as our quotation marks and indented paragraphs to distinguish visually between quotations and text. Hence, scholars disagree over how much of what follows was actually written by Diocles in the first century BC: the whole description of Stoic dialectic, i.e. sections 49 to 83 of Book VII? Or a more limited portion: sections 49 to 53, or 49 and 50, or section 49 alone? Various other authorities, such as Chrysippus, Antipater and Diogenes of Babylon, are quoted along the way, but we do not know how much comes from their texts, nor whether Diogenes Laertius is quoting them at first hand or took the quotations over from Diocles. In short, our knowledge of Stoic dialectic, and hence of Stoic ideas about language generally, depends to a large extent upon a text which *may* be a fairly accurate summary of a work of the first century BC; or it may be a heavily updated and reworked version composed by Diogenes Laertius himself and therefore dating from the third century AD, by which time grammar had long since acquired a standard form in the ancient world.

Reading

A summary of the problems with references to more detailed discussions is given by:

Karlheinz Hülser, *Die Fragmente zur Dialektik der Stoiker I* (Stuttgart–Bad Cannstatt: frommann-holzboog 1987), pp. xlvi–xlix.

A compelling case for accepting only sections 49 to 53 as derived from the work of Diocles of Magnesia is made by:

Jaap Mansfeld, 'Diogenes Laertius on Stoic philosophy', *Elenchos* 7 (1986), 295–382; the relevant discussion is found on pp. 351–73.

Each successive unit is a subset of the previous one: *lexis* 'writable sound' is a subset of *phōnē*, all sounds, and *logos* 'meaningful sound' is a subset of *lexis*:

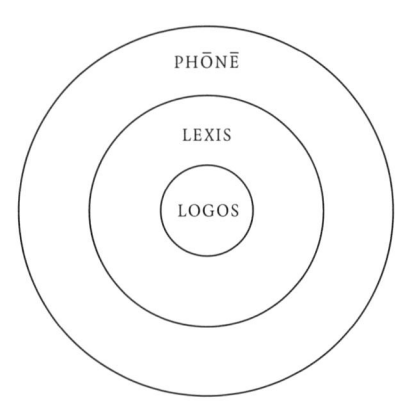

```
        PHŌNĒ
      ┌────────┐
      │  LEXIS │
      │  ┌──┐  │
      │  │LOGOS│
      │  └──┘  │
      └────────┘
```

The contrast between *lexis*, the linguistic unit of form – whether simply its letters, or with regard to its morphological structure – and *logos*, the linguistic unit of meaning, was an important one in ancient linguistic thought, and, as we shall see in chapter 5, it took on theological significance in the early days of Christianity. The Stoics, in the quest for truth, were concerned with the meaningful aspect of speech, both as it was used to express truth or falsehood (rhetoric) and as a tool to distinguish the true from the false (dialectic). Consequently, they took an interest in the 'virtues' and 'vices' of speech – such qualities as idiomatic use of language, lucidity, conciseness, appropriateness and elegance on the one hand, and barbarisms (malapropisms and mistakes in the form of a word) and solecisms (wrong collocations, whether offending against syntax or against sense) on the other. Definitions too were carefully scrutinised, still under the heading of 'speech'.

The other branch of Stoic dialectic was the study of what was represented in speech. Here the Stoics entered upon a discussion of mental representations and of the entities represented by the spoken utterance, namely, the *sēmainomenon*, 'that which is signified' (the term corresponds closely to Saussure's *signifié*) and the *lekton*, 'that which may be put into words'. (The interpretation of both terms is hotly debated by present-day philosophers and semioticians.) The study of these important elements was the prelude to a categorisation of types of sentences and propositions, the stuff of dialectic proper in the eyes of later writers.

Thus, although the Stoics concerned themselves only with dialectic and rhetoric, and did not (so far as we know) write grammars, they went sufficiently deeply into linguistic issues to earn the respect of many generations of grammarians as well as of dialecticians and rhetoricians. Just how great their influence was on the subsequent constitution of grammar as a discipline, and on the form taken by the ancient grammar as a text, is a controversial subject, as we shall see in chapter 4. The best-known thinker to develop their linguistic ideas was St Augustine (see box 5.5, p. 100 below), who sets out a fully-fledged doctrine of the sign in his treatise on dialectic. The nature of the sign

3.2 Varro: linguistic analysis from first principles

During the Golden Age of Greece, in the decades around 400 BC, Italy was a cultural backwater. The city-state of Rome, founded according to ancient tradition in 753 BC, was engaged upon a lengthy programme of conquest and consolidation, little by little expanding its territory to take in almost the whole of the Italian peninsula. By the third century BC Romans were looking across the sea, coming into conflict with Greece and the Phoenician colony of Carthage, in present-day Tunisia. With the passing of time, literary and cultural pursuits began to attract the interest of a people previously devoted to agriculture and warfare. Teachers and all the trappings of civilisation were imported from the Greek world, to the point where it became a commonplace that most

---

Box 3.3 Pythagoras and the Pythagoreans

Pythagoras was a Greek from the island of Samos who travelled around Egypt and the Near East in order to study the kinds of knowledge and modes of perception cultivated in the various mystery centres still active at that time. Eventually he settled at Crotona in southern Italy in 530 or 529 BC (a full century before Plato's lifetime). Although Pythagoras himself left no writings, so far as we know, we hear a good deal about his teachings from later writers – Plato, Aristotle, the historian Plutarch, and members of his school such as Philolaus and Iamblichus. As Plato was later to do, Pythagoras stressed the importance of mathematics as a vital part of the training of anyone who would attain to true wisdom. Through mathematics one could come to an understanding of what non-arbitrary knowledge was like: there is no room for personal opinion about the number of angles in a triangle or the sum of their degrees. Pythagoras is credited with a number of insights which lie at the root of all subsequent work on mathematics, including the theorem which bears his name. It was numbers and their relations – proportions – which seemed to Pythagoras to underlie all natural phenomena, from acoustics to geometry to astronomy.

Another feature of Pythagorean thought is a tendency to perceive processes in the world as being the outcome of the play of pairs of opposing forces – fundamental polarities. The Greeks at large recognised that the physical properties of the natural world were derived from the interaction of four basic qualities: hot, cold, wet, dry. These four qualities in combination give rise to the four elements – fire, air, water, earth – out of which all living beings are composed. But the Pythagoreans identified many other fundamental dichotomies: finite and infinite, odd and even, one and many, right and left, male and female, rest and motion, straight and curved, light and dark, good and evil, square and oblong. The Pythagorean respect for mathematics as the representative *par excellence* of absolute truth, their interest in proportions, and their fondness for antitheses lived on in Plato's teaching, in the linguistic writings of the Roman scholar Varro, and in countless other manifestations.

features of Roman intellectual and cultural life owed their origin to the Greeks. One of the sources of Greek influence was the Greek province in the 'toe' of Italy, present-day Calabria, settled by Greeks in the eighth century BC. From there various ideas filtered north and were assimilated into the general intellectual inheritance of the Romans.

Amongst the most influential thinkers of the Greek colony in southern Italy was the school of the Pythagoreans (box 3.3). Pythagorean ideas filtered into Greek and Roman intellectual life, deeply influencing Plato (among others). We can find traces of them too, along with signs of Platonic and Stoic doctrine, in the linguistic thought of one of the greatest of all Roman scholars, Marcus Terentius Varro (116–27 BC). Varro lived when Roman civilisation was at its most creative: amongst his contemporaries were the poet Vergil, the military leader and historian Caesar, and the philosopher and orator Cicero. Varro himself was a polymath of extraordinary breadth of learning. He was versed in Greek and Latin literature, in Roman history and antiquities, and in Greek philosophy, which he had studied in Athens. His writings were so numerous that St Augustine said of him five centuries later: 'He read so much that I wonder how he ever found the time to write anything; and he wrote so much that I can hardly believe that anyone could read it all.'[2] He wrote on practically every subject known: mathematics, chronology, agriculture, history, law, philosophy, literary history and language; and he also wrote satires, poems, speeches and letters. Although his writings were influential for many centuries after his death, only a few have come down to us: his work on agriculture (*De re rustica*), part of his longest treatise on language, and scattered snippets of his other writings.

His principal work on language, the *De lingua latina* ('On the Latin language'), composed between 47 and 45 BC, is known to us from a single copy damaged at beginning and end, an eleventh-century manuscript from the monastery of Monte Cassino in southern Italy. It contains just six of the original twenty-five books, Books V to X. Because Varro recapitulates the contents of the entire work here and there as he goes along, we know how this section relates to the whole. He divided the work into three main parts reflecting the threefold nature of speech, as he saw it:

1. The imposition of names upon things.

2. Modifications in the form of the original words, i.e. *declinatio*.

3. Bringing words together to express a meaning.

- Book I: dedication (to Cicero) and introduction.
- Book II to IV: the principles of etymology, with arguments for and against it.
- Book V to VII: examples of etymology in different areas of Latin vocabulary.
- Books VIII to X: the role of analogy and anomaly in language.
- Books XI to XIII: examples of analogy.
- Books XIV to XXV: the 'conjoining' of words, apparently along the lines of the Stoic analysis of different types of propositions.

Only Books V to X have survived, containing the latter part of the discussion of etymology and the first part of that of analogy. The disappearance of the rest is one of our saddest losses, for what Varro has to say about language is like nothing else that has come down to us from the ancient world. The *De lingua latina* is not a grammar – plenty of those survive from the later Roman empire – but rather a treatise on fundamental linguistic issues.

Varro, like Plato, is anxious to discover unchanging, absolutely true aspects of language. The surface phenomena cannot serve as a starting-point; initially, the linguistic phenomena and processes must be connected with analogous processes in the world beyond language. Only so can language be redeemed from its arbitrariness; and only then is it appropriate to answer linguistic questions solely with reference to linguistic phenomena. This reasoning runs through ancient and medieval linguistic thinking (see section 6.2 below). Varro uses the Pythagorean dichotomies as his starting-point. Some of them, like the distinction between one and many, can readily be applied to a language like Latin, where oneness and multiplicity are encoded in distinct singular and plural noun and verb forms, whereas others do not at first sight look likely to lend themselves to application to language. When in Book V Varro introduces his lengthy series of etymological examples with a basic classification of Latin vocabulary, he takes the rest/motion dichotomy as his point of departure. For either rest or motion to take place, four elements are required: a thing (*corpus* 'a body, material substance') that is at rest or in motion; the place where resting or motion comes about; the time at which resting or motion occurs; and the activity. Varro emphasises the inseparability of these four primal elements: motion is impossible without a body that is moving and space for it to move in; and activity has to take place in time. From this Varro draws a linguistic conclusion: 'Because there are four basic kinds of things, there are correspondingly four basic kinds of words' (V 13).[3] The etymologies which occupy the next two books are organised according to these four classes, words pertaining to place and body in Book V, and words pertaining to time and activity in Book VI (the latter subdivided into the three fundamental human activities, thinking, speaking and doing). Book VII, which deals with the vocabulary of poetry, is also structured around these four basic classes.

The etymological books are often skimmed over in accounts of Varro's work, for his approach to etymology appears to be quite alien to ours. Yet although he accepts that many words do (or did) possess some degree of intrinsic rightness, he recognises all the causes of mismatch between present-day words and their original *raison d'être* that Socrates identifies in the *Cratylus*: some words have disappeared, some were incorrectly formed in the first place, others have changed out of all recognition, and of course some are borrowed from foreign languages (V 3). How are we to go about reconstructing the reason for any given word? Not by means of the tools of nineteenth-century comparative philology – systematic phonological correspondences, cognate forms and the like. Rather, Varro invokes four 'causes': the addition, loss, transposition and alteration of letters/speech-sounds (for the term *littera*, often misleadingly translated 'letter', see box 4.4, p. 61 below) or syllables.[4] In focussing attention upon these processes of change, he at once defines the principles on which etymology was based until well into the modern era, and signals an aspect of language which has attracted relatively little attention in modern linguistics: processes of change. Whereas modern etymologies are presented as a succession of states, Varro and other ancient etymologists preferred to concentrate on what went on *between* one state and the next: what processes were at work? Charting the end points of the processes of change interested only one ancient writer, the grammarian Priscian (early sixth century AD: see section 4.10 below). Varro goes on to describe four levels of etymological explanation:

1. compound words such as *viocurus* 'road-overseer' (from *via* 'road' + *cura* 'responsibility'), which are transparent even to the common herd;
2. poetic neologisms such as *clupeare* 'beshield' (from *clupeum* 'shield'), which 'old-fashioned grammar' understands;
3. words in common use such as *oppidum* 'town', so called because it is fortified for strength (*ops*) and because people have need (*opus*) of such a place in which to lead their lives; such explanations are offered by philosophy;[5]
4. the fourth level Varro describes as that of the 'sanctuary and the mysteries of the king', and gives no example (V 7–8).

He sees an ascending hierarchy in these levels, rising from the transparently obvious compounds, their structure clear even to the 'common herd', through the attainments of 'old-fashioned grammar' up to the levels of 'philosophy' and the mysteries. Quite what he means by this final level is unclear. A scholar who has studied Varronian etymology in detail, Wilhelm Pfaffel, surmises that Varro's 'king' is the original name-giver, and that Varro believes that the etymological method required to uncover such words is reconstruction, a technique he occasionally employs.[6] (Modern etymologists feel comfortable only with the first two levels – unless Pfaffel's explanation is right.)

Having worked his way through the etymologies of a large chunk of Latin vocabulary, Varro turns in Book VIII to a different issue, the role of the forces of analogy and anomaly in language. Which is more important, the drive to level out and achieve similarity, or the force which creates irregularities and dissimilarity? Varro dramatises the issue in a manner rather similar to Plato's procedure in his dialogues. Although he does not introduce named speakers, he sets out the arguments on either side so vividly that nineteenth-century readers imagined that Varro was documenting a great debate between rival schools.

In broad terms, the issue was as follows. Like the Greeks, Varro was interested in the roles of nature and convention in language. Like Plato, he believed that error could easily creep into the original process of naming 'because people, unskilled and isolated, gave names to things just as the fancy took them';[7] the inherently regular force of nature, on the other hand, can be observed in the inflected case and verb forms, which are rarely subject to human caprice. But what if a mistake crept in? Should one follow reason and correct it? Or should one simply kowtow to usage? The argument that usage should be followed was invoked to justify an anomalous, apparently mistaken form. That is, although the word was acknowledged to be irrational, there was no point trying to correct it since it was well established. Even as we talk of *trousers* and *scissors* without 'rationalising' them to *trouser and *scissor, the Romans spoke of *scalae* 'stairs' and *scopae* 'broom', both plural in form though singular in meaning. Logically, shouldn't the words be grammatically singular – *scala and *scopa – to correspond to the oneness of the objects they denote? Analogy was thus aligned with logic, and anomaly with usage.

Varro devotes a good deal of space to this issue because of his deep-seated concern with the inherent rationality of language, its regularity, or as some might say, its 'scientific' nature. He is as concerned as Pythagoras or Plato before him to discover absolute, non-arbitrary truths; but unlike Plato, he believes it is possible to find them in language. Plato had sought them in words themselves, hoping in vain to find a regular correspondence between sound and outer reality; Varro was well aware of the possibilities and limitations of this approach, as is demonstrated in his study of etymology. Once again, he thinks the issue through from first principles (probably with some help from his Greek sources). In order to establish whether analogy is at work he first has to establish what classes of words may properly be compared with one another. He proceeds by dichotomies. The first basic division is between those words which inflect, producing new words, and those which do not. Words of the inflecting kind are of two sorts, names and verbal elements. Each of these categories subdivides further: within each one, some words are prior, others later. Thus, 'man' (*homo*) and 'writes' (*scribit*) are prior, 'knowledgeable' (*doctus*) and 'knowledgeably' (*docte*) are later, as shown in the tree diagram.

```
                              WORDS
                             /      \
                     INFLECTING      UNINFLECTING
                    /          \
                NAMES           VERBAL ELEMENTS
                /    \            /        \
            prior   later      prior       later
              |       |          |           |
             man  knowledgeable writes  knowledgeably
             homo    doctus     scribit     docte
```

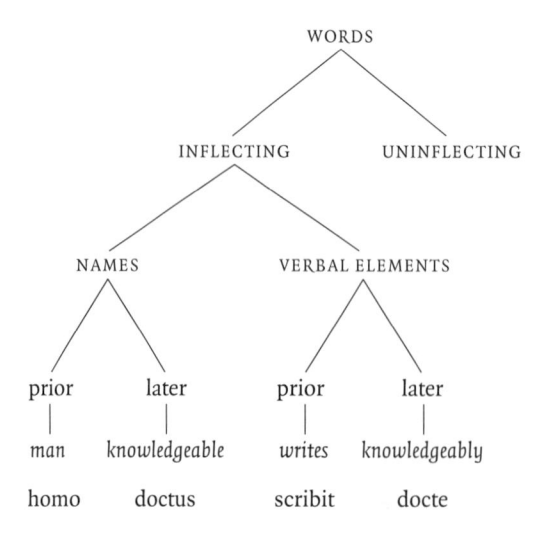

Clearly, Varro is not talking about derivational priority: ontological priority is at issue. Just as you cannot talk about a man without presupposing place, or about an action without presupposing time, you cannot use the word 'knowledgeable' without presupposing a person or 'knowledgeably' without presupposing an action.

Later Varro returns to the inflecting word classes, applying a different set of parameters to them. Words inflected by nature are divided into four classes:

1. those which have case but not tense, e.g. *docilis* 'docile', *facilis* 'easy';
2. those with tense and not case, e.g. *docet* 'teaches', *facit* 'makes';
3. those which have both case and tense, e.g. *docens* 'teaching', *faciens* 'making';
4. those which have neither, e.g. *docte* 'learnedly', *facete* 'wittily'.[8]

Case and tense are the features which underlie his new categorisation. Both have distinctive formal exponents in Latin, and form is an aspect of language of which Varro was far more conscious than his contemporaries (and indeed more so than almost anyone else in Christian Europe for a good 1,500 years to come). For him, analysing the word classes was merely the prelude to something far more important: the discussion of *declinatio*. Basically, *declinatio* means any kind of change in a word. Literally, it means a sort of 'falling off', 'declining' in both the literal and the grammatical sense. Since it covers alterations in both nominal and verbal morphology 'inflection' is the closest English term. In Varro's view it is a phenomenon of immense importance in language. What is its role? Only a very limited stock of words was originally created, he says, and after all this is a good thing, since it means that we are not obliged to overburden our memories. *Declinatio* was invented as a way of reducing the need for more of those primitive words. Through *declinatio* we can create new words from old ones without needing to invent totally new forms. For example, if the original stock contained one thousand words, and we have five hundred ways of modifying each one, then we will produce some 500,000 new words!

Five hundred ways of modifying each word? Even the inflection-happy Latin verb comes nowhere near generating 500 forms from a single stem. But Varro's view of *declinatio* is more comprehensive than ours of 'inflection'. He identifies two types:

- natural inflection (*declinatio naturalis*), corresponding to our 'inflectional morphology';
- arbitrary inflection (*declinatio voluntaria*), representing the act of name-giving or word-creation that corresponds to some extent to our 'derivational morphology'.

Varro discusses this distinction at some length. Since ancient Rome was a slave-owning society, he conjures up an image of three men who have each just bought a slave from a slave-dealer by the name of Artemidorus in the town of Ephesus, in Ionia, on the western coast of what is now Turkey.[9] One owner might give his slave the name *Ephesius*, after the town in which he bought him; the second might prefer to commemorate the province, and calls his new slave *Ion*; while the third instead wants to remember the slave dealer rather than the place (was it a particularly good deal?), and calls his slave *Artemas*. These names are the ultimate example of arbitrarily chosen names, and as if to corroborate that, each name stands in a different relationship to the word from which it was formed: *Ephesus–Ephesius, Ionia–Ion, Artemidorus–Artemas*. This formal diversity is what Varro regards as 'arbitrary'. (Of course, it is arbitrary from the point of view of the language as a whole, and not from that of the individual language user. Had the slave-owners attempted to create new names along the lines of *Ephesas – *Ionius – *Artem, the other members of their household might well have protested at the barbarous, un-Latin nature of the names. Even the most highhanded master was bound by the constraints of the language.) Once the household started to use the names, however, each person was obliged to inflect them in exactly the same way; inflectional morphology offers minimal opportunities for choice.

Varro thereby establishes a distinction between the act of name-giving and the inflection of those names once in use. This distinction, close to the modern one between derivational and inflectional morphology, is of vital importance for any kind of linguistics in which importance is attached to word form as well as to word meaning. Until this fundamental distinction is grasped, it will be all but impossible to study language historically; it will be difficult to arrive at an economical descriptive grammar of a language; in short, it will be impossible to construct an accurate description of its morphology. That gives us some sense of Varro's achievement. But the distinction and its potential were not understood by Varro's successors. The grammarians who came after him worked in a tradition permeated by the semantic concerns of dialecticians, which encouraged them to look at linguistic phenomena in semantic, or at most in functional, terms, relegating purely formal issues to the status of an awkward leftover. Although several later grammarians quoted from the *De lingua latina*, none of them saw the relevance of this distinction to their own needs. It was not rediscovered until late in the Middle Ages.

In trying to establish what may be compared with what, Varro invoked another Pythagorean notion: proportions. Even as Pythagoras had worked with ratios, or proportions, in arithmetic, geometry and music, so Varro now tried to identify them in language. He describes a grid which has been reconstructed as follows:[10]

	1	2	4
	10	20	40
	100	200	400
	[Nominative	Genitive	Dative]
[Masc.]	albus	albi	albo
[Fem.]	alba	albae	albae
[Neut.]	album	albi	albo

Each axis of the grid is significant. The vertical axis of the linguistic grid gives masculine, feminine and neuter forms of the same adjective, *albus* 'white'. They differ only in gender, even as in the numerical grid 1, 10 and 100 differ only in order of magnitude. The horizontal axis of the linguistic grid sets out several of the inflected case forms – the nominative (subject), genitive (possessor) and dative (indirect object). These forms are qualitatively different in that they cannot function in the same way in a sentence. Analogously, 1, 2 and 4 are qualitatively distinct in Pythagorean arithmetic, which focussed on the unique properties of 'unity', 'duality', 'fourness' and so on. The purpose of the table is to emphasise the importance of knowing which forms are in fact comparable; otherwise, false analogies will result. This is a point which Varro demonstrates with a number of linguistic examples.

Despite the fact that he was frequently quoted by later grammarians, those aspects of Varro's linguistic doctrine which we find most striking seem to have made little impression upon his Roman readers. They seem to have studied him selectively, reading right over those parts which were so radically different from what they were used to that they had no way of grasping them or using them. When, after centuries of oblivion, the *De lingua latina* was rediscovered by Boccaccio in 1355, it was studied with great excitement by Italian Humanists, and played a part – just how much has yet to be established – in the shaping of linguistics during the Renaissance.

In his search for ways of identifying aspects of language which were not arbitrary, but partook of reality, Varro stands in the ancient stream which was to persist up to the Renaissance and beyond: the drive to rescue language from its arbitrariness and conventionality, and so intrinsic unimportance, by demonstrating that it in some way reflected the structure of reality. The method he chose to do this was far-reaching: he went right back to first principles, applying ways of thinking associated with the Pythagoreans. By looking for proportions, and so ascribing greater importance to the relationships between items than to the items themselves, he worked in a manner reminiscent of twentieth-century structuralism. In elaborating this line of thought he was drawn to studying linguistic form more precisely than any of his contemporaries or successors until late in the Middle Ages.

Further reading

Reading on the Stoics

Background

A. A. Long, *Hellenistic Philosophy: Stoics, Epicureans, Sceptics*, 2nd edn (London: Duckworth 1986), ch. 4.

Stoic linguistic doctrine

Marc Baratin, 'La constitution de la grammaire et de la dialectique', in Sylvain Auroux, ed., *Histoire des idées linguistiques 1: La naissance des métalangages en Orient et en Occident* (Liège and Brussels: Mardaga 1989), pp. 186–206, esp. pp. 192–7.

Marc Baratin, 'Aperçu de la linguistique stoïcienne', in Peter Schmitter, ed., *Geschichte der Sprachtheorie 2: Sprachtheorien der abendländischen Antike* (Tübingen: Narr 1991), pp. 193–216.

Michael Frede, 'Principles of Stoic grammar', in John M. Rist, ed., *The Stoics* (Berkeley, CA: University of California Press 1978), pp. 27–75.

A. C. Lloyd, 'Grammar and metaphysics in the Stoa', in A. A. Long, ed., *Problems in Stoicism* (London: Athlone 1971), pp. 58–74.

A. A. Long, 'Dialectic and the Stoic sage', in his *Stoic Studies* (Cambridge: Cambridge University Press 1996), pp. 85–106, repr. from John M. Rist, ed., *The Stoics* (Berkeley, CA: University of California Press 1978), pp. 101–24.

Karlheinz Hülser, 'Stoische Sprachphilosophie', in Marcelo Dascal et al., eds., *Sprachphilosophie/Philosophy of Language/La philosophie du langage* 1 (Berlin and New York: de Gruyter 1992), pp. 17–34.

J. Lohmann, 'Über die stoische Sprachphilosophie', *Studium Generale* 21 (1968), 250–57.

Sources for Stoic linguistic doctrine

Diogenes Laertius, *Lives of the Philosophers* VII 41–83. English translation in *Diogenes Laertius II*, transl. R. D. Hicks, Loeb Classical Library no. 185 (Cambridge, MA: Harvard University Press and London: Heinemann 1979), pp. 151–93.

Sextus Empiricus, *Against the Mathematicians* VIII (= *Against the Logicians* II) 67–86. English translation in *Sextus Empiricus II*, transl. R. G. Bury, Loeb Classical Library no. 291 (Cambridge, MA: Harvard University Press and London: Heinemann 1983), pp. 271–81.

Sextus Empiricus, *Against the Mathematicians (Adversus Mathematicos I)*, transl. D. L. Blank (Oxford: Clarendon 1998).

These passages and many others have been assembled and given a German translation, together with scholarly notes and bibliography, by:

Karlheinz Hülser, *Die Fragmente zur Dialektik der Stoiker*, 4 vols. (Stuttgart–Bad Cannstatt: frommann-holzboog 1987–8).

More advanced studies

A. A. Long, 'Language and thought in Stoicism', in his *Problems in Stoicism* (London: Athlone 1971), pp. 75–113.

Jonathan Barnes, 'Meaning, saying and thinking', in Klaus Döring and Theodor Ebert, eds., *Dialektiker und Stoiker. Zur Logik der Stoa und ihrer Vorläufer* (Stuttgart: Steiner 1993), pp. 47–61.

Michael Frede, 'The Stoic notion of a *lekton*', in Stephen Everson, ed., *Companions to Ancient Thought 3: Language* (Cambridge: Cambridge University Press 1994), pp. 109–28.

Mariano Baldassarri, *Introduzione alla logica stoica* (Como: Libreria Noseda 1984), esp. ch. 3 ('L'enunciabile').

Urs Egli, 'Stoic syntax and semantics', in Jacques Brunschwig, ed., *Les Stoïciens et leur logique* (Paris: Vrin 1978), pp. 135–54; and in *Historiographia Linguistica* 13 (1986), 281–306; and in Daniel J. Taylor, ed., *The History of Linguistics in the Classical Period*, Studies in the History of the Language Sciences 46 (Amsterdam and Philadelphia: John Benjamins 1987), pp. 107–32.

Wolfram Ax, *Laut, Stimme und Sprache. Studien zu drei Grundbegriffen der antiken Sprachtheorie*, Hypomnemata 84 (Göttingen: Vandenhoeck & Ruprecht 1986), pp. 138–211.

D. M. Schenkeveld, 'Studies in ancient grammar III. The Stoic ΤΕΧΝΗ ΠΕΡΙ ΦΩΝΗΣ', *Mnemosyne* 43 (1990), 86–108.

Further reading

Reading on Varro

The De lingua latina

Varro, De lingua latina, 2 vols., transl. Roland G. Kent, Loeb Classical Library no. 333–4 (Cambridge, MA: Harvard University Press and London: Heinemann 1977).

Editions and translations of individual books

There are many editions with parallel translation (into various languages) and commentary of individual books of the De lingua latina. Two particularly useful ones are:

Varron: La langue latine, Livre VI, ed. Pierre Flobert (Paris: Les Belles Lettres 1985).
Varro – De Lingua Latina X, ed. Daniel J. Taylor, Studies in the History of the Language Sciences 85 (Amsterdam and Philadelphia: John Benjamins 1996).

Secondary literature

The introduction to Taylor, Varro – De Lingua Latin X (see above), contains a useful summary of current thinking about Varro's place in ancient linguistic thought, and a detailed account of the manuscript history, with references to further literature.

- Daniel J. Taylor, 'Varro and the origins of Latin linguistic theory', in Irène Rosier, ed., L'héritage des grammairiens latins de l'Antiquité aux Lumières (Louvain and Paris: Peeters 1988), pp. 37–48.
- Jean Collart, 'L'œuvre grammaticale de Varron', in his (et al.) Varron, grammaire antique et stylistique latine (Paris: Les Belles Lettres 1978), pp. 3–21.
- Jean Collart, Varron grammairien latin (Paris: Les Belles Lettres 1954).
- Franco Cavazza, Studi su Varrone etimologo e grammatico (Florence: La Nuova Italia 1981).
- Wilhelm Pfaffel, Quartus gradus etymologiae: Untersuchungen zur Etymologie Varros in 'De lingua Latina', Beiträge zur klassischen Philologie 131 (Königstein/Ts.: Hain 1981).
- Wilhelm Pfaffel, 'Wie modern war die varronische Etymologie?', in Historiographia Linguistica 13 (1986), 381–402; and in Daniel J. Taylor, ed., The History of Linguistics in the Classical Period, Studies in the History of the Language Sciences 46 (Amsterdam and Philadelphia: John Benjamins 1987), pp. 207–28.
- Jean Stéfanini, 'Remarques sur l'influence de Varron grammairien, au Moyen Age et à la Renaissance', in Jean Collart et al., Varron, grammaire antique et stylistique latine (Paris: Les Belles Lettres 1978), pp. 185–92.

4 From literacy to grammar: describing language structure in the ancient world

4.1 From literacy to grammar

In the *Cratylus* Socrates refers to 'those who are skilled in vowels and consonants',[1] and Aristotle mentions grammarians (*grammatikoi*). In any literate society there are teachers whose job it is to impart the basic skills of reading, writing and numeracy. In ancient Greece the origins of the profession are encoded in the name: *grammatikos* (the singular of *grammatikoi*) is visibly derived from *gramma* 'letter' (plural *grammata*). Of course, one can teach someone to read without any grammatical concepts more sophisticated than 'letter', 'sound' and 'word': equivalent terms are found in all literate societies, and in most, if not all, preliterate societies. In other words, the ability to read and write – and by implication to devise a writing system – does not presuppose an extensive repertoire of linguistic concepts, still less a well-developed system of grammar or theoretical linguistics. What is it that gives the impetus to move on to that stage? In ancient India the desire to preserve an older, more 'correct' form of pronunciation was the spur for the description of the articulatory phonetics of Sanskrit; in the medieval Arab world the need of foreign converts to Islam for instruction in Arabic, the language of the Qur'ān, together with a feeling of nostalgia for the ancient language of the Beduin, lay behind the first grammars; but in the Greek world the motivation for the writing of grammars is less clear.

4.2 The Hellenistic world and the scholarship of Alexandria

The era of Socrates, Plato and Aristotle – the Golden Age of Athens (see box 3.1, p. 39 above) – was a period of extremely rapid intellectual change, and it was followed by three centuries of consolidation, the Hellenistic age (box 4.1). Greek scholarship during this era came to centre on written texts. Scholars sifted through the inherited stock of knowledge, developing it and organising it. And there was a lot of work to be done. Many texts were now in existence, both literary and technical in content. There was as yet no such thing as printing, and this has enormous implications for the nature of

> **Box 4.1 Alexander the Great, the Hellenistic world, and their Byzantine heirs**
>
> Aristotle's most celebrated pupil was Alexander, prince of Macedonia (356–323 BC), in northern Greece. Aristotle was his tutor for several years. In 336 BC Alexander succeeded to the throne and embarked upon an ambitious programme of conquests, consolidating the conquest of Greece which his father had carried out, and moving eastwards and southwards across Turkey, Egypt, the Near East and Persia to the borders of India, where he died in a skirmish. The huge territory he acquired was divided up by his generals into separate kingdoms, and it is these which are collectively known as 'the Hellenistic world'. They brought a veneer of Greek civilisation to the various peoples living in them, some of whom had writing systems and literatures of their own going back centuries. Via the schools scattered throughout this vast territory, the Greek language, Greek grammar, Greek literature, philosophy and science were disseminated across the Near East. When the Arabs arrived, bringing Islam with them, in the seventh century, it was a form of Greek civilisation that they encountered here.
>
> In 168 BC Greece itself was conquered by Rome, and in the course of the first century BC the Hellenised territories of the Near East were incorporated into the Roman empire. Greek remained the lingua franca of much of the area, however. In AD 330 the capital of the Greek world was transferred from Rome to Byzantium, a town on the Bosphorus, the straits between the Black Sea and the Mediterranean, by Emperor Constantine the Great. (The town was renamed Constantinople 'Constantine's city', and kept that name until it was captured by the Turks in 1453, when it was changed to Istanbul.) Christianity was adopted as the state religion later in the fourth century, and soon missionaries from Byzantium began to play a role in converting neighbouring peoples, simultaneously bringing them within the Byzantine cultural sphere. In this way not only the areas which had once been part of the Hellenistic world, such as modern Jordan and Iraq, but other regions, such as Armenia, Georgia and Kievan Rus', came under the influence of Byzantine civilisation and Orthodox Christianity.
>
> *Reading*
> F. W. Walbank, *The Hellenistic World* (London: Fontana 1992).

scholarship in the ancient world. Printing permits one to produce an infinite number of identical copies of the same text. Before literacy became widespread it was the custom to pass on even very long texts by word of mouth, the village singer teaching his son, and the son passing the tales on to his son in turn, and so on down the generations. Just as no two performances of a piece of music are identical, so no two recitals of an epic are the same; when they are written down, it is one particular performance which is selected and preserved. Thus, different versions of the 'same' text began to be copied out – and so were available for comparison. As Greek scholars pored over transcripts of Homer's great poems, the *Iliad* and the *Odyssey*, attempting to reconcile the different versions, a new specialisation emerged: textual criticism. The textual critic attempted to establish which parts of the text were genuine and which were later interpolations, which parts had been correctly transmitted and which were garbled, and which showed signs of significant omissions. Even when a work was written down by its author, problems remained. As you know from your own experience, when you copy out any lengthy text by hand, you invariably make mistakes: you miss out a word, skip a line, repeat words or even whole lines. It is extremely difficult to make a perfect copy of any but the shortest text. Even author's originals – autograph manuscripts, as they are called – contain such mistakes. And of course successive copyists might introduce deliberate (as well as accidental changes) into the text. The textual critic had plenty to do.

Hellenistic scholars, particularly those in Alexandria, the cultural centre of the Hellenistic world, were famed for the study of literary texts. As they pondered the epics of Homer and Hesiod, the lyrics of Sappho and Pindar, and the plays of Aeschylus and Euripides, they realised that they were lacking basic tools to help them in their work, the tools that modern textual critics take for granted: symbols to indicate textual corruption, signs to indicate the position of word accent (Ancient Greek had a system of pitch accents not indicated in the earliest orthography), glossaries of difficult archaic and dialectal words, monographs on literary problems such as the identity of Homer or the amount of time taken up by the action in a comedy. One by one, Hellenistic scholars filled the gaps. Aristophanes of Byzantium, for example (ca 257–180 BC and not connected with Aristophanes the celebrated comic playwright of fourth-century Athens), devised a system of symbols to represent pitch accents which is still used in printing Ancient Greek texts. He also assembled lists of difficult vocabulary from ancient literary texts, the forerunners of today's dictionaries. As he edited texts he had to deal with garbled word forms, many of them archaic words which had gone out of use centuries earlier. How was he to decide whether or not a form was correct? He realised that one very powerful tool was analogy. If he could establish that an unfamiliar word was formed and inflected on exactly the same model as a familiar one, then he could reconstruct the desired form with confidence. But here he found himself in the role of a pioneer, for little attention had hitherto been paid to morphological patterns. Scholars who approached language from a philosophical standpoint, like the Stoics, were interested above all in semantic categories which might or might not have morphological exponents; purely formal phenomena were of no interest to them. Aristophanes therefore drew up a list of five criteria for use in identifying fully comparable forms: the words in question must be of the same gender, case, termination, number of syllables and sound (or accent). His pupil Aristarchus (ca 216–144 BC) added a sixth criterion: compound words should not be compared with simple (uncompounded) ones. This list tells us that a number of metalinguistic notions were in existence by the second century BC; but it is inconclusive as to whether a systematic way of describing morphology, in the form of a descriptive grammar, as yet existed. The word 'grammar' had not yet acquired the relatively narrow sense it has today, when it usually denotes the rules governing the structure of a language. Throughout Antiquity, 'grammar' – *tekhnē grammatikē* in Greek, *ars grammatica* in Latin – meant literary and textual criticism with all relevant ancillary studies, rather like the German *Philologie*. A pupil of Aristarchus, Dionysius Thrax (ca 170–ca 90 BC), famed for his

Homeric criticism, outlined the contents of the discipline of grammar in his day like this:

Grammar is the practical study of the normal usage of poets and prose writers. It has six parts:
1. competence in reading aloud observing prosody [= accents and vowel length];
2. interpretation, with particular attention to the figures of speech encountered in the text;
3. explanation in simple terms of difficult words and allusions;
4. investigation of the true meaning (*etymologia*) of words;
5. analysis of analogy;
6. criticism of poems, the finest branch of this subject.²

Much of this programme reflects the literary preoccupations of the Alexandrians – reading aloud; comprehension of difficult words, allusions and figures of speech; and criticism, whether textual or literary. The interest in the 'true meaning' of words reflects the pervasive concern with etymology (in the sense in which that term is used in Plato's *Cratylus*) in the ancient world. Only one item in the list comes close to the concerns of a grammarian narrowly defined: the fifth, the analysis of analogy. Although many scholars have been tempted to assume that 'analogy' must here imply full-scale morphological analysis tantamount to 'grammar' in the narrow sense, it is as possible that it simply referred to Aristophanes's and Aristarchus's criteria for identifying comparable forms.

4.3 The first grammars in the West

Who wrote the first grammar in the West? Controversy surrounds this issue. It was assumed for a long while that this distinction – or at any rate, the distinction of writing the earliest grammar to survive – belonged to Dionysius Thrax. But recently both views have been challenged. It now looks more likely that the first systematic grammars were written during the first century BC, after Dionysius's death in 90 BC, and that the grammar thought to be his work, the *Tekhnē grammatikē* ('Art of Grammar'), belongs to a later epoch, perhaps as late as the fourth century AD (see box 4.2). We have a fair amount of information about Greek grammars from the first century AD and later in the form of fragments of grammars preserved on papyrus rolls excavated in Egypt (which by that time was part of the Hellenistic cultural sphere), and a few complete treatises. One of the earliest grammatical fragments so far discovered dates from the first century AD. Here is the full text:

A meaningful utterance (*logos*) is a prose collocation of word forms (*lexis*) revealing a complete thought. Its parts are nine: proper noun, common noun, participle, pronoun, article, verb, preposition, adverb, conjunction.

The proper noun is a word form which signifies the individual nature of an object or concept, without tense but with cases, such as 'Homer', 'Paris'.

The common noun is a word form which applies to many objects, without person or tense, such as 'poet', 'person'.

The participle is a word form which takes articles and cases, and shows distinctions of tense, such as 'saying', 'known'. Hence it is called 'participle', in that it participates in aspects of both noun and verb.

Box 4.2 Who wrote the *Tekhnē grammatikē*?
Even during the Middle Ages many of the scholars of Byzantium had doubts about the authenticity of the *Tekhnē grammatikē* (although that did not keep them from using it as their chief elementary textbook), and the question was reopened in modern times by the Italian scholar Vincenzo Di Benedetto, who published a massive monograph on the subject in 1957–8. All scholars today accept the first five chapters as genuine. In them, Dionysius outlines the contents of the discipline of grammar (see p. 55 above), and then discusses reading aloud, accents, punctuation and the genre of rhapsody. It is the status of the rest of the work which is in dispute. The remaining chapters look like a self-contained grammar of a type common in both Greece and Rome in late Antiquity, starting with chapters on the smaller linguistic units – the *gramma* (letter/speech-sound), syllable and word – and then on each word class: noun, verb (and conjugation), participle, article, pronoun, preposition, adverb, conjunction. The arguments are of two kinds, internal (based on evidence from the text of the grammar itelf) and external:

1. The programme set out in the opening paragraph is not followed after chapter 5.
2. The first five chapters have almost no connection with the rest of the work, suggesting that they were added later as a kind of introduction to an existing self-contained grammar.
3. There are significant discrepancies between the doctrine ascribed to Dionysius Thrax by early sources and that of the *Tekhnē grammatikē*.
4. The only passages quoted from the *Tekhnē grammatikē* by writers earlier than the fourth century AD come from the first five chapters.
5. The earliest copies of the *Tekhnē grammatikē* date from the fifth century AD.
6. The extant Greek grammars dating from the first to fourth centuries AD are not based upon the *Tekhnē grammatikē*, but show the kind of fluctuation and experimentation that was characteristic of grammar in the better-documented Roman world *before* it was given definitive form in the mid-fourth century by Donatus (see section 4.6 below).

Supporters of the authenticity of the *Tekhnē grammatikē* argue that there is no reason why such a work should not have been written in the late second century BC, and that it could in any case have undergone substantial modification in the centuries between its composition and the earliest surviving manuscript copies. Given that new papyrus fragments are still being excavated in Egypt, it is possible that a definitive answer will soon appear. In the meantime, this book will adopt the position that the status of the *Tekhnē grammatikē* is analogous to that of Donatus's two grammars in the Roman world – the outcome at a fairly late date of several centuries of consolidation and abbreviation, and the definitive textbook in the Byzantine world throughout the Middle Ages.

Reading
Alan Kemp, 'The *Tekhnē grammatikē* of Dionysius Thrax translated into English', *Historiographia Linguistica* 13 (1986), 169–89, reprinted in Daniel J. Taylor, *The*

4.3 The first grammars in the West

> *History of Linguistics in the Classical Period*, Studies in the History of the Language Sciences 46 (Amsterdam: John Benjamins 1987), pp. 169–89.
>
> Alan Kemp, 'The emergence of autonomous Greek grammar', in Peter Schmitter, ed., *Geschichte der Sprachtheorie 2. Sprachtheorien der abendländischen Antike* (Tübingen: Narr 1991), pp. 302–33. [Useful summary of the arguments, pp. 307–15.]
>
> Vincenzo Di Benedetto, 'Dionisio Trace e la Techne a lui attribuita', *Annali della Scuola Normale Superiore di Pisa*, 2nd ser., 27 (1958), 169–210, and 28 (1959), 87–118. [The article that reopened the debate: for enthusiasts only!]
>
> Vivien Law and Ineke Sluiter, eds., *Dionysius Thrax and the Technē Grammatikē*, 2nd edn, The Henry Sweet Society Studies in the History of Linguistics 1 (Münster: Nodus 1998). [Collection of articles on the authenticity problem.]

The pronoun is a word form used demonstratively instead of the noun, assigning order to the persons, such as 'I', 'he'.

The article is a word form with case which is placed before or after another word inflected for case and shows distinctions of gender, as in (in the nominative case) *ho, hē, to* 'the' [cf. German *der, die, das*].

The verb is a word form showing activity or receiving action with tense and person, such as 'I write', 'it is being written' [these are single-word forms in Greek: *lego, graphetai*].

The preposition is an uninflected word form which stands before the word classes in composition. These are the prepositions: *ana* 'up to', *kata* 'down to', *dia* 'through', *meta* 'after', *para* 'beside', *anti* 'against', *amphi* 'around', *huper* 'over', *apo* 'from', *peri* 'about', *en* 'in', *eis* 'into', *pro* 'before', *pros* 'toward'.

The adverb is an uninflected word form which is placed before or after the verb and not compounded with it, signifying quantity, quality, time, place, negation, agreement, prohibition, exhortation, interrogation, exclamation, comparison or doubt. Indicating quantity: 'frequently', 'rarely'. Quality: 'well', 'nicely'. Time: 'now', 'yesterday', 'tomorrow'. Place: 'here', 'there', 'outside'. Negation: 'not'. Agreement: 'yes'. Prohibition: *mē* [the negative particle used in negative commands]. Exhortation: 'what!', 'encore!'. Interrogation: 'where?'. Exclamation: 'if only!' [cf. Spanish *ojalá*]. Comparison: 'like'. Doubt: 'pretty much', 'perhaps'.

The conjunction is a word form linking the parts of discourse. It is used with copulative, disjunctive, causal, rational, interrogative, hypothetical, or expletive force. The following conjunctions are copulative: 'but', 'on the one hand', 'both . . . and', 'and', ' . . . as also', 'and also' . . . Disjunctive: [the fragment ends here].[3]

Apart from the digressions on the various types of adverbs and conjunctions, this passage is extremely concise, consisting mostly of a series of definitions of the parts of speech. It may have formed part of a longer text in which, once the initial definitions had been set out, the word classes were discussed one by one, such as we see in some of the other papyri. Even in this short fragment, however, we can glimpse something of the twofold origin of the ancient grammar. The Stoic concern for the distinction between *logos* and *lexis* is manifest in the opening definition. Each of the word classes listed is described as a *lexis*, focussing attention on its formal properties, the concern in earlier centuries of poets and orators. The definitions include where possible both semantic and formal elements. The fact that the proper and common noun are treated as distinct parts of speech even though they lack morphological differentiation (unless you count number; and note that the Greeks did not use capital letters to distinguish proper names) is a reminder of the semantic preoccupations of Stoic linguistic analysis. (Aristarchus, and in the Roman world Palaemon, were reputed to have combined them into a single word class: see box 4.3.) For the most part the author concentrates single-mindedly upon the definitions; his few digressions are semantic in nature, classifying first adverbs and then conjunctions according to their meaning. This fascination with semantic categories, and a tendency to regard them as more interesting than purely formal ones, pervades many ancient grammars, as we shall see.

4.4 Grammar in the Roman world

Even as the Greek *grammatikos* was trying to improve upon the work of his predecessors, contributing to the proliferation of grammars both short and long, his Roman counterpart, the *grammaticus*, was doing the same. Indeed, there is every reason to suppose that the Romans learnt about grammar from the Greeks, although precisely what they learnt is controversial. The Romans had a lingering sense of cultural inferiority when they compared themselves with the Greeks, neatly articulated in a famous line by the Roman satirist Horace: *Graecia capta ferum victorem cepit*, 'captive Greece captivated her brutish conqueror'.[4] Up until the first century BC Greek was the language of much of Roman intellectual life. Roman philosophers, for instance, used Greek for their writings until Cicero created a philosophical metalanguage for Latin and used it in his own philosophical works. Well-to-do families ensured that their sons received a good training in the language by having a Greek slave, a *paedagogus*, as a live-in teacher (and some of these slaves were highly educated in their own right). Young Roman men often went off to the universities at Athens or Rhodes to complete their education. All this meant that the Romans had to engage with Greek as a *foreign* language in a way that the Greeks had never had to engage with any other single language. And as the Roman empire (established in 27 BC) spread east and westward, Latin was customarily imposed upon the subject population as the official language, creating a need for formal instruction in it. If we were to compare the linguistic awareness of the Greeks with that of the Romans, we would have to say that the Greeks for the most part experienced their language from within, as native speakers, and this is reflected above all in their interest in philosophy and rhetoric; and this approach also coloured the grammars they wrote. Meaning – semantic classification – took precedence over form, because as native speakers, teachers and pupils could take the forms for granted. The relationship to language in the Roman world was more complex. The Romans began their intellectual development with what they took over from the Greeks, as they themselves freely acknowledged; they thus inherited the native-speaker-oriented way of looking at language. At the same time, many of them were exposed to a different type of linguistic experience through studying Greek as a foreign language. Often this took place at such an early age that it was closer to growing up in a bilingual family than to formal rule-based instruction; but all the same, in the European context it is in the Roman world that we first see

4.4 Grammar in the Roman world

Box 4.3 The parts of speech (word classes)

We have already seen how Aristotle drew up a list of the constituents of the meaningful utterance (*logos*) in the *De interpretatione*, and a partly overlapping list of the constituents of the utterance-as-form (*lexis*) in the *Poetics*. Other thinkers drew up different lists to suit their own purposes. Grammarians regarded the ability to identify every element in a sentence as an important part of a child's training, and they invariably included a list of word classes, or 'parts of the sentence', in their grammars. (Because *oratio*, the Latin equivalent of the Greek *logos*, can be translated 'speech' as well as 'sentence' or 'utterance', *partes orationis* is traditionally rendered 'parts of speech'. The term *word class* was introduced by Leonard Bloomfield in 1914.) The fragmentary Greek grammars of the first century AD recognise nine word classes: proper noun, common noun, participle, article, pronoun, verb, preposition, adverb, conjunction. Donatus and several other Roman grammarians have a somewhat different list: noun (combining the proper and the common noun), pronoun, verb, adverb, participle, conjunction, preposition, interjection. This list did not include the article, for Latin had none, but on the other hand it separated the interjection off from the adverb as a distinct part of speech. The *Tekhnē grammatikē* likewise combined the two types of noun into a single word class, but, apart from changing the order of the parts of speech by placing the verb next to the noun, retained the characteristic Greek list: noun, verb, participle, article, pronoun, preposition, adverb, conjunction. Priscian (see section 4.10 below) was later to take over the Greek order in his Latin grammar, the *Institutiones grammaticae*, as did those medieval grammarians in the Byzantine cultural sphere who based their doctrine on the *Tekhnē grammatikē*.

How do these lists compare with any list that you might have learnt? For one thing, the adjective is missing from both Greek and Roman lists: since the Greek and Latin adjective declines like a noun and functions substantivally, there was no reason to give it the status of a separate word class. Only when grammarians began to study languages like English, French and German did they find morphological justification for giving it independent status. As for the participle, which modern analysis subsumes under the verb because it is derived from a verbal stem, ancient grammarians argued that since it is a hybrid, derived from a verb but inflecting like a noun, it deserves to be considered an independent part of speech.

Reading

B. Colombat, ed., *L'adjectif: perspective historique et typologique* (= *Histoire, Epistémologie, Langage* 14.1 (1992)). [Collection of articles on the history of the identification of the adjective, with an accompanying anthology of texts, printed in *Archives et Documents de la Société d'Histoire et d'Epistémologie des Sciences du Langage* (SHESL), 2nd ser., 6 (1992).]

J. Lallot, 'Origines et développement de la théorie des parties du discours en Grèce', *Langages* 92 (1988), 11–23.

F. Charpin, 'La notion de partie du discours chez les grammairiens latins', *Histoire, Epistémologie, Langage* 8.1 (1986), 125–40.

grammars written from the opposite point of view, looking at language from the outside, as it were.

According to the traditional story, grammar was introduced to Rome by a Greek, the Stoic Crates of Mallos, who arrived in Rome on a diplomatic mission in 169–8 BC. During his stay he slipped and broke his leg, and whiled away his convalescence by giving lectures on grammar. Nineteenth- and early twentieth-century scholars speculated endlessly on the content of Crates's teaching, and tried to ferret out evidence of Stoic doctrine in Roman grammars. Nowadays scholars tend to view the question as somewhat futile, given that we know nothing whatever about what Crates actually taught, and not as much as we would like about Stoic grammatical doctrine. The current consensus is that the Roman grammatical tradition emerged out of an amalgamation of the Stoic-inspired logical analysis of propositions and the more formal concerns of Alexandrian textual critics.

Varro refers to *grammatici* as though they were a familiar phenomenon in the first century BC, and we know that grammar teaching was well established by the middle of the century – so much so that the famous historian Suetonius (ca 69 AD – after 122 AD) compiled a biographical handbook about the most celebrated (or in some cases notorious) grammarians and rhetoricians of his day, *De grammaticis et rhetoribus*, 'On Teachers of Grammar and Rhetoric', a work which is still extant. Many of the people he describes – Palaemon, Valerius Probus, Pansa and others – wrote long and scholarly treatises on grammar which were often quoted by their successors, but not a single work by any of these scholars survives. The few short passages reproduced out of context by later writers are not enough to give us any idea of the structure of their works or of what they considered important.

4.5 Quintilian and the ideal education

Our main source of information about grammar and grammatical instruction in the Roman world in this early period is a text which belongs not to the discipline of grammar but to that of rhetoric: a work on the proper education of the orator, *Institutio oratoria*, 'Educating the Orator', by Marcus Fabius Quintilian(us) (ca 35 AD–ca 100 AD). Originally from Spain, Quintilian was the head of the leading school of rhetoric in Rome. Far from having the frivolous or morally somewhat questionable reputation it has in many quarters today, rhetoric was the cornerstone of Roman life: professional advancement depended upon being able to argue one's case well in the Senate, in the lawcourts, or at the imperial court. Boys destined for a high-flying political career needed to be carefully schooled in rhetoric so that they could later make their way in the highest echelons of Roman society through their eloquence and their command of the classical authors. In view of what was at stake (at any rate in the eyes of ambitious parents), Quintilian devotes a fair amount of space to what he regards as the ideal education for the young orator. But he does not restrict his account to the actual professional training in rhetoric. Instead, he argues that the orator, by reason of his responsible position in society, must possess well-developed moral qualities. Since

Box 4.4 Terminology 1: *littera*

The Latin term *littera* looks temptingly like our 'letter', but the similarity is misleading. *Littera*, like its Greek equivalent, *gramma*, was a more complex entity than our 'letter'. The *littera* had three properties: its name, e.g. 'double-u'; its shape, e.g. W; and its sound-value, e.g. /w/:

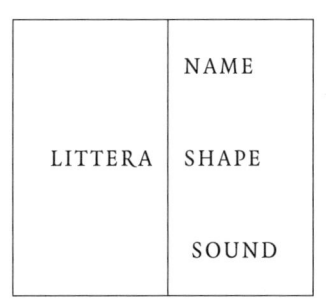

	NAME
LITTERA	SHAPE
	SOUND

Finding a single equivalent for *littera* or *gramma* in a modern language is thus next to impossible. At different times they correspond to 'speech-sound', 'phoneme', 'letter' and 'grapheme', or to all of these simultaneously. But ancient writers could contrast 'letter' and 'speech-sound' when they wanted to, by restricting *littera* to the sense of 'letter' and contrasting it with *elementum* (Greek *stoikheion*), 'element, minimal unit'.

ELEMENTUM	SPEECH-SOUND
LITTERA	LETTER

Thus it is wrong to claim that ancient writers confused letter and sound; in most ancient texts it is quite clear which is meant.

Reading

David Abercrombie, 'What is a "letter"?', in his *Studies in Phonetics and Linguistics* (London: Oxford University Press 1965), pp. 76–85, repr. from *Lingua* 2 (1949), 54–63.

Françoise Desbordes, '*Elementa*. Remarques sur le rôle de l'écriture dans la linguistique antique', in Henri Joly, ed., *Philosophie du langage et grammaire dans l'Antiquité* (Brussels: Ousia and Grenoble: Université des Sciences Sociales 1986), pp. 339–55.

Françoise Desbordes, 'La prétendue confusion de l'écrit et de l'orale dans les théories de l'Antiquité', in Nina Catach, ed., *Pour une théorie de la langue écrite* (Paris: CNRS 1988), pp. 27–33.

José Antonio Puentes Romay, 'Algunos aspectos de la doctrina acerca de las letras en los gramáticos latinos', *Euphrosyne* 19 (1991), 143–58.

moral training is best begun in earliest childhood, education in the early years is of the foremost importance. Quintilian examines this early education in some detail in Book I of the *Institutio oratoria*. He tells us how children should be taught to write – by tracing letters incised in their wax tablets – and discusses the relative merits of education at home and at school. Grammar gets three chapters to itself (I iv–vi), from which we can gain some impression of what the grammar-teacher taught toward the end of the first century AD.

First, Quintilian announces that grammar is divided into two parts:

1. *recte loquendi scientia* 'knowledge of how to speak correctly';
2. *poetarum enarratio* 'interpretation of the poets'.

Grammarians have to teach the division of the letters/speech sounds (Latin *littera*, like the Greek *gramma*, denotes both: see box 4.4) into vowels, semivowels (our continuants) and mutes (our plosives), and Quintilian goes into some detail over orthographical problems. He then moves on to the parts of speech, giving a brief history of opinions about how many should be identified. Children should learn to inflect nouns and verbs correctly, he says, and should be aware of irregularities of gender and case. He goes on to discuss the 'virtues and vices' of speech, which for the most part correspond to what were traditionally known as 'figures of speech' (see box 4.9 below).

Later he discusses the issue of authority and usage in grammar. Speakers have their norms to follow, writers theirs. Four factors govern speech: reason (i.e. analogy and etymology); the usage of very ancient writers, especially religious ones; the authority of literary authors, particularly orators and historians; and usage or custom. Each force plays a part in language, and Quintilian exemplifies them all and tries to assess their relative merits. Although this topic only occasionally made its way into grammatical treatises, the Romans continued to be aware of it as a linguistic issue for several centuries: echoes of the debate appear in the fourth and fifth centuries in the grammars of Charisius, Diomedes, Augustine, Audax and Victorinus.

Quintilian's sketch of grammar thus includes the letters/speech sounds, the parts of speech, and the virtues and vices of speech. As we shall see, this three-part curriculum foreshadows the structure of many a Latin grammar. Later, Quintilian surveys Greek and Latin literature, picking out the works an orator should know. But rhetoric naturally occupies the bulk of his book. Quintilian's description of the ideal education of the orator corresponds in broad outline to what we know of educational practice, at least in urban settings (box 4.5). Rhetoric and associated studies thus came to dominate the Roman curriculum (box 4.6). Although philosophy was in principle highly prized, in practice it took second place to rhetoric. A Roman who wanted to make a serious study of philosophy had to go to the Greek world, to Athens or to Rhodes, whereas for a good training in rhetoric he could stay at home. The ultimate goal of Roman education – to turn out good orators – cast its shadow over the earlier stages of schooling, in that the grammar-teachers (*grammatici*) shaped their instruction to act as a preparation for rhetorical training; indeed, one grammarian, Diomedes, integrated some preparatory

> **Box 4.5 Ancient education**
> In its very earliest stages, education in ancient Greece and Rome centred on the 3 Rs: reading, writing and arithmetic. The Roman boy might be sent to the school of the *litterator* from seven to about twelve, or if his parents were well-off, they might buy a well-educated Greek slave, a *paedagogus*, to educate him at home. (The Aesop who compiled *Aesop's Fables* was just such a *paedagogus*.) Around twelve the boy would move on to a school run by a grammarian, or *grammaticus*, whose job it was to introduce him to the great literature of the past, the badge then as now of a cultivated member of society. While studying the prescribed texts, the 'classics' par excellence – Vergil's epic poem, the *Aeneid*; the comedies of Terence; the speeches of Cicero; and the historical writings of Sallust – the boy would be introduced to the basic concepts of grammar as analytical tools. If he progressed further, he would enter the school of the *rhetor*, the teacher of rhetoric, in his late teens, and master the techniques of public speaking that would open the door to a career as a lawyer, equipped to play an active part in the affairs of the nation in the Senate or the imperial court. (Greek education, in contrast, had philosophy as its ultimate goal.) Access to education depended not only upon gender and social status but upon place of residence: small country towns rarely boasted instruction above the elementary level.
>
> Reading
> H.-I. Marrou, *A History of Education in Antiquity* (London: Sheed and Ward 1956), part 3, chs. 4–6.
> Stanley F. Bonner, *Education in Ancient Rome from the Elder Cato to the Younger Pliny* (London: Methuen 1977), esp. part 3.
> Alan D. Booth, 'Elementary and secondary education in the Roman Empire', *Florilegium* 1 (1979), 1–14.
> Robert A. Kaster, *Guardians of Language: The Grammarian and Society in Late Antiquity* (Berkeley, CA: University of California Press 1988), ch. 1.

training in rhetoric into his grammar. But most of the *grammatici* concentrated on the study of grammar and the great literary authors, the common heritage of all educated Romans. The perennial school favourites – Vergil, Cicero, Terence, Sallust – were occasionally supplemented by other writers such as the satirists Horace and Juvenal, and the epic poets Lucan and Statius. In order to understand the numerous allusions in their works pupils were introduced to a certain amount of history, geography, mythology and astronomy, and various textbooks on these subjects have come down to us. Likewise, about thirty Latin grammars and a number of treatises on metrics and orthography have survived, most of them dating from the third to early fifth centuries AD, the so-called 'Late Latin' era (as opposed to the Golden Age of Latin literature, the first century BC, or the Silver Age, the first and second centuries AD). For this reason their authors are known as the *Late Latin grammarians*. These grammars fall into two broad groups depending upon their writer's orientation: predominantly semantic or predominantly formal. As we shall see, those of a predominantly semantic orientation – the *Schulgrammatik* type – reflect the needs of native speakers, whereas those

Box 4.6 Studying under the rhetoricians: the *ars rhetorica*
Rhetoric, often described as the art of speaking well, traced its origin back to Aristotle and the Sophists. In the Greek world Aristotle's *Rhetoric*, a lost treatise by Hermagoras (second century BC), and a complete course by Hermogenes (ca AD 200), and at Rome Quintilian's *Institutio oratoria*, the *Rhetorica ad Herennium* attributed to Cicero, and several works by Cicero (106–43 BC) himself gave the discipline its canonical form. It had five parts, corresponding to the five stages in the composition of a speech:

- invention (*inventio*): choice of subject
- arrangement (*dispositio*): organisation of the subject-matter
- expression (*elocutio*): clothing the subject-matter in fitting words
- memorisation (*memoria*): committing the discourse to memory using special techniques
- delivery (*pronuntiatio*): pronouncement of the discourse with dignity and elegance, using suitable gestures

The overlap with both grammar and dialectic was obvious from earliest times, when Socrates was so anxious to demarcate the respective territory of rhetoric and dialectic. By the end of Antiquity grammar, rhetoric and dialectic had been brought together within the framework of the Seven Liberal Arts (box 5.6, p. 101 below).

Brief surveys
Brian Vickers, *In Defence of Rhetoric* (Oxford: Clarendon 1988), ch. 1.
Françoise Desbordes, 'La rhétorique', in Sylvain Auroux, ed., *Histoire des idées linguistiques 1. La naissance des métalangages en Orient et en Occident* (Liège and Brussels: Mardaga 1989), pp. 162–85.
Françoise Desbordes, 'Agir par la parole: la rhétorique', in Peter Schmitter, ed., *Geschichte der Sprachtheorie 2. Sprachtheorien der abendländischen Antike* (Tübingen: Narr 1991), pp. 395–426.

Longer works
Françoise Desbordes, *La rhétorique antique* (Paris: Hachette Supérieur 1996).
M. L. Clarke, *Rhetoric at Rome: A Historical Survey*, 3rd edn (London and New York: Routledge 1996).
George A. Kennedy, *A New History of Classical Rhetoric* (Princeton, NJ: Princeton University Press 1994).
James J. Murphy and Richard A. Katula, eds., *A Synoptic History of Classical Rhetoric*, 2nd edn (Davis, CA: Hermagoras 1994).
William J. Dominik, ed., *Roman Eloquence: Rhetoric in Society and Literature* (London and New York: Routledge 1997).
Richard L. Enos, *Roman Rhetoric: Revolution and the Greek Influence* (Prospect Heights, IL: Waveland 1995).

which concentrate on form – the *regulae* genre – are geared to foreign students of Latin.

4.6 Donatus and the *Schulgrammatik* genre

In many respects the needs of young Romans embarking upon the study of Latin literature were similar to those of young Greeks about to plunge into the epics of Homer and the great Greek tragedies. The inflectional patterns of their native tongue were their birthright; what they needed was a conceptual framework with which to analyse the stylistic devices encountered in the texts. Because their needs were so similar to those of their Greek counterparts, Roman grammarians were able to adapt the basic type of grammar in use in the Hellenistic world to their own purposes, taking over many of the fundamental notions identified by the Greeks. The literary context of the study of grammar may explain why Roman grammarians preferred to adapt Greek models instead of building on Varro's work: his *De lingua latina* could have provided the inspiration for a well-organised *formal* description of Latin. But formal categories were of less interest to the Late Latin grammarians than the mix of semantic, formal and functional categories developed by the Greeks, and for this reason they took up the Greek type of grammar and modified it to suit their own needs. The grammatical genre which resulted is known as the *Schulgrammatik* ('school grammar') genre. (This not wholly appropriate name – for why should the label of 'school grammar' be reserved for one type of grammar and not another? – was bestowed upon a particularly important lost work of the type by the German classicist Karl Barwick in 1922.[5]) Grammars of *Schulgrammatik* type are characterised by four features:

- rigorously hierarchical structure;
- systematic structure within chapters;
- logical organisation reflecting the presumed logical structure of language;
- tendency to foreground semantic categories and correspondingly to relegate formal categories to second place or omit them altogether.

Some fifteen Latin grammars of this type have come down to us (box 4.7), but only one complete early Greek one, the *Tekhnē grammatikē* mentioned in section 4.3 above. Many more, both Greek and Latin, must once have existed.

To get acquainted with the *Schulgrammatik* genre (and at the same time to prepare the ground for the next two chapters) let us look at the two most famous grammars of the Roman world, the *Ars minor* ('Shorter Grammar') and *Ars maior* ('Longer Grammar') by Aelius Donatus. They were studied continuously up to the sixteenth century, and provided a model for countless other works well into the early modern period; indeed, their influence lived on indirectly into twentieth-century Britain via *Kennedy's Latin Primer*, a famous school textbook from which generations of boys and girls learnt their Latin. Donatus, active in Rome in the years around AD 350, owed some of his

> **Box 4.7 Latin grammars wholly or partly of the *Schulgrammatik* genre**
>
> Scaurus, *Ars grammatica* (Rome, second century?) [unpublished]
>
> Asper, *Ars* (uncertain date and provenance, but probably early) [GL 5.547–54]
>
> Sacerdos, *Artes grammaticae* (Rome, late third century) [GL 6.417–546]
>
> Probus, *Instituta artium* (?Palestine, or ?originally from Africa moving to Rome; grammar written between 305 and 320) [GL 4.47–192]
>
> (Maximus) Victorinus, *Ars* (early fourth century) [GL 6.187–205]
>
> Donatus, *Ars minor* and *Ars maior* (Rome, ca 350) [GL 4.355–402; ed. L. Holtz, 1981], transl. Wayland John Chase, *The Ars Minor of Donatus, for 1000 Years the Leading Textbook of Grammar*, University of Wisconsin Studies in Social Sciences and History 11 (Madison, WI: University of Wisconsin 1926), repr. in Peter H. Salus, *On Language: Plato to von Humboldt* (New York: Holt, Rinehart and Winston 1969), pp. 92–103.
>
> Marius Victorinus, *Ars grammatica* (Rome, ca 350, or possibly written a few years earlier, while he was still in Africa) [GL 6.3–173; ed. I. Mariotti, 1967]
>
> Charisius, *Ars grammatica* (originally from Carthage; thought to have written grammar while teaching in Constantinople, ca 362) [GL 1.1–296; ed. K. Barwick, 2nd edn 1964]
>
> Diomedes, *Ars grammatica* (?Constantinople, ca 370–380) [GL 1.299–529]
>
> Augustine, *Ars breviata* (originally from Thagaste and Carthage; wrote grammar while at Cassiciacum, Italy, 386–7) [ed. C. F. Weber, 1861]
>
> Dositheus, *Ars grammatica* (eastern Roman empire, late fourth century) [GL 7.376–436; ed. J. Tolkiehn, 1913]
>
> Audax, *Excerpta* (Africa, late fourth century) [GL 7.320–62]
>
> Consentius, *Ars de nomine et verbo* (Narbonne, first half of the fifth century) [GL 5.338–404]
>
> Anonymus Bobiensis, *Ars grammatica* (Italy, fifth century?) [GL 1.533–65; ed. M. De Nonno, 1982]
>
> Priscian, *Institutiones grammaticae* (originally from Caesarea in Mauretania (Roman north Africa); wrote grammar in the years 526–7 while teaching at Constantinople) [GL 2 and 3.1–377]
>
> Note
> GL = *Grammatici Latini*, ed. Heinrich Keil, 8 vols. (Leipzig: 1855–80, repr. Olms: Hildesheim 1961, 1981). Many of the texts included in the *Grammatici Latini* have been re-edited recently; the editor's name and date of publication are listed above, where relevant.

fame to his ex-pupil St Jerome, who mentions his old teacher three times in his widely read writings on the Bible. Otherwise, we know almost nothing about Donatus's life; all we have to go on are his works. Like many other ancient grammarians, he wrote commentaries on some of the literary texts he taught: the comedies of Terence and the poems of Vergil. But his reputation rests on his two grammars. The *Ars minor*, aimed

4.6 Donatus and the *Schulgrammatik* genre

> **Box 4.8 The ancient book**
>
> In ancient Greece and Rome the commonest writing material was *papyrus*, a paper-like substance made from a reed which grew prolifically along the Nile. Instead of binding separate sheets together down one edge, as we do, the ancient practice was to glue up to twenty sheets together into a long roll. The amount of text that one could fit onto such a roll was known as a *book* (Latin *liber*, pl. *libri*), and ancient writers used it as a convenient unit roughly equivalent to a longish chapter. Thus, when we say that Donatus's *Ars maior* is 'divided into three books', we should think of a single work consisting of three fairly lengthy chapters headed 'Book I' 'Book II' and 'Book III'. Gradually, however, Christians in the second and third centuries took to using little booklets of folded sheets stitched together down one edge. Since papyrus was too brittle to be sewn securely, animal skins, stretched and cured in a special way, were used instead. (Sheets made from sheepskin were often called *parchment*, whilst the term *vellum* usually denoted sheets made out of calfskin.) Once bound, usually with wooden boards covered with leather or parchment, these *codices*, or books in the modern sense, were much more durable than papyrus. If an ancient text was transcribed from a papyrus roll into a parchment or vellum codex it had a good chance of surviving on into the Middle Ages and so to us. If, on the other hand, it failed to be transcribed, as probably happened to the grammars of Pansa and Remmius Palaemon, then it was lost. By the fourth century, codices accounted for the lion's share of ancient book production. Although papyrus was still in use here and there into the eighth century, almost all the grammars that have come down to us are preserved in parchment codices.
>
> *Reading*
>
> Naphtali Lewis, *Papyrus in Classical Antiquity* (Oxford: Clarendon 1974).
>
> L. D. Reynolds and N. G. Wilson, *Scribes and Scholars: A Guide to the Transmission of Greek and Latin Literature*, 3rd edn (Oxford: Clarendon 1991), ch. 1.
>
> David Diringer, *The Book Before Printing: Ancient, Medieval and Oriental* (New York: Dover 1953, repr. 1982), chs. 4 and 5.

at beginners, deals solely with the parts of speech, in question-and-answer form, in just eleven pages. The *Ars maior*, a more advanced work, is divided into three *books* (box 4.8):

> **Book I.** Sound (*vox*), letter/speech-sound (*littera*), syllable, metrical feet, accents, punctuation.
>
> **Book II.** Parts of speech: noun, pronoun, verb, adverb, participle, conjunction, preposition, interjection.
>
> **Book III.** Barbarisms, solecisms, other faults, metaplasms, schemes, tropes.

An ascending hierarchical structure is visible throughout the three books. Book I works upward from the physical starting-point of speech, vocal sound, to larger units, *litterae*

2   A Greek youth sits reading a papyrus roll (ca 470 BC).

and syllables. (The *morpheme*, a unit which straddles the meaning–form divide, was unknown to ancient and medieval scholars; it is first mentioned in 1896.) Book II deals with each word class in turn. Book III deals mostly with collocations of words coming under the loose modern heading of 'figures of speech' (box 4.9). (This third book, found in a number of grammars of *Schulgrammatik* type, seems to be a characteristically Roman feature with no Greek equivalent.) Ancient writers recognised four linguistic levels, neatly summed up in this oft-repeated saying: 'Every sentence can be divided

> **Box 4.9 The virtues and vices of speech**
>
> Had the Late Latin *ars grammatica* been based upon Varro's *De lingua latina*, there is every reason to suppose that its final section would have consisted of an analysis of the structure of propositions such as we find in Stoic logic. Instead, the preoccupation of rhetoricians and literary critics with stylistics meant that the study of deviations from the norms of 'correct speech' became part of the traditional domain of the grammarian. Such deviations from the norm were of two kinds: the 'vices' (*vitia*) of speech, usages not to be imitated; and the 'virtues' (*virtutes*) of speech, which were regarded as an adornment to discourse. These were further subdivided into six major categories:
>
> *Vices of speech*
> - barbarisms: faults in individual word-forms, e.g. *infantibu' parvis* 'little chil'en', for *infantibus parvis* 'little children';
> - solecisms: faults in collocations of words, e.g. **torvum**que *repente clamat* 'stern and suddenly he cries', for *torve* 'sternly';
> - other faults: a mixed bag of items, some of which turn up in medieval grammars reclassified as virtues.
>
> *Virtues of speech*
> - metaplasms: alterations in the form of a word, e.g. metathesis;
> - schemes: figures of collocation, e.g. alliteration;
> - tropes: semantic alterations, e.g. metaphor, metonymy, synecdoche, periphrasis, hyperbole, sarcasm.
>
> Book III of Donatus's *Ars maior* popularised the study of these figures as a part of the grammatical curriculum, for their usefulness in textual analysis, whether of the *Aeneid* or of the Bible, was obvious. Even in the central and late Middle Ages, when Books I and II of the *Ars maior* fell from favour, Book III was copied and recopied, often in conjunction with Books XVII and XVIII of Priscian's *Institutiones grammaticae*. Together these two texts provided a complete course in syntax, both figurative (Donatus) and non-figurative (Priscian).
>
> Reading
> Marc Baratin and Françoise Desbordes, 'La "troisième partie" de l'*ars grammatica*', *Historiographia Linguistica* 13 (1986), 215–40; and in Daniel J. Taylor, *The History of Linguistics in the Classical Period*, Studies in the History of the Language Sciences 46 (Amsterdam and Philadelphia: John Benjamins 1987), pp. 41–66.
> Marc Baratin, *La naissance de la syntaxe à Rome* (Paris: Minuit 1989), part 2.

into words, and words can be divided into syllables, and syllables into litterae, but there is nothing into which litterae can be divided.'[6] The *Ars maior* is structured around those four levels, the two which lack meaning being discussed together in Book I, the word being dealt with in Book II, and levels above the word in Book III. (Because *logos* and *oratio* denoted *any* meaningful element, from 'word' to 'sentence', there was no room for intermediate syntactic units like 'phrase' and 'clause', and these did not appear in a strictly technical sense in European grammars until the nineteenth century.) This rough isomorphism between the structure of the linguistic treatise and the perceived structure of what it describes – language – is visible in the earliest years of the Latin linguistic tradition, when Varro seems to take it for granted that the structure of his *De lingua latina* arises from the threefold nature of speech.[7] Although Donatus and his contemporaries recognised four rather than three linguistic levels (and they make use of Varro's triad), the number of books into which they divided their grammars was variable; nonetheless, the basic progression from the smallest unit to largest remained a feature of the *Schulgrammatik* genre. The structure of the *Ars maior* is thus linear, sequential and cumulative, progressing upwards through linguistic units from the smallest to the largest: *littera*, syllable, word, complete utterance. The parts of speech are not in themselves hierarchically organised: there was no intrinsic reason why the noun should come first, the pronoun second and the verb third (although many ancient and medieval scholars tried to find some justification for the traditional order). Each word class is therefore presented as being on a par with all the rest.

Ancient writers were convinced that language was at root a natural phenomenon, even if words themselves and their inflections were arbitrary. Since they were sure the world was rationally organised, they felt that the structure of language must be intrinsically logical. It was incumbent upon the grammarian to recognise the logical structure underlying linguistic phenomena and represent it as faithfully as possible. Each chapter in a work of *Schulgrammatik* type such as the *Ars minor* or the *Ars maior* was organised systematically according to the norms of dialectic, like language itself. Each one opens with a definition followed by a list of the properties, or attributes, of the unit defined; and then each property is discussed in turn, with examples. At the end of the chapter come miscellaneous remarks on subjects which did not fit in under any other heading, in recognition either of the irredeemably arbitrary element of language or of the grammarian's inadequacy. The methodical nature of the presentation thus makes it easy to find your way around. If, for example, you want to read about tense in the verb, you run through the list of properties at the start of the chapter on the verb. Having established that tense is the sixth property, you scan the text (either a written copy or the version inscribed upon your memory) until you come to it. In an age when the index did not exist, and tables of contents were rare (for such aids did not become routine until the thirteenth century), systematic organisation was vital.

The chapter on the noun from the *Ars minor* shows these organising principles in action:[8]

What is a noun?	The chapter opens with a definition of the
It is a part of speech which has case and	noun, followed by a list of its
signifies either an object or a notion,	properties. The definition of the noun
and is either proper or common.	includes both a formal element – case –
How many properties does the noun have?	and a semantic one. The proper/
Six.	common distinction mentioned here is

4.6 Donatus and the *Schulgrammatik* genre

What are they?

Quality, comparison, gender, number, composition, case.
What constitutes quality?

There are two types of quality: a noun is either the name of one individual, and is said to be 'proper', or the name of many individuals, and is said to be 'common'.
How many degrees of comparison are there?
Three.
What are they?
Positive, like 'knowledgeable', *doctus*; comparative, like 'more knowledgeable', *doctior*; and superlative, like 'most knowledgeable', *doctissimus* [cf. 'big – bigger – biggest'].
Which nouns can undergo comparison?
Only common nouns which signify quality or quantity [i.e. adjectives]: quality, e.g. 'good', 'bad'; quantity, e.g. 'large', 'small'.
How many noun genders are there?
Four.
What are they?
Masculine, like *hic magister*, 'this teacher'; feminine, like *haec musa*, 'this muse'; neuter, like *hoc scamnum*, 'this bench'; and common, like *hic et haec sacerdos*, 'this priest and this priestess'. In addition, there are nouns of three genders, such as *hic et haec et hoc felix*, 'this happy man/woman/thing', and there are epicene or promiscuous nouns, such as *passer*, 'sparrow', and *aquila*, 'eagle'.
How many types of noun number are there?
Two.
What are they?
Singular, as in 'this teacher', and plural, as in 'these teachers'.

a remnant of the bygone practice of identifying proper and common nouns as separate word classes.

Instead of defining each property, Donatus simply exemplifies them. (Diomedes and Priscian are more generous with their definitions, but most of the Roman grammarians adopt the same practice as Donatus, exemplifying rather than defining the properties.)

Where no obvious metalinguistic term existed, the Romans (like the Greeks before them) pressed a very general catch-all term into service, giving it a technical sense. Thus, the proper/common distinction was labelled 'quality' (*qualitas*); gender was called 'kind' or 'type' (*genus*); and 'voice' (the active/passive distinction) was also called *genus*, although some grammarians preferred to use the term *significatio* 'meaning'.

The adjective was regarded as one of the semantic subtypes of the noun in both Latin and Greek because it inflected almost identically to the noun and functioned substantivally. It was not until the sixteenth century that it was given the status of a word class in its own right.

The ancient understanding of grammatical gender was different from ours. Instead of regarding it as *intrinsic* to the noun – so that, for instance, *sacerdos* is a noun which is *either* masculine when denoting a male referent ('priest') *or* feminine when denoting a female referent ('priestess') – they described the noun as at once *potentially* masculine *and* feminine. Hence the categories 'common gender' and 'noun of three genders' (our adjectives).

Epicene nouns always belong to one and the same grammatical gender, no matter whether the individual sparrow or eagle (or whatever) is male or

How many types of noun composition are there?
Two.
What are they?
Simple, e.g. 'decent', 'potent', and compound, e.g. 'indecent', 'impotent'.
In how many ways may noun compounding take place?
Four:
> from two full forms, e.g. *suburbanus* ['near the city', < *sub* + *urbanus*];
> from two bound forms, e.g. *efficax* ['effective', < *ex* + *fac*-] and *municeps* ['citizen of a town', < *munio* + *capio*];
> from a full form and a bound form, e.g. *insulsus* ['insipid', < *in* + *salsus*];
> from a bound form and a full form, e.g. *nugigerulus* ['trivia merchant', < *nugae* + *gerulus*];
> sometimes from several forms, e.g. *inexpugnabilis* ['impregnable', < *in* + *ex* + *pugnabilis*], *inperterritus* ['indomitable', < *in* + *per* + *territus*].

How many noun cases are there?
Six.
What are they?
Nominative, genitive, dative, accusative, vocative, ablative. Nouns, pronouns and participles of all genders are declined through these cases in the following manner.

Magister 'teacher' is a common noun of the masculine gender, singular number, simple form, nominative and vocative

female. So even if you were talking about a sparrow sitting on her eggs, you would still use masculine modifiers – *hic passer* – because the noun *passer* is grammatically masculine.

The cases are listed here in the order used almost universally in the west up to the mid-nineteenth century. Only after they had become acquainted with the grammars of ancient India, did European scholars realise that here was nothing sacred about this order, and that other sequences might be pedagogically more effective. Thus, British school grammars now use the order nominative, vocative, accusative, genitive, dative, ablative, whereas American ones still retain the old order. Some European countries use slightly different orders.

The paradigms (model nouns declined through all cases) were usually set out in running text rather than in the case, which will be declined thus: nominative *hic magister* 'this teacher' [subject], genitive *huius magistri* 'this teacher's', dative *huic magistro* 'for this teacher', accusative *hunc magistrum* 'this teacher' [direct object], vocative *o magister* 'teacher!', ablative *ab hoc magistro* 'from this teacher'; and in the plural, nominative *hi magistri* 'these teachers' [subject], genitive *horum magistrorum* 'these teachers'', dative *his magistris* 'for these teachers', accusative *hos magistros* 'these teachers' [direct object], vocative *o magistri* 'teachers!', ablative *ab his magistris* 'from these teachers'.

Musa 'muse' is a common noun of the feminine gender, singular number, simple form, nominative and vocative case, which will be declined thus: nominative *haec musa* 'this muse' [subject], genitive *huius musae* 'this muse's', dative *huic musae* 'for this muse', accusative *hanc musam* 'this muse' [direct object], vocative *o musa* 'O muse!', ablative *ab hac musa* 'by this muse'; and in the plural, nominative *hae musae* 'these muses' [subject], genitive *harum musarum* 'these muses', dative *his musis* 'for these muses', accusative *has musas* 'these muses' [direct object], vocative *o musae* 'O muses!', ablative *ab his musis* 'from these muses'.

Scamnum 'bench' is a common noun of the neuter gender, singular number, simple form, nominative, accusative and vocative case, which will be declined thus: nominative *hoc scamnum* 'this bench' [subject], genitive *huius scamni* 'of this bench', dative *huic scamno* 'for this bench', accusative *hoc scamnum* 'this bench' [direct object], vocative *o scamnum* 'bench!', ablative *ab hoc scamno*

visually more striking form of columns or tables, a practice which continued in some countries (notably Italy) into the early modern period.

The Greeks had always declined the definite article along with the noun in their paradigms because the Greek article is clearly marked for gender in the nominative and accusative cases singular and displays no morphological syncretism amongst the cases. Since Latin lacks an article, Roman grammarians pressed the demonstrative adjective *hic* 'this' into service in its stead. To disambiguate one frequent instance of syncretism (with the dative) in noun paradigms, the ablative case was always marked with the preposition *ab* 'from, by' in addition to the demonstrative adjective.

The nine muses were the goddesses of the arts. Despite its pagan associations, *musa* remained the usual model of the first declension, firmly etched into the memories of many generations of schoolchildren, until the sixteenth century, when the embattled German Humanist Nicodemus Frischlin, grumbling that *musa* 'doesn't mean anything', replaced it with *mensa* 'table'.[9] Three centuries later, the banishment of the muses brought the young Winston Churchill up against the irrational reality of the adult world with a jolt. Having memorised the declension of *mensa*, he asked his teacher what it meant:

> '*Mensa* means a table,' he answered.
> 'Then why does *mensa* also mean "O table",' I enquired, 'and what does "O table" mean?'
> '*Mensa*, "O table", is the vocative case,' he replied.
> 'But why "O table"?' I persisted in genuine curiosity.
> ' "O table" – you would use that in addressing a table, in invoking a

'from this bench'; and in the plural, nominative *haec scamna* 'these benches' [subject], genitive *horum scamnorum* 'of these benches', dative *his scamnis* 'for these benches', accusative *haec scamna* 'these benches' [direct object], vocative *o scamna* 'benches!', ablative *ab his scamnis* 'from these benches'.

Sacerdos 'priest' is a common noun of the common gender, singular number, compound form, nominative and vocative case, which will be declined thus: nominative *hic et haec sacerdos* 'this priest and this priestess' [subject], genitive *huius sacerdotis* 'this priest's/priestess's', dative *huic sacerdoti* 'for this priest/priestess', accusative *hunc et hanc sacerdotem* 'this priest and this priestess' [direct object], vocative *o sacerdos* 'O priest/priestess!', ablative *ab hoc et ab hac sacerdote* 'from this priest and from this priestess'; and in the plural, nominative *hi et hae sacerdotes* 'these priests and these priestesses' [subject], genitive *horum et harum sacerdotum* 'these priests' and these priestesses' ', dative *his sacerdotibus* 'for these priests/priestesses', accusative *hos et has sacerdotes* 'these priests and these priestesses' [direct object], vocative *o sacerdotes* 'O priests/priestesses!', ablative *ab his sacerdotibus* 'from these priests/priestesses'.

Felix 'a happy man/woman/thing' is a common noun of every gender, singular number, simple form, nominative and vocative case, which will be declined thus: nominative *hic et haec et hoc felix* 'this happy man/woman/thing' [subject], genitive *huius felicis* 'of this happy man/woman/thing', dative *huic felici* 'for this happy man/woman/thing', accusative *hunc et hanc felicem et hoc felix* 'this happy man/woman and this happy thing' [direct object], vocative *o felix* 'O happy man/woman/thing!', ablative *ab*

table.' And then seeing he was not carrying me with him, 'You would use it in speaking to a table.'

'But I never do,' I blurted out in honest amazement.

'If you are impertinent, you will be punished, and punished, let me tell you, very severely,' was his conclusive rejoinder.[10]

hoc et ab hac et ab hoc felice uel felici 'from this happy man/woman/thing'; and in the plural, nominative hi et hae felices et haec felicia 'these happy men/women and these happy things' [subject], genitive horum et harum et horum felicium 'of these happy men/women/things', dative his felicibus 'for these happy men/women/things', accusative hos et has felices et haec felicia 'these happy men/women and these happy things' [direct object], vocative o felices et o felicia 'O happy men/women and O happy things!', ablative ab his felicibus 'from these happy men/women/things'.

As for those nouns which end in *a* or *o* in the ablative singular, what do they end in in the genitive plural?

In *rum*, and in *is* in the dative and ablative plural.

As for those nouns which end in *e* or *i* or *u* in the ablative singular, what do they end in in the genitive plural?

If the *e* is short, in *um*; if it is long, in *rum*; if they end in *i*, in *ium*; if in *u*, in *uum* with two *u*'s.

What do the dative and ablative plural of these nouns end in?

All of them end in *bus*.

These paragraphs are a brief guide to the correlation of the endings of the ablative singular and the genitive, dative and ablative plural. This information would only make sense to a native speaker; anyone else would require a properly organised account of the Latin noun declensions (box 4.10).

If we were to represent the structure of this chapter diagrammatically, it would look like the figure on p. 76. A hierarchical structure like a rather complicated tree diagram is implicit in the way that the information is organised. (No ancient grammar actually sets out diagrams like this: rather, such a structure is implicit in the text of this and every other chapter of the Ars minor and of most other ancient grammars.) Hierarchical organisation possesses one major advantage: it clarifies the relationship between any particular unit and the units above and below. For example, it is apparent that 'feminine' is one of the four genders of the noun, which is in turn one of the eight word classes. While such vertical relationships are well brought out, horizontal relationships are far less clear. What, for instance, is the relationship between the common noun and the common gender? Does number in the noun have a connection with number in the verb? Do the same processes of compounding apply to all word classes? Such questions cannot easily be accommodated within the hierarchical model, which breaks down when applied to horizontal relationships – relationships

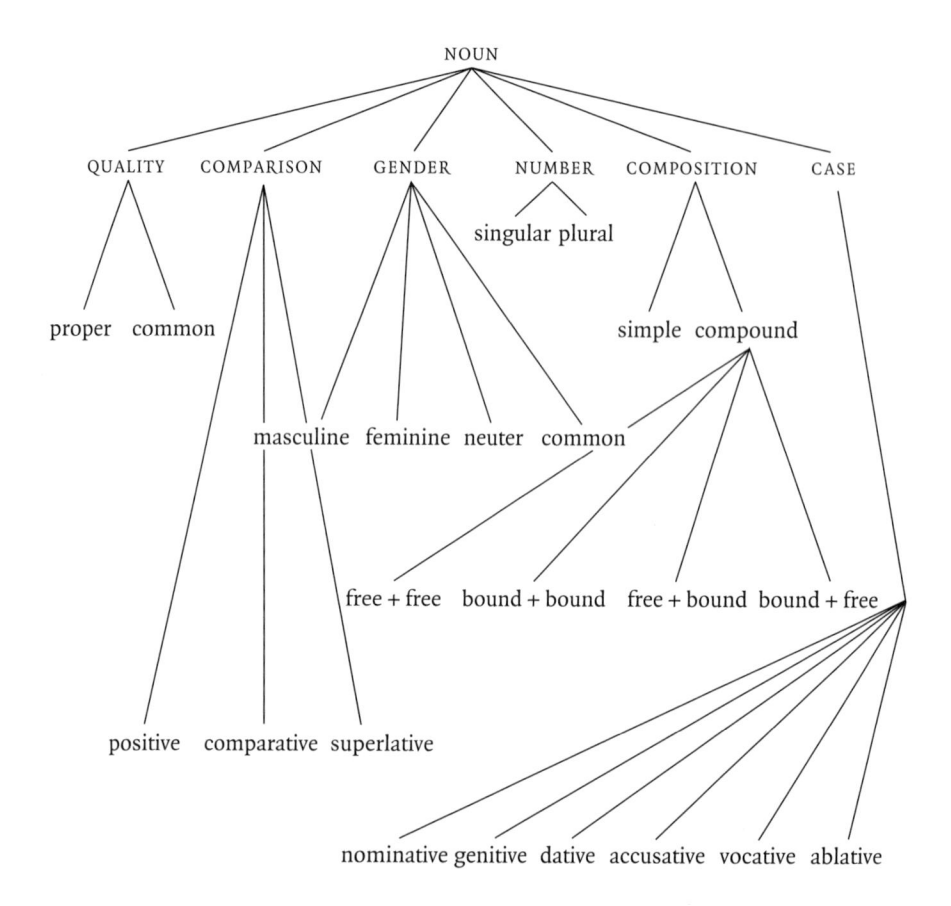

```
                                    NOUN
              ┌──────┬──────────┬────────┬────────┬──────────┬──────┐
           QUALITY COMPARISON GENDER  NUMBER  COMPOSITION  CASE
                                           singular plural

         proper common                              simple compound

                           masculine feminine neuter common

                                   free + free  bound + bound  free + bound  bound + free


          positive comparative superlative

                             nominative genitive dative accusative vocative ablative
```

of equality. In both syntax and historical linguistics, the heavy use of tree diagrams has recently brought to light the limitations of the model. In other spheres of life, too, hierarchical models lead to difficulties in dealing simultaneously with diversity and equality. This has been apparent in the social, racial and political issues that have come to the fore since the middle of the nineteenth century, which the ancient hierarchical mode of thinking – deeply ingrained into western minds through education and administrative structures – is incapable of dealing with. From time to time people try to break away from it in order to develop new modes of thought, new ways of conceptualising relationships, but so far the European intellectual and socio-political mainstream has rejected most such attempts, unconsciously permeated by the habits of thought of the ancient world.

Donatus's grammars show us how this way of thinking was incorporated into textbooks intended for use with young people. From the third century BC to the fifth century AD one textbook after another, in every conceivable subject, was drawn up along these lines, shaping the thought patterns of one generation after another. At first sight grammar lent itself admirably to this treatment. But in practice the inability of the hierarchical model to cope with horizontal relationships brought grammarians up

4.6 Donatus and the *Schulgrammatik* genre

Box 4.10 Latin inflectional morphology

Many languages – English, French and Chinese, for example – rely on a relatively fixed word order to define the relationship of nouns or noun-substitutes in a sentence: 'That cat has caught a bird' is drastically different from 'That bird has caught a cat.' In Latin, as in the majority of the older (and some modern) Indo-European languages, word order played a less important role in establishing these relationships; rather, they were specified by the endings of nouns. Although the number of such relationships is potentially huge, Indo-European languages tend to have a relatively small number of distinct forms, assigning several functions to each one. In Latin, six such formally distinct categories, called 'cases', were recognised by ancient grammarians. In the examples below, the italicised word or words would be in the case indicated in bold in a Latin sentence.

- **nominative:** the subject ('the *cat* arched its back') or subjective completion ('that *dog* is a *mutt*').
- **genitive:** possessive, equivalent to English *of* or *'s* ('the *dog's* fangs', 'the colour *of the tail*').
- **dative:** indirect object ('we put out the milk *for the cat*', 'she gave *the dog* a pat').
- **accusative:** direct object ('the cat scratched *the dog*'), and used after prepositions involving motion *towards* a place ('the dog slunk towards its *kennel*').
- **vocative:** used when directly addressing someone ('*Simiot*, come here!'; 'Down, *Grenser*!').
- **ablative:** a miscellaneous category which has taken over some of the functions of the Indo-European instrumental ('lashed out *with its claws*'), but tends to occur chiefly after prepositions indicating the *place where* something is happening or the *place away from* which something is moving ('the cat perched on *the fence*', 'the dog ran away from *the cat*').

Each of these case functions was represented by a distinct morphological exponent, an ending which coalesced with the stem of the noun. In the course of time, phonological changes took place at the junction of stem and ending. For instance, the ending of the accusative singular was -m. When this met a stem ending in a vowel, no change was normally necessary:

ecclesia-m, fluctu-m, die-m

However, if the stem ended in -o, the -o- became -u-:

*iusto-m > iustu-m

And if the stem ended in a consonant, the original syllabic m̥ generated an epenthetic -e-:

*reg-m̥ > reg-e-m

Five distinct patterns of endings resulted from the fusion of the original endings with the five possible stem vowels. (Consonant-stem nouns were assimilated into the pattern of i-stem nouns.) Varro was the first to point out the existence of such patterns, *declensions*, which his successors called *ordines* 'series' or *declinationes* (*ordo* and *declinatio* in the singular). They refined his list until, some time in the second half of the fourth century, it reached the form it has kept to this day:

First declension:	a-stems, e.g. *musa*
Second declension:	o-stems, e.g. *magister, scamnum*
Third declension:	i- and consonant-stems, e.g. *sacerdos, felix*
Fourth declension:	u-stems, e.g. *fructus*
Fifth declension:	e-stems, e.g. *facies*

Latin verbs were also heavily inflected, changing their endings to indicate modifications of person, number, tense, mood and voice. Verbs, like nouns, underwent various phonological changes when a standard set of endings fused with different stem vowels. The inflectional patterns which resulted (*conjugations*) were called *coniugationes*, 'conjugations', or *ordines*, or sometimes *declinationes*. They were initially numbered as follows:

1. a-stems, e.g. *amare*
2. e-stems, e.g. *docere*
3. i-stems, e.g. *legere, audire*

From the grammarian Sacerdos (third century AD) on, it became increasingly common practice to divide the third conjugation into two, the ĭ-stems and the ī-stems:

1. a-stems, e.g. *amare*
2. e-stems, e.g. *docere*
3. ĭ-stems, e.g. *legere*
4. ī-stems e.g. *audire*

This is the solution preferred by modern grammarians.

Any modern Latin grammar will show you how contemporary teachers conceptualise the structure of the language. Many grammars have tables of paradigms at the end to give you an overview of the inflectional morphology.

Reading
Daniel J. Taylor, 'Latin declensions and conjugations: from Varro to Priscian', *Histoire, Epistémologie, Langage* 13.2 (1991), 85–109.

against the biggest problem in western linguistics: how to relate meaning and form in a single framework.

How does Donatus handle issues of form?

- Inflectional and derivational morphology are treated as parallel phenomena.
- Derivational morphology is given more coverage than inflectional morphology because of its semantic consequences in generating new lexemes.
- No attempt is made to give complete coverage of inflectional morphology: Donatus exemplifies each gender rather than each declension. Thus, he gives

one paradigm of a noun of the first declension (*musa*), two of the second (*magister* and *scamnum*), and two of the third (*sacerdos* and *felix*). What of the fourth and fifth? They are not represented at all, nor are the numerous subtypes and irregular types. Similarly, unless you already know Latin, the instructions in the final paragraphs on how to generate the genitive, dative and ablative plural once you know the ablative singular are unlikely to help you. Of course, Donatus's audience consisted of young Romans, familiar from earliest childhood with a form of Latin (even if in many respects the spoken Latin of the fourth century AD was significantly different from that of writers of the first century BC such as Vergil and Cicero). What his pupils needed in their grammar lessons was an introduction to grammatical taxonomy, learning how to attach the correct metalinguistic label to forms they already knew. Thus, to be shown an example of a noun of each gender declined together with a demonstrative adjective helped to make them aware of the system behind the initially baffling plethora of endings. Once the Roman child realised that *hoc* always marked a neuter noun, then he could transfer that knowledge from *hoc scamnum* 'bench' to *hoc vulgus* 'crowd' or *hoc nomen* 'name' or *hoc genu* 'knee', dissimilar though they are in form and meaning. Donatus operates on the same policy in his chapter on the verb, where he declines only one example in full – a third-conjugation verb, *legere* 'to read'. Again, the native speaker could recognise that the label 'first person singular, future indicative active' applied not only to the form *legam* 'I shall read', but equally well to such apparently dissimilar forms as *docebo* 'I shall teach' and *ero* 'I shall be': one example will do for the native speaker.

- More space is allocated to semantic categories than to formal ones: thus, in the *Ars maior* Donatus lists a great range of semantic subtypes of the common noun with some formal ones interspersed. Here is the complete list, with a selection of Donatus's examples:

corporeal, e.g. 'man', 'earth', 'sea'
incorporeal, e.g. 'piety', 'justice', 'dignity'
primitive, e.g. *mons* 'hill'
derivative, e.g. *montanus* 'hilly'
diminutive, e.g. *monticulus* 'hillock'
nouns of Greek origin which continue to be inflected according to the Greek
    declension pattern, e.g. *Calypso, Pan*.
nouns of Greek origin inflected like Latin nouns, e.g. *Ulixes* (cf. the Greek
    Odysseus)
nouns midway between Greek and Latin, e.g. *Achilles*
homonyms
synonyms
patronymics, e.g. *Atrides* 'son of Atreus'
possessives, e.g. *Agamemnonius* 'belonging to Agamemnon', 'Agamemnonian'
epithets, e.g. 'large', 'strong'
epithets signifying quality, e.g. 'good', 'bad'

epithets signifying quantity, e.g. 'big', 'small'
epithets signifying nationality, e.g. 'Greek', 'Spanish'
epithets signifying one's homeland, e.g. 'Theban', 'Roman'
epithets signifying number, e.g. 'one', 'two'
epithets signifying order, e.g. 'first', 'second'
epithets signifying relationship, e.g. 'father', 'brother'
epithets signifying relation, e.g. 'right', 'left'
generic, e.g. 'body', 'animal'
specific, e.g. 'stone', 'person', 'wood'
verbal nouns, e.g. *doctor* 'teacher', *lector* 'reader' [from the verbs *docere* 'to teach', *legere* 'to read']
nouns similar to participles, e.g. *demens* 'demented', *sapiens* 'wise', *potens* 'powerful'
nouns identical to verbs, e.g. *comedo* 'a spendthrift' [homonymous with the verb *comedo* 'I devour']; *palpo* 'a flatterer' [homonymous with the verb *palpo* 'I caress']

- There is no unit comparable to our 'morpheme' straddling the meaning–form divide. Donatus and his contemporaries speak in terms of *litterae* (see box 4.4 if your memory needs refreshing) and 'syllables', and occasionally of 'endings' (*terminationes*). Otherwise, their morphological metalanguage was almost non-existent.[11]

What Donatus's grammars achieve is to provide an inventory of such basic notions as gender, derivation, composition, number, case, tense, person, mood, voice and conjugation. They set out an extensive semantic classification of types of noun, adverb and conjunction. What they do not do is to provide a comprehensive description of the inflectional morphology of Latin. There are insufficient paradigms to exemplify the many different inflectional patterns of Latin nouns, verbs and participles (pronouns are relatively well covered in the *Ars minor*); there are no rules for the formation of adverbs, nor for generating the comparative and superlative of adjectives. Nor are there any rules on word order, on agreement, or on the use of the moods and tenses. In short, any non-native speaker attempting to learn Latin as a foreign language from these grammars alone would fail (if not already discouraged by the fact that they are in Latin from start to finish). They are clearly targeted at an audience of native speakers who have already mastered the forms of their mother tongue; what Donatus does is to make such people aware of the various morphosemantic categories of their language, and to give them a technical vocabulary with which to label those categories. Nevertheless, Donatus's grammars swiftly gained popularity for reasons we can only guess at. Their brevity and their systematic structure, both of which would have made them easy to memorise, no doubt helped. But the fact that they dealt so inadequately with morphological phenomena created problems which were to challenge the ingenuity and creativity of countless teachers for centuries to come.

4.7 After Donatus: the commentators

A generation or so after Donatus wrote the Ars minor and the Ars maior – possibly still within his lifetime – the focus of grammatical education began to change. Originally the purpose of studying grammar had been to learn to appreciate and imitate the style of literary texts such as Vergil's Aeneid and Cicero's speeches. Grammarians often wrote commentaries on such texts, as we have seen. But at the end of the fourth century one noted grammaticus, Servius by name, the author of an exhaustive commentary on the works of Vergil, composed a commentary on the Ars maior. And his was the first of many (box 4.11). It seems that a change was coming over Roman education. Perhaps standards were felt to be slipping. At any rate, mastering the contents of Donatus's grammars now became as important an activity as assimilating the literary set texts. Several factors might have contributed: the telegraphic brevity of Donatus's style; ambivalence amongst Christian parents and teachers vis-à-vis the secular or sometimes out-and-out pagan nature and morally dubious content of many of the great literary texts of the first century BC; and the effects of linguistic change over the five centuries since those texts were written (box 4.12).

What issues interested the commentators? At the most basic level, they simply wanted to ensure that their pupils had understood the text. Pompeius, for instance, spells out the implications of Donatus's definition of the noun in these words:

A noun is a part of speech which has case and signifies an object or a notion, and is either proper or common. No noun in the world can exist without these three things: it may not lack case; there is no such thing as a noun which is not either corporeal or incorporeal; and there is no such thing as a noun which is not either proper or common. No noun can exist without these three things. The noun attracts these things to itself of its nature. Choose any noun you like. 'Hector' has all of this: 'Hector' has case; Hector can be seen and touched, so it is corporeal; and 'Hector' is the name of an individual, so it is a proper noun. So you see that no noun can exist without these three things.[12]

Box 4.11 Late Latin commentators on Donatus's grammars

  Servius (Rome, late fourth century) [GL 4.405–48]
  Sergius (?Rome, ?late fourth century: but a number of works clearly not all
     by the same author go under the name 'Sergius') [GL 4.475–565]
  Sergius (pseudo-Cassiodorus) (fifth century) [Migne, Patrologia Latina
     70.1219–40]
  Pompeius (Roman North Africa, fifth century) [GL 5.95–312]
  Cledonius (Constantinople, latter part of the fifth century) [GL 5.9–79]

GL = Heinrich Keil, Grammatici Latini, 8 vols. (Leipzig: Teubner 1855–80, repr. Hildesheim: Olms 1961, 1981)

> **Box 4.12 The changing Latin language**
>
> Latin was still very much a living language in the fourth and fifth centuries, the native language or first foreign language of millions of Roman citizens from Portugal to Palestine, from Britain to North Africa. But the educated citizen of Seville, Carthage or even Rome couldn't help noticing that the everyday spoken language was now very different from that of the writings of Vergil or Cicero. Several features stand out:
>
> - phonological changes affecting in particular the vowels of unstressed syllables, leading to thoroughgoing syncretism in the inflectional morphology;
> - increased reliance upon prepositions to spell out syntactic relationships;
> - a preference for a simpler, coordinating, sentence structure, as against the complex subordinating constructions packed with telegraphic participial phrases characteristic of Classical literary style;
> - lexical changes, e.g. *caballus* for *equus* 'horse', *cattus* for *feles* 'cat'.
>
> St Jerome adopted these features in his Latin translation of the Bible, the Vulgate, a move which, while it made the sacred text more easily comprehensible, also contributed to the scorn with which traditionally educated Romans viewed Christianity, already associated with the lower, linguistically less sophisticated, strata of society. One well-educated Christian, a woman called Proba, enterprisingly tried to rescue her faith from the charge of illiteracy by retelling the life of Christ entirely in lines and phrases from Vergil's *Aeneid*. Others undertook to versify bits of the Bible in their own right: Juvencus put the Gospels into verse, Arator did Acts of the Apostles, and Caelius Sedulius composed parallel prose and verse versions of the Gospel story, all with the aim of giving the central texts of Christianity a veneer of linguistic sophistication comparable to that of the great classical literature of the first century BC.
>
> *Reading*
> József Herman, *Vulgar Latin* (University Park, PA: Pennsylvania State University Press 2000).

Pompeius thus tries to lead his pupils to experience nounness. Many of his colleagues preferred a more sharply intellectual approach, applying the methods of analysis they knew from their study of dialectic to Donatus's definitions. This is how Servius works his way through Donatus's definition of the noun:

A noun is a part of speech which has case and signifies an object or a notion, and is either proper or common. The definitions of the word classes ought to be formulated in such a way that they distinguish each one from the other classes and show what is peculiar to the class being defined. Therefore when Donatus said that the noun was a part of speech, he distinguished it from whistling and clapping and other inarticulate sounds. When he said 'which has case', he distinguished it from verbs, adverbs, prepositions and conjunctions. When he said that it signifies 'an object or a notion', this is what is peculiar to it ... And he added another feature peculiar to it, that it signifies something which is 'either proper or common'. For a proper noun pertains to one individual, e.g. 'Hector', and a common noun pertains to many, e.g. 'person'.[13]

Definitions apart, the grammarians found plenty of other matters to comment on. Sometimes they went into the etymology of the metalinguistic terms; sometimes they added information lacking in Donatus, such as ways of identifying the five declensions; and they considered problems such as the relationship of grammatical gender to the sex of real-world beings, and whether the pronoun 'I' has a vocative case. (How do you address yourself when you're talking to yourself? 'O I'? 'O me'? Or just plain 'Hey, you!'?) Individual grammarians worried to a greater or lesser extent about metalinguistic matters such as the significance (or lack of it) of the order in which the parts of speech were listed.

4.8 Regulae grammars: foreigners and form

By a little after AD 100 the Roman empire had expanded right across Europe (see map 1). At its height it extended from Hadrian's Wall, close to the modern border between Scotland and England, to the Iberian peninsula, covering most of western Europe, Hungary, the Balkans and Greece, Turkey, the shores of the Black Sea, much of the Near East, and the coast of North Africa. In succeeding centuries portions were reclaimed by neighbouring kingdoms and tribes, but for several hundred years the empire posed a huge educational problem, for large parts of this area were inhabited by people whose native language was not Latin. The 'barbarians', as they were called (unless they were Greek), sent their children to Roman schools so that they would learn Latin and pick up the trappings of civilisation, and more importantly, be assimilated into the dominant culture. But how they were taught Latin is a mystery. The indigenous type of grammar in the West is the *Schulgrammatik* type represented by the *Ars maior*, in which, as we have seen, few concessions are made to the need of foreign learners for a full description of the forms of the language. In the first and second centuries AD the only aids for foreigners trying to read Vergil were bilingual glossaries; in other words, the problem was tackled initially on the lexical level. Texts dealing with Latin morphology appear in large numbers in the fifth and sixth centuries: they are known as *regulae* grammars (box 4.13).

A number of ancient grammars bear the word *regulae* or its Greek equivalent, *kanones*, in their titles. *Regula* (*regulae* is the plural form) means 'a rule, ruler, model, standard, pattern, paradigm'. One grammarian, Consentius, explains the term in these words: 'a *regula* covers a large number of nouns which follow the same pattern by making a generalisation'.[14] The term was applied to formal patterns only; in practice, therefore, it is closer to our 'paradigm' than to our 'rule'. Significantly, virtually all the surviving *regulae* texts were written in areas were Latin was not the first language of the population – North Africa, Palestine, Constantinople. Their contents and structure are rather heterogeneous: the family resemblance is by no means so strong as it is amongst grammars of the *Schulgrammatik* genre, for two reasons. First, each one represents an individual teacher's attempt to cope with his pupils' needs on his own initiative, without any model to follow. Secondly, it was not a question of helping the pupil to 'recollect' grammar, a process of which there is perhaps still a residual echo in works of the *Schulgrammatik* type. Writers of *regulae* grammars were concerned with the arbitrary

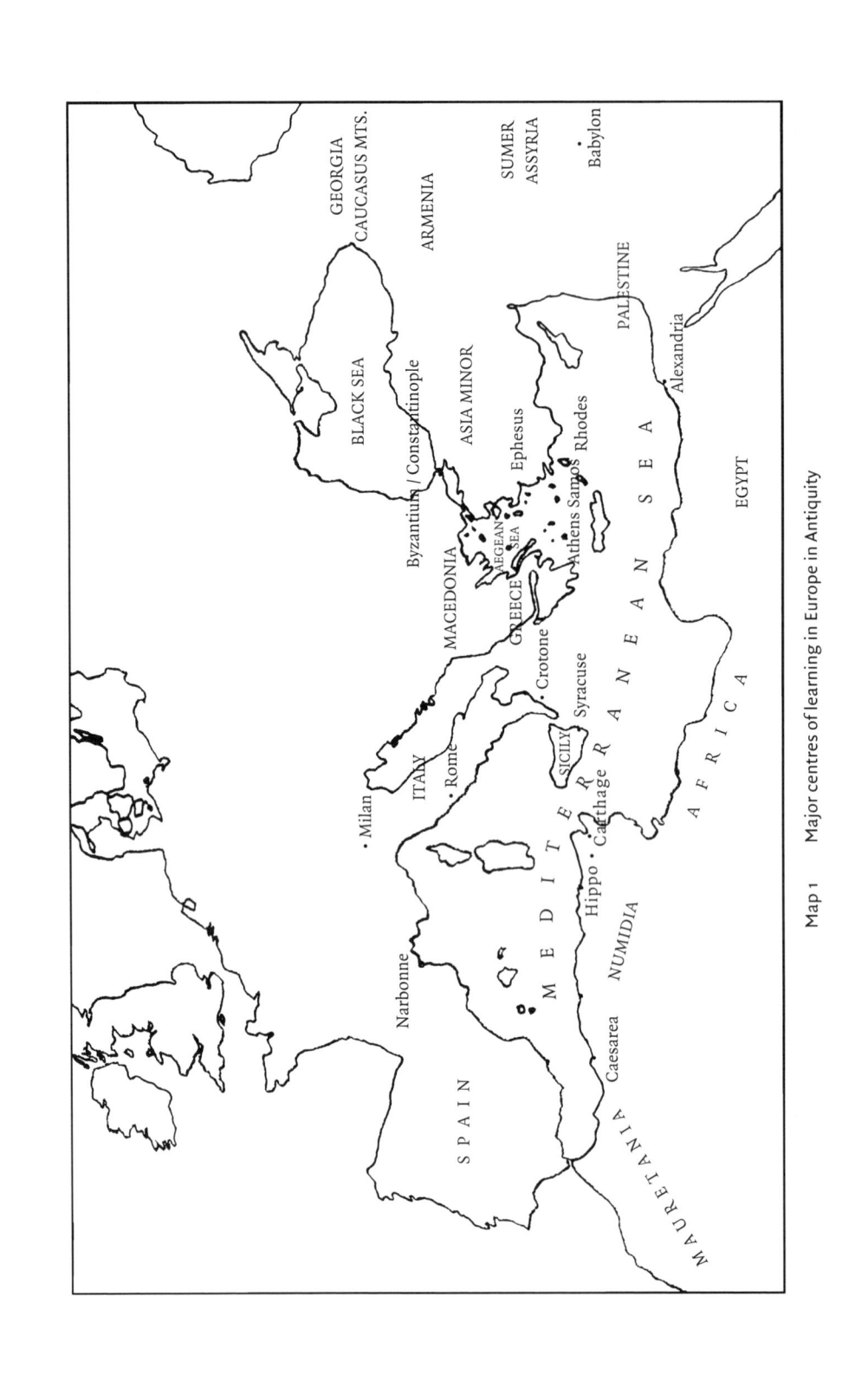

Map 1   Major centres of learning in Europe in Antiquity

4.8 *Regulae* grammars: foreigners and form

> **Box 4.13** *Regulae* grammars
>
> Probus, *Catholica* (the work so called is probably a separately transmitted version of Book II of Sacerdos's *Artes grammaticae* (see box 4.7) [GL 4.3–43]
>
> Martianus Capella, *De nuptiis Philologiae et Mercurii*, Book III (Africa, first half of the fifth century) [ed. J. Willis, 1983]; transl. William Harris Stahl with E. L. Burge, *Martianus Capella and the Seven Liberal Arts 2. The Marriage of Philology and Mercury* (New York: Columbia University Press 1977), pp. 64–105, esp pp. 87–104 (§§290–324).
>
> Phocas, *Ars de nomine et verbo* (Rome, fifth century) [GL 5.410–39; ed. F. Casaceli, 1974]
>
> Priscian, *Institutio de nomine et pronomine et verbo* (originally from Caesarea in Mauretania; wrote grammar while teaching in Constantinople in the early decades of the sixth century) [GL 3.443–56; ed. M. Passalacqua, 1992 and 1999]
>
> Eutyches, *Ars de verbo* (Constantinople, first half of the sixth century) [GL 5.447–89]
>
> pseudo-Augustine, *Regulae* (Africa, fifth or sixth century) [GL 5.496–524]
>
> *Fragmentum Bobiense de nomine et pronomine* (sixth century) [GL 5.555–66; ed. M. Passalacqua, 1984]
>
> pseudo-Palaemon, *Regulae* (date and provenance very uncertain) [GL 5.533–47]
>
> GL = Heinrich Keil, *Grammatici Latini*, 8 vols. (Leipzig: Teubner 1855–80, repr. Hildesheim: Olms 1961, 1981) References to more recent editions are given where possible.

forms of a particular language, Latin. They had to think empirically, working out for themselves how to organise their material. Some set out their collections of material as alphabetically organised reference works. (In fact, however, the student was probably expected to memorise these works, as he would the *Ars minor*.) Phocas, for instance, lists all the possible nominative (citation) endings of nouns in alphabetical order and tells you what gender and declension they belong to. Thus, if you come across an unfamiliar noun ending in -*a*, Phocas will inform you that it could belong to a masculine or a feminine noun of the first declension, or alternatively to a neuter noun of the third declension. Eutyches provides an analogous guide to the conjugations of verbs. Other grammarians, such as pseudo-Augustine and pseudo-Palaemon, provide a selection of paradigms, although their coverage of Latin inflectional morphology is far from complete. Thus, when it came to engaging with the purely formal side of language, Roman grammarians were far from confident about how to proceed. They frequently opted for alphabetical order as the main organising thread of their work, which betrays their total bafflement over how to bring these disparate bits of information into some kind of relationship with each other. And that is natural. They lacked the key that has enabled us to see the order which lies behind all the disparate forms: the historical understanding of how these forms have evolved through time. Only from the mid-nineteenth century were Europeans in a position to structure their accounts of the inflectional morphology of Latin or Greek in a manner consistent with its own internal logic.

4.9 Integrating meaning and form

What happened when a grammarian wished to combine the relatively theoretical, logically organised information contained in a grammar of *Schulgrammatik* type with an account of inflectional morphology, usually alphabetically organised, along the lines of a *regulae* grammar? Several of the grammarians of the later Roman empire took up the challenge. Interestingly, they could not see their way to a thoroughgoing fusion of such disparate types of information; instead, they put them into separate sections. Priscian (see section 4.10), for example, writing his huge *Institutiones grammaticae* shortly after 500, structures his work so as to place *Schulgrammatik* information about the traditionally recognised properties of the noun (much of it cribbed from Donatus's *Ars maior*) into Books I to V, and then gives a separate, minutely detailed description of noun inflection in Books VI and VII. In Book VIII he returns to the *Schulgrammatik* model for his description of the properties of the verb, only to switch again to *regulae* information in Books IX and X, where he discusses the formation of the perfect base form. Thus, although Priscian and several other grammarians (Sacerdos, Charisius, Diomedes, Probus) attempted to integrate meaning and form in their grammars, in practice all they managed to do was to alternate lengthy chunks of *Schulgrammatik* and *regulae* text.

4.10 Priscian

Along with Donatus, Priscian was one of the most influential grammarians of the ancient world. The nature of his influence was utterly different, however: whereas Donatus taught children (and their teachers) *what* to think about language, in terms of a basic structure and metalanguage, Priscian taught them *how* to think. His works, and in particular his monumental *Institutiones grammaticae*, provided theoretical argumentation to take issue with, and a huge corpus of data on which to test the theory.

Priscian, a native of the province of Mauretania in Roman North Africa, taught at Constantinople, the capital of the Byzantine empire, early in the sixth century AD. To judge from his writings, most of his pupils were native speakers of Greek with a high level of competence in Latin. Priscian himself was a prominent figure at the court, publishing several panegyrics to Emperor Anastasius alongside his pedagogical works. Even as a *grammaticus* he was wide-ranging, writing on numerals, weights and measures, rhetoric and metrics as well as on grammar proper.

Each of his three works on Latin grammar was destined to become enormously influential in the course of the Middle Ages, in different ways. Each throws light on a different aspect of language study in late Antiquity. Let us look at them one by one.

Partitiones: *classroom pedagogy*

The full title of the work known as the *Partitiones* ('Divisions', 'Analyses') goes like this: 'Analyses of the Twelve First Lines of the *Aeneid*' (*Partitiones duodecim versuum Aeneidos principalium*). What Priscian does is to examine each word in the first line of each book of Vergil's epic poem, the *Aeneid*, in minute detail. The *Partitiones* is fifty-six pages long in a modern edition – nearly five pages on each verse! What does Priscian find to say? After analysing the metrical structure of the line, he considers each word in it. He runs through the properties of that word class, and takes up the grammatical relations: what case is it in? how do you know? what other words are derived from it? Here is a specimen:

Signum quae pars orationis? What part of speech is 'sign'?
A noun.
Proper or common?
Common.
Primitive or derived?
Primitive.
Give derivatives formed from it.
The diminutive *sigillum* 'seal'; the verbs *signo signas* 'point out' and *signio signis* 'mark with a sign', as well as a verb compounded from this latter, *insignio insignis* 'to mark', from which *insignitus* 'distinctive' comes. In addition, *significo significas significat* 'signify', and *signifer* 'standard-bearer', and *antesignanus* 'front-line soldier', literally 'one who fights in front of the signs', and *designo* 'denote', from which we get 'designate', and *resigno* 'open, disclose', as Virgil says in Book IV of the *Aeneid*: 'he opens his eyes to death'. *Signum* is a homonym: it means 'seal', 'statue', 'battle-standard', 'signal'.[15]

The question-and-answer format allows us to listen in on a lesson in progress: the lively opening interchange (or interrogation) gives way to a mini-lecture from the teacher. This kind of analysis of a series of chosen head-words came to be known as 'parsing' (after the Latin word for 'word class, part of speech': *pars orationis*). The *Partitiones* was not much used in the early Middle Ages, but was rediscovered around 800 and helped inspire a new grammatical genre, the **parsing grammar** (as we'll see in box 7.3, p. 145 below).

The Institutio de nomine: *a framework for formal description*

A much shorter work of Priscian's, the *Institutio de nomine et pronomine et verbo* ('Instruction on the Noun, Pronoun and Verb'), was if anything more influential than the *Partitiones*. Only fourteen pages long, the *Institutio de nomine* deals exclusively with the inflecting parts of speech – the three mentioned in the title plus the participle. It belongs to the *regulae* genre in that it deals with form alone, but – as later readers realised – its importance lies in the fact that it is more systematic than any other *regulae* work. Priscian classifies nouns, pronouns, verbs and participles according to their inflections. Nouns are arranged by declension; pronouns are divided into primitive and derived classes, another form-based classification; verbs are grouped by conjugation, and participles by their tense, which leads to a formal classification. Thus, shortly after AD 500 we find what was lacking in Donatus's day – a systematic form-based description of Latin. Let us look more closely at Priscian's procedure. The work opens with these words:

All the nouns which Latin speech employs are inflected according to the five declensions, which got their order from the sequence of the vowels forming their genitive case. The first declension is thus that in which the genitive ends in the diphthong *ae*, e.g. *hic poeta, huius poetae* 'this poet, this poet's'. The second is that in which the genitive ends in ī e.g. *hic doctus, huius doctī* 'this knowledgeable man, this knowledgeable man's'. The third ends in ĭs, e.g. *hic pater, huius patrĭs* 'this father, this father's'. The fourth ends in ūs, e.g. *hic senatus, huius senatūs* 'this senate, of this senate'. The fifth ends in *ei* pronounced as two separate syllables, e.g. *hic meridies, huius meridiei* 'this noon, of this noon'.

The nominative of the first declension therefore has two final letters, *a* and *s*, and three endings, *a*, *as* and *ēs*, as in *haec syllaba, huius syllabae* 'this syllable, of this syllable', *hic Aeneas, huius Aeneae* 'this Aeneas, of this Aeneas', *hic Anchisēs, huius Anchisae* 'this Anchises, of this Anchises'.

All nouns ending in *a*, whether they are Greek or Latin in origin, masculine or feminine or common, belong to the first declension.[16]

Right at the opening of the work Priscian thus makes clear the basis on which nouns are divided into declensional classes, and then goes on to discuss the various possible nominative endings of each declension, commenting on the correlation between noun ending and gender. As you will have noticed, he uses terms like 'genitive case', 'masculine/feminine/common gender' and so on without explaining them: this work is obviously not intended for beginners. Although someone who already knew Latin well could probably reconstruct all the regular paradigms of the inflecting word classes from what follows, a foreign learner could not: too much is taken for granted, and Priscian frequently refers the reader to his *magnum opus*, the *Institutiones grammaticae*, for further details. (And of course, as in virtually all ancient grammars, source and target language are the same.) In other words, what Priscian provides is the framework for a comprehensive description of Latin forms, but the details are not filled in. What later teachers appreciated about the *Institutio de nomine* was the succinct and systematic framework it provided for the description of Latin inflectional morphology. For this reason it proved to be extremely helpful to early medieval teachers in non-Latin-speaking areas who were grappling with the problem of how to organise comprehensive descriptions of the forms of Latin, as we'll see in chapter 6.

The Institutiones grammaticae: *theory and data*

The *Institutiones grammaticae* ('Grammatical Doctrine') is Priscian's most famous work by far. It is on a totally different scale from the *Partitiones* or the *Institutio de nomine*: it is eighteen books, or nearly 1,000 printed pages, in length. In some respects it is a fusion of *Schulgrammatik* and *regulae* genres. Broadly speaking, its structure is that of Donatus's *Ars maior* (and indeed it cannibalises a good deal of the *Ars maior* as it goes along). But it also incorporates a vast amount of *regulae*-type material on the way (Books VI, VII, IX, X), so that by the end Priscian has recorded absolutely everything there is to know about Latin inflectional and derivational morphology in the five-and-a-half books (312 pages) on the noun and the three books (178 pages) on the verb (not to mention what he has to say on the other word classes). Priscian gives many examples from literary works. His Greek audience is reflected in the fact that he occasionally draws upon Greek sources, notably Herodian (mid-to-late second century AD), and, particularly in his discussion

> **Box 4.14 Apollonius Dyscolus**
>
> Apollonius Dyscolus, 'the grumpy' (nobody knows for sure why he was called that!), lived and worked in Alexandria in Egypt toward the middle of the second century AD. His son Herodian was also a grammarian of some repute. Of Apollonius's extensive grammatical writings only a few have come down to us: treatises on the pronoun, the adverb, and the conjunction, and almost the whole of a four-book work on syntax. It is this upon which Priscian drew for his discussion of syntax. Apollonius discusses the following topics in his *Syntax*:
>
> > **Book I:** preliminary remarks, syntax of the article
> > **Book II:** syntax of the pronoun
> > **Book III:** syntax of the verb, including agreement and grammaticality
> > **Book IV** syntax of prepositions (the lost portion dealt with the syntax of adverbs and conjunctions)
>
> For Apollonius, syntax is a function of semantics, the external representation of the meaning of individual words in combination.
>
> *Translations*
> Fred W. Householder, *The Syntax of Apollonius Dyscolus*, Studies in the History of Linguistics 23 (Amsterdam: John Benjamins 1981).
> Jean Lallot, *Apollonius Dyscole, De la construction (syntaxe)*, 2 vols. (Paris: Vrin 1997).
> Vicente Bécares Botas, *Apolonio Díscolo, Sintaxis* (Madrid: Gredos 1987).
>
> *Studies*
> David L. Blank, 'Apollonius Dyscolus', in W. Haase and H. Temporini, ed., *Aufstieg und Niedergang der römischen Welt* 2. Principat 34.1 (Berlin and New York: de Gruyter 1993), pp. 708–30.
> Ineke Sluiter, *Ancient Grammar in Context: Contributions to the Study of Ancient Linguistic Thought* (Amsterdam: VU University Press 1990), ch. 2.
> David L. Blank, *Ancient Philosophy and Grammar: The Syntax of Apollonius Dyscolus*, American Classical Studies 10 (Chico, CA: Scholars Press 1982).

of syntax, Apollonius Dyscolus (box 4.14). In so doing, he bypassed many indigenous Roman developments, even discussing the parts of speech in the Greek order: noun, verb, participle, pronoun, preposition, adverb, interjection, conjunction. He did not hesitate to introduce concepts from the Greek grammatical tradition; thus, *species*, 'derivational state' (corresponding to the Greek *eidos*), the property of being primitive or derived, is brought into the list of properties of the parts of speech, an innovation which permitted Priscian to discuss derivational morphology more systematically than had previously been possible in the Roman tradition.

What makes the *Institutiones grammaticae* unique among the surviving ancient grammars of Latin is that its last two books are devoted to syntax. The last twelve books of Varro's *De lingua latina* had dealt with the 'conjoining' of words; to judge from the solitary paragraph from this section that has come down to us, its doctrine was modelled

> **Box 4.15 Becoming aware of transitivity**
>
> The Stoics are often credited with being the first to notice transitivity; amongst grammarians, Apollonius Dyscolus mentions the notion at several points in his *Syntax* without formally introducing it. Both that fact and his fluctuating terminology (*diabasis, metabasis*) suggest that it may have been a less formalised notion for him than it was for Priscian, who discusses it several times in his *Institutiones grammaticae*, calling it *transitio personarum*, 'transition of persons'. Priscian's understanding of it, and consequently that of the medieval syntacticians who relied upon him, differed somewhat from ours. This is how he describes it:
>
> It can happen that actions proceeding from the nominative [our 'subject'] to inflected case forms may be understood with respect either to transition of persons or with respect to one and the same person. It happens with transition of persons in 'Aristophanes taught Aristarchus', 'I respected you', 'you said to me' . . .
> The same thing may happen with one and the same person, as in 'Phemius taught himself'. The transition of teaching here takes place, not to another person, but to Phemius himself.
>
> Priscian thus introduces what we call *transitive* and *reflexive* sentences. Later, he mentions *intransitive* utterances, i.e. those which do not make the transition from one person to another, such as 'a tall man is running past'; because the nominal elements are in the nominative case, they have no transitivity. The accusative and ablative, however, when they are transitive, require free-standing prepositions; free-standing prepositions [as opposed to bound prepositions] always denote transitivity.
>
> Contrary to our understanding of the notion, Priscian sees nouns and noun-substitutes as possessing transitivity.
>
> *Reading*
> Anneli Luhtala, 'On the concept of transitivity in Greek and Latin grammars', in Gualtiero Calboli, ed., *Papers on Grammar 3* (Bologna: Clueb 1990), pp. 19–56.
> Anneli Luhtala, *On the Origin of Syntactical Description in Stoic Logic*, The Henry Sweet Society Studies in the History of Linguistics 7 (Münster: Nodus 2000).

on the Stoic analysis of propositions. Donatus had devoted the third book of the *Ars maior* to figures of speech (broadly speaking), many of which involved collocations of words – phrases, clauses or whole sentences; but a systematic treatment of syntax was apparently new to the Latin grammatical tradition. Like Apollonius, Priscian stressed the complete parallelism of the four levels of analysis – *littera* (see box 4.4 above), syllable, word and sentence. The syntactic properties of the pronoun occupied large parts of Book XVII, along with a more general discussion of agreement; Book XVIII dealt with constructions involving nouns and verbs, including the various phenomena later gathered together under the heading of 'government', i.e. constructions involving two nominal elements, such as the ablative absolute, or comparative and possessive constructions. Priscian works through the peculiarities of each mood and voice one by one. One notion he took over from his Greek sources was to be of particular significance in after years: the notion of transitivity (box 4.15). The emphasis on literary usage – Priscian illustrates each point with examples from Greek and Latin authors – encourages him to cultivate a sensitivity to subtler aspects of syntactic usage than are noticed by syntacticians who restrict themselves to a more pedestrian corpus. Priscian comments occasionally on ellipsis and on what 'is understood', *subauditur*, and makes use of the traditional 'figures' as a descriptive framework for apparently anomalous syntactic phenomena. Parts of his discussion of syntax would now be regarded as falling into the domain of pragmatics. Overall, his model of syntax was word-based – a dependency model rather than a constituency model. Priscian was interested primarily in how one word affects another – the classic grammarian's approach, as contrasted with that of the logician, who is characteristically interested in the structure of propositions. When the *Institutiones grammaticae* was rediscovered, around 800, and studied in conjunction with Aristotle's writings on dialectic (for this see chapter 7), it stimulated medieval scholars to turn their minds to syntactic problems.

Further reading

Reading on grammar in the Ancient World

The emergence of grammar

Henri Joly, 'Platon entre le maître d'école et le fabriquant de mots. Remarques sur les "grammata" ', in H. Joly, ed., *Philosophie du langage et grammaire dans l'Antiquité* (Brussels: Ousia and Grenoble: Université des Sciences Sociales 1986), pp. 105–36.

Wolfram Ax, 'Sprache als Gegenstand der alexandrinischen und pergamenischen Philologie', in Peter Schmitter, ed., *Geschichte der Sprachtheorie 2: Sprachtheorien der abendländischen Antike* (Tübingen: Narr 1991), pp. 275–301.

Dirk M. Schenkeveld, 'Scholarship and grammar', *La philologie grecque à l'époque hellénistique et romaine* (= *Entretiens sur l'Antiquité* classique 40 (1993)), 263–306.

Michael Frede, 'The origins of traditional grammar', in Robert E. Butts and Jaakko Hintikka et al., eds., *Historical and Philosophical Dimensions of Logic, Methodology and Philosophy of Science* (Dordrecht and Boston: Reidel 1977), pp. 51–79.

Daniel J. Taylor, 'Rethinking the history of language science in Classical Antiquity', *Historiographia Linguistica* 13 (1986), 175–90; and in Daniel J. Taylor, ed., *The History of Linguistics in the Classical Period*, Studies in the History of the Language Sciences 46 (Amsterdam and Philadelphia: John Benjamins 1987), pp. 1–16.

John E. Joseph, 'On replotting the beginnings of Western language theory', in Kurt R. Jankowsky, ed., *History of Linguistics 1993*, Studies in the History of the Language Sciences 78 (Amsterdam and Philadelphia: John Benjamins 1995), pp. 27–35.

The earliest grammars

Alfons Wouters, *The Grammatical Papyri from Graeco-Roman Egypt. Contributions to the Study of the 'Ars Grammatica' in Antiquity*, Verhandelingen van de Koninklijke Academie voor

Wetenschappen, Letteren en Schone Kunsten van België, Klasse der Letteren 41, no. 92 (Brussels 1979).

Grammar in the Roman world

Jürgen Blaensdorf, 'Cratès et les débuts de la philologie romaine', *Ktema* 13 (1988), 141–7.

Daniel J. Taylor, 'Roman language science', in Peter Schmitter, ed., *Geschichte der Sprachtheorie 2: Sprachtheorien der abendländischen Antike* (Tübingen: Narr 1991), pp. 334–52.

C. Suetonius Tranquillus, *De grammaticis et rhetoribus*, ed. with transl. and comm. by Robert A. Kaster (Oxford: Clarendon 1995).

Quintilian, *Institutio oratoria*, transl. H. E. Butler, Loeb Classical Library 124–8 (Cambridge, MA, and London: Harvard University Press 1920–2).

Robert A. Kaster, 'Islands in the stream: the grammarians of late Antiquity', *Historiographia Linguistica* 13 (1986), 323–42; and in Daniel J. Taylor, eds., *The History of Linguistics in the Classical Period*, Studies in the History of the Language Sciences 46 (Amsterdam and Philadelphia: John Benjamins 1987), pp. 149–68.

Robert A. Kaster, *Guardians of Language: The Grammarian and Society in Late Antiquity* (University of California Press: Berkeley 1988).

Even Hovdhaugen, 'The teaching of grammar in Antiquity', in Peter Schmitter, ed., *Geschichte der Sprachtheorie 2: Sprachtheorien der abendländischen Antike* (Tübingen: Narr 1991), pp. 377–91.

Louis Holtz, *Donat et la tradition de l'enseignement grammatical: étude sur l'Ars Donati et sa diffusion (IVe-IXe siècle) et édition critique* (Paris: CNRS 1981), esp. pp. 1–244.

The structure of grammars

Manfred Fuhrmann, *Das systematische Lehrbuch. Ein Beitrag zur Geschichte der Wissenschaften in der Antike* (Göttingen: Vandenhoeck & Ruprecht 1960).

Pierre Swiggers and Alfons Wouters, 'Philosophical aspects of the *Tékhnē grammatikē* of Dionysius Thrax', in Pierangiolo Berrettoni, ed., *Grammatica e ideologia nella storia linguistica* (Perugia: Istituto di Linguistica 1996).

Marc Baratin, 'Sur la structure des grammaires antiques', in J. De Clercq and P. Desmet, ed., *Florilegium Historiographiae Linguisticae* (Louvain-la-Neuve: Peeters 1994), pp. 143–57.

Vivien Law, 'The mnemonic structure of ancient grammatical doctrine', in Pierre Swiggers and Alfons Wouters, ed., *Ancient Grammar: Content and Context* (Leuven and Paris: Peeters 1996), pp. 37–52.

Vivien Law, 'Late Latin grammars in the early Middle Ages: a typological history', *Historiographia Linguistica* 13 (1986), 365–80; and in D. J. Taylor, ed., *The History of Linguistics in the Classical Period*, Studies in the History of the Language Sciences 46 (Amsterdam and Philadelphia: John Benjamins 1987), pp. 191–206; repr. in Vivien Law, *Grammar and Grammarians in the Early Middle Ages* (London: Longman 1997), pp. 54–69. [Introduces distinction between *Schulgrammatik* and *regulae* genres.]

Further reading

Priscian

R. H. Robins, 'Priscian and the context of his age', in Irène Rosier, ed., *L'héritage des grammairiens latins de l'Antiquité aux Lumières* (Paris and Louvain: Peeters 1988), pp. 49–55, repr. in his *Texts and Contexts: Selected Papers on the History of Linguistics*, The Henry Sweet Society Studies in the History of Linguistics 5 (Münster: Nodus 1998), pp. 151–8.

Guglielmo Ballaira, *Prisciano e i suoi amici* (Torino: Giappichelli 1989).

M. Salamon, 'Priscianus und sein Schülerkreis in Konstantinopel', *Philologus* 123 (1979), 91–6.

Marc Baratin, 'Les difficultés de l'analyse syntaxique', in *Histoire des idées linguistiques* 1: *La naissance des métalangages en Orient et en Occident* (Liège and Brussels: Mardaga 1989), pp. 228–42, esp. pp. 231–42.

W. Keith Percival, 'On Priscian's syntactic theory: the medieval perspective', in Hans Aarsleff, Louis G. Kelly and Hans-Josef Niederehe, eds., *Papers in the History of Linguistics*, Studies in the History of the Language Sciences 38 (Amsterdam and Philadelphia: John Benjamins 1987), pp. 65–74.

Manfred Glück, *Priscians Partitiones und ihre Stellung in der spätantiken Schule*, Spudasmata 12 (Hildesheim: Olms 1967).

5 Christianity and language

5.1 The arrival of Christianity

With Christianity a completely new force burst upon the spiritual and intellectual life of Europe. No area of intellectual endeavour was unchanged, least of all linguistics. The language policy and transformed educational priorities of the Church, and the far-reaching programmes of education undertaken in regions previously untouched by Greco-Roman civilisation, created new external conditions for language study, while the few enigmatic mentions of language in the Bible spurred the best minds of the age to take up the challenge of reconciling new ideas with old. The centuries from late Antiquity to the central Middle Ages, from approximately 400 to 1200, are characterised by the permeation of traditional Greco-Roman ideas about language with Christian attitudes – a 'conversion', so to speak, of linguistics to Christianity.

Why was Christianity so important? Religion is peripheral to most people's lives in the West today, but in terms of world history, we are the odd ones out. Up until the Renaissance, people all round the world were aware of the existence of a spiritual world and took religious observances very seriously. On the wane for centuries, this awareness disappeared in Europe around the time of the Renaissance, replaced for almost everyone by tradition, and has been fading away in other parts of the world too. A second factor which gave Christianity and the Christian Church a far greater importance than they possess today was the collapse of the institutional structures of the Roman empire under the pressure of successive waves of Germanic peoples. The deposition of the last Roman emperor, Romulus Augustulus, in 476 provides a symbolic date for the end of the empire. Except in Italy, where the old schools of the *grammatici* seem to have lingered on, schools and the other trappings of civilised society very nearly disappeared. It was the Church which took over responsibility for the maintenance of literacy and learning in western Europe until late in the Middle Ages: the Church was simultaneously teacher, librarian and transmitter of Greco-Roman civilisation. The great thinkers and writers of the Middle Ages, from Bede to Aquinas, owed their education to the Church and dedicated their finely honed intellects to furthering its intellectual life. Even the universities, which appeared from the thirteenth century on, began as religious institutions, although they little by little asserted their independence from the Church authorities. Thus, to regard the fact that all intellectual life during the Middle Ages took place under the aegis of the Church as symptomatic of a restrictive, blinkered outlook is a serious misunderstanding. It is thanks to the Church that literacy endured and spread throughout Europe; it is because of the activities of individuals who dedicated their lives to the service of the Church that the literature and learning of Greece and Rome survived at all. The position of the Church with regard to intellectual life and education was comparable to that of the state in many countries, including Britain, today; indeed, the control of the higher Church authorities over the content of the school curriculum was much less than that exerted by the government in most contemporary western countries.

Let's look briefly at the historical background. Christianity took shape during the first centuries of the Christian era in Palestine and neighbouring regions. In some respects, the new religion looked a little like the mystery cults of the ancient Near East – Mithraism is the best known – and it responded to similar spiritual needs. But there the similarities ended. For one thing, Christianity quickly became a religion of the Book, like Judaism before it and Islam later. Its sacred Scriptures were assembled into the 'Book' *par excellence*, the Bible (the Greek word *biblion*, pl. *biblia*, means 'book') by early in the third century (see box 5.1). More importantly, and more shockingly, the basis of Christianity was the certainty that a divine being had incarnated into a human body and

---

Box 5.1 The Bible

The central teachings of Christianity are presented in the Bible, a vast work in two unequal halves: the Old Testament, originally written in Hebrew and Aramaic (a Semitic language closely related to Hebrew), in 46 books; and the New Testament, originally written in Greek, in 27 books. There are some further books with a claim to inspired authorship, the Apocrypha, which have not been accepted into the canon of recognised writings. (The canon differs slightly in different branches of the Church: the King James translation of the Bible into English, used by the Church of England since 1611, has 49 Old Testament books, for instance.) The authoritative translation of the Bible into Latin, called the *Vulgate*, was made by St Jerome (see box 5.3 below) from the Hebrew and Greek original text.

Reading

F. F. Bruce, *The Books and the Parchments*, 4th edn (London: Pickering and Inglis 1984). [A history of the Bible with useful background information.]

P. R. Ackroyd and C. F. Evans, eds., *The Cambridge History of the Bible* 1. *From the Beginnings to Jerome* (Cambridge: Cambridge University Press 1970).

F. Gladstone Bratton, *A History of the Bible: An Introduction to the Historical Method* [London: Robert Hale 1961). [Parts 2 and 3 deal with the making of the Old and New Testaments, while ch. 11 discusses early translations.]

Bruce M. Metzger, *The Early Versions of the New Testament: Their Origin, Transmission, and Limitations* (Oxford: Clarendon 1977), ch. 7. [The Latin versions.]

had lived for a while on earth. Earlier religions – the mystery cults, Judaism and Roman paganism alike – were well aware of the workings of the gods and of the creative Word in the world, and now and again their religious teachers had foretold the incarnation of a sublime spiritual being; but many of their adherents found it difficult to accept that this event had actually taken place. Christians now began the long-drawn-out task of pondering its implications for world history and human existence. The easiest part of the establishment of the new religion was completed first – the creation of institutional structures (see box 5.2). After an initial period during which Christianity led a relatively informal existence as an underground movement popular chiefly amongst the lower classes, its adherents often being subjected to persecution by Roman state authorities, it was given official recognition in 313 by Emperor Constantine the Great, and later in the fourth century became the state religion of the Roman empire.

It was in the latter part of the fourth century that the first great writers of the Church were active (see box 5.3). Tertullian, Ambrose, Augustine, Jerome, and in the East Origen, Clement of Alexandria, John Chrysostom, Gregory of Nyssa and many others dedicated themselves to pondering questions of Christian doctrine which were fundamental for a clear intellectual grasp of the faith, such as whether Christ was wholly divine, wholly human, or somehow both human and divine at the same time. The Church authorities felt that it was wrong to leave individual Christians to make up their own minds on such crucial issues. So there arose the notion of 'correct belief', orthodoxy, and of proscribed, incorrect, belief: heresy. The distinction between orthodoxy and heresy was reinforced by the holding of great councils with bishops in attendance from all over Christendom in order to resolve particularly controversial matters. Christianity thus became a religion based upon precedent transmitted in the form of creeds and theological treatises.

It is this, as much as anything, which makes it clear just how remote southern Europeans now felt from what had been people's normal way of experiencing the world a few centuries before. For most people, tradition had now replaced inner vision as the main means of relating to the spiritual dimension. In northern and western Europe in contrast, the numerous accounts of visions that survive from late Antiquity and the earlier Middle Ages suggest that the boundary between everyday consciousness and a kind of consciousness that still permitted some degree of clairvoyance was somewhat more fluid than it is today.

Despite great efforts by the Church authorities to ensure uniformity of belief, the Christian world gradually fragmented, mirroring the political split of the Roman empire. For in 395 the sprawling territory of the empire was divided into two halves:

- the western, or Roman, empire, with its capital at Rome, including Italy and areas to the north, south and west of it;
- the eastern, or Byzantine, empire, with its capital at Constantinople, including Greece and areas to the north and east of it.

In some respects the division did no more than formalise the existing linguistic and cultural divide between Greek and Latin speakers. Latin had never managed to extend its domain in the East beyond legal, administrative and military circles. Greek intellectuals

Box 5.2 The Church and its members

At the local level *priests* guided the population of their parish in leading a Christian life, teaching them the basic tenets of belief through a creed, a summary of the fundamentals of the faith, and introducing them to the contents of the Bible through the graphic stories recounted in it, from which they would draw a moral in their sermons. *Bishops* watched over the activities of the priests in their diocese, a relatively large territory with its centre in a city. Over the bishops of a given country presided an *archbishop*. In the Catholic western half of the Roman empire the *pope* (originally simply the bishop of Rome) was the supreme authority, responsible only to God. In the Orthodox East the authority of the pope was not recognised; rather, the *patriarchs* played an equivalent role within their own territories. As for the ordinary Christian man or woman, most contented themselves with living as upright a life as they could manage, giving alms to the poor, fasting during Lent, and attending services regularly. A substantial minority (far more than do today) dedicated themselves wholly to the religious life. Many joined communities of likeminded persons, becoming *monks* or *nuns*, and spent their entire lives in monasteries (men) or convents (women), devoting themselves to a strict regime of prayer, physical work and study. Often, parents gave a child to a monastery, where he or she lived as an *oblate*, receiving an education. Such children frequently became monks or nuns on reaching adulthood. A few individuals preferred to live in isolated spots as *hermits* or *anchorites*, or felt called to the active but perilous life of the *missionary*.

You'll have noticed how hierarchically the clergy was organised, from priests to bishops and beyond. In many respects the structure and even the ritual and pomp and ceremony of the Catholic Church was modelled upon the structures and ceremonial of the Roman empire. But when it came to the ecclesiastical hierarchy, Church writers invoked a different parallel: with the nine orders of angels. Although nowadays we don't hear much about spiritual beings other than angels (and not much about them), early Christians knew that angels were the lowest in a whole series of heavenly beings, and they set up nine grades within the Church reflecting this hierarchy:

Heavenly hierarchy	Ecclesiastical hierarchy
Seraphim	Bishop
Cherubim	Priest
Thrones	Deacon
Exusiai	Subdeacon
Powers	Acolyte
Principalities	Exorcist
Archai	Lector
Archangels	Psalmist
Angels	Doorkeeper

Reading
Bernard Hamilton, *Religion in the Medieval West* (London: Arnold 1986).

> **Box 5.3 The Fathers of the Church**
>
> Certain early theologians, up to the middle of the fifth century, were revered in after years as the 'Fathers' of the Church. The first to use Latin for theological writing, previously the preserve of Greek, was Tertullian (c. 155–c. 222), from Carthage in Roman North Africa. Toward 400 a number of particularly articulate and erudite scholars steeped in classical learning – several were professors of rhetoric – emerged in both east and west. Eight were later singled out as the great 'Doctors' or 'Teachers' (Latin *doctor* means 'teacher') of the Church:
>
> | The Four Doctors of the Latin Church | The Four Doctors of the Greek Church |
> |---|---|
> | Ambrose, 339–397 | Athanasius, ca 296–373 |
> | Jerome, ca 346–420 | Gregory of Nazianzus, 329–389 |
> | Augustine, 354–430 | Basil the Great, ca 330–379 |
> | Gregory, ca 540–604 | John Chrysostom, ca 347–407 |
>
> The four Latin Doctors are often depicted on the sides of the pulpit in European cathedrals. They are easily recognisable from their headgear: Augustine and Ambrose wear bishop's mitres, Jerome the flat cardinal's hat, and Pope Gregory the Great the papal tiara.
>
> *Reading*
>
> Jacques Fontaine, *La littérature latine chrétienne*, Que Sais-Je? 1973 (Paris: Presses Universitaires de France 1970).
>
> William G. Rusch, *The Later Latin Fathers* (London: Duckworth 1977).

regarded it as incapable of reproducing the nuances of Greek, and rarely bothered to read or to translate the writings of their Roman counterparts (whereas Greek theological writings were often translated into Latin soon after they appeared). Little by little Greek, always the language of scholarly discourse, crept back into use in administrative contexts. And differences in outlook assumed greater strength as time passed. The views of the western Church were coloured by the Roman background and training of its chief writers, with their somewhat legalistic outlook and emphasis on order, organisation and authority. They early on began to insist on the Church's role as an intermediary between God and the human being. Only through the Church, they declared, could Christians hope to learn the truth about spiritual matters. Individuals were discouraged from seeking spiritual knowledge on their own initiative for fear that heresy would creep into the Church. The eastern Church laid less emphasis upon this, for it was influenced more by the heritage of Greek philosophy, and placed greater emphasis on the individual's ability to attain knowledge of higher matters directly. The differences between the two branches of the Church continued to grow, and the tension between them increased until a formal break took place, the Great Schism, traditionally dated to the year 1054. From that time on we can speak of the *Catholic Church* with its seat at Rome, and the *Orthodox Church*, a term which subsumes a number of independent (autocephalous) churches, in the Greek East, of which the Greek Orthodox and the Russian Orthodox are the best known today.

5.2 The Bible on language

The Bible says remarkably little about language. Nonetheless, those few passages were to shape medieval linguistic thinking profoundly. Interpreting their meaning was by no means an easy task, for they are couched in the form of stories or enigmatic pronouncements which use everyday words to hint at spiritual mysteries. Because so much in the Bible is difficult to understand, a tradition of *exegesis*, or interpretation, had grown up amongst Jewish scholars, and was continued and developed by Christians. The Fathers of the Church created a body of Christian exegesis which showed how the Old Testament could be read as foreshadowing the New, and spelling out the moral implications of the more puzzling stories of the Old Testament and the teachings of Christ and St Paul in the New (see box 5.4). No medieval Christian would have tried to study the Bible unaided; either the parish priest or the writings of a revered exegete would have been their guide. The view that all Christians have the right to read the Bible unaided and to think their own thoughts about it was one of the cornerstones of Protestantism during

---

Box 5.4 Interpreting the Bible: the techniques of exegesis

The Bible is full of stories which at first sight seem out of place in a text claiming to be divinely inspired – irrelevant or even morally dubious. What was a good Christian to make of them? The grammarians and rhetoricians of late Antiquity had devised a rich metalanguage for describing figurative uses of language; Christian exegetes, eager to rescue the learning of the past, redeployed this doctrine to arrive at a morally and doctrinally appropriate reading of the Scriptures. Augustine devoted his *De doctrina christiana* ('Christian Instruction') to explaining how the whole world, from snakes and diamonds to names and numbers, constitutes a vast system of signs which we must learn to read if we are to understand the Scriptures aright. Certain types of interpretation became particularly popular:

- literal, requiring a knowledge of biblical history and geography, and of the unusual terms found in the Scriptures;
- allegorical, showing how an earthly phenomenon represents a spiritual one;
- anagogical, whereby Old Testament events are shown to prefigure those of the New Testament;
- tropological, revealing the significance of a phenomenon for moral action. Joseph's coat of many colours, for instance, represents the virtues granted us by God, which we should cherish as long as we live.

Reading

G. R. Evans, *The Language and Logic of the Bible: The Earlier Middle Ages* (Cambridge: Cambridge University Press 1984) [pp. 1–8 describe how the Fathers explain the need for exegesis].

Beryl Smalley, *The Study of the Bible in the Middle Ages*, 3rd edn (Oxford: Blackwell 1983), ch. 1.

G. W. H. Lampe, ed., *The Cambridge History of the Bible 2. The West from the Fathers to the Reformation* (Cambridge: Cambridge University Press 1969), ch. 6.

the Reformation in the sixteenth century; up to that time, personal interpretations of the Scriptures were strongly discouraged (as they are in the Catholic Church to this day) because of the dangers of misunderstanding, error and heresy. To look at what the Bible says about language and try to interpret it for themselves was something which no medieval layperson would have ventured to do. Let us do what they would have done, and take as our guide to the biblical passages of linguistic interest a revered exegete: St Augustine, the most influential thinker of western Christianity (see box 5.5).

Box 5.5 St Augustine (354–430)

Augustine was born in the province of Numidia, in Roman North Africa, the son of a pagan father and Christian mother. He was given a good education, but as far as religion was concerned, he wavered. As a young man he was what we would call a 'seeker', searching for a spiritual path and outlook that would make sense of the world and his own inner experiences. First he was attracted to Manichaeism, an enormously popular religion in the Near and Middle East, which saw the cosmos as a battleground between the forces of good and evil. Later he turned to Neoplatonism, a development of Plato's teaching which (like Plato) recognised truth as existing only outside the material world (see box 2.4, p. 27 above). It was when he was at the height of a successful career as professor of rhetoric in Milan that he arrived at Christianity. Abandoning his previous career, he entered the Church, and quickly became bishop of Hippo, a town in North Africa. As a Christian theologian he wrote voluminously, and very many of his interpretations of difficult points of belief became part of the accepted doctrine of the Church.

Perhaps it was his professional interest in rhetoric that led him to concern himself particularly with linguistic issues. At any rate, he is the first Christian that we are aware of who wrote on linguistic questions from a Christian standpoint. (Several of the Late Latin grammarians, such as Pompeius and Priscian, were Christians too, but their grammars are scarcely touched by their faith.) Augustine was convinced that the best path to knowledge of divine and incorporeal matters was via what is perceptible to our senses, so in 387, while he was preparing for baptism, he started to compose a series of textbooks on the Seven Liberal Arts (see box 5.6). This was a major project, demanding as it did an in-depth knowledge of a wide range of subjects from rhetoric to astronomy. His grammar, which is in many ways rather similar to Donatus's *Ars maior*, contains only a few hints of his higher design. The book on dialectic, unfinished though it is, outlines a theory of the sign (see box 5.7). As for the other textbooks, the only one he got around to completing in the way he intended, many years later, was the one on music. The use of language in the service of Christianity remained a major concern of his, and he returned to the subject several times, notably in the dialogue *De magistro* ('The Teacher') and in the treatise *De doctrina christiana* ('Christian Instruction').

Reading

Henry Chadwick, *Augustine* (Oxford and New York: Oxford University Press 1986).

John M. Rist, *Augustine: Ancient Thought Baptized* (Cambridge: Cambridge University Press 1994).

> **Box 5.6 The Seven Liberal Arts**
>
> Every culture passes on a body of knowledge to the next generation, and in Europe and Asia this knowledge has, at least since the first millennium BC, been divided up into compartmentalised disciplines. By the fourth century AD a division was emerging that was to remain definitive until the Renaissance. It consisted of seven disciplines, the Liberal Arts, divided into two groups:
>
> - *trivium* ('threefold path'), comprising the language arts (*artes sermocinales*): grammar, rhetoric and dialectic;
> - *quadrivium* ('fourfold path'), comprising the mathematical arts (*artes arithmeticae*): arithmetic, music, geometry, astronomy.
>
> Although for much of the Middle Ages the Seven Liberal Arts represented an ideal curriculum rather than the actual one, many writers gave them pride of place in their account of learning. Isidore of Seville placed them at the start of his famous encyclopedia, the *Etymologies*, published in 636, while in the fifth century Martianus Capella devoted an entire treatise to them, *The Marriage of Philology and Mercury*. Both works were widely studied during the Middle Ages.
>
> Grammar was viewed as the origin and foundation of all the rest, the most basic (in both senses of the word). It was often depicted as a woman teacher leading young children on to higher things, brandishing a penknife for use not only in sharpening quill pens but also in excising the mistakes of her pupils.
>
> *Reading*
> David L. Wagner, *The Seven Liberal Arts in the Middle Ages* (Bloomington, Indiana: Indiana University Press 1983), chs. 1 and 2.
> Ilsetraut Hadot, *Arts libéraux et philosophie dans la pensée antique* (Paris: Etudes Augustiniennes 1984).

The origin of language: Adam names the creatures (Genesis 2: 19–20)

Right at the beginning of the Bible, just after the Creation of the world has been described, God brings the newly created animals to Adam, the first man, so that he could name them:

> From the ground God formed every wild animal and every bird in the sky, and he brought them to the man so the man could name them. Whatever the man called each living thing, that became its name. The man gave names to all the tame animals, to the birds in the sky, and to all the wild animals.[1]

This is the closest the Bible comes to describing the origin of language. Adam plays the part of Plato's name-giver, assigning names to birds and animals. What language did he use? Augustine reminds us that even if there was one original *Adamic* language, it disappeared when the Tower of Babel was built (see next passage). There is no point, he remarks severely, attempting to discover what language it was. Like generations of

> **Box 5.7 Augustine's early theory of the sign**
>
> Throughout his life, first in his professional capacity as a teacher of rhetoric and later as a Christian preacher and teacher, Augustine reflected on signs and how they work. That signs – words in particular – were an unavoidable intermediary in the search for truth he could not deny, much as he would have preferred to do without them. His first description of signs occurs in his textbook on dialectic:
>
> A word (*verbum*) is a sign of any sort of thing. It is spoken by a speaker and can be understood by a hearer. A thing is whatever is sensed or is understood or is hidden. A sign is something which is itself sensed and which indicates to the mind something beyond the sign itself... When, therefore, a word is uttered for its own sake, that is, so that something is being asked or argued about the word itself, clearly it is the thing which is the subject of disputation and inquiry; but the thing in this case is called a *verbum*. Now that which the mind not the ears perceives from the word and which is held within the mind itself is called a *dicibile*. When a word is spoken not for its own sake but for the sake of signifying something else, it is called a *dictio*. The thing itself which is neither a word nor the conception of a word in the mind, whether or not it has a word by which it can be signified, is called nothing but a *res* in the proper sense of the name. Therefore, these four are to be kept distinct: the *verbum*, the *dicibile*, the *dictio*, and the *res*. 'Verbum' both is a word and signifies a word. 'Dicibile' is a word; however, it does not signify a word but what is understood in the word and contained in the mind. 'Dictio' is also a word, but it signifies both the first two, that is, the word itself and what is brought about in the mind by means of the word. 'Res' is a word which signifies whatever remains beyond the three that have been mentioned [sc. *verbum*, *dicibile* and *dictio*].
>
> The *dicibile*, literally 'that which can be uttered', 'sayable', corresponds approximately to the Stoic *lekton* (p. 41 above). Many scholars have pointed out the Stoic antecedents of Augustine's theory of the sign.
>
> For further reading on Augustine's theory of the sign, see p. 111.

medieval Christians, Augustine puzzled over how the fish got their names. Some people, he tells us, held that God had suggested the correct names of the fish to human beings. But Augustine rejects this idea, saying that if this had been the case, then the mystical significance of the fish names would have been obvious, which it is not (apparently overlooking the fact that he has just argued that the original names have in any case disappeared with the original language). Augustine was a firm conventionalist, and claimed to abhor etymological speculation into the reasons why things bore the names they did. All the same, he was not above deploying etymologies in time-honoured fashion to strengthen his argumentation in both his theological writings and his sermons.

5.2 *The Bible on language*

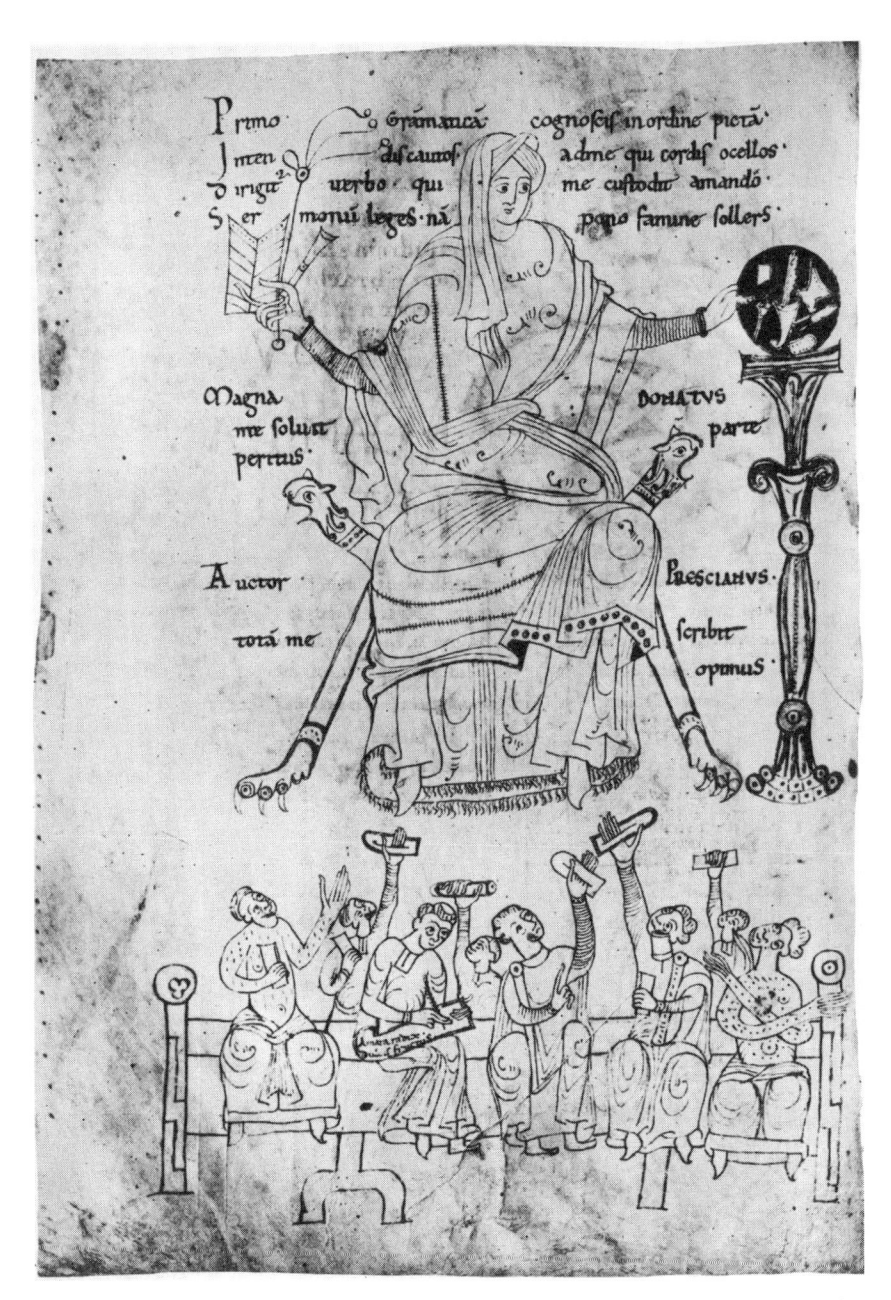

3 Image from a twelfth-century copy of Martianus Capella's allegory. Grammar presides over a class of children one of whom has just written 'Bitter is the root but sweet the fruit' (of learning). In one hand Grammar holds a round box containing surgical implements, including a scalpel for excising mistakes, and in the other a pen and two pages ruled for writing, and also a whip. Florence Biblioteca Mediceo-Laurenziana, Cod S. Marco 190 f. 15.

The origin of linguistic diversity: the Tower of Babel (Genesis 11: 1–9)

The origin of languages and the dispersal of the human race into warring tribes were closely linked:

At this time the whole world spoke one language, and everyone used the same words. As people moved from the east, they found a plain in the land of Babylonia and settled there.
    They said to each other, 'Let's make bricks and bake them to make them hard.' So they used bricks instead of stones, and tar instead of mortar. Then they said to each other, 'Let's build a city and a tower for ourselves, whose top will reach high into the sky. We will become famous. Then we will not be scattered over all the earth.'
    The Lord came down to see the city and the tower that the people had built. The Lord said, 'Now, these people are united, all speaking the same language. This is only the beginning of what they will do. They will be able to do anything they want. Come, let us go down and confuse their language so they will not be able to understand each other.'
    So the Lord scattered them from there over all the earth, and they stopped building the city. The place is called Babel since that is where the Lord confused the language of the whole world. So the Lord caused them to spread out from there over the whole world.[2]

Augustine, like other western readers, regarded the origin of linguistic diversity as a catastrophic event, divine punishment for human arrogance. Whatever the original, Adamic, language might have been, it had been lost for ever as a result of this episode. (Augustine's successors were not so cautious, and many of them identified the original language with Hebrew.) In the eastern Church some exegetes took a less negative view of the Babel episode. In the Syrian Church, Išoʿdad of Merv (in present-day Turkmenia, then part of the Syriac-speaking cultural area) explained that God had confused the languages and dispersed the nations so that human beings would grow in intelligence and wisdom and so that the earth would be peopled and cultivated.[3]

The redemption of languages (Acts of the Apostles 2: 1–11)

Could the 'fall' of language at Babel be redeemed? Augustine pointed to the story of Pentecost, or Whitsun, in the New Testament:

When the day of Pentecost came, they [the disciples of Christ] were all together in one place. Suddenly a noise like a strong, blowing wind came from heaven and filled the whole house where they were sitting. They saw something like flames of fire that were separated and stood over each person there. They were all filled with the Holy Spirit, and they began to speak different languages by the power the Holy Spirit was giving them.
    There were some religious Jews staying in Jerusalem who were from every country in the world. When they heard this noise, a crowd came together. They were all surprised, because each one heard them speaking in his own language. They were completely amazed at this. They said, 'Look! Aren't all these people that we hear speaking from Galilee? Then how is it possible that we each hear them in our own languages? We are from different places: Parthia, Media, Elam, Mesopotamia, Judea, Cappadocia, Pontus, Asia, Phrygia, Pamphylia, Egypt, the areas of Libya near Cyrene, Rome (both Jews and those who had become Jews),

Crete and Arabia. But we hear them telling in our own languages about the great things God has done!'[4]

In explaining this passage Augustine contrasts the humility of the faithful with the arrogance of the builders of the Tower.[5] Whereas their arrogance had led to dispersal and misunderstanding, humility will lead to a new unity of languages and peoples in the Church with Christ as its head. In his more optimistic moods Augustine felt that this was already taking place with the conversion of an ever-growing number of distant peoples. Some exegetes preferred to interpret this passage differently, as foretelling a future when people will understand one another perfectly no matter what language they speak.

Meaning, form and the speech act: the incarnation of the Word (John 1:1–3 and 23)

At the beginning of the Gospel of St John two linguistic terms – *word* and *voice* – appear in an unwonted context:

In the beginning was the Word [*Logos*], and the Word was with God, and the Word was God. The same was in the beginning with God. All things were made by him; and without him was not any thing made that was made...
[John the Baptist] said, 'I am the voice [*phōnē*] of one crying in the wilderness...'[6]

Why 'Word'? Why 'voice'? In English the term 'Word' is difficult to comprehend in this context, for it is much more limited in its scope than the *logos* of the Greek original. *Logos* denoted 'reason, rational principle', the inherently rational principle underlying all spiritual and earthly phenomena, and also the utterance-as-meaning. Medieval western scholars read the New Testament not in the original Greek but in Latin translation, however, and there the equivalent term was *verbum*. Narrower in scope than *logos*, *verbum* was still broader than 'word' in that it could mean 'meaningful utterance, proverb, verb, word-as-meaning'. Both *logos* and *verbum* thus denote the meaningful aspect of the word. In Greek and Latin these terms contrasted with others which denoted the word as form (*lexis*) or sound (*lexis* or *phōnē* in Greek, *vox* in Latin). Because John the Baptist described himself as the 'voice' (*phōnē*, *vox*) of one crying in the wilderness, Augustine based his exposition of this part of St John's Gospel on the opposition between *verbum* and *vox*: what was the relationship between the 'voice crying in the wilderness', John the Baptist, and Christ, the divine Word? Augustine here uses a distinction from linguistics to shed light upon a theological problem; and at the same time he gives the clearest description of the speech act that anyone (to our knowledge) had presented up to that time. He discussed the subject several times, both in the lengthy theological treatise *De Trinitate*[7] and in his sermons. The following version was originally presented as a sermon on the feastday of John the Baptist, 24 June, in the year 401:

What is *vox*? What is *verbum*? What are they? Listen to what you experience within yourselves, and you will be able to answer your own question. *Verbum*, if it does not have meaning, is not *verbum*. *Vox*, on the other hand, can be called *vox* even if it is just a meaningless noise, like a cry, but cannot be called *verbum*. Suppose someone groans: it is a *vox*. Suppose they wail: it is a *vox*. The sound is formless and conveys a noise without any meaningful content to the ears. *Verbum*, however, unless it means something, unless it conveys something to the ears and mind, is not called *verbum*. So as I was saying, if you shout, it is a *vox*; if you say 'a person', it is a *verbum*, or if you say 'cattle', or 'God', or 'the world', or whatever. I have termed all these 'meaningful *voces*', not empty noises which teach us nothing. If you have now made this distinction between *vox* and *verbum*, listen to something really surprising about John the Baptist and Christ. The *verbum* is enormously valuable even without the *vox*, while the *vox* is worthless without the *verbum*. Let me see if I can explain this. Imagine you want to say something. What you want to say is already conceived in your heart. It is stored up in the memory, made ready by your will, and lives in your understanding. What you want to say is not in any language. The content which you wish to say, stored up in your heart, is not in any language – not in Greek or Latin or Punic or Hebrew or any other. The content is simply conceived in your heart, ready to go forth. So, as I said, there is something, some opinion, some thought, conceived in your heart, ready to go forth and be introduced into a listener. The *verbum* is thus already known to the person whose heart it is in, already known to the person who is to utter it, but not yet known to the hearer. So here is the *verbum*, already formed, already complete, waiting in the heart. It wants to go forth and be communicated to a hearer. The person who has conceived the *verbum* waits for the person he is to say it to, keeping the *verbum* in his heart. Does he happen upon a Greek? He looks for a Greek *vox* in which it can go forth to the Greek. Does he run into into a Roman? He looks for Latin words in which it can go forth to the Roman. Does he come across a Carthaginian? He looks for Punic words in which it can go forth to the Carthaginian. Remove the differences between the hearers, and that *verbum* conceived in the heart is not in Greek or Latin or Punic or any other language. It simply seeks a *vox* in which to go forth which will help the listener...

Now, I already know what I want to say and am keeping it in my heart. I look for the assistance of a *vox*. Before that *vox* is voiced in my mouth the *verbum* is stored up in my heart. The *verbum* thus preceded my *vox*, and in me the *verbum* comes first, the *vox* later. But as far as you are concerned, the *vox* arrives at your ears first so that you can understand, so that the *verbum* can be introduced into your mind. You would have no way of knowing what took place in me before the *vox* unless it took place in you after the *vox*. Therefore, if John the Baptist was the *vox*, and Christ the *verbum*, Christ existed before John, but within God; Christ came after John, but within us...

Everyone who voices the *Verbum* is the *vox* of the *Verbum*. What the sound of our voice is to the *verbum* which we bear in our hearts, every pious prophetic soul was to that *Verbum* of which it was said: 'In the beginning was the *Verbum*, and the *Verbum* was with God, and the *Verbum* was God. This was in the beginning with God.' What mighty *verba*, indeed what splendid *voces* the *Verbum* made, stored up in the heart! What awe-inspiring prophets the *Verbum* made as He waited within the Father! He sent patriarchs, he sent the prophets, he sent countless great forerunners. The *Verbum*, still remaining within the Father, sent out *voces*, and after all these preliminary *voces*, the unique *Verbum* came in his vehicle, as it were, in his *vox*, in his flesh. So gather together in one, as it were, all the *voces* which preceded the *Verbum*, and put them all into the person of John the Baptist.[8]

Augustine draws upon his congregation's familiarity with the everyday experience of conversation to explain a complex theological issue. He describes how the would-be speaker stores up what he wants to express, the *verbum*, in a non-linguistic form before sending it out as a spoken word, a *vox*, to his listener, in whose mind it calls up the corresponding *verbum*. As we learn from *De magistro* ('The Teacher'), a dialogue about language he wrote in 389, Augustine believed that we do not learn directly from the words we hear; rather, the spoken words help to call up a mental image of the truth that we have within us. They are but a sign pointing to a pre-existing inner truth. Developing this line of thought in his sermon, Augustine next reminds us that the divine *Verbum*, Christ, existed in God long before the Incarnation, sending out messengers – *voces*, as it were – to prepare the way for his incarnation into a human body. The *Verbum* himself then put on physical form, incarnating into a human body, and this physical vehicle is in a sense the *vox* through which the *Verbum* becomes manifest and known to us. (Augustine's shifting analogies are characteristic of the kaleidoscopically metamorphosing viewpoints of patristic and medieval exegesis.) The *vox*, whether it takes the form of the prophets and St John the Baptist, or the body of Christ, is merely a messenger or a vehicle, for what really matters is the *Verbum*, Christ Himself.

These analogies are not merely decorative. Even as grammar could be used to throw light upon a theological point, so theology affected the way people thought about linguistic phenomena. Although in its original context the linguistic aspect of the *verbum*/*vox* dichotomy is incidental to Augustine's theological point, the way in which he develops that contrast had the profoundest of implications for the study of language over the next thousand years. What are its implications? Up until now, the Latin terms *verbum* and *vox* had been metalinguistic terms without any religious connotations, unlike the Greek *logos*, which had always had deeper associations (see section 3.1 above). From Augustine on, no Latin-speaking Christian could hear either word without immediately thinking of their religious associations (although if the context was a grammatical discussion of the verb – also *verbum* – those associations would be suppressed). They regarded the *verbum*, 'word-as-meaning', as the real core of language. By contrast, the *vox*, 'word-as-form', was secondary, just the outer covering that the word-as-meaning put on when it wanted to become manifest. As Augustine declared in his sermon, 'The *verbum* is enormously valuable even without the *vox*, whereas the *vox* is worthless without the *verbum*.' Augustine compared the word to a living being in an analogy full of resonances for his medieval readers:

The word consists of sound and meaning. The sound belongs to the ears and the meaning to the mind. Don't you think, then, that in the word, as in any living creature, the sound is the body and the meaning is, as it were, the soul of the sound?[9]

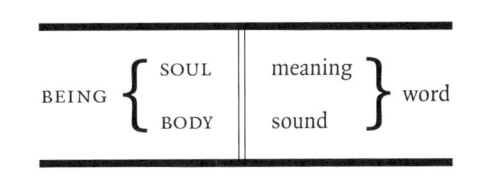

$$\text{BEING} \begin{cases} \text{SOUL} \\ \text{BODY} \end{cases} \begin{array}{c} \text{meaning} \\ \text{sound} \end{array} \bigg\} \text{word}$$

You have only to think of premodern western attitudes to the body and to physical aspects of existence to realise the implications. Do you remember the three etymologies of *soma*, the Greek word for 'body', which Plato quoted in the *Cratylus* (p. 22 above)? All three see the body as subordinate to the soul, whether as its safe, or its sign, or its tomb. Medieval western writers went further still. Although some of them associated the Latin word for 'body', *corpus*, with *custodia*, 'safe-keeping', most preferred to bring out the rank side of corporeal nature: in the seventh century, Isidore of Seville tells us that the body is called *corpus* 'because it perishes in a state of corruption', *quod corruptum perit*,[10] and that is mild beside the widespread explanation of *corpus* as *cordis pus*, 'heart's pus'. Almost everything you read from the early centuries of Christianity up to the fifteenth century is pervaded by a sense of resentment and loathing for the physical side of existence, for it presented Christians with daily evidence of the fall of humans from their previous spiritual nature. This is not just a cliché; on the contrary, it was a very deep-rooted feeling. Sin – the sin committed by Adam and Eve in the Garden of Eden when they ate the forbidden fruit of the Tree of Knowledge – was the cause of our having to put these bodies on in the first place, and the bodies themselves drag us down ever deeper into sin. To counteract this disastrous slide, the more spiritually inclined Christians adopted various practices intended to bring the body under control – fasting, going without washing, wearing a scratchy hair shirt next to the skin, and so on. The goal of all their striving was the spiritual, the unchanging, the uncorrupted, the permanent and absolute.

In these circumstances, the more physical aspect of language, *vox*, did not stand a chance. The focus of attention was inevitably *verbum*, the meaningful aspect of the word, the part that partakes of the spiritual and points to something invisible. What were the consequences of this outlook for language study during the Middle Ages?

5.3 Medieval priorities: focus on the spiritual

At all times and in every country, people prefer to acquire knowledge that they consider to be of lasting validity – 'true' knowledge. What kind of knowledge answers that need varies from one community to another. Even on a small scale we see it within the contemporary academic world, when for example a university professor in Beijing in the 1980s decided to translate Charles Hockett's *Course in Modern Linguistics* (1958) for the use of his class, regarding it as much more practical than the Chomskyan linguistics then being taught in most parts of Europe and the Anglo-American world, or when European medievalists find that they are no longer 'speaking the same language' as their American colleagues; in other words, the questions one group of scholars asks, and the answers they find satisfying, may well differ from those of another group working on the same problems. The gap between medieval and modern western views of what constitutes worthwhile knowledge is far greater. Whereas we to a large extent equate knowledge with what we can see and measure, with what is sense-perceptible and susceptible to quantitative analysis, medieval scholars dismissed this kind of knowledge as unreliable because it dealt only with what was constantly changing. Plants, animals, even mountains and empires, all come and go. Knowledge about such matters is therefore ephemeral and worthless – unless it can be shown to point beyond the transient phenomena to some enduring spiritual reality. Language too was caught up in this everlasting flux, constantly changing. The study of language 'in and for itself' so characteristic of nineteenth- and much twentieth-century scholarship was precisely what medieval scholars wanted to avoid. To focus on language 'in and for itself' would mean condemning oneself to an endless vicious circle – trying to explain the ephemeral by reference to the ephemeral. Medieval scholars attempted to escape this everlastingly futile round by seeking out those aspects of language which were in some way linked with unchanging spiritual realities. They did so in two ways, by focusing on what they regarded as the spiritual aspects of language, and by searching for features of language pointing beyond language itself to some higher truth.

5.4 Form or meaning? Which branch of linguistics?

Given that linguistic form, the *vox*, was dismissed as the 'body' of the word, quite as transient and uninteresting as all other temporal phenomena, medieval scholars saw no point in developing those branches of linguistic study which focussed on form. This included both speech sounds and word forms. Hence, we cannot look for any development of phonetics, phonology or morphology by medieval theoreticians. If the individual word forms were insignificant, then differences between languages were also unimportant: remember how Augustine regards the language in which the *verbum* chooses to come to expression as a minor detail contingent upon external circumstances. Consequently, the idea that compiling descriptive grammars 'adds to the stock of knowledge', and that this might be a desirable end in itself, was as foreign to the medieval as to the ancient mentality; descriptive grammars were written only in response to pressing practical need. By the same token, comparative grammar was unknown. Nor was charting the changes that languages have undergone through time regarded as a worthwhile occupation. Linguistic change was acknowledged, of course, for everything in the visible world was known to be in a state of flux; but what was the point of studying the random and arbitrary changes to which words, like all other earthly phenomena, were subject? It was enough to identify the processes of change which were at work; the precise details of sound changes were felt to be a waste of time. Consequently, we will not find a historical approach to language. So there was no phonetics, no phonology, no morphological analysis; no interest in linguistic diversity, either in space or in time, so no comparative or descriptive grammar (with one exception which we shall come to in chapter 6), no historical linguistics, no areal typology or anthropological linguistics. In other words, this characteristically medieval mind-set rules out those branches of linguistics which, as we shall see, owe their modern development to a major change in ways of thinking which took place at the Renaissance. What was left?

Medieval thinkers were drawn to any aspect of language which was primarily to do with meaning. Lexical and sentence meaning, illocutionary force, sentence structure, studied today under the headings of semantics, pragmatics and syntax – the list is relatively short. And, as linguists today well know, these areas are less clearly delimited than those listed earlier. In these latter areas one rapidly finds oneself involved in questions which have very little to do with language at all – questions of perception, or cultural relativity, or formal logic. All these areas impinge upon conceptual issues or real-world problems which are represented in words or encoded in language, but where the notions or phenomena are primary and the words are secondary. Left to themselves, medieval scholars would have preferred to concentrate on those aspects of language which pointed most obviously to extra-linguistic reality. But circumstances – and Church policy – pointed them in a different direction.

Further reading

General

Useful background to many of the issued surveyed in this chapter is to be found in:
William R. Cook and Ronald B. Herzman, *The Medieval World View: An Introduction* (Oxford and New York: Oxford University Press 1983), part I.

Language in the ancient Church

Gustave Bardy, *La question des langues dans l'Eglise ancienne* 1 (Paris: Beauchesne 1948).
Pierre Swiggers, 'Les Pères de l'Eglise', in Sylvain Auroux, ed., *Histoire des idées linguistiques* 2 (Liège: Mardaga 1992), pp. 76–82. [A brief outline of the thinking of some western Church Fathers on linguistic, mostly grammatical, issues.]
Ю. М. Здельштейн, 'Проблемы языка в памятниках патристики', in А. В. Десницкая and С. Д. Кацнельсон, ed., *ИСТОРИЯ ЛИНГВИСТИЧЕСКИХ УЧЕНИЙ: средневековая Европа* (Leningrad: Nauka 1985), pp. 157–207. [A fairly comprehensive introduction to the thinking of the Church Fathers, eastern as well as western, on a number of linguistic issues.]

Augustine's writings on language: the principal sources

B. Darrell Jackson and Jan Pinborg, ed. and transl., *Augustine: De dialectica* (Dordrecht and Boston: Reidel 1975).
The Works of Saint Augustine: A Translation for the 21st Century. Sermons III/8 (273–305A) on the Saints, transl. Edmund Hill (New York: New York City Press 1994). [Sermon 288 is on pp. 110–18. The Latin text is to be found in J. P. Migne, *Patrologia Latina* 38 (Paris: J. P. Migne 1845), cols. 1302–8.]
Saint Augustine: Christian Instruction (De doctrina Christiana), transl. John J. Gavigan 2nd edn (Washington, DC: Catholic University of America Press 1950), pp. 1–235.

About Augustine's linguistic thought

A recent book covering all aspects of Augustine's linguistic thought, with useful bibliography:
Sebastiano Vecchio, *Le parole come segni. Introduzione alla linguistica agostiniana* (Palermo: Novecento 1994).

The Tower of Babel and the origin of language

Arno Borst, *Der Turmbau von Babel. Geschichte der Meinungen über Ursprung und Vielfalt der Sprachen und Völker*, 4 vols. (Stuttgart: Hiersemann 1957–63), 2. [Ch. 1 sets out the views of the Latin Church Fathers; pp. 391–404 are devoted to Augustine.]
Hubert Bost, *Babel: Du texte au symbole* (Geneva: Labor et Fides 1985), pp. 135–44.
Sebastiano Vecchio, *Le Parole come segni. Introduzione alla linguistica agostiniana* (Palermo: Novecento 1994), ch. 5 (pp. 71–93).

Gilbert Dahan, 'Nommer les êtres: exégèse et théories du langage dans les commentaires médiévaux de Genèse 2,19–20', in Sten Ebbesen, ed., Geschichte der Sprachtheorie 3: Sprachtheorien in Spätantike und Mittelalter (Tübingen: Narr 1995), pp. 55–74. [Views of later medieval commentators.]

Augustine's theory of the sign

The literature on this subject is extensive. A few of the more approachable contributions are these:

Christopher Kirwan, 'Augustine on the nature of speech', in Stephen Everson, ed., Language (Cambridge: Cambridge University Press 1994), pp. 188–211.

John M. Rist, Augustine: Ancient Thought Baptized (Cambridge: Cambridge University Press 1994), ch. 2.

Clifford Ando, 'Augustine on language', Revue des Etudes Augustiniennes 40 (1994), 45–78. [Shows how Augustine's ideas on language are connected with his philosophical thought.]

Robert A. Markus, 'St Augustine on signs', Phronesis 2 (1957), 60–83, repr. in his Augustine: A Collection of Critical Essays (Garden City, NY: Doubleday 1972), pp. 61–91.

B. Darrell Jackson, 'The theory of signs in St Augustine's De doctrina christiana', Revue des Etudes Augustiniennes 15 (1969), 9–49, repr. in Robert A. Markus, ed., Augustine: A Collection of Critical Essays (Garden City, NY: Doubleday 1972), pp. 92–147. [Outlines Augustine's theory of the sign – not only from the De doctrina christiana – and its sources.]

Drago Pintarič, Sprache und Trinität. Semantische Probleme in der Trinitätslehre des hl. Augustinus, Salzburger Studien zur Philosophie 15 (Salzburg and Munich: Pustet 1983). [A richly documented analysis of Augustine's concept of the 'inner word', pp. 94–110.]

Hans Ruef, 'Die Sprachtheorie des Augustinus in De dialectica', in Sten Ebbesen, ed., Geschichte der Sprachtheorie 3: Sprachtheorien in Spätantike und Mittelalter (Tübingen: Narr 1995), pp. 3–11.

Hans Ruef, Augustin über Semiotik und Sprache. Sprachtheoretische Analysen zu Augustins Schrift 'De Dialectica' (Bern: Wyss Erben 1981).

6   The early Middle Ages

6.1   Linguistic thought in the Middle Ages

With this chapter we enter the western Middle Ages properly speaking – the millennium between Priscian and the Northern Renaissance, roughly 500 to 1500. Throughout this period scholars across Europe dedicated themselves to the twofold task of working through what they had inherited from Greco-Roman Antiquity, and of reconciling that inheritance with Christian doctrine. This long-drawn-out process took place in stages defined both by the character of the linguistic thinking of the epoch and by the classical writings on language known at the time. For by no means all the ancient writings on language that we have met in earlier chapters were known in every part of western Europe continuously from the end of Antiquity. Some monastic libraries had half-a-dozen Late Latin grammars, others a different half-dozen, and a few especially well-stocked collections had ten or more. Rarely did any two libraries own quite the same selection. Some texts were virtually unknown for hundreds of years, coming back into circulation after a lapse of several centuries. Thus, Priscian's *Partitiones* and in some areas his *Institutiones grammaticae*, and Aristotle's *Categories* and *De interpretatione* were unknown up until a little before 800; Aristotle's remaining logical writings and the *Metaphysics* until around 1150; and Varro's *De lingua latina* until 1355. For this reason alone it would be wrong to regard linguistic thought in the Middle Ages as a monolithic whole. And throughout these centuries, people's interests and priorities changed, as did their views on the best ways to teach and present linguistic doctrine. The history of linguistic thought during the Middle Ages can be divided into four broad stages:

1. the *early Middle Ages* (500–800), during which western European scholars grappled with the need to write descriptive grammars of Latin for the use of non-native speakers, using Donatus's two grammars and Late Latin commentaries on them along with Priscian's brief *Institutio de nomine* as the starting-point for their own descriptive grammars;
2. the *central Middle Ages* (800–1100), from the Carolingian Renaissance to the twelfth-century Renaissance, a period during which the rediscovery of Aristotle's *Categories* and *De interpretatione* and Priscian's *Institutiones grammaticae*

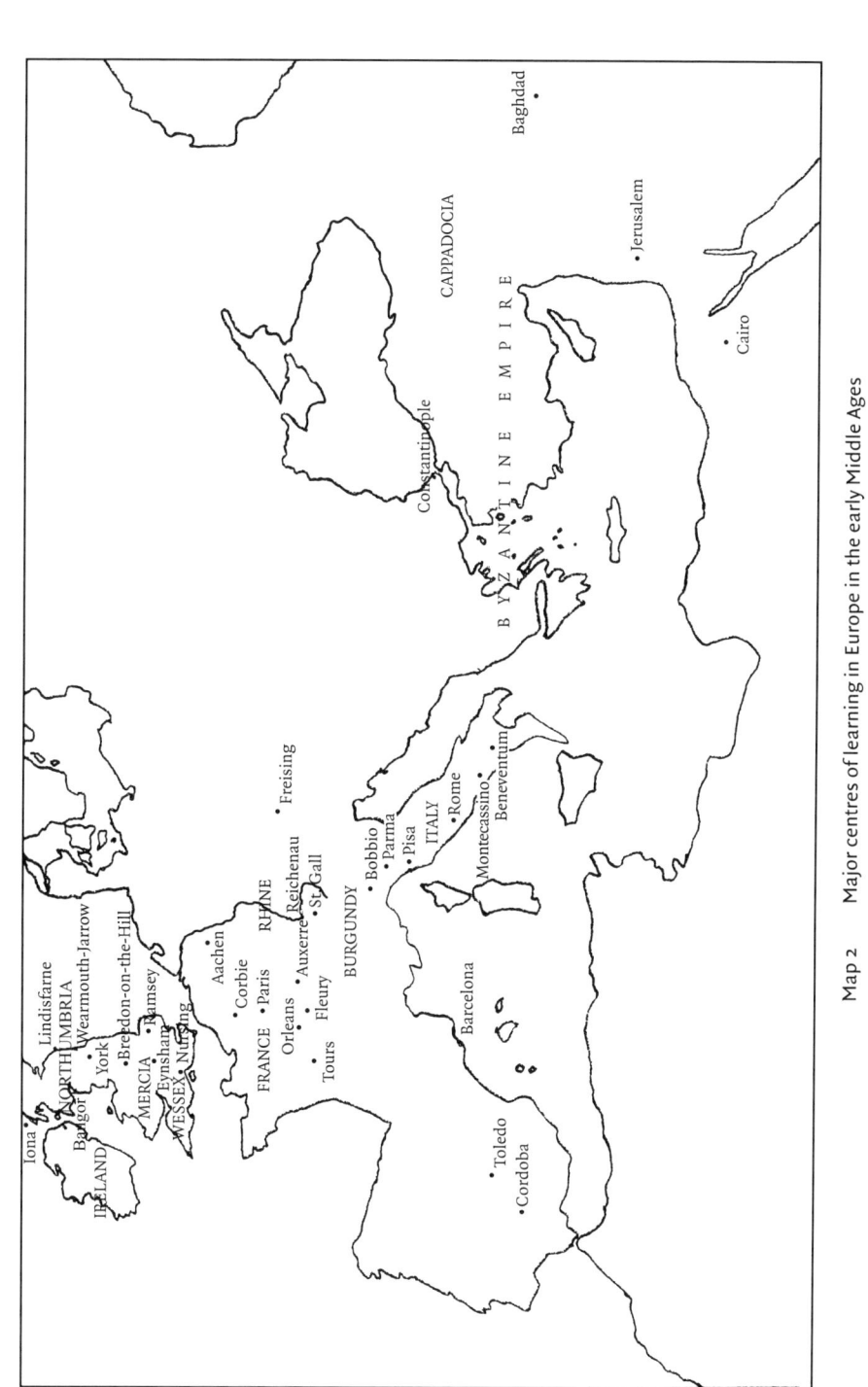

Map 2   Major centres of learning in Europe in the early Middle Ages

> **Box 6.1 The Church and culture**
>
> With our contemporary view of the Church as an institution which occupies a peripheral place in most modern societies, having failed to assimilate the scientific, technological and economic preoccupations of our present culture, we are inclined to regard the Church's preeminent position in the Middle Ages with dismay. How, we ask, could culture not have been stifled under its dominion? In fact the position of the Church with regard to culture was comparable to that of the state today, with equal potential for paternalism, authoritarianism, or genuine care. It took on responsibility for the provision of schools and institutions of higher learning, for libraries and archives, for the 'publication' and dissemination of books and ideas, and also for the provision of social welfare: care for the sick, elderly, orphaned and homeless. In many parts of Europe monks took the lead in cultivating hitherto untilled land and in introducing innovatory agricultural and industrial processes. That some members of the Church betrayed ignorance of classical culture, like the eighth-century priest who thought Venus was a man, or intolerance, as in the ubiquitous diatribes against 'the lying tales of the heathen', testifies to the diversity of experience and opinion to be found in early medieval Europe – no less diverse than that to be found in present-day Britain, where an MP can boast of never having read a poem and a Minister of Education can betray a woeful lack of familiarity with Shakespeare's writings. It was the monks and nuns of the decades around 800 who, with the permission and encouragement of their superiors, dedicated their lives to the laborious task of copying out the whole gamut of Classical Latin literature, from the risqué plays of Terence and forthright epigrams of Martial to Ovid's tales of pagan gods and goddesses. Without these eighth- and ninth-century copies, many of the most famous works of ancient literature would not be known to us today.
>
> *Reading*
>
> Bernhard Bischoff, 'Benedictine monasteries and the survival of Classical literature,' in his *Manuscripts and Libraries in the Age of Charlemagne*, transl. and ed. by Michael Gorman (Cambridge: Cambridge University Press 1994), pp. 134–60; originally published in German and Italian versions: 'Das benediktinische Mönchtum und die Überlieferung der klassischen Literatur', *Studien und Mitteilungen zur Geschichte des Benediktiner-Ordens und seiner Zweige* 92 (1981), 165–90; 'I monaci benedettini e la tradizione classica', *Atti dei Convegni Lincei* 51 (1982), 35–56.
>
> William R. Cook and Ronald B. Herzman, *The Medieval World View: An Introduction* (New York and Oxford: Oxford University Press 1983), ch. 6.
>
> Bernard Hamilton, *Religion in the Medieval West* (London: Arnold 1986).
>
> Carl A. Volz, *The Medieval Church from the Dawn of the Middle Ages to the Eve of the Reformation* (Nashville, TN: Abingdon 1997), chs. 1 and 2.

sparked off a rethinking of the nature and role of grammar, and the parsing grammar took over from the Insular elementary grammar as the chief aid to grammatical pedagogy;

3. the *later Middle Ages*, or Scholastic era (1100–1350), in which, inspired by the discovery of further works of Aristotle's, scholars in the new universities strove to create a theoretical as well as a practical approach to the study of language, while their colleagues in schools developed the verse grammar;
4. the *end of the Middle Ages* (1350–1500), during which people became increasingly aware of their vernaculars and began to teach Latin through the medium of the vernacular (and even, here and there, to experiment with grammars of the vernacular), and, in northern Europe, to try out visually striking ways of presenting grammatical doctrine, such as tables and columns.

In this chapter we shall survey aspects of the study of language in the earlier Middle Ages, focusing upon those parts of Europe north of the Alps which had relatively recently been converted to Christianity and thereby joined the mainstream of European intellectual life (see box 6.1). As we saw in chapter 5, Christianity brought a renewed emphasis upon those aspects of language which seemed to point beyond material life on earth to spiritual matters. Left to themselves, western Christians might well have preferred to concentrate on the transcendental nature of language; but the Church adopted a language policy which compelled them to focus on linguistic structure – the nuts and bolts of language – as well. Let us begin with a glimpse of the very unfamiliar ways of thinking about the higher aspects of language which we find in the early Middle Ages, and then move to the more earthly and material, and hence to us more accessible, consequences of the Church's language policy.

6.2 Language as a pointer to higher things: medieval *littera* theory and correlative thinking

By and large, scholars in the seventh and eighth centuries found it difficult to see any kind of higher meaning in grammatical doctrine about the word classes and their properties. (Early in the ninth century, the grammarian Smaragdus was to sketch the outlines of a spiritual interpretation of such phenomena as the eightfoldness of the parts of speech, and the mysteries of gender and number.) Only the smallest and the largest linguistic units – the *littera* and the use of figures and tropes – seemed to have potential for pointing to a meaning beyond the strictly literal and earth-bound. Figurative usage was the subject of a number of treatises by early medieval scholars, who found in the ancient doctrine of figures and tropes (see box 4.9, p. 61 above) a useful exegetical tool for explaining the many passages in the Bible in which the literal meaning is hard to understand. By reading such passages figuratively, commentators such as Bede could arrive at an appropriate interpretation (see box 6.2).

It is not so difficult to see how tropes such as allegory, irony and hyperbole might apply to the Bible. How did early medieval scholars arrive at a higher interpretation of the *littera*? The following passage comes from one of the numerous little treatises on the *littera* written in the seventh and eighth centuries. The work begins with some basic points, many (but not all) borrowed from ancient writers. Which elements do you think are medieval?

Box 6.2 The Venerable Bede: interpreting the figurative language of the scriptures
Bede (673–735) spent his life as a priest and monk in the community of Wearmouth-Jarrow, situated near the northeast coast of England close to the modern city of Newcastle. Within a few years of his death his reputation for uncommon erudition had crossed the Channel: the missionary St Boniface, working in Germany, asked his English correspondents to send him some of the writings of Bede, that 'candle of the Church lit by the Holy Spirit'. Bede left an enduring mark upon the daily life of Europe by popularising a system of dating events according to the number of years before or after the birth of Jesus, rather than according to the regnal years of monarchs. His learning embraced many spheres: the Bible, on which he wrote a series of commentaries, the last of them enriched by the smattering of Greek which he picked up by studying a bilingual Greek–Latin copy of Acts of the Apostles which had found its way from Sardinia to England; saints' lives; English history (his *Ecclesiastical History of the English People* is to this day one of our chief sources of information about the early history of England); natural history and chronology; and language. He never wrote a grammar as such, however, but compiled works on three other aspects of language: orthography, metrics, and figures and tropes. In all three books he strove to show how traditional Roman doctrine applied equally to Christian texts, as he makes clear in the introduction to his work on figures and tropes, *De schematibus et tropis*:

In order that you, my beloved son, and indeed all who choose to read these words may know that holy Scripture takes precedence over all other writings not only by virtue of its authority, in that it is divine, and its utility, in that it leads to eternal life, but also because of its antiquity and its very use of rhetoric, I have decided to demonstrate by means of examples gathered from its pages that there is not one of these schemes [=figures] and tropes which teachers of classical rhetoric boast of which did not appear in it first.

Bede carried out his promise, exemplifying each of Donatus's figures and tropes with an instance from the Bible or a Christian writer. The passage in which the prophet Elijah taunts the pagan guardians of the unresponsive idol Baal was a perfect example of irony: 'Pray louder!' he said. 'If Baal really is a god, maybe he is thinking, or busy, or travelling! Maybe he is sleeping so you will have to wake him!' (I King 18: 27). Allegory, a particularly important trope to medieval exegetes, was illustrated at length. Bede's treatise and those of several other early medieval scholars showed less confident writers and readers how to assimilate the rich metalinguistic repertoire they found in the grammars of Antiquity into their Christian studies.

Reading
George Hardin Brown, *Bede the Venerable* (Boston: Twayne 1987).
Benedicta Ward, *The Venerable Bede* (London: Chapman 1998).
Lawrence T. Martin, 'Bede as a linguistic scholar', *American Benedictine Review* 35 (1984), 204–17.
Margot H. King, '*Grammatica mystica*, a study of Bede's grammatical curriculum', in Margot H. King and Wesley M. Stevens, eds., *Saints, Scholars and Heroes: Studies in Medieval Culture in Honour of Charles W. Jones* (Collegeville, MN: Hill Monastic Manuscript Library 1979), 1, pp. 145–59.

6.2 Language as a pointer to higher things

> Benedetto Clausi, 'Elementi di ermeneutica monastica nel *De schematibus et tropis di Beda*', *Orpheus* n.s. 11 (1990), 277–307.
>
> Bede, *Libri II De Arte Metrica et De Schematibus et Tropis; The Art of Poetry and Rhetoric*, Latin text and English translation by Calvin B. Kendall (Saarbrücken: AQ 1991) [Kendall takes the text of a single manuscript, St Gall, Stiftsbibliothek, 876, as the basis of his text and translation of Bede's works on metrics and figures and tropes].
>
> Bede, *De schematibus et tropis*, ed. by Calvin B. Kendall, *Corpus Christianorum Series Latina* 123A (Turnhout: Brepols 1975), pp. 142–71. [Critical edition of the Latin text only.]
>
> Gussie Hecht Tanenhaus, 'Bede's *De schematibus et tropis* – a translation', *Quarterly Journal of Speech* 48 (1962), 237–53, repr. in J. M. Miller et al., eds., *Readings in Medieval Rhetoric* (Bloomington, IN: Indiana University Press 1973), pp. 96–122.

What is the *littera*? The minimal element (*elementum*) of an articulate spoken word (*vox*). What is an element? The grasping of meaning (*sensus*). What is meaning? The manifestation of thought expressed through the spoken word.	*Elementum* means simultaneously 'minimal unit' and 'speech sound' (as opposed to 'letter'): see box 4.4, p. 61 above.
Which comes first, the spoken word (*vox*) or the word-as-meaning (*verbum*)? The spoken word comes before the word-as-meaning because before the air is struck by the tongue, the spoken word bursts into sound.	Compare this with what Augustine had to say (section 5.2 above).
The spoken word (*vox*) has three forms: organised, muddled, and the third arising from ringing or striking.	Presumably the author is here referring to articulate and inarticulate human speech, and the various noises objects give off when struck.
There are three ways in which we come to speak correctly: through training, through reading, and through usage.	Although three was a number of special significance to all Christians because of its association with the three persons of the Trinity, the Irish were especially fond of triads. This triad of triads, together with the reference below to the three sacred languages (Latin, Greek and Hebrew), and the use of the Hiberno-Latin term *glorificatio* for 'manifestation', might well point to an Irish origin for this treatise.
The *littera*, as we said, is to be considered from three points of view: shape, name	Whereas ancient authors meant the sound-value of a *littera* when they

and value. The shape pertains to the eyes, the name to the ears, and the value to thought.	referred to its *potestas* 'value, power', our author regards the *potestas* of the *littera* as its ability to point to spiritual matters perceptible only to thought.
A sentence may be broken down into words (*verba*), words into syllables, and syllables into *litterae*, but there is nothing into which *litterae* may be broken down.	Note the familiar levels of analysis.
In Hebrew *littera* is called *sephir*, as when the Old Testament says *Careat sephir*, i.e. 'city of letters'. In Greek *littera* is called *gramma*, and the Romans call it *littera*. Philosophers call the *littera* 'atom', i.e. the tiniest spark of fire or ember of sunbeam.	'Careatsephir' is a medieval version of the Hebrew place-name Qiriath-sepher[2] which is glossed on its two occurrences in the Latin Vulgate translation of the Bible as 'city of letters'.
Littera is, as it were, *legitera*, because it provides an itinerary for readers (*legentibus **iter**).[1]	This etymology, the comment about 'atom', the analytical sequence of linguistic units from sentences down to *litterae*, and a definition similar to that given at the start of the passage, occur in the first five sentences of Sergius's *De littera*,[3] a Late Latin commentary on the first book of the *Ars maior* which was widely read in the seventh and eighth centuries.

After this introduction each of the *litterae* is discussed individually. From the section on the letter A you can see what kinds of things the author considered important:

A is a vowel.
How many strokes is it made of? Three strokes. Hence it is described as threefold in sound and in shape.
How many names does it have? Three names. It is called *aleph* in Hebrew, *alpha* in Greek, and *a* in Latin.
Why is *a* the first of the letters? Because it stands first in 'Adam', the first human name, and in *anima* 'soul', and in 'angel' that existed eons ago, when souls were created by the living God.
What does its twofoldness signify? The two Testaments, the Old and the New.
Three strokes form the letter A. What do they signify? They represent the Trinity.
When *a* is thought of as a unit, what does it signify? The one God.
Why? The three persons [of the Trinity] are called the one God.
A is an adverb of number meaning 500.[4]

As you can see, the author finds the shape of the letter the most fruitful of its three aspects for his line of thought. Its names in the three sacred languages merit a sentence, but its sound comes a very poor third. That enigmatic aside about the *littera* being threefold in sound as well as in shape is never elaborated upon. Most of the questions concentrate on the way in which the *littera* points beyond itself to some spiritual truth, the 'value' apparent to thought referred to in the introduction.

Frustrating as this may be to a modern phonetician, many early medieval thinkers found this a more satisfying way of studying the *litterae* than to treat them as purely ('merely', they would have said) physical phenomena. They wanted to escape from the arbitrariness and futility of the material world, subject as it was to constant change and deterioration. Language, like all other human phenomena, partook of the bodily nature which was a constant reminder of our Fall from Paradise. How could it be redeemed? Uncovering a link between the form of the letters and spiritual truths was a way which appealed to some – even if it lent itself to parody (see box 6.3).

Another path was to seek correlations between linguistic phenomena and other planes of existence – the microcosm, the macrocosm, and the Scriptures. Let's take a few examples from grammars written in the eighth and ninth centuries.

How many vowels are there? Five.
What are they? A e i o u.
Why five?
Because the body has five senses and the mind has five too.
What are the senses of the body? Sight, hearing, taste, smell and touch.
What are the senses of the mind? Love, fear, joy, sadness, hatred.
Why do the vowels not occur together in the alphabet?
Because the consonants are supported by the vowels in the same way that a house is supported by pillars.
Why does *a* come first? It forms part of an ascending series, for *a* resounds in the chest, *e* in the throat, *i* within the jaws, *o* within the teeth, and *u* right at the tip of the lips.[5]

The kind of reasoning used in this passage is quite different from what we are accustomed to. For a start, we would not dream of asking 'why?' about a matter of fact such as the precise number of vowels a language has, nor to seek the answer in a correlation with nonlinguistic phenomena such as the senses. The grammarian uses what anthropologists call 'correlative thinking' to pair the five vowels with two other fivefold phenomena, the senses of the body and the mind. No precise matching up of the vowels to corresponding senses is required; what matters is the fivefoldness. What the author wants to achieve is to show that the linguistic phenomenon – the existence of five vowels – is not something which exists in isolation, without meaning; the correlation with the fivefoldness of the senses shows that there is a fivefold counterpart to the vowels in the human being. As for the order in which the vowels occur in the alphabet, a modern writer would seek a historical answer, accounting for the order of the vowels in our alphabet by looking at the order in which they stand in the Phoenician alphabet, from which ours is ultimately derived. Instead, this anonymous grammarian tries to

> **Box 6.3 The first linguistic parody**
>
> The solemn authoritativeness of the grammarian – a vital part of the image – lent itself to spoofs and lampoons. In the middle of the seventh century someone who called himself Virgilius Maro Grammaticus – Virgil the Grammarian, almost certainly a pseudonym – wrote a pair of grammars which superimposed a sprinkling of parody upon the well-established tradition of grammatical discourse to conceal a serious objective: the subversion of the spurious authority of the grammarian, and along with it the Church's parallel claim to being the custodian of the sole route to truth. Virgilius depicts rival grammarians battling for fourteen days and nights over the vocative of *ego* 'I'; well, how *do* you address yourself when you talk to yourself? (The fifth-century grammarian Pompeius discusses this matter for the better part of a page without a whiff of humour!) But in Virgilius's book, such lighthearted moments serve to disguise an earnest message about epistemological and linguistic pluralism. Latin, Virgilius says, is 'so huge and profound that in order to expound it fully one must use a multiplicity of methods, words, forms and meanings'. Thus, although there are undeniably parodistic elements in Virgilius's work, it would be a mistake to categorise the whole thing as a parody. A clearer case is a treatise by one Sergilius, who describes himself as the disciple of Virgilius, who, together with his teacher Æneas (yes!), taught us how to move 'from strokes, dots and crosses to letters, from letters to articulate words, and other marvels analogous to these'. Sergilius's little tract gives the names of the strokes of each letter in the three sacred languages in this way:
>
> P. These strokes are called *urban irban* in Hebrew, *urbusta irbusta* in Greek, and in Latin a straight line from above and a semicircle to the right.
>
> We have no reason to suppose that Sergilius knew something about the vocabulary of Greek and Hebrew which has escaped the notice of modern scholars; everything suggests that he was lampooning treatises like Virgilius's.
>
> *Reading*
> *Virgilio Marone Grammatico, Epitomi ed Epistole*, ed. with Italian transl. by Giovanni Polara and Luciano Caruso (Naples: Liguori 1979).
> Vivien Law, 'Learning to read with the *oculi mentis*: the word-play of Virgilius Maro Grammaticus', in V. Law, *Grammar and Grammarians in the Early Middle Ages* (London and New York: Longman 1997), ch. 11.
> Vivien Law, *Wisdom, Authority and Grammar in the Seventh Century: Decoding Virgilius Maro Grammaticus* (Cambridge: Cambridge University Press 1995). [Pompeius's discussion of the vocative of *ego* is translated on pp. 8f. and Virgilius's on pp. 109–11.]

link the order of the written symbols with the part of the vocal tract in which he felt them resonate. The apparently arbitrary order of the symbols in the alphabet reflects the physical process of speaking as it takes place in the body.

Different correlations were used by a Byzantine Greek commentator on the *Tekhnē* attributed to Dionysius Thrax when asking about the seven vowels of Greek:

> Why does the writer of the *Tekhnē* define the number of the vowels as seven?
> Our answer is either that he made them equal to the number of strings of Apollo's lyre, or that they imitate the planets of the sky, for the planets are seven in number – Saturn, Jupiter, Mars, Sun, Venus, Mercury and Moon. The vowels depend on the planets: they say that *a* depends on the moon, *e* on Mercury, *ē* on Venus, *i* on the Sun, *o* on Mars, *u* on Jupiter, and *ō* on Saturn.[6]

Instead of looking to the human body for a correlation, this author looked outwards to the universe and to Greek mythology for his correlations. Although the commentator links each vowel with a specific planet, starting with the Moon, closest to the Earth, and finishing with the remotest, Saturn (the three outer planets had not yet been discovered), it is the sevenfoldness which matters most: the linguistic sevenfoldness finds its validation and its redemption from arbitrariness in the sevenfoldness of the macrocosm (see box 6.4).

Correlations could also be found in another domain, in the Bible. In the *Liber in partibus Donati* ('Book about Donatus's Parts of Speech'), written in northeastern France by the Carolingian grammarian Smaragdus around 805, we read: 'The Latin language is totally comprehended and brought to fulfilment in its eight parts.' Smaragdus then quotes Donatus: 'Many people have held that there are more or fewer parts of speech.' Smaragdus continues:

However, the universal Church sometimes observes the number eight, which I am sure is divinely inspired. Because the elect tend to come to knowledge of the Trinity through knowing Latin, and with it as their guide race on to their blessed heavenly homeland, it was inevitable that the Latin language should be contained within the number eight. That number often turns out to be sacred in the Holy Scriptures. For example, eight souls were saved from the waters of the Flood by the wooden ark, and similarly those who are saved by the water of baptism and the wood of the Cross in this world will enjoy the eight Beatitudes of the gospel in the kingdom that is to come.[7]

Smaragdus thus justifies Donatus's position – that there are eight parts of speech and neither more nor fewer – by showing how central a number eight is in the Bible. (He lists several more instances of eightfoldness after the ones quoted here.) Smaragdus too thought correlatively, seeking out instances of eightfoldness and emphasising the significance of this number. In trying to appreciate what this meant to him and his contemporaries we need to bear in mind that they experienced numbers differently from us – not as mere quantities, but as qualitatively distinct entities. They knew, for instance, that two bore within it a tension which is resolved in three. Several early medieval scholars compiled treatises listing all the ones, twos, threes, and so on to be found in the Bible and in the external world.

Box 6.4 Macrocosm and microcosm

People in ancient and medieval Europe were keenly aware of the interconnectedness of human beings with the world in which they live. Their understanding took a different form from ours, however. Whereas we stress the evolution of the human body from forebears akin to today's animals, and picture ourselves as participants in the global ecosystem or the global economy – a cog in a huge system – pre-Renaissance thinkers saw each human being as containing the whole universe in miniature within him- or herself. Each aspect of the human being, the microcosm, thus corresponded to some aspect of the macrocosm outside. In the seventh century Virgilius Maro Grammaticus developed this theme along the following lines:

It is by no means inappropriate that our instructors ... thought of man by the name of 'microcosm', for within himself he contains everything the visible world is made of: earth in his body, fire in his soul, water in his fluidity and air in the swiftness of his thoughts; the sun in the radiance of his wisdom, the moon in the uncertain and unstable conditions of wealth and youth, a blossoming meadow in the nobility of his virtues and the equanimity of his mild temper, mountains in the heights of generosity, hills in the succession of the family line, valleys in the humbling experiences of tribulation, fruit trees in the fruits of largess; barren trees, rugged places and mucky bogs, thorns and thistles in his evil ways and insatiable greed, snakes and cattle in simplicity and prudence, and the teeming, surging sea in the storm-tossed depths of the heart of man and in reason itself.

Ancient and medieval thinkers alike were convinced that it was a waste of time to try to understand the human being in isolation: man had no meaning without the universe. And likewise, the universe was incomprehensible without man. The modern view of *homo sapiens* as a chance latecomer to the earth's surface (a notion that has only become widespread since the latter part of the nineteenth century) would have seemed to pre-Renaissance thinkers to deny meaning as much to the universe as to man. Instead, their sense of the deep interconnectedness of human beings and the outer world offered them a way of finding meaning in the study of language. If you regarded language as simply an arbitrary means of communication, you had to concede that there was no point in studying it except in order to learn to use it more effectively. But if you saw in it another microcosm – a microcosm of man as well as of the universe – then it opened up new possibilities for insight.

Reading

George-Perrigo Conger, *Theories of Macrocosms and Microcosms in the History of Philosophy* (New York: Columbia University Press 1992).

M.-Th. d'Alverny, 'L'homme comme symbole. Le microcosme', *Simboli e simbologia nell'alto medioevo* 1, Settimane di Studio del Centro Italiano di Studi sull'Alto Medioevo 23 (1976), 123–95.

F. Saxl, 'Macrocosm and microcosm in mediaeval pictures', in his *Lectures* I (London: The Warburg Institute 1957), pp. 58–72.

A. J. Gurevich, 'Macrocosm and microcosm', in his *Categories of Medieval Culture* (London: Routledge & Kegan Paul 1985), ch. 3 (pp. 41–91).

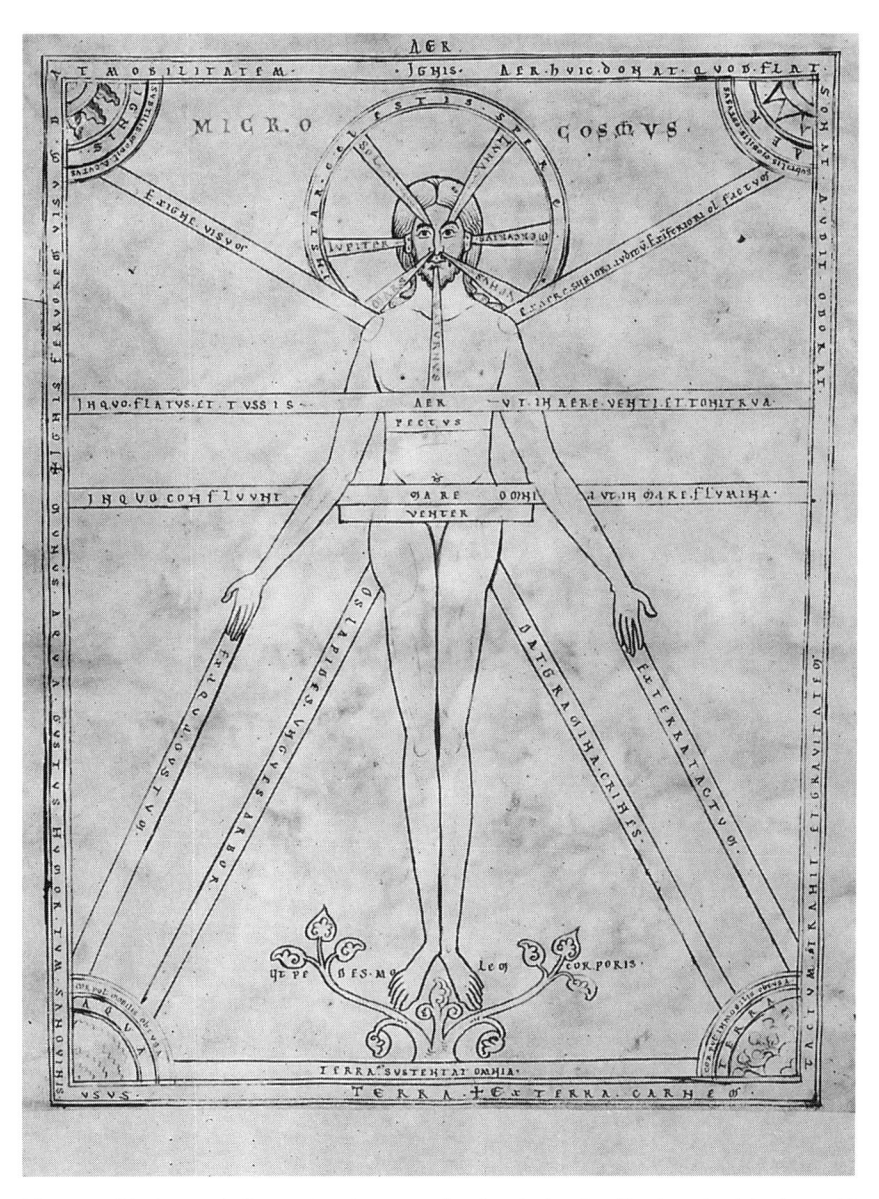

4   Diagram of the human being as the microcosm showing the head as like the celestial sphere with the seven planets attached to the eyes, ears, nose and mouth, and the four elements are given their appropriate link to various parts of the body, signalled with captions such as 'As the feet bear the weight of the body so the earth carries everything' and 'Air gives him the possibility of breathing, making sounds, hearing and smelling' (Regensburg, ca 1150). Munich, Bayerische Staatsbibliothek, Clm 13002.

In all three examples – and there are many others – the grammarian was at pains to connect the linguistic phenomenon under discussion with something outside language – the human being (microcosm), the cosmos (macrocosm), or the Bible (sacred history). In this way, what would otherwise have been a trivial and intrinsically meaningless point of grammar is linked with extralinguistic reality, and so reflects something of the harmony and majesty of the planets or the sublime promise of the Scriptures.

6.3 The language policy of the Church: a push towards linguistic materialism?

In the early centuries of Christianity the lands surrounding the eastern Mediterranean were a complex linguistic zone in which a relatively large number of languages were spoken, and several – Greek, Coptic, Aramaic and Syriac, to name only the principal ones – had a long-established written form as well. Eastern Christians therefore translated the Scriptures into their own language and used their native tongue for theological writings and commentaries, as well as in the day-to-day life of the Church. As neighbouring peoples were converted it seemed natural to create alphabets for their languages and continue the policy of translation, as was done for Armenian, Georgian and Gothic in the fourth century, and for Old Church Slavonic in the ninth. The difficult task of mastering a foreign language was thus confronted in the East by only a small number of individuals – those engaged in the work of translation and those who were destined to become leaders of the Church in their area, who spent time studying in Constantinople or Jerusalem and returned with first-hand knowledge of major texts and doctrinal disputes.

In the West the linguistic situation was utterly different. When the Church, following in the wake of the Roman empire, spread northwards and westwards out of its Mediterranean heartland, it found no local languages with an established literary tradition. On the territory of present-day France, Spain, Portugal, Britain, Germany, Switzerland, Austria and Hungary, Latin had been the language of Roman administration, education and culture. The Church adopted the same policy, insisting that those of its western converts who wished to play an active role in ecclesiastical and cultural life learn Latin. Church services, the liturgy, hymns, prayers, the Bible, commentaries, ecclesiastical law, church records – all were in Latin. In short, the adoption of Roman Christianity meant the adoption of the Latin language as the medium of religious life, and therefore of virtually all intellectual activity.

The contrasting language policies of the Orthodox and Roman churches had far-reaching consequences for the intellectual involvement of their adherents. Where the life of the Church could be maintained in the native language of the believers, as was the case in most of the Orthodox East, the relationship of Christians to their sacred texts was in principle direct: all literate individuals could study the Scriptures for themselves and participate with a certain degree of understanding in services. To advance further, to study commentaries on the Scriptures, required an intellectual effort, but nonetheless theological issues were within the grasp of the Byzantine man in the street. In the fourth century Gregory of Nyssa, a theologian from Cappadocia, in what is now eastern Turkey, reported with amazement on a visit to Constantinopole: 'If I ask for my bill, the reply is a comment about the virgin birth; if I ask the price of bread, I am told that the Father is greater than the Son; when I ask whether my bath is ready, I am told that the Son was created from nothing.'[8] In the West such debates were conducted in Latin, and so remained the preserve of the highly educated few. There was thus a much greater gulf between the merely functionally literate and the well educated in the West than was the case in much of the East. Basic literacy in the East unlocked a great range of literature in the native tongue; throughout much of the West it was merely the first step on the laborious path to a working knowledge of a foreign language, Latin. In northern and western Europe, where the new converts were native speakers of Germanic or Celtic languages, a huge amount of effort had to be expended on the teaching and learning of Latin. To maintain the life of the Church each generation needed to be trained anew in the Latin language.

The language policy of the Church of Rome thus had momentous consequences for the development of linguistics in the West. Whereas in the East literate persons could continue to relate to their language on an only partly conscious level, focusing on language in use – rhetoric and dialectic – literate westerners were obliged to become aware of linguistic form at the most basic level: grammar. Thus, although the western Church, like its eastern counterparts, preached that good Christians should turn away from physical and material things and devote themselves to the spiritual, on the linguistic plane its policies had the opposite effect. Instead of devoting themselves from the outset to the 'soul' of the word – its meaning – young westerners were expected to spend years grappling with its 'body' – declensions and conjugations – before they could advance to the goal of their studies. Very many never got so far. Of course, this is an over-stark view of the situation, for the monastic pupil, and indeed the layman, would be receiving a certain amount of religious instruction in vernacular sermons concurrently with his or her Latin studies; nonetheless, most individuals remained totally dependent upon the interpretation provided by the priest.

6.4 The linguistic conversion: creating descriptive grammars of Latin

As missionaries from Rome pushed into areas ever more remote from the Mediterranean centre of the old empire they found themselves obliged to make provision for the linguistic as well as the doctrinal instruction of their converts. In Ireland, converted in the fifth century, in England, converted during the seventh, in Germany, converted during the eighth, in Bohemia and Hungary, converted during the tenth and eleventh centuries, and in Scandinavia, converted during the eleventh and twelfth, the requirement to carry out religious duties in Latin posed a serious challenge to the educational capacity of the Church. It was easy enough to drill young oblates in basic literacy so that they could recite psalms and prayers in church, but quite another matter to teach native speakers of Old Irish, Old English, Old High German, Old Norse, and early forms of Czech, Polish and Hungarian enough Latin to understand the complex language of theologians like Tertullian or Ambrose, let alone to write it themselves. The existing grammars – the works of the Late Latin grammarians – were, as we have seen, written for native speakers of Latin or people who already possessed near-native competence; there was nothing specifically designed for foreigners who had no direct access to native speakers. The teaching aids which we take for granted – progressive textbooks with carefully graded exercises, readers, dictionaries, not to mention tapes, videos, computer courses, summer courses abroad, and the Internet – were non-existent. How did people go about mastering Latin as a foreign language?

First, we must remember that the great majority of those who were struggling to learn Latin in the early Middle Ages were oblates living in monasteries or convents. Since the daily routine of their lives included seven services a day, totalling at least four hours of exposure to Latin daily, they rapidly built up a passive knowledge that no modern student could hope to possess. (A comparable modern situation would be the way in which millions of people throughout the world today are exposed to English through English-language media, soap operas and pop songs reinforced by formal instruction.) For most medieval pupils, their acquaintance with Latin was initially through the spoken word, for books were scarce and not normally put into the hands of young children (see boxes 6.5 and 6.6). This, as we shall see, had important consequences for the kinds of linguistic analysis pursued during the earlier Middle Ages. Passive exposure to a spoken form of Latin during church services was supplemented by systematic instruction using descriptive grammars – textbooks of Latin as a foreign language.

Supplementing Donatus

The *Ars minor* was the starting-point in teaching Latin, yet it was far from ideal as a textbook for foreigners. It had the advantage of conveying definitions and descriptions of basic grammatical phenomena extremely concisely, and in pedagogically convenient question-and-answer form; but it took for granted a knowledge of Latin morphology, conjugating only one verb in full and declining an unrepresentative selection of nouns (see section 4.6 above). Seventh- and eighth-century teachers had no wish to abandon it and start again, however, for it possessed enormous authority and was, after all, a convenient basic summary. They had two choices: to compile additional material to use alongside it, or to make additions and modifications to the text itself.

Compiling additional material: Declinationes nominum

The easiest solution was to assemble the missing material in independent treatises without attempting to incorporate it into the carefully planned structure of the *Ars minor*. Because Latin nouns and verbs are fairly complex in their morphology (see box 4.10 if your memory needs refreshing), their inflection needs to be set out in some detail. What several early teachers in the British Isles and across the Channel did was to compile collections of noun and verb paradigms, each one introduced briefly

6.4 The linguistic conversion: creating descriptive grammars

Box 6.5 Memory and learning

In the Middle Ages, 'learning' meant 'learning by heart', as is still the case in many parts of the world today. A child just starting on Donatus's *Ars minor*, for instance, would copy out from dictation as much of the text as a wax tablet could hold, and memorise it before the next lesson, when the wax would be smoothed over and reused. If the lesson was not firmly lodged in the memory, it was lost. In copies of advanced commentaries on Donatus we often find that Donatus's statements are given in abbreviated form, reduced either to the first couple of words or to the first letter of each word – just enough to jog the well-schooled memory. The learning process is concisely depicted in this scene from the *Colloquy* of Ælfric Bata, an Englishman writing early in the eleventh century. The *Colloquy* – like the better-known one by his teacher, Ælfric of Eynsham – was a dialogue designed to help expand pupils' vocabulary and knowledge of everyday Latin:

My dearest classmates! Quick, get your books and sit in your seats. Read and memorise your assignments so that first thing tomorrow morning you can recite quickly and then learn more from our teacher so that when you're old you'll be able to read from memory in all Latin books and understand something in them, in order to teach others again and be upright. For to read books and not understand is to forget them, according to Cato's proverb.

Before you deplore the apparent inhumanity of this method of teaching, think about the context. For one thing, very few individuals in the early Middle Ages would ever own a book in their lives, parchment being an expensive commodity (see box 6.6). Failing eyesight was another consideration: glasses were not invented until the end of the thirteenth century. The more you had stored up in the 'bookchest of your memory', the more you would have to draw upon in old age. Thirdly, through the act of memorising, people were trained to observe the structure of the works they read down to the very last details, a method of reading which enormously facilitated assimilating the text.

Reading

Pierre Riché, 'Le rôle de la mémoire dans l'enseignement médiéval', in Bruno Roy and Paul Zumthor, eds., *Jeux de mémoire: aspects de la mnémotechnie médiévale* (Montreal: Presses de l'Université de Montréal and Paris: Vrin 1985), pp. 133–48.

Vivien Law, 'Memory and the structure of grammars in Antiquity and the Middle Ages', in Mario De Nonno, Paolo De Paolis and Louis Holtz, eds., *Manuscripts and the Tradition of Grammatical Texts from Antiquity to the Renaissance* 1 (Cassino: Università degli Studi di Cassino 2000), pp. 9–58.

Gail Ivy Berlin, 'Memorization in Anglo-Saxon England: some case studies', in W. F. H. Nicolaisen, ed., *Oral Tradition in the Middle Ages* (Binghamton, NY: Medieval and Renaissance Texts and Studies 1995), pp. 97–113.

Mary Carruthers, *The Book of Memory: A Study of Memory in Medieval Culture* (Cambridge: Cambridge University Press 1990).

David W. Porter, 'The Latin syllabus in Anglo-Saxon monastic schools', *Neophilologus* 78 (1994), 463–82. [A lively analysis of how Ælfric Bata's *Colloquy* would have been used.]

> Scott Gwara, ed., and David W. Porter, transl., *Anglo-Saxon Conversations: The Colloquies of Ælfric Bata* (Woodbridge: Boydell 1997). [Entertaining vignettes of eleventh-century classroom life.]

and followed by a list of examples and sometimes a concluding remark, as in this example:

Another long feminine noun: *haec area* 'courtyard' *areae areae aream area area*, and in the plural *areae arearum areis areas areae areis*. Here are some more examples: *galea* 'helmet', *aranea* 'cobweb', *Iudea* 'Judea', *Galilea* 'Galilee', *uinea* 'vineyard', *spontanea* 'voluntary', *caerea* 'waxy'. These nouns end in -*ae* [in the genitive singular.][9]

> **Box 6.6 What price grammar?**
> Toward the end of the seventh century Julian of Toledo grumbled that he wanted to include more in his commentary on Donatus, 'but it is too long to write, given that parchment is rarely bestowed upon us by our prince'. The relatively large number of medieval manuscripts containing grammars that have survived shows that many princes (and bishops and abbots) did regard grammar as a high-priority subject, unlike Julian's patron. In the year 1044 the cathedral chapter of Barcelona bought a copy of Priscian's *Institutiones grammaticae* from the Jew Raymundo Senisfredo for the price of a house and a piece of land. That work, being by far the longest ancient grammar, vying with the Bible in length, was often its owner's most valuable movable possession. As a result, copies not infrequently ended up in the hands of Jewish money-lenders, acquiring Hebrew jottings in the process. At the back of one such copy, originally from Italy but now in the library of Trinity College, Cambridge (MS R.9.11), there is a list of the items sold off in a household clearance that took place in England some time during the thirteenth century:
>
>> I received this from the effects of Mr R.:
>> For the bench etc. 5 shillings.
>> For the parchment 3 shillings.
>> For the linen 2 shillings.
>> For the rug etc. 5 shillings.
>> For the ring 3 shillings.
>> For the Priscian 12 shillings.
>> Also 5 shillings and 7 pence which I found in his chest, and 6 pence owed to him by Gregory.
>
> Mr R.'s single most valuable possession was thus his copy of the *Institutiones grammaticae*, fetching more than twice as much as either his furniture or his carpet.
>   Early modern printers were well aware of the commercial potential of grammars and other schoolbooks: Donatus's *Ars minor* was the second book ever printed (the Bible was the first), by Johannes Gutenberg, the western inventor of printing; and it was the very first book printed by William Caxton, the first printer in England.

6.4 The linguistic conversion: creating descriptive grammars

5 Hereford cathedral library. Some libraries regarded their books as so precious that they were chained to the shelves.

Since each paradigm with its accompanying matter constituted a self-contained paragraph, teachers could experiment by rearranging them in any order they liked. Generally they started by grouping all the nouns belonging to the same declension together, but within each declension they might group them by gender, or by termination, or even by language of origin (Latin/Greek/Hebrew: some of the most important words in the life of the western Church were borrowed from Hebrew, like *pascha* 'Easter', or from Greek, like 'Church' itself, *ecclesia*). Verbs were easier, for the four conjugations provided an adequate way of organising regular verbs, and irregular ones could just be grouped together at the end. As for pronouns, two principal methods of classification were in use, one following the noun declensions, the other based on Priscian's different system. Historically speaking, the importance of these little treatises, just called *Declinationes nominum* ('Declensions of Nouns'), humble little collections of paradigms though they are, is greater than it might appear at first sight. In the ancient world, few people had been able to see any inner logic in the formal structure of language, and alphabetical order had been imposed as an artificial ordering criterion. Now, for the first time in the history of linguistics in western Europe, people began to look for intrinsic ordering criteria in Latin morphology. No two *Declinationes nominum* treatises are organised alike. The experimentation gives us a glimpse into these first attempts to make sense of form.

Modifying the Ars minor: *Asporius and the Insular elementary grammarians*

Even as some teachers were compiling additional material to use along with Donatus's text, others began to experiment with modifications to the *Ars minor* itself. One solution was that of the unknown author of the Christian *Ars minor*, a lightly altered version of the *Ars minor* which substituted examples from Christian vocabulary for Donatus's pagan ones – *ecclesia* 'church' for his *musa* 'a muse', *templum* 'temple' for his *scamnum* 'stool' – and added a few extra paradigms to obtain coverage of the fourth and fifth declensions.[10] More thoroughgoing changes were made by Asporius (also known as Asperius or Asper), probably active around 600 in Ireland or Burgundy. Asporius began by copying out the first few lines of the *Ars minor*. When he arrived at Donatus's first examples of proper names, 'Rome, Tiber', he replaced them with Christian ones: 'Jerusalem, Jordan, Zion'. He then added a few more for good measure: 'Michael, Peter, Stephen, Isaiah, Aaron, Ezekiel', all biblical names, and noted the common nouns which correspond to each one: 'angel, apostle, martyr, prophet, priest, king'. His example of the comparison of adjectives is *sanctus sanctior sanctissimus* 'holy, holier, holiest', replacing Donatus's *doctus doctior doctissimus* 'learned, more learned, most learned'. When he got to the paradigms he at first followed Donatus fairly closely, using a word with Christian overtones to exemplify the declension of one noun of each gender:

Donatus	Asporius
magister (m.) 'a teacher'	*iustus* (m.) 'a just man'
musa (f.) 'a muse'	*ecclesia* (f.) 'a church'
scamnum (n.) 'a bench'	*ieiunium* (n.) 'a fast'

But instead of moving on to the common gender next, as Donatus does, Asporius suddenly realised that not all neuter nouns decline like *ieiunium*, and he added paradigms of several others: *pectus, nomen, murmur*, and six more. Soon another masculine paradigm occurred to him, and then a neuter he'd left out, and a couple more feminines. In the process he ended up remedying Donatus's deficiencies: all five declension patterns are represented rather than just the three covered by Donatus, and many slightly irregular types are declined as well. But the overall effect is chaotic, for Asporius abandoned Donatus's guiding principle of gender without putting anything else in its place. Asporius is an intriguing case of a monastic teacher becoming aware as he goes along of Donatus's inadequacies and doing his best to rectify them. The fact that his work was widely read by eighth- and early ninth-century teachers shows that his contemporaries were quick to recognise its usefulness.[11]

Some of Asporius's successors in the British Isles tried to improve upon Donatus in a more systematic manner, drawing upon Asporius's grammer and the *Declinationes nominum* texts for inspiration and material. Characteristically, these new works, the **Insular elementary grammars** (Insular here has the specialised medievalists' sense of 'from the British Isles'), followed the *Ars minor* (often interpolating material from the *Ars maior*), replacing Donatus's examples with Christian ones, until they reached the noun paradigms. Then they switched to a text which provided a more comprehensive treatment – either an existing version of the *Declinationes nominum* or the introduction to Priscian's *Institutio de nomine*, which, as we have seen (section 4.10 above), offered the framework for a complete description of Latin inflection without actually filling in the details. By slotting in a paradigm (often borrowed from a *Declinationes nominum* text) of each type mentioned by Priscian and collecting lengthy lists of examples, Insular teachers could be confident that their pupils would learn all they needed to know about the Latin noun, pronoun and verb. Indeed, they often went to great lengths to be comprehensive, trying to provide paradigms of every conceivable subtype. Tatwine, for instance, writing towards 700 at the monastery of Breedon-on-the-Hill in the central English kingdom of Mercia (in what is now Leicestershire), identified nearly twenty distinct subtypes within the first declension alone, where modern Latinists identify one or at most two distinct patterns.[12] (He achieved this by regarding derivational affixes such as -tura, -gena, -gera, -fica as part of the inflectional ending where we would say that the final -a common to all these affixes is the only relevant morpheme.) His younger contemporary, Boniface, writing in Wessex, at the monastery of Nursling, in Hampshire, went to the opposite extreme, giving just one paradigm for each declension.[13] A balanced solution, giving paradigms of each morphologically distinct subtype, was only arrived at after considerable experimentation.

6.5 Developing an awareness of word structure: morphological metalanguage and visual representation

As we have seen, ancient and early Christian thinkers lived very much within their native tongue, as it were, conscious of word and sentence meaning and their pragmatic effect, conscious too of the morphological exponents of semantic categories, but in general showing less interest in the formal structure of words and sentences. The foreign learners of the early Middle Ages stood in a different relationship to Latin, viewing it from the outside, noticing first the letters and sounds, and then word forms and sentence structure. The contrast between natives' and foreigners', internal and external, approaches to language was rendered even more acute by the fact that whereas ancient grammar was to a large extent aural-based, medieval grammarians were obliged to depend upon the written word.

The aural/oral basis of ancient grammar is vividly apparent in the Latin words for 'word':

verbum	saying, proverb, word-as-meaning (and also 'verb')
vox	voice, utterance, word-as-form
dictio	word (from *dicere* 'to say')
pars orationis	part of an utterance, word class (*oratio* 'speech, connected utterance' comes from *orare* 'to speak, declaim, pray')

When Late Latin grammarians wished to analyse word structure, their metalanguage was phonological rather than morphological in origin. They spoke of adding or dropping 'syllables' or 'speech sounds'. Terms such as 'root', 'stem', 'morpheme' and 'suffix' are of relatively modern origin, appearing from the sixteenth century on (see box 10.12, p. 248 below). Medieval grammarians were thus obliged to work with a repertoire of notions which was far from ideally suited to morphological analysis (see box 6.7).

Teachers throughout the Middle Ages relied upon the so-called word-and-paradigm model. When they wanted to describe the forms of an inflecting word class, they chose an example and set out its forms one after the other in the traditional

Box 6.7 Terminology 2: Describing the parts of a word

In the course of the Middle Ages scholars gradually became aware that, when it came to describing the constituent parts of a word, they faced a metalinguistic lacuna. For us, that lacuna is very revealing of their holistic way of thinking. Early medieval grammarians, like their ancient predecessors, frequently used phonological terminology – *littera* and 'syllable' – in describing morphological phenomena. The strictly morphological terminology available for describing the parts of a word was limited to two terms:

- *praepositio loquellaris* 'preposition bound to a word': this denoted both bound prefixes such as *dis-* and *re-* and elements such as *sub-* and *super-* which may also occur as free forms belonging to the class of prepositions;
- *terminatio* 'termination, ending'.

There was no term for what was left once prefix and termination had been removed – our 'root' – but 'word', *dictio*. *Dictio* thus had to do double duty, denoting both the complete word form and a part of it, the root. Significantly, given the early medieval penchant for seeing correlations between language and the human being, a parallel terminological lacuna existed in the early medieval terms for 'body': Old English *bodig* denoted both the whole human form and what we now call 'trunk', using a loanword from Latin.

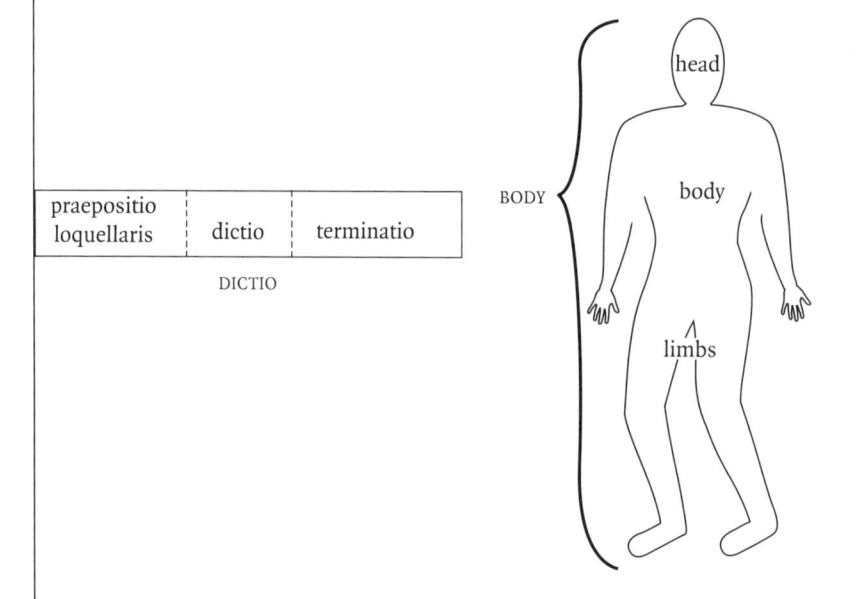

praepositio loquellaris	dictio	terminatio

DICTIO

BODY { head / body / limbs }

Both 'trunk' and 'root' in a linguistic sense appear first in English during the Northern Renaissance, 'trunk' in 1494 and 'root' in 1530. The terms corresponding to our *free form* and *bound form* similarly convey an image of the entity in one of two

6.5 Developing an awareness of word structure

> states: 'whole' (*nomen integrum*) or 'damaged' (*nomen corruptum*) – a far cry from the building-block metaphors of our current terminology.
>
> Reading
> Vivien Law, 'Geschichte der morphologischen Forschung I.8. The Middle Ages', in Geert Booij, Christian Lehmann and Joachim Mugdan, eds., *Morphologie/Morphology* I.1 (Berlin and New York: de Gruyter 2000), pp. 76–90.

sequence inherited from the Late Latin grammarians. But whereas we are used to seeing paradigms set out in columns, one form below the other, early medieval teachers used running text for paradigms; that is, the paradigms were copied out continuously without any visual distinction from the surrounding text. Lists of examples, on the other hand, were often copied out in columns. This mode of presentation reflects a primarily oral–aural mode of teaching and study (and bear in mind that 'silent' reading in the Middle Ages was often done with the lips moving, sounding the words out to oneself!): paradigms, which consist of the same word repeated with minor variations, could easily be read out from running text without detriment to clarity of expression, whereas examples in lists were more safely presented in columns to emphasise their lack of contextual meaning. Only very occasionally did teachers and scribes in the seventh,

6 Extract from an early medieval copy of the *Ars Ambianensis*. St Gall, Stiftsbibliothek, 877 (Switzerland, s. ix in.), p. 178 (278). Can you pick out the paradigms?

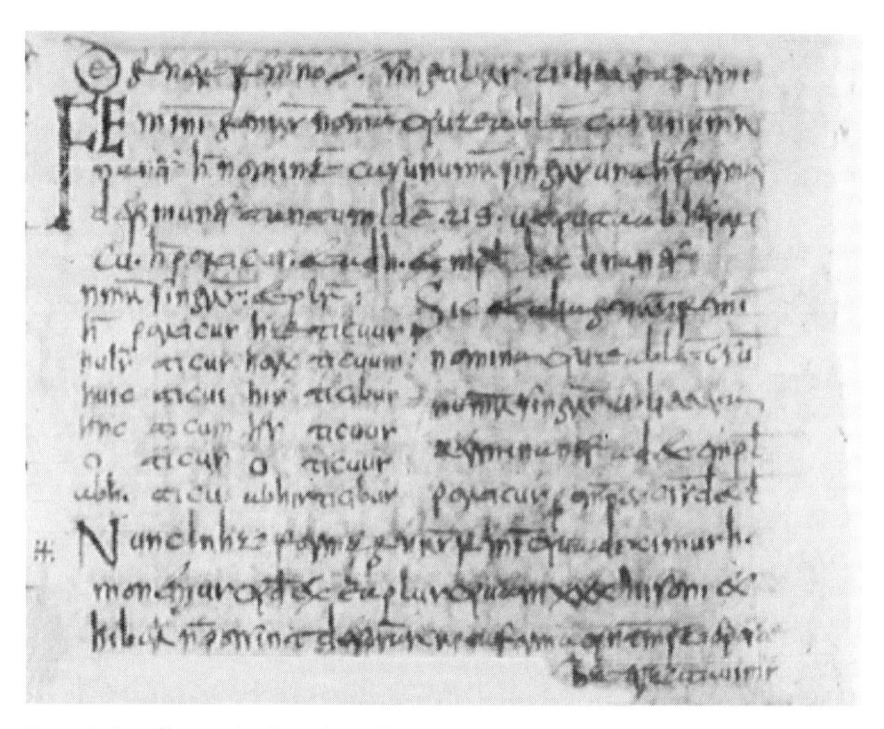

7 Transcription of *haec porticus* from the Bobbio manuscript.

eighth and ninth centuries notice the visual potential of columns and tables for paradigms as well, and try to set the paradigms off from the text.

The manner in which a paradigm is presented often has consequences for the perception of morphological structure. After all, it is much easier to identify the part of a word common to all the forms in the paradigm when they are set out one above the other than when they stand next to one another on the same line. As long as it remained customary to set out paradigms in running text, facilitating reading aloud, the basis of analysis remained an aural–oral unit: the syllable. Not only did grammarians describe morphological operations in terms of 'adding' or 'dropping' *litterae* or syllables; even their attempts at abbreviating paradigms were affected. In these examples the letters in square brackets were omitted by the scribe, as you can see from the facsimile. What would you reconstruct as the root? What principle has the scribe used in abbreviating the paradigm?

(1) h[aec] porticus   hae [por]ticuus
     hui[u]s [por]ticus   har[um] [por]ticuum
     huic [por]ticui   his [por]ticibus
     hanc [por]ticum   has [por]ticuus
     o [por]ticus   o [por]ticuus
     ab h[ac por]ticu   ab his [por]ticibus

This is the paradigm of *porticus* 'portico', a fourth-declension noun, as set out in a copy of Probus's *Instituta artium* in a seventh-century manuscript copied by an Irish scribe

6.5 Developing an awareness of word structure

8   Transcription of *haec uirtus* from the Corbie manuscript.

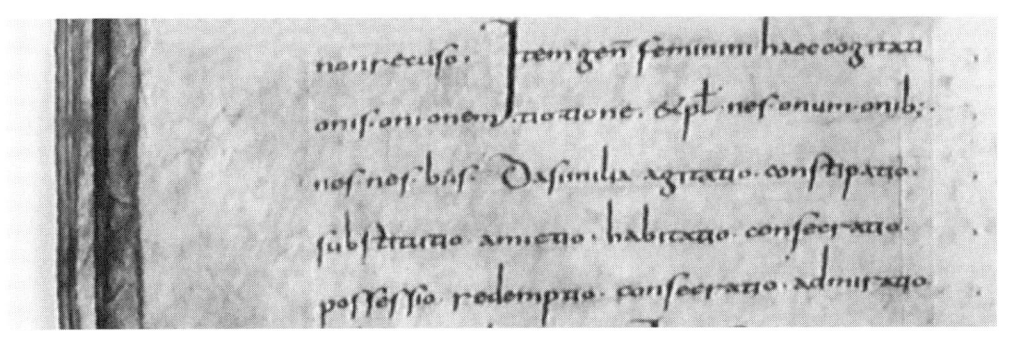

9   Transcription of *haec cogitatio* from the Corbie manuscript.

at the monastery of Bobbio, in northern Italy.[14] Throughout the plural the scribe has written -*uus* where we would expect -*us* endings, possibly to indicate the length of the vowel, but equally possibly through confusion with the (correct) -*uum* ending of the genitive plural – or alternatively from confusion with words ending in -*quus*.

(2)   hae[c] uirtus [uir]tutis [uirtu]ti [uirtu]tem [uir]tus [uirtu]te [uirtu]tes [uirtu]tum [uirtuti]bus [uirtu]tes [uirtu]tes [uirtuti]bus

The paradigm of *uirtus* 'courage' from an early ninth-century copy of the *Declinationes nominum* made at Corbie, an important monastery in northern France.[15] Again, can you identify the principle which underlies the abbreviation of the forms? (The scribe wasn't totally consistent at the outset.)

(3)   haec cogitatio [cogitatio]nis [cogitati]oni [cogitati]onem [cogita]tio [cogita]tione, et pl[uraliter] [cogitatio]nes [cogitati]onum [cogitati]onibus [cogitatio]nes [cogitatio]nes [cogitationi]bus.

On the same page of the Corbie manuscript we can see another way of tackling the problem, this time in the paradigm of *cogitatio* 'thought', again in running text.

In (1), the Bobbio scribe tried to abbreviate the paradigm; but instead of eliminating the entire shared portion, *portic(u)*, he drops only the first syllable, *por*. In the first of the two instances from the Corbie manuscript (2), the scribe gives only the final syllable (except in the first two forms). Once again, this method of abbreviation does not coincide with a modern root-based analysis, partly because we would consider the entire shared portion, *uirtut-*, to be the root, partly because 'stems' of different lengths result from the scribe's counting backwards from the end. In (3) the segmentation is based not on syllables but on perceptual salience: the part selected is the one which leaps out at the viewer/hearer.

Early medieval scholars perceived the word as the minimal semantic unit, and the transition to handling the word as a 'physical' object with an analysable structure did not come easily. Their mentality was holistic rather than analytical, as we can see from their way of thinking in a great many other domains – natural history, anthropology, cosmology and even arithmetic. What mattered was the meaning of the entity – the mystical significance of the hedgehog, or the number 4, or the letter B, or the word as a whole. Chopped up into pieces, dissected, analysed, reduced to a mere quantity or a string of units, the entity lost its significance. The natural inclination of seventh- and eighth-century scholars was to continue to work in a holistic way, looking for higher meaning; but where language was concerned, Church policy forced them to turn their attention to the physical appearance and form of words. From this time on, western scholars began to elaborate the basic notions of morphological analysis – but it came hard. If the uncompounded word was the minimal semantic unit, how could one break it down into smaller parts? People had to *learn* to see the word as an entity made up of component parts, which meant that, little by little, they had to develop a mechanistic way of thinking. The problem was analogous to that which a beginner in zoology might face in trying to identify the constituent parts of a worm or an eel: without dissecting it – which means killing it – how can one determine where its body stops and its tail begins?

Seventh- and eighth-century teachers and scribes engaged in a good deal of experimental morphological analysis, trying out tables and segmenting nouns and verbs using various criteria. As they did so, they became increasingly aware of the word as something with visual form and a shape of its own. The inherited metalanguage based on the perception of the word as a spoken, oral–aural unit no longer seemed wholly appropriate. Initially in seventh-century Irish circles, but more generally in the eighth and ninth centuries, two new terms were pressed into service in the sense of 'word form': *litteratura*, literally 'lettering, written form', and *superficies*, literally 'surface'. Both terms clearly reflect the new emphasis on the study of language via the written medium. By the twelfth century they had fallen out of use again, and the aurally based terms predominated once more. By then, however, people were learning to visualise language in a different way, as we shall see in chapter 8.

Further reading

Background

Peter Brown, *The Rise of Western Christendom: Triumph and Diversity AD 200–1000* (Oxford: Blackwell 1996).

William B. Cook and Ronald B. Herzman, *The Medieval World View: An Introduction* (New York and Oxford: Oxford University Press 1983), chs. 1–6.
Jean Leclercq, *The Love of Learning and the Desire for God: A Study of Monastic Culture*, 2nd edn (London: SPCK 1978).
Joseph H. Lynch, *The Medieval Church: A Brief History* (London: Longman 1992), chs. 2 and 3.
David Nicholas, *The Evolution of the Medieval World: Society, Government and Thought in Europe, 312–1500* (London: Longman 1992), part 1.
Pierre Riché, *Education and Culture in the Barbarian West, Sixth through Eighth Centuries* (Columbia, SC: University of South Carolina Press 1976), esp. ch. 8.
Philippe Wolff, *Western Languages AD 100–1500* (London: Weidenfeld and Nicolson 1971), transl. from *Les origines linguistiques de l'Europe occidentale*, 2nd edn (Toulouse: Association des Publications de l'Université de Toulouse–Le Mirail 1982).

Bibliography

V. Law, 'Grammar in the early Middle Ages: a bibliography', in her *Grammar and Grammarians in the Early Middle Ages* (London: Longman 1997), ch. 14, updated from the version originally published in *History of Linguistic Thought in the Early Middle Ages*, ed. V. Law, Studies in the History of the Language Sciences 71 (Amsterdam: John Benjamins 1993), pp. 25–47 (=*Historiographia Linguistica* 20 (1993), 25–47).
Pierre Swiggers, 'L'héritage grammatical gréco-latin et la grammaire au Moyen Age', *Mediaeval Antiquity*, ed. A. Welkenhuysen, H. Braet and W. Verbeke (Leuven: Leuven University Press 1995), pp. 159–95. [A bibliographical essay.]

The language policy of the Church and the first grammars of Latin as a foreign language

Vivien Law, *The Insular Latin Grammarians* (Woodbridge: Boydell and Brewer 1982), chs. 1, 3, 5.
V. Law, 'Linguistics in the earlier Middle Ages: the Insular and Carolingian grammarians', in her *Grammar and Grammarians in the Early Middle Ages* (London and New York: Longman 1997), ch. 4, repr. from *Transactions of the Philological Society* 83 (1985), 171–93.
Anneli Luhtala, 'Early medieval grammar', in E. F. K. Koerner and R. E. Asher, eds., *Concise History of the Language Sciences* (Oxford: Pergamon 1995), pp. 121–9.
V. Law, 'The study of Latin grammar in eighth-century Southumbria', in her *Grammar and Grammarians in the Early Middle Ages* (London and New York: Longman 1997), ch. 5, repr. from *Anglo-Saxon England* 12 (1983), 43–71.
Michael Herren, 'Die Anfänge der Grammatikstudien auf der britischen Inseln: Von Patrick bis zur Schule von Canterbury', in *Medialität und mittelalterliche insulare Literatur*, ed. Hildegard L. C. Tristram (Tübingen: Narr 1992), pp. 57–79.
Louis Holtz, 'Continuité et discontinuité de la tradition grammaticale au VIIe siècle', in J. Fontaine and J. N. Hillgarth, eds., *Le septième siècle: changements et continuités* (London: Warburg Institute 1992), pp. 41–57.
V. Law, 'Geschichte der morphologischen Forschung: the Middle Ages' [in English], in G. Booij et al., *Morphologie/Morphology* 1.1 (Berlin and New York: de Gruyter 2000), pp. 76–90. [Survey of the history of morphology in the Middle Ages.]

Edoardo Vineis and Alfonso Maierù, 'Medieval linguistics', in Giulio Lepschy, ed., *History of Linguistics 2: Classical and Medieval Linguistics* (London and New York: Longman 1994), pp. 134–189, transl. from the Italian original in G. Lepschy, ed., *Storia della linguistica* (Bologna: il Mulino 1990), 11–100.

Language as a pointer to higher reality

Friedrich Ohly, 'Vom geistigen Sinn des Wortes im Mittelalter', in his *Schriften zur mittelalterlichen Bedeutungsforschung* (Darmstadt: Wissenschaftliche Buchgesellschaft 1977), pp. 1–31; first published in *Zeitschrift für deutsches Altertum und deutsche Literatur* 89 (1958), 1–23.

Jean Jolivet, 'Quelques cas de "platonisme grammatical" du VII au XIIIe siècle', *Mélanges offerts à René Crozet* 1 (Poitiers: Société d'Etudes Médiévales 1966), pp. 96–9.

Vivien Law, 'Learning to read with the *oculi mentis*: the word-play of Virgilius Maro Grammaticus', in her *Grammar and Grammarians in the Early Middle Ages* (London and New York: Longman 1997), pp. 224–45.

Two texts on the *litterae* were printed by Hermann Hagen, *Anecdota Helvetica* (Leipzig: Teubner 1870, repr. as volume 8 of the *Grammatici Latini*), pp. 302–7. [The third text Hagen prints is an excerpt from *The Marriage of Philology and Mercury* by Martianus Capella.]

Texts

Researchers in this field habitually use texts that have not yet been edited alongside those that are available in print, going to the libraries where they are kept to read them and transcribe the text from them by hand (photocopying medieval manuscripts is not permitted!), or alternatively buying a microfilm copy from the library to work with at home. This requires some degree of training in paleography, the study of the different scripts in use during the Middle Ages, and of codicology, the study of the physical structure of manuscript codices. Grammatical texts from this period mentioned in this chapter which are available in print include:

Ars Asporii, ed. H. Hagen, *Anecdota Helvetica* (=GL 8, Leipzig: Teubner 1880), pp. 39–61.

Christian Ars minor, ed. V. Law, 'Erchanbert and the interpolator: a Christian Ars minor at Freising (Clm 6414)', in V. Law, ed., *History of Linguistic Thought in the Early Middle Ages*, Studies in the History of the Language Sciences 71 (Amsterdam and Philadelphia: Benjamins 1993), pp. 223–43, at pp. 231–8.

Ars Bonifatii (Boniface), ed. C. J. Gebauer and B. Löfstedt, Corpus Christianorum Series Latina 133B (Turnhout: Brepols 1981), 13–99.

Ars Tatuini (Tatwine), ed. M. De Marco, Corpus Christianorum Series Latina 133 (Turnhout: Brepols 1968), 1–93.

7 The Carolingian Renaissance

7.1 The notion of 'renaissance'

Between Classical Antiquity and our own day lie a series of renaissances, so-called 'rebirths' of a past phase of history, or more accurately revivals of interest in an earlier period. The Italian Renaissance, *the* Renaissance *par excellence*, is the best known, but every survey of European history reveals others: the Carolingian Renaissance, the Ottonian Renaissance, the Twelfth-Century Renaissance, and then, after the Italian Renaissance, the Northern Renaissance. After that the label 'renaissance' disappears, and instead we talk about Neo-Classicism, the Gothic revival, the pre-Raphaelite movement. Even the late twentieth-century preoccupation with roots and heritage, with manifestations as diverse as reconstructions of Civil War battles, Anglo-Saxon villages, historical theme parks, Elizabethan feasts, and companies which will trace your family tree, is in its own way a 'renaissance' of the past. Although such renaissances are invariably brief, they occupy a disproportionately important place in historical surveys of all kinds, from intellectual history to the history of art and architecture. Why? Isn't a retreat into the past a form of escapism, at best antiquarianism, at worst a failure to get to grips with the present?

In fact, almost paradoxically, each such period presages the appearance of something new. Latent in them is the germ of the next phase of development. Yet how can an interest in the past lead to the future? All back-to-the-past movements have certain elements in common. They commence with widely felt dissatisfaction with the present. Trapped in a dead end, people cast around for alternatives; but since the present offers none and the future is inaccessible, they look back with nostalgia to an era when architects designed people-friendly buildings, composers wrote music everyone liked, politicians were honest, and life was generally rosier. That very process of looking back to the past dislodges one from the problems of the present and creates an opening for new ideas – space for the future, as it were. What grows up in that space may not look much like the past that inspired it, any more than the pine tree looks like the cone. The importance of a renaissance lies not so much in the rebirth of the past – though this is often its most conspicuous feature – as in the loosening from the

7.2 The Carolingian Renaissance

The *Carolingian Renaissance*, in the decades around 800, is the first major back-to-the-past movement in European history. Let's look at what led up to it. In 476 the Roman empire succumbed definitively to the pressure of migrants from the East: that was the year in which the last emperor of Roman stock was deposed and replaced by a Germanic chieftain. One by one Germanic tribes carved out kingdoms on the territory of the former Roman empire: Lombards and Ostrogoths in Italy, Burgundians in eastern France, Franks in northern France, Anglo-Saxons in England, Visigoths in Spain and Vandals in North Africa. All these peoples were converted to Christianity in the course of the fifth, sixth and seventh centuries (see sections 6.3 and 6.4 above). Little by little, as their territory was consolidated and Christianity took ever deeper hold, individuals emerged who began to wonder about the intellectual life of ancient Rome, so often alluded to by Bible exegetes such as Augustine and Jerome. Perhaps the most influential of all such individuals in the early Middle Ages was Charlemagne (reigned 768–814), a member of the Carolingian dynasty. Charlemagne began his career by unifying the domains occupied by the Franks, i.e. German-speaking territory on both sides of the Rhine and in the Low Countries. (It was several centuries before all the Germanic-speaking people on the territory of modern France adopted a form of speech descended from Latin as their own language.) In recognition of his conquests (coupled with more devious political intentions) Pope Leo III crowned Charlemagne emperor on Christmas Day in the year 800. The revival of the ancient Roman title of emperor is symptomatic of the strongly felt desire of this generation to establish a link with the past of imperial Rome (even if Charlemagne himself was reluctant to accept the political implications of the pope's act). Charlemagne, when not preoccupied with military campaigns, saw himself as a patron of intellectual life, like the Emperor Augustus in the most glorious days of ancient Rome. He gradually assembled all the leading scholars of Europe at his court in Aachen (Aix-la-Chapelle): Peter of Pisa and Paul the Deacon (Paulus Diaconus) from Italy; Theodulf of Orléans from Spain; several scholars from Ireland; and, most importantly for the history of linguistics, Alcuin of York from England.

Charlemagne and his team of scholars instigated a number of projects. Every bishop was required to set up a school in his diocese open to anyone who was capable of benefiting from education, a measure which, where it was implemented, began the long-drawn-out process of making education available outside the network of monasteries. New editions of the Bible and of the Benedictine Rule, the regulations which governed life in the monasteries, were undertaken in order to purge them of the textual errors which had slipped in with the passing of time, and with a view to ensuring uniformity throughout the kingdom. Even the handwriting used in copying books was redesigned, for many different varieties – by no means all equally legible – were in use in different monasteries. The result is known as *Caroline minuscule*, a clear and harmonious

7.2 The Carolingian Renaissance

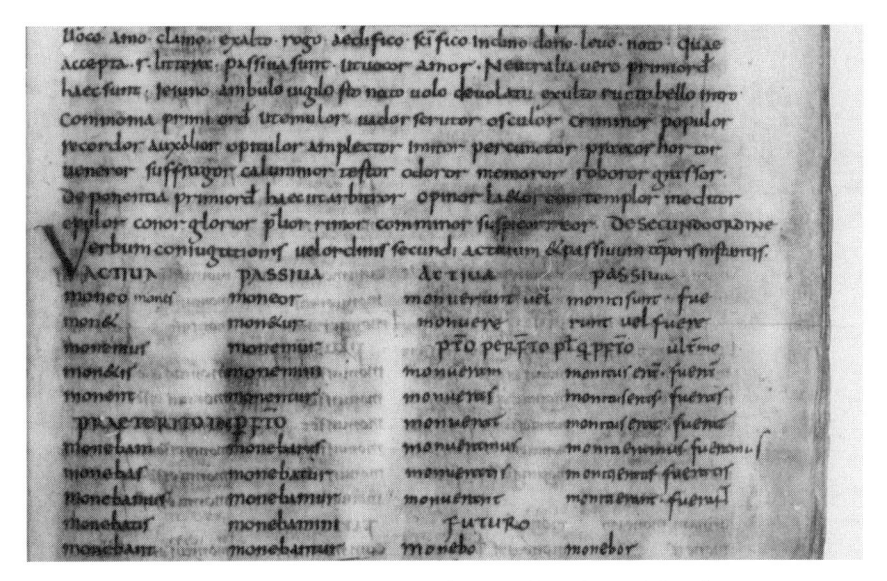

10   Paradigms from the *Ars Bonifacii* copied out in a fine Caroline minuscule hand.

script which, revived by the Humanists in the fifteenth century, became the ancestor of our modern printed letter forms. In all these reforms a striving for uniformity and standardisation across a wide geographical area is apparent. So too is the feeling that authority is to be found in the past – in ancient copies of the Bible and the Benedictine Rule.

But the Carolingians looked back to the ancient world in another area as well, turning their interest to the literature of ancient Rome. During the seventh and eighth centuries very little Classical Latin literature had been read, and then only by a small number of exceptionally learned scholars such as Adamnán of Iona (Ireland) and Bede at Wearmouth-Jarrow in Northumbria (northeastern England). Vergil's poetry and a few historical texts were read here and there, but for the most part pre-Carolingian scholars preferred to put all their effort into studying the writings of the Church Fathers, a major project in its own right. In the decades toward 800 the scholars around Charlemagne rediscovered a number of long-forgotten classical authors: the historians Suetonius and Livy, and the poets Ovid, Juvenal and, a little later, Horace. Full of nostalgia for the Roman past, Charlemagne, Alcuin and their colleagues adopted classical names and composed poetry modelled on the writings of the ancients. As they strove to imitate the syntactic and stylistic complexities of the most accomplished writers of ancient Rome, they became aware of aspects of Latin that had previously gone unnoticed. If the greatest authors of Rome had known how to express themselves with such eloquence, surely the ancient grammarians had written with comparable profundity about their language. What, they wondered, had the grammarians actually said about language? Of course all these Carolingian scholars had received their initial instruction in Latin from an ancient work, Donatus's *Ars minor*, modified to accommodate the needs of pupils in a setting Donatus had never dreamt of, as we saw in chapter 6; but in their enthusiasm for the ancient world the Carolingians' attitude towards the Insular

> **Box 7.1 Text and manuscript**
>
> What is the difference between a *text* and a *manuscript*? The *text* lived originally in the head of the author as he (or rarely she) found appropriate words in which to clothe the ideas. Sometimes it was composed in its entirety in the author's mind and then recited orally, only later to be written down on papyrus, parchment or paper. Later still, modern scholars **edit** it, reconstructing the author's original version as accurately as they can, and print the result with a **critical apparatus** at the foot of the page, listing all the variants they find in each copy of the text. No matter what medium it is presented in, from papyrus roll to CD-ROM or Web site, the text remains the same. A *manuscript*, on the other hand, is a physical artefact – a handwritten copy of one or more texts. Most medieval manuscripts were made of parchment sheets sewn together and bound with wooden boards covered with leather up until the fourteenth century, when paper, introduced from the East (ultimately from China), swiftly displaced the animal skins of which parchment was made. Although much cheaper and more easily obtainable than parchment, paper is far less durable. Many kinds of nineteenth- and early twentieth-century paper, in particular, crumble away very rapidly due to the manufacturing process used.
>
> Like any other volume in a library, every medieval manuscript has its own identificatory shelfmark. This is made up of several elements:
>
> | *Oxford,* | *Bodleian Library,* | *Additional* | *C.144* |
> |---|---|---|---|
> | city | library | collection | number |
>
> The **shelfmark** (or **classmark**) may be cited in abbreviated form after its first occurrence in an article or scholarly book. Scholars often also give the place where the manuscript originated (provenance) and its approximate date of origin, using standard Latin terminology. For example, this information for the Oxford manuscript just mentioned would take the form: 'central Italy, s. xi in.', meaning 'copied in central Italy at the beginning of the eleventh century'. In this system, *s.* stands for *saeculo* 'in the ... century', *in.* (*ineunte*) means 'at the beginning', *med.* (*medio*) means 'in the middle', and *ex.* (*exeunte*) means 'at the end'. You can indicate which half or quarter of a century a manuscript dates from like this: s. viii^1 (first half of the eighth century), s. x^2 (second half of the tenth century), s. ix$^{2/4}$ (second quarter of the ninth century, i.e. ca 825–850). Of course, knowing when a *manuscript* was copied doesn't tell you when the *texts* in it were composed – but at least you know the texts can't be any later than the manuscript! Or, as scholars would say, a manuscript copied in the first half of the ninth century furnishes a *terminus ante quem* for the texts it contains of *ca* 850.
>
> To indicate whereabouts in the manuscript a given text is to be found, most libraries use a system a little different from that used in printed books. Modern books are **paginated**; that is, the front and back of each leaf are separately numbered. Most medieval manuscripts are **foliated**; that is, each leaf, or **folio**, has its own number. The front of the folio, i.e. the right-hand page, is called the **recto**, and the back, or left-hand page, is called the **verso**. A work that occupies the first four pages (in modern parlance) of a manuscript would thus be said to run from folio 1 recto to

folio 2 verso, normally abbreviated to 'ff. 1r-2v'. If, as is common from the twelfth century on, the page is divided into columns, the first column is indicated by the letter *a* and the second by the letter *b* (and so on).

elementary grammars of the previous generations changed. One Carolingian teacher wrote:

Donatus's grammars have been corrupted and spoilt by every Tom, Dick and Harry adding just what he feels like from other authors or slipping in declensions, conjugations and other stuff of this sort. One can hardly find them as pure and whole as when they left his hand except in ancient manuscripts.[1]

Ancient manuscripts were the key: hitherto unknown grammars languishing unread at the bottom of monastery book-chests were unearthed and brought back into circulation, pored over and eagerly copied by the first generation of Carolingians (see box 7.1). Whereas Donatus's works had been the only ancient grammars of *Schulgrammatik* type available in the seventh and eighth centuries, now other grammars were discovered: Augustine's *Ars breviata* and the works of Audax, Scaurus and Dositheus. Their popularity was short-lived, however; after the middle of the ninth century they found few readers. On the other hand, *regulae* grammars, dealing explicitly with Latin morphology, gained new readers well into the eleventh century: Phocas and Eutyches in the first instance, but also the *regulae* attributed to Augustine and Palaemon. Whereas hitherto *regulae* grammars had served as sources supplementary to Donatus, now they were studied and commented on in their own right by such authors as the wandering Irish teacher Sedulius Scottus or the energetic commentator Remigius of Auxerre.

The scribal activity of the Carolingians was vitally important in the transmission of the Latin grammars of late Antiquity. Basically, if an ancient grammar was copied during the Carolingian era, then provided it passed through the common perils listed in box 7.2 it will have survived to the present day, often in a manuscript dating from this period (see box 7.2). However, of all the ancient writers rediscovered during the Carolingian Renaissance, two had an impact which extended far beyond the Carolingian period; indeed, they were still being studied during the Italian Renaissance seven hundred years later: Priscian and Aristotle. Let us look at how they affected Carolingian linguistic thought.

7.3 The rediscovery of Priscian's *Institutiones grammaticae*

As we saw in section 4.10, Priscian, teaching shortly after 500 in Constantinople, had written a series of grammars which were rather different in orientation from those being produced in Rome. Because his students were native speakers of Greek, Priscian concentrated on Latin inflectional and derivational morphology and syntax. Thus, his concise *Institutio de nomine et pronomine et verbo* outlines the various inflectional

Box 7.2 What's happened to all the medieval manuscripts?
Although the parchment codices of the Carolingian era, bound in wooden boards covered with vellum, were a good deal more robust than our flimsy modern paperbacks, vast numbers of them fell victim to one hazard or another. Fire, floods, and even bookworms (a kind of beetle) were common perils. So too in the early and central Middle Ages were attacks by marauders such as the Vikings, who sacked the monasteries of Lindisfarne, Jarrow and Iona between 793 and 795, or the Magyars, who pillaged St Gall in the winter of 925–6. Fashion had its part to play as well: when a text had outlived its usefulness, or people found the old-fashioned handwriting too difficult to read, they carefully scraped the ink away in order to reuse the parchment. (Such recycled volumes, called *palimpsests*, challenge the ingenuity of the modern scholar, who is eager to read the eradicated earlier text, to develop all sorts of technological aids. Nineteenth-century scholars tried out chemical reagents which showed up the faint original text for a few minutes but as they dried, left a permanent purple smear across the page, making it impossible for anyone else ever to read it again. Recently, less damaging techniques such as ultraviolet lamps and computer enhancement have been introduced.) In the Renaissance, medieval manuscripts faced a two-pronged attack. With the dissolution of the monasteries in England (1536) and their decline elsewhere, their libraries were often appropriated by unscrupulous potentates and scholars, finding their way centuries later into the great national collections such as the British Library in London and the Bibliothèque Nationale in Paris. Ironically, printing, the very process which immortalised the texts they contained, destroyed many manuscripts, for once the texts had been typeset, printers often discarded the manuscripts or used the parchment to reinforce bookbindings. Wars too have taken a heavy toll down to the present day. Every time a manuscript is lost, that bit of history is gone forever. In order to counteract the steady process of attrition, the Hill Monastic Manuscript Library of St John's Abbey and University, Collegeville, Minnesota, has embarked upon a huge project to microfilm the entire contents of European manuscript collections, but it is too late for some, such as the libraries of Strasbourg and Metz, burnt in 1870–1 during the Franco-Prussian War; the library of the university of Leuven (Louvain), burnt down in both the First and the Second World Wars; the library of Chartres cathedral, destroyed in 1944; and the archives of Sarajevo, destroyed in 1992.

Librarians today go to great lengths to ensure the security of the manuscripts in their collections, requiring prospective readers to establish their credentials and demonstrate that they really *need* to handle the original volumes (for many collections prefer you to work with a microfilm copy instead to minimise wear and tear); keeping a watchful eye on readers as they work; and insisting that only pencil be used in the vicinity of manuscripts. One Cambridge college library counts every page of the manuscript before and after consultation, a sad indictment of the behaviour of a few unscrupulous individuals.

Reading
L. D. Reynolds and N. G. Wilson, *Scribes and Scholars: A Guide to the Transmission of Greek and Latin Texts*, 3rd edn (Oxford: Clarendon 1991), ch. 3.

7.3 Rediscovery of Priscian's Institutiones grammaticae

classes of nouns, pronouns, verbs and participles, but takes for granted such theoretical issues as how each class is to be defined. That work (along with Donatus's grammars) was the starting-point for the form-based account of Latin of the Insular elementary grammars (see chapter 6 above). Priscian's massive *Institutiones grammaticae*, on the other hand, describes at great length both Latin inflections, copiously exemplified with passages from literary authors, and also Latin syntax, leavened with a modicum of theorising about grammatical categories and concepts. In this concern with linguistic theory and metatheory Priscian's interests diverged from those of the more pedagogically inclined Romans. During the seventh and eighth centuries the *Institutiones grammaticae* were used only by a very small number of scholars, notably Virgilius Maro Grammaticus and Aldhelm. Around 800 there was a sudden growth in interest. Manuscript copies were multiplying swiftly, as we can see from the number of surviving copies (a very approximate guide, for we don't know how many were destroyed as the centuries passed): from the eighth century we have only a few fragments, whereas from the ninth and tenth centuries 61 mostly complete copies have survived, and from the eleventh and twelfth centuries 283. Alcuin, the monk from York who was summoned to the Continent by Charlemagne, was influential in popularising it around 800: the earliest Carolingian copies come from monasteries close to Tours, where he was abbot between 796 and 804 (see box 7.3). Alcuin himself drew upon the *Institutiones grammaticae* in two works, a grammar, *Dialogus Franconis et Saxonis de octo partibus orationis* ('Dialogue of the Frank and the Saxon on the Eight Parts of Speech'), and a *florilegium*, or collection of extracts, largely from Books 17 and 18, on syntax.

Getting to grips with a thousand-page grammar is no easy task, yet Carolingian teachers were convinced of the fundamental importance of the *Institutiones grammaticae* for a well-grounded knowledge of Latin. Much of the effort of scholars from the ninth century to the twelfth was channelled into working through the *Institutiones*, digesting its doctrine, comparing it with other grammars, and pondering its implications. Some teachers, such as Ursus of Beneventum and Gozbert, made abbreviated versions to help their students. (Shortly after 1000 the Anglo-Saxon scholar Ælfric based his grammar of Latin written in Old English on one such abbreviated version, the *Excerptiones de Prisciano*.) Toward the middle of the ninth century Walahfrid Strabo, a monk at Reichenau, an important monastery and cultural centre on an island in Lake Constance, rewrote the familiar doctrine of the *Ars minor* in Priscian's words. Manuscript copies of the *Institutiones grammaticae* were glossed, or annotated, with translations of difficult words, explanations of tricky points of doctrine, and parallel passages from other grammarians.

Priscian's heightened awareness of grammatical concepts and metalanguage was another aspect of his work which caught the attention of his Carolingian readers. Whereas in the Late Latin grammars of the fourth and fifth centuries technical terminology is normally introduced with a minimum of comment, Priscian ponders his terminology at length. For instance, he lavishes nearly four pages on an explanation of what it means to say that a word can be 'defective', i.e. lacking a part of its paradigm (like the English verb *can*), and two pages on the nature of time and tense.[2] His reliance upon Greek sources also raised issues which needed clarification. Instead of employing the time-hallowed terminology and definitions of the Late Latin tradition, Priscian often

> **Box 7.3 Alcuin of York (c. 735–804)**
>
> Alcuin, born and brought up in the kingdom of Northumbria, in northeastern England, could well have spent his entire life at the important religious centre of York Minster had he not agreed to travel to Rome on an errand on behalf of the archbishop of York. When he was passing through Parma, in Italy, he happened to meet Charlemagne, who invited him to join his court. As a result of this encounter he spent over a decade at the court, up until 794, when he became abbot of Tours, where he stayed until his death. His move to the Continent enabled him to play a part in the redirection of intellectual life that characterised the Carolingian Renaissance. He was involved in the drafting of royal policy documents, in theological controversy, in the preparation of a revised text of the Bible, and even in the reforming of Latin pronunciation. Naturally he took a keen interest in the study of grammar, writing an orthographical treatise; an introduction to grammar in dialogue form, the *Dialogus Franconis et Saxonis de octo partibus orationis*; and a collection of excerpts from Priscian's *Institutiones grammaticae*. The existence of this last work, the first of its kind, and the fact that the early Continental manuscripts of the *Institutiones grammaticae* radiate outwards from Tours, strongly suggests that Alcuin was responsible for popularising this work, which was to become so significant in the history of linguistics in the central and late Middle Ages.
>
> *Reading*
>
> S. Allott, *Alcuin of York, c. A.D. 732 to 804 – His Life and Letters* (York: William Sessions 1974).
>
> John Marenbon, *From the Circle of Alcuin to the School of Auxerre* (Cambridge: Cambridge University Press 1981).
>
> J. R. O'Donnell, 'Alcuin's Priscian', in John J. O'Meara and Bernd Naumann, eds., *Latin Script and Letters AD 400–900* (Leiden: Brill 1976), pp. 222–35. [On Alcuin's florilegium from the *Institutiones grammaticae*.]
>
> Louis Holtz, 'Priscien dans la pédagogie d'Alcuin', in M. De Nonno, P. De Paolis and L. Holtz, eds., *Manuscripts and Tradition of Grammatical Texts from Antiquity to the Renaissance* I (Cassino: Università degli Studi di Cassino 2000), pp. 289–326.

simply translated the differently worded definitions he found in his Greek sources. Thus, Donatus defines the noun like this:

Nomen est pars orationis cum casu corpus aut rem proprie communiterve significans.
A noun is a part of speech marked for case which signifies an object or a concept in either a proper or a common manner.[3]

Priscian, on the other hand, follows the Greek tradition in defining it like this:

Nomen est pars orationis, quae unicuique subiectorum corporum seu rerum communem vel propriam qualitatem distribuit.
A noun is a part of speech which assigns common or proper quality to each relevant object or concept.[4]

Although these definitions are very similar in substance (apart from Priscian's omitting all references to case), they are worded quite differently. Terms such as *subiectum* and *qualitas* signalled to a Latin reader not grammar but dialectic. Anyone familiar with the writings of Aristotle in Latin translation, or with popularising textbooks on logic, would have a nodding acquaintance with such terms – but not necessarily in quite the same sense. Here was a potential source of confusion to Carolingian scholars. All the same, they realised that Priscian's teachings, difficult as they were, offered the hope of a subtler understanding of language than had hitherto been possible: alluring, illuminating, challenging. (But he also offered them the possibility of a new approach to teaching: see box 7.4.)

7.4 Linking grammar with the laws of thought: the Carolingian discovery of Aristotelian logic

Priscian's writings, exciting as they were, left the Carolingians dissatisfied in one important respect: they rarely stepped outside the linguistic sphere to show how language might be linked to extralinguistic reality. That, as we saw in chapter 5, was a matter of urgent concern to medieval thinkers. Mere grammatical phenomena were of no interest in themselves; their only claim upon the attention of a good Christian was as a means to an end, the comprehension of God's will as revealed in the Scriptures. But if one could show that they were in some way linked with external reality, then their apparent arbitrariness was slightly lessened. One way of achieving this was correlative thinking; the painstaking study and application of dialectic, the laws which structure logical thought, was another. Aristotle's works on dialectic had been inaccessible to virtually all westerners since the end of Antiquity, however (see box 7.5). Only toward 800 did dialectic find a new audience. Once again, Alcuin may well have been the moving spirit behind the change. He and his circle studied Porphyry's *Isagoge*, Aristotle's *Categories* and *De interpretatione*, Boethius's commentaries and some related works, and began to experiment with the techniques of logical disputation. But even this was a modest beginning: the other works of the *Organon* were not rediscovered until the middle of the twelfth century.

The Carolingian application of dialectic to grammar

Logic has an immediate bearing on language. Logic uses language as a tool, and logicians have to become aware of the possibilities and limitations of their tools before starting work. Once people begin to study logic, they begin to think in a different way about language. They are no longer satisfied with language-internal questions such as 'How do you decline a noun?' or 'What are the properties of the verb?' Concerned above all with truth and falsehood, they now want to know how a linguistic utterance relates to the world out there. How does a word relate to what it denotes? Are linguistic categories identical to the categories we use for analysing reality? The questions are close to those which Plato was asking in the *Cratylus*, but with one significant difference: most Carolingian scholars agreed – or were prepared to agree when

> **Box 7.4 Learning by asking: the parsing grammar**
>
> Even though Priscian himself taught students at an advanced level, one of his works, the *Partitiones* (see section 4.10 above), seems to have inspired a new grammatical genre used for the most part at a relatively elementary level: the parsing grammar. Instruction in question-and-answer form was an important part of elementary grammatical pedagogy as far back as we can trace it. Donatus's *Ars minor* was in that form, and at least one of the surviving Greek grammatical papyri, as well as elementary texts in other subject areas. Where we get a glimpse of the classroom setting in a little more detail, we can see that the teachers asked the questions and the pupils answered – a metamorphosis of Socrates's enlivening attempts to draw latent knowledge out of his pupils into a framework for the memorisation and rote response that took place in a great many ancient classrooms, we may surmise. After the end of Antiquity question-and-answer form was seldom used until the Carolingian Renaissance, when it resurfaces – with a difference: the roles are now reversed. Alcuin portrays the ignorant pupils begging the omniscient master to fill them with information – the 'empty bucket' approach to pedagogy. Carolingian teachers – Peter of Pisa is the first so far known – devised a new kind of grammar. Instead of asking relatively abstract questions such as 'What is a noun?' or 'What are the properties of the adverb?', they chose a particular noun (or pronoun, or verb...) as the focus of each chapter, and posed questions about it (*parsing* it) in much the same way as Priscian does with each word from the lines of the *Aeneid* that he analyses in the *Partitiones*. Some of the resulting parsing grammars are so concise that they look like drills to accompany Donatus; others range quite widely across the whole field of grammar and into the lower reaches of dialectic, as does *Magnus quae vox*, an anonymous work probably of the tenth century. (Because parsing grammars are almost always anonymous and often lack distinctive titles, they tend to be known by their first few words, normally 'What part of speech is...?'.) The most popular later medieval elementary grammars, *Magister quae pars* ('What parts of speech is "teacher"?') and *Dominus quae pars* ('What part of speech is "Lord"?'), and the so-called *Ianua* (*Poeta quae pars*), are all parsing grammars.
>
> Reading
>
> V. Law, 'Memory and the structure of grammars in Antiquity and the Middle Ages', in M. De Nonno, P. De Paolis and L. Holtz, eds., *Manuscripts and Tradition of Grammatical Texts from Antiquity to the Renaissance* 1 (Cassino: Università degli Studi di Cassino 2000), pp. 9–58, esp. pp. 24–32.

wearing their dialectician's hat – that words themselves were largely arbitrary (see box 7.6).

Naturally it took the Carolingians a long time to work through the content of the newly rediscovered discipline of dialectic and learn how to apply it to these questions. Grammar, as the best-developed and most closely related intellectual discipline, was the testing-ground where they tried out the new ideas. In the course of the ninth, tenth and eleventh centuries dialectic was applied to grammar in many different contexts. Let's take two domains as examples.

> **Box 7.5 The transmission of Aristotle's writings**
>
> Lost for a couple of centuries after his death in 322 BC, Aristotle's writings were edited and brought back into circulation late in the first century BC. From then on they were intensively studied in schools in the Hellenistic world (which included the hellenised Near and Middle East as well as Greece itself) and were translated into the *lingua franca* of that region, Syriac (a Semitic language closely related to Hebrew). With the coming of the Muslim Arabs in the seventh century, many of Aristotle's works were translated into Arabic, either directly from the Greek or via the existing Syriac translations, and Arab philosophers and scientists joined in the work of interpreting Aristotle and reconciling his teaching with that of their faith in the great cultural centres of the Islamic empire: Baghdad, Cairo, Cordoba, Toledo.
>
> In the West the situation was different. Up to the third century AD knowledge of Greek was fairly commonplace amongst educated Romans, but gradually it became a rarity. As firsthand acquaintance with the Greek language waned, access to Aristotle's writings became ever more difficult. By the beginning of the sixth century the problem was so acute that a Roman senator by the name of Anicius Manlius Severinus Boethius (480–524/5) embarked upon the great project of translating Aristotle's complete works into Latin and writing commentaries upon them. He started with the works on logic, beginning with the *Categories*, *De interpretatione*, *Prior* and *Posterior Analytics*, *Topics* and *Sophistical Refutations*, together with the introduction (*Isagoge*) by the Neoplatonist philosopher Porphyry. Unfortunately he got no further, for his political activities as a highly placed Roman senator brought him under suspicion of treason. Theodoric, the Ostrogothic king of Italy, had him imprisoned and executed. (During his imprisonment he wrote *The Consolation of Philosophy*, a profound and beautifully expressed meditation upon the vicissitudes of Fortune which inspired many generations of medieval thinkers.) Thus, the only works of Aristotle's that had been translated into Latin by the end of Antiquity were the works on logic – so nothing on metaphysics, ethics, psychology, natural history, or physics. Many centuries were to pass before these works became accessible to western Christians.
>
> But even the works on logic translated by Boethius did not spring to instant popularity. Logic, or dialectic, as it was usually called, was a subject which seems to have interested very few scholars between Boethius's death and the Carolingian Renaissance. Martianus Capella, Cassiodorus and Isidore of Seville included accounts of it as part of their outline of the Seven Liberal Arts in their encyclopedias, and it was from these summaries that seventh- and eighth-century scholars drew such knowledge of the subject as they possessed.
>
> *Reading*
> J. Marenbon, 'Boethius: from antiquity to the Middle Ages', in his, ed., *Medieval Philosophy* (London and New York: Routledge 1998), pp. 11–28.
> J. Barnes, 'Boethius and the study of logic', in M. Gibson, ed., *Boethius: His Life, Thought and Influence* (Oxford: Blackwell 1981), pp. 73–89.
> O. Lewry, 'Boethian logic in the medieval West', in M. Gibson, ed., *Boethius: His Life, Thought and Influence* (Oxford: Blackwell 1981), pp. 90–134.

> L. Minio-Paluello, 'Les traductions et. les commentaires aristotéliciens de Boèce', in his *Opuscula: The Latin Aristotle* (Amsterdam: Hakkert 1972), pp. 328–35, repr. from Studia Patristica 2.2 (*Texte und Untersuchungen zur Geschichte der altchristlichen Literatur* 64 (1957)), 358–65.

Definitions

Vast numbers of philosophical disputes turn on problems of definition – ultimately, problems of meaning. Definitions are the very cornerstone of dialectic: if they are not correctly formulated, one's entire argument will collapse. Consequently, the formulation of accurate definitions was a vital part of the training of the medieval dialectician. This skill was of very wide applicability, of course, for all the scholarly disciplines required a precise use of terminology if they were to reach conclusions which could be accepted by everyone. Even at the most elementary level, schoolchildren could learn how to define terms and structure a proposition. Grammar, as the most widely studied subject of all, provided a ready testing-ground for the new techniques.

Porphyry's *Isagoge*, an introduction to Aristotle's logical writings (see box 7.4 above), provides instructions on the most economical ways in which to structure a definition so as to include all the members of a class and exclude all non-members.[5] (More detailed discussions of the formulation of definitions were to be found in a work by a contemporary of Donatus's, Marius Victorinus, which many medieval readers believed was by Boethius.) Porphyry begins with the traditional definition of *homo*, 'man' (in the sense of 'human being'):

homo	est	animal	rationale	mortale	risus	capax
man	is	a-being	rational	mortal	of-laughter	capable

'Man is a rational mortal being able to laugh.'

'Man', *homo*, is the term to be defined. The first thing which has to be indicated is the *genus* to which it belongs: *animal*. 'Man' is a subset, a species, of the genus 'animal'. Next one must indicate what distinguishes man from other species within the genus 'animal': the quality of being rational, which other living beings, such as mosquitoes and catfish, do not share. This is the *differentia*, the distinguishing feature. Thirdly, however, one has to indicate the *communio*, the property shared by all species within the genus: the quality of being mortal. Finally, one must indicate what is unique to this class amongst all beings of all genera, its *proprietas*: the ability to laugh. All human beings can laugh, which neither animals nor angels can. How might you analyse this rather longer definition of a pig from a French manuscript of the second half of the ninth century?

porcus	est	animal	mortale	irrationale	cibum capiens	quadrupedale	grunnibile[6]
the-pig	is	a-being	mortal	irrational	food-taking	four-footed	able-to-grunt

'The pig is a mortal, irrational, four-footed being able to grunt which forages for food.'

Carolingian grammarians took up this new tool with enthusiasm. Peter of Pisa, one of the Italian scholars Charlemagne summoned to his court, included a detailed analysis

7.4 Linking language with the laws of thought

Box 7.6 Early theories of the sign

If you've had even a slight brush with modern linguistics you'll have come across the famous theory of the sign associated with the Swiss linguist Ferdinand de Saussure (1857–1913). As Saussure himself knew quite well, he was by no means the first person to raise the question. Aristotle sets out a theory of the sign at the start of his *De interpretatione*, while the Stoics had a well-developed theory of their own. Neither the Late Latin nor the early medieval grammarians take up the subject, however. It was the Carolingians who reintroduced it into grammar with a few allusions here and there. Alcuin, for instance, has this little exchange near the beginning of his *Dialogus Franconis et Saxonis de octo partibus orationis*:

TEACHER: Tell me first what the starting-point of your conversation should be.
PUPILS: Why, the *littera*, of course.
TEACHER: Good idea – or at least, it would have been if you hadn't just said something about philosophy. Since you have, you ought to start your conversation with the utterance (*vox*), which is the reason the *litterae* were invented; or perhaps we ought to go back further still and ask what conversation consists of.
PUPILS: Please tell us, teacher. We haven't any idea what conversation consists of.
TEACHER: All conversation or discourse consists of three things: things, concepts and utterances. The things are what we perceive with the reasoning faculty of the mind. The concepts are what we learn the things with. The utterances are what we set out the things that we have grasped (*res intellectae*) with, for which reason, as I said, *litterae* were invented.

Alcuin's formulation – especially his use of the term *res intellecta* – foreshadows the thinking of the Speculative grammarians (section 8.2 below).

A different account was given by Remigius of Auxerre, a writer of commentaries on a great range of grammatical and literary texts toward the end of the ninth century. In his commentary on Donatus's *Ars major* he writes:

After the utterance (*vox*) Donatus defines the *littera*, and he does well to do so after the utterance, because the *littera* is the sign of the utterance. Signs are either signs of things or signs of signs. 'Earth', for example, is the sign of a thing, i.e. a substance, whereas the letters with which the noun *earth* is written are the sign of a sign, i.e. of a noun which signifies a thing.

Remigius – less of a philosopher than Alcuin – is not interested in the difference between real-world objects and our percepts or concepts; rather, he focuses on the twofold nature of the sign.

By the twelfth century philosophers were grappling with the sign, and with semantic problems generally, in a far subtler manner. Thierry of Chartres, giving a series of lectures on Boethius's *De Trinitate* in the years around 1140, declared:

Meaning (*significatio*) is the union of the thing and its name. We don't call the thing alone the meaning, but include the word signifying it. Meaning includes the signified (*significatum*) as much as the signifying element (*significans*).

> Thierry's use of the term *significatum* 'signified' is close to Saussure's use of *signifié*, its etymological descendant. We shall see its further development in the next chapter.
>
> Reading
> Eugenio Coseriu, *Die Geschichte der Sprachphilosophie von der Antike bis zur Gegenwart: Eine Übersicht*, 2 vols. (Tübingen: Narr 1975). [A convenient overview of ancient and medieval theories of the sign, though not including Carolingian ones.]

of Donatus's definition of the verb in his grammar. Donatus had defined the verb like this:

Verbum est pars orationis cum tempore et persona sine casu aut agere aliquid aut pati aut neutrum significans.[7]
The verb is a part of speech with tense and person, without case, signifying action or passivity or neither.

Peter comments:

How many things must we look out for in this definition?
Five.
What are they?
Species, genus, communio, differentia, proprietas. This is how these five things are to be identified.
Species is when it says 'a verb', for what is specific pertains to one individual, whereas what is generic pertains to many. 'Verb' is a specific noun because when this whole word class is mentioned in accordance with its nature it is a specific noun.
Genus is when it says 'a part of speech', for there are other parts of speech as well.
Communio is when it says 'with tense and person', for tense and person are common to the verb, the pronoun and the participle. The verb has person in common with the pronoun and tense in common with the participle.
Differentia is when it says 'without case', because it differs from the noun, the pronoun and the participle in that these parts of speech have case while the verb does not.
Proprietas is when it says 'action or passivity or neither', because the other parts of speech do not have this.[8]

Do you agree with Peter's analysis? He overlooks the fact that participles can also be active or passive! At any rate, this example and many others like it show that the structure of definitions was an issue which caught the attention of the Carolingians, and they worked intensively upon it.

An equally popular issue was the identification and classification of various types of definition. Marius Victorinus had drawn up a list of some fifteen types;[9] grammarians decided that they could make do with six. Sedulius Scottus, an itinerant Irish teacher who spent much of his professional life in France, describes them thus in his commentary on the *Ars maior*:

According to the grammarians there are six types of definition.
The first is definition according to substance, e.g. 'A noun is a part of speech with case.'

The second is definition according to the sound [of the word], e.g. 'The noun (*nomen*) is, as it were, a note (*notamen*).'
The third is the definition which assigns it to a species, e.g. 'signifying an object or concept and either proper or common'.
The fourth is in terms of its properties, e.g. 'The noun has six properties.'
The fifth is quantitative, e.g. 'There are eight parts of speech.'
The sixth is etymological, e.g. '*homo* "man" is so called from *humus* "soil", and *humus* gets its name from *humor* "moisture".'[10]

Quite routinely, questions about the nature of definitions were included in Carolingian grammars at a fairly elementary level. Pupils were thus being encouraged to develop a level of metalinguistic awareness substantially higher than that customary amongst their eighth-century predecessors.

When teachers and pupils become interested not only in the content of a discipline, but also in how that content is presented, they distance themselves from their subject-matter. This cultivation of a meta-level of discourse – the ability to talk about how one talks about something – fosters the faculty of thinking objectively and critically about the discipline: how it is presented, how it is related to other disciplines, whether it could or should change in any way. Hence, not only the intellectually adventurous work of the great philosophers, but also the humbler work of scrutinizing definitions, had its part to play in making an ever-widening circle of people aware of some of the assumptions that had been made by the great authorities of the past. As the central Middle Ages drew on, scholars became increasingly inclined to criticise Donatus, Priscian and other ancient writers on major theoretical issues as well as on points of detail.

Dialectic and the content of grammar

Definitions, important as they were, were a technical tool to grammarians; linguistic phenomena were the real focus of their interest. All the same, Carolingian grammarians believed they had more in common with dialecticians than many of their present-day counterparts would, for they were convinced that the linguistic categories they studied corresponded directly to phenomena in the real world. In this respect, too, dialectic held out the promise of new insights. Initially, however, few scholars were capable of making connections across the two disciplines. Alcuin gives us a hesitant glimpse of the alternative possibilities in his grammar, the *Dialogue of the Frank and the Saxon on the Eight Parts of Speech*. The grammar for the most part purveys the well-known doctrine of Donatus's *Ars maior* with bits of Priscian's *Institutiones grammaticae* (and other works) interspersed, in the form of a conversation between a fourteen-year-old Frankish boy and a fifteen-year-old Saxon. Occasionally, when the Saxon can no longer cope with the Frank's questions, they turn to the teacher:

FRANK: First of all, give me a definition of the verb.
SAXON: No, let's ask the teacher what the definition of the verb is according to philosophy.
PUPILS: Teacher, does this important part of speech have its own philosophical definition, like the noun?

TEACHER: It has a subtle and noble definition: the verb is an utterance (*vox*) which signifies by convention, with tense, and signifies something definite and predicated.
PUPILS: Explain this definition to us, father.
TEACHER: When I say *lego* 'I am reading', I signify the activity of someone who is reading. A Greek would signify this activity using a different utterance, and that is why the verb is described as signifying by convention. It takes tense. It is definite in that it signifies something fixed, and predicated in that activity and passivity are predicated of a person. But you two, get on with your practice. I'll deal with this elsewhere.
PUPILS: Anything you say![11]

The 'philosophical' definition comes from Aristotle's *De interpretatione*. Alcuin says no more about it here; his intention was simply to alert his pupils to the fact that philosophers too thought about language, and on occasion their 'subtle and noble' thoughts differed from those of grammarians.

Succeeding generations penetrated more deeply into the new doctrine. In the middle of the ninth century the celebrated Irish scholar, John Scottus Eriugena, a contemporary of Murethach and Sedulius Scottus's, acquired a reputation as a theologian. He arrived at the Frankish court from Ireland around 860, and died in or around 877. He was unquestionably the greatest scholar in the West in the ninth century. He could read Greek and was well versed in the writings of the Greek Fathers of the Church. He translated the works of the Neoplatonist Dionysius the Areopagite (later of importance in the rise of western mysticism) into Latin. His best known work, however, is on the frontiers of theology, philosophy and cosmology: the *Periphyseon*, a treatise on Nature and all its works, ranging from God and the heavenly hierarchies to the created world and the constitution of man. Eriugena's interest in dialectic is already apparent in the *Periphyseon*. For example, he uses Aristotle's ten categories as a framework for investigating the nature of God. In addition, he composed a commentary on parts of Priscian's *Institutiones grammaticae*. In it, he looks at Priscian's statements with Aristotelian eyes. Priscian's terminology, for instance, with its aroma of dialectic, attracted his attention. Priscian's definition of the noun, as we saw above, is this:

Nomen est pars orationis, quae unicuique subiectorum corporum seu rerum communem vel propriam qualitatem distribuit.[12]
The noun is a part of speech which assigns common or proper quality to each relevant object or concept.

Qualitas 'quality' functions both as a metalinguistic term and as the Latin name of one of the ten categories, the property of being 'white' or 'grammatical', and so on. Eriugena comments:

You should be aware that Priscian used *qualitas* here to stand for all the other properties, even though we read in the philosophical work called *Categoriae* in Greek that there are ten categories which include everything there is. Nonetheless, *qualitas* is so broad in its scope that it can be used for all ten, except for substance. *Qualitas* is very rarely used for 'substance' but is very frequently employed in lieu of the other nine [sic!]. Authors often use the term *qualitas* for quantity, relation, position, location, time, possession, activity and passivity.[13]

Eriugena goes on to demonstrate that all these properties are implicit in Priscian's definition. His Priscian commentary is pervaded through and through with the dialectician's distinctive type of interest in language – the first medieval instance of a philosopher grappling with grammatical issues.

A century later, the monastery of St Gall, in what is now Switzerland, became a flourishing centre of dialectical studies. Indeed, one of its most important scholars, Notker the German (ca 950–1022), translated Aristotle's *Categories* and *De interpretatione* into the language of his pupils, Old High German, and added some glosses of his own. In the latter part of the ninth century an anonymous scholar tried to correlate Priscian's grammatical categories with Aristotle's real-world ones, taking as his basis Priscian's twenty-seven classes of common noun. He begins with an introduction in which he distinguishes between linguistic and logical categories:

The eight parts of speech in grammar show clearly what words are in themselves. The ten categories of Aristotle, on the other hand, which belong to logic, show what the parts of speech signify beyond themselves, and secondarily what they are in themselves. Nature shows us the same sequence in children, for they learn to understand what the word 'person' (*homo*) is predicated of before they learn the forms 'person', 'person's', 'persons', 'persons' '. Ever since languages began, everyone has had to learn to understand words; only later did some people begin to study the form of words.[14]

The author then tells us that scholars are uncertain which word class corresponds to which of the ten categories, and that it is agreed that five of the categories are covered by nouns – substance, quantity, quality, relation, possession. After these introductory points he goes on to discuss each of the types of common noun and shows how it fits into one or another of the categories, arguing each case with careful reference not only to the *Categories* but also to Porphyry's *Isagoge*.

Thus, whereas ancient grammarians had drawn unselfconsciously upon their knowledge of dialectic to frame more-or-less watertight definitions, Carolingian scholars, full of enthusiasm for the newly discovered works by Aristotle, began to compare the possibilities held out by the new discipline with the familiar opportunities opened up by grammar. The resulting confrontation between logic and grammar has never been far from the forefront of linguistics from that day to this.

Further reading

Cultural and educational aspects of the Carolingian Renaissance

Giles Brown, 'Introduction: the Carolingian Renaissance', in R. McKitterick, ed., *Carolingian Culture: Emulation and Innovation* (Cambridge: Cambridge University Press 1994), pp. 1–51.

John J. Contreni, 'The Carolingian Renaissance: education and literary culture', in Rosamond McKitterick, ed., *The New Cambridge Medieval History* 2: *c. 700–c. 900* (Cambridge: Cambridge University Press 1995), ch. 27 (pp. 709–57).

David Ganz, 'Book production in the Carolingian empire and the spread of Caroline minuscule', in R. McKitterick, ed., *The New Cambridge Medieval History* 2, *c. 700–c. 900* (Cambridge: Cambridge University Press 1995), ch. 29 (pp. 786–808).

John Marenbon, 'Carolingian thought', in, R. McKitterick, ed., *Carolingian Culture: Emulation and Innovation* (Cambridge: Cambridge University Press 1994), pp. 171–92.

John Marenbon, *Early Medieval Philosophy (480–1150): An Introduction* (London: Routledge and Kegan Paul 1983).

M. Haren, *Medieval Thought: The Western Intellectual Tradition from Antiquity to the Thirteenth Century* (London: Macmillan 1985), pp. 59–116.

Pierre Riché, *Ecoles et enseignement dans le Haut Moyen Age* (Paris: Aubier 1979), pp. 69–79, 261–6.

John Marenbon, 'Alcuin, the Council of Francfort and the beginnings of medieval philosophy', in R. Berndt, ed., *Kristallisationspunkt karolingischer Kultur*, Quellen und Abhandlungen zur mittelrheinischen Kirchengeschichte 80 (Mainz: Gesellschaft für mittelrheinische Kirchengeschichte 1997), pp. 603–15.

Edoardo Vineis, 'Grammatica e filosofia del linguaggio in Alcuino', *Studi e saggi linguistici* 28 (1988), 403–29.

Carolingian grammar

Vivien Law, 'The study of grammar under the Carolingians', in her *Grammar and Grammarians in the Early Middle Ages* (London and New York: Longman 1997), pp. 129–53, repr. with corrections from R. McKitterick, ed., *Carolingian Culture: Emulation and Innovation* (Cambridge: Cambridge University Press 1994), pp. 88–110. [Surveys main trends, with bibliography.]

Louis Holtz, 'Les innovations théoriques de la grammaire carolingienne: peu de chose. Pourquoi?' in I. Rosier, ed., *L'héritage des grammairiens latins de l'Antiquité aux Lumières* (Paris and Louvain: Peeters 1988), pp. 133–45.

V. Law, 'Carolingian grammarians and theoretical innovation', in her *Grammar and Grammarians in the Early Middle Ages* (London and New York: Longman 1997), pp. 154–63; first published in A. Ahlqvist, ed., *Diversions of Galway* (Amsterdam 1992), pp. 27–37. [A reply to Holtz 1988.]

L. Holtz, 'Les nouvelles tendances de la pédagogie grammaticale au Xe siècle', *Mittellateinisches Jahrbuch* 24/25 (1989/1990), 163–73.

L. Holtz, 'L'enseignement de la grammaire au temps de Charles le Chauve', in *Giovanni Scoto nel suo tempo: l'organizzazione del sapere in età carolingia* (Spoleto: Centro italiano di studi sull'alto medioevo 1989), pp. 153–69.

L. Holtz, 'L'enseignement des maîtres de grammaire irlandais sur le continent au IXe siècle', in J.-M. Picard, ed., *Ireland and Northern France AD 600–850* (Dublin: Four Courts Press 1991), pp. 143–56.

Margaret Gibson, 'Milestones in the study of Priscian, circa 800-circa 1200', *Viator* 23 (1992), 17–33.

Anneli Luhtala, 'Syntax and dialectic in Carolingian commentaries on Priscian's *Institutiones grammaticae*', in V. Law, ed., *History of Linguistic Thought in the Early Middle Ages*, Studies in the History of the Language Sciences 71 (Amsterdam and Philadelphia: John Benjamins 1993), pp. 145–91 (= *Historiographia Linguistica* 20 (1993), 145–91).

A. Luhtala, ' "Priscian's definitions are obscure": Carolingian commentators on the *Institutiones grammaticae*', in V. Law and W. Hüllen, eds., *Linguists and their Diversions: A Festschrift for R. H. Robins on his 75th Birthday* (Münster: Nodus 1996), pp. 53–78.

Texts

As is the case with pre-Carolingian grammars, by no means all Carolingian grammatical texts have been edited, and scholars must often travel to the libraries where the manuscripts are kept in order to read them, or order a microfilm. Works mentioned in this chapter that are available in print include:

Alcuin, *Dialogus Franconis et Saxonis de octo partibus orationis*, in J.-P. Migne, *Patrologia Latina* 101, 854–902.

Cunabula grammaticae artis Donati, in Migne, PL 90, 613–32.

Johannes Scottus Eriugena's Priscian commentary, ed. A. Luhtala, 'Early medieval commentary on Priscian's *Institutiones grammaticae*', *Cahiers de l'Institut du moyen âge grec et Latin* 71 (2000), 115–88.

Murethach (Muridac), *In Donati artem maiorem*, ed. L. Holtz, Corpus Christianorum Continuatio Mediaevalis 40 (Turnhout: Brepols 1977).

Peter of Pisa, *Ars*: a facsimile of the text of one manuscript is available in *Sammelhandschrift Diez. B. Sant. 66. Grammatici Latini et Catalogus Librorum*, ed. by B. Bischoff (Graz: Akademische Druck- und Verlagsanstalt 1973), pp. 3–66.

Remigius, *In artem maiorem Donati commentum*, ed. H. Hagen, *Anecdota Helvetica* (=GL 8, Leipzig: Teubner 1880), pp. 219–74, supplemented by J. P. Elder, 'The missing portions of the *Commentum Einsidlense* on Donatus's *Ars grammatica*', *Harvard Studies in Classical Philology* 56–7 (1947), 129–60.

Sedulius Scottus, *In Donati artem maiorem*, ed. B. Löfstedt, Corpus Christianorum Continuatio Mediaevalis 40B (Turnhout: Brepols 1977).

Smaragdus, *Liber in partibus Donati*, ed. B. Löfstedt, L. Holtz, A. Kibre, Corpus Christianorum Continuatio Mediaevalis 68 (Turnhout: Brepols 1986).

8 Scholasticism: linking language and reality

8.1 Universities and universals

Up to the eleventh century almost all the scholarly work of the Christians of western Europe had taken place in the great monasteries: Fleury, Corbie, Freising, Reichenau, St Gall, Ramsey and many others. Monasteries were the setting of virtually all intellectual life, except in Italy. But during the central Middle Ages, from the ninth to the eleventh century, partly in response to Charlemagne's edict, schools were being set up in towns, usually closely associated with a cathedral. With the expansion of towns in the eleventh and twelfth centuries the cathedral schools grew in size and significance. If you wanted to get involved in the intellectual issues of the days, you might well study at one of the great cathedral schools of northern France – Reims, Laon, Orléans, Notre-Dame de Paris or Chartres – or perhaps across the Channel at Salisbury or Canterbury. Monastic schools continued to be important centres of learning, but the more open cathedral schools attracted many, while in Italy secular schools teaching law and medicine drew young men with their eye set upon a professional career.

Early in the thirteenth century some of these schools grew into the first universities, notably Paris, celebrated for the Arts, philosophy and theology, and Oxford, also famed for Arts and theology. By 1300 there were universities all across western Europe, from Lisbon to Cambridge, Toulouse to Naples. Several things distinguished a university from a monastic or cathedral school:

- a structured course spread over several years with well-defined stages;
- a core of prescribed texts on which students were to attend lectures a set number of times;
- the granting of degrees;
- public recognition, usually in the form of a charter from the pope.

Most students spent several years in the Faculty of Arts, where they attended lectures by the masters on Priscian's *Institutiones grammaticae*, Aristotle's logical works, and often his writings on ethics and natural history as well. When they graduated, they could stay on to become Masters of Arts in their turn, or they could go on to one of the higher faculties

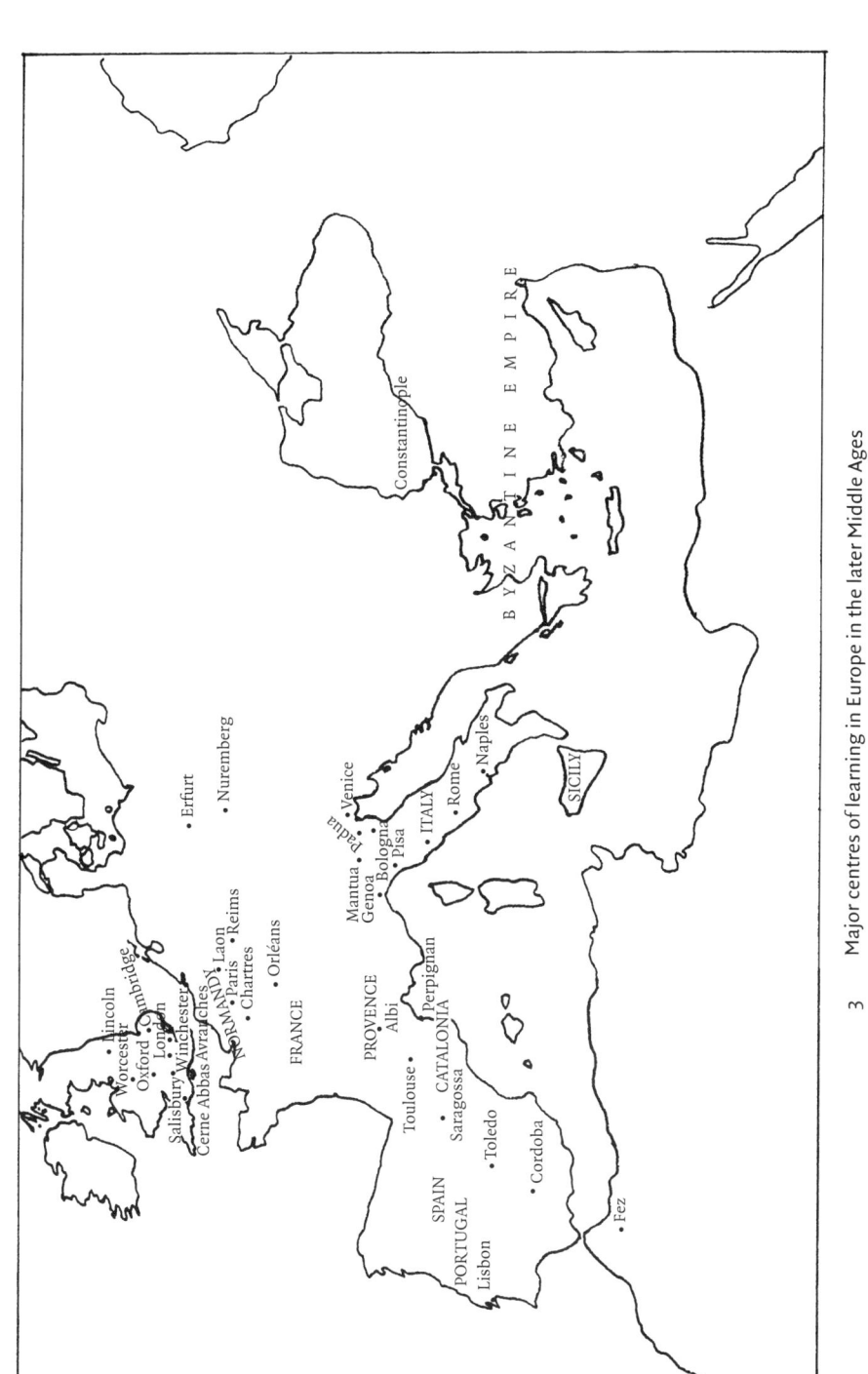

3 Major centres of learning in Europe in the later Middle Ages

11 Sculpture of Grammatica, one of the Seven Liberal Arts, who sits watching over two of her young pupils, while below them a studious grammarian – Donatus or Priscian – contemplates his book. Chartres cathedral, west portal.

to study theology, law or medicine. A few universities, Oxford and Cambridge among them, had a Faculty of Grammar whose role was to train teachers for the grammar schools, where Latin was taught, the language which gave access to the knowledge accumulated in centuries of painstaking scholarship and meditation (box 8.1).

One of the most urgently debated issues in the cathedral schools and the fledgeling universities was that of universals. This was a problem which arose out of the study of dialectic. In the first chapter of Porphyry's *Isagoge* medieval scholars found this statement:

As to whether genera and species really exist or are purely mental constructs, and, if they exist, whether they are material or immaterial, and whether they are separate from sense-perceptible things or are contained within them – on all of this I am reserving judgement. It is a profound matter which deserves further investigation.[1]

What is a genus or a species? The ontological status of an individual is easy to define: my cat is called 'Simiot', and I can point to her as an actual existing thing. But what

8.1 Universities and universals

12 Representation of grammar, from Gregorius Reisch's *Margarita philosophica nova* 'New pearl of philosophy', published in Strasbourg in 1515. Grammatica leads her young pupil with a hornbook setting out the alphabet towards a tower which she is unlocking with a key marked *congruitas*, one of the central domains of medieval syntax. On the ground floor Donatus is teaching his beginners, and on the next floor up Priscian is lecturing to more advanced pupils. Only after passing through those preparatory stages could the pupil rise to the other Liberal Arts: logic, represented by Aristotle; rhetoric and poetry, represented by Marcus Tullius Cicero; arithmetic, represented by Boethius; music, represented by Pythagoras; geometry, represented by Euclid; and astronomy, represented by Ptolemy. Higher still, Plato presides over physical philosophy, as the caption has it, and Seneca over moral philosophy, while right at the summit the celebrated theologian Peter Lombard represents theology and metaphysics.

> **Box 8.1 From the parts to the Arts: the position of grammar**
> Even after the founding of the universities, with the possibility they offered of specialising in law, medicine or theology, Latin grammar remained the fundamental subject to be mastered at school, and was a central part of the Arts curriculum at every university. This was not to every student's liking; then as now, grammar was perceived as a dry and difficult subject by very many pupils. One anonymous commentator on Priscian's *Institutiones grammaticae* quotes a verse which warns against trying to rush on with the Arts without having mastered the parts of speech, the core of grammar:
>
> > Qui nescit partes in uanum tendit ad artes.
> > Artes per partes, non partes disce per artes.
>
> > if you don't know the parts,
> > You'll strive in vain for the Arts.
> > Learn the Arts through the parts,
> > Not the parts through the Arts.

about the species 'domestic cat'? Or the genus 'cat family'? The terms 'domestic cat' and 'cat family' do not here denote individuals; the status of what they signify is very unclear (box 8.2). Are they simply abstractions constructed out of all the individuals we have ever encountered? This was the position adopted by a number of scholars labelled Nominalists (because they held that generic terms like 'cat' and 'human' had no reality beyond the word). Or at a certain level, be it at the level of the concepts we form, be it at the level of supersensible realities, is there some reality that transcends all the individuals, as the Realists maintained?

You can see the shades of Plato and Aristotle standing behind this twelfth-century debate. And yet Plato's writings were all but unknown: only the *Timaeus* was available in the West at this date. What medieval scholars knew of his Theory of Forms came from Neoplatonist writers such as Porphyry, Plotinus and Calcidius (for the Neoplatonists see box 2.5, pp. 30–31 above). As for Aristotle, up until the middle of the twelfth century only two of his treatises on logic, the *Categories* and the *De interpretatione*, were widely available in the Latin West. Although his other logical writings had also been translated by Boethius at the beginning of the sixth century, they were not generally known; and his writings on subjects such as ethics and natural history had not been translated at all, so were inaccessible to all but the tiniest handful of western Christians. In the twelfth century this began to change (see box 8.3). Boethius's translations of the remaining logical writings were rediscovered and came into circulation under the name of the 'new logic', *logica nova*, alongside the existing works, 'old logic', *logica vetus*. One by one Aristotle's other writings arrived in the schools and universities in Latin translation, amongst them the *Physics* and the *Metaphysics*, both translated by 1150. The arrival, one by one, of these new Aristotelian texts in the cathedral schools gave rise to a bubbling sense of intellectual excitement. The challenge to permeate Aristotelianism with Christianity was one which these scholars, and their thirteenth-century successors,

> **Box 8.2 Who was the first to distinguish between signification and reference?**
> In the year 1080 Anselm, prior of the monastery of Bec in Normandy, and later archbishop of Canterbury, wrote a philosophical dialogue called 'On "Literate"' (De grammatico). The Latin word he chose to exemplify the problem of paronyms, grammaticus, here means not 'grammarian' or 'grammatical', but 'possessing grammar', 'educated', or, as its translator renders it, 'literate'. Now, Priscian tells us that the distinctive property of nouns (don't forget that adjectives such as 'literate' were classed as a type of noun) is to signify substance (or being) and quality. Anselm's question is how this word, and countless others like it, can simultaneously signify both the substance, i.e. a literate individual, and the quality of being literate which inheres in any literate individual. His solution is that the word signifies the quality in itself, but signifies the substance only indirectly.
>
> At about the same time, a commentator on Priscian's *Institutiones grammaticae*, the anonymous author of the *Glosule in Priscianum*, was grappling with the same problem. He introduced a new technical term to clarify the distinction: *nominatio*, 'reference'. Thus, the word *homo*, 'human being', *signifies* the quality of being human and simultaneously *denotes* individual human beings. This debate was taken further by philosophers such as Abelard and William of Conches, and was developed in new directions by both logicians and theologians in the latter part of the twelfth century, with the help of the *logica nova*, the newly discovered logical works of Aristotle's.
>
> *Reading*
> A. de Libera and I. Rosier, 'La pensée linguistique médiévale 3. L'analyse de la référence', in S. Auroux, ed., *Histoire des idées linguistiques* 2 (Liége: Mardaga 1992), pp. 137–58.
> K. M. Fredborg, 'Speculative grammar', in P. Dronke, ed., *A History of Twelfth-Century Western Philosophy* (Cambridge: Cambridge University Press 1988), pp. 177–95, esp. pp. 181–6.
> D. P. Henry, transl. and comm., *The De Grammatico of St Anselm: The Theory of Paronymy* (Notre Dame, IN: University of Notre Dame Press 1964).

rose to with enthusiasm, and the ensuing period of rapid intellectual growth and change is known as the *Twelfth-Century Renaissance*.

Even to the grammarian, the arrival of these works held out exciting new prospects. Everyone who worked with language was obliged to confront its essential arbitrariness, and that, as we saw in chapter 5, was something which medieval scholars found very painful. Occasionally one writer or another spotted some linguistic feature which seemed to correspond to one aspect or another of extra-linguistic reality: the four grammatical genders paralleling the four elements, the five vowels corresponding to the five senses, and so on. Now, with the new-found interest in universals, the question could be formulated slightly differently: where should one look in language to find universals? Scholars scrutinised Priscian's *Institutiones grammaticae*: here if anywhere, in the authoritative grammar of Antiquity, the answer would surely be found.

> **Box 8.3 The twelfth-century rediscovery of Aristotle**
>
> Only a few of Aristotle's writings on logic – notably the *Categories* and the *De interpretatione* together with Porphyry's *Isagoge* (these three works were known as the *logica vetus* or 'old logic') – were widely studied in the West in the central Middle Ages. The remainder of the logical writings, like all of his writings on other subjects, from ethics to metaphysics and natural philosophy, were inaccessible to western Christians. But as the Christian West was getting to grips with Aristotelian logic, the East was absorbing Aristotelian science and metaphysics, as we saw in box 7.5. By the middle of the twelfth century, the rest of Aristotle's logical writings, the *logica nova*, had become available.
>
> From early in the twelfth century, Christians began to realise that other works of Aristotle's were in circulation in the Greek East and in the Islamic world. Some adventurous scholars travelled from northern Europe to the shores of the Mediterranean to join in the work of translation. Some translators, like James of Venice, William of Moerbeke and Robert Grosseteste, worked directly from the original Greek text; others took a more circuitous route. In Sicily and in Spain, notably in Toledo, Christians, Jews and Muslims might all collaborate on a translation. One celebrated account describes how a Jew and a Christian worked together on a translation of *De anima* ('On the soul'), a work by Avicenna, an Arab philosopher. The Jewish scholar, Avendeuth, writes to the archbishop of Toledo, the dedicatee of the translation: 'You have here the book translated from Arabic at your command with me reading out the individual words in the vernacular and Archdeacon Dominicus rendering them into Latin one by one.' Quite how this passage should be interpreted is controversial, especially given that not all the manuscripts describe the event in exactly the same way, but one reading is that Avendeuth translated the Arabic text orally into Old Spanish, and Dominicus then recorded it in Latin. Thus, many steps could intervene between Aristotle's original and the Latin text which finally filtered through to the universities of Christian Europe.
>
> *Reading*
>
> B. G. Dod, 'Aristoteles Latinus', in N. Kretzmann, A. Kenny, J. Pinborg and E. Stump, eds., *The Cambridge History of Later Medieval Philosophy* (Cambridge: Cambridge University Press 1982), pp. 45–79. [Surveys what is known about individual translators and lists all known Latin translations of each work of Aristotle's, with dates.]
>
> David C. Lindberg, 'The transmission of Greek and Arabic learning to the West', in his, ed., *Science in the Middle Ages* (Chicago and London: University of Chicago Press 1978), pp. 52–90.
>
> Marie-Thérèse d'Alverny, 'Translations and translators', in Robert L. Benson and Giles Constable, eds., *Renaissance and Renewal in the Twelfth Century* (Oxford: Clarendon 1982), pp. 421–62. [Surveys the translators with ample bibliographical references.]
>
> S. van Riet, ed., *Avicenna Latinus: Liber de anima I-II-III* (Louvain: Peeters and Leiden: Brill 1972), pp. 95*–105*. [Discusses interpretations of the Avendeuth passage.]

> **Box 8.4 Applying Aristotle's four causes to grammar**
>
> As grammarians experimented with the new ideas they found in Aristotle's works, they realised – as did their colleagues in other disciplines – that one of the most easily transferable points of doctrine was the theory of the four causes (see section 2.5 above). The four causes, or parameters, could be applied to anything – to the elements which enter into a construction, for example, or to the grammatical text itself. This is how one anonymous commentator on *Priscianus minor*, the syntactical books of the *Institutiones grammaticae*, writing around 1200, applies them to the work under study:
>
> It is thus apparent what the subject or material cause to be expounded in this book which we have in our hands is: speech is the subject or material cause.
>   The efficient cause is Priscian, handing down the teaching.
>   The formal cause is twofold: the form of presentation and the form of the treatise. The form of presentation is the mode of procedure (*modus agendi*), which is three- or fourfold, viz. defining, dividing, prescribing, proscribing and exemplifying. The form of the treatise is the division of the work into separate well-defined books, chapters and sections.
>   The final cause is twofold: the internal goal and the external goal. The internal goal is knowledge of the matters which are dealt with in this discipline. The external goal is threefold, proximate, remote and ultimate. The proximate goal is that we should possess knowledge of grammar. The remote goal is philosophy, or perfection of our intellectual soul. The ultimate goal is the blessedness or happiness toward which all the disciplines are oriented.
>
> Note how the study of grammar is placed in a broader context: the development of our intellectual soul, or mind, and the quest for spiritual fulfilment.

Indeed, Priscian does mention 'the generic and specific forms of things, which existed in mentally cognisable form in the divine mind before they went forth into bodies',[2] and the theologian Abelard (1079–1142) identified Priscian's 'generic and specific forms' with the Platonic Forms.[3] On the face of it, Aristotle's newly discovered writings should have been irrelevant to grammarians, for none of them dealt with language in its own right; but it was precisely because of that that they proved inspirational. They offered a new way of thinking about extra-linguistic reality which held out points of contact with language which grammarians and philosophers rushed to develop. From the middle of the twelfth century on, linguistics was dominated by attempts by grammarians of every theoretical persuasion to master the new Aristotelian doctrine and work out its implications for language (see box 8.4). The new ideas pervaded linguistic thinking at every level, from humble school grammars to the subtlest semantic reasoning about the nature of the Trinity. Let's consider the impact of two very different areas of Aristotelian theory: motion and epistemology.

8.2 Aristotle's *Physics*: from motion to phonetics and syntax

At first sight an unlikely source of inspiration to medieval grammarians, Aristotle's ideas about motion were taken up by thinkers in a great range of disciplines, from optics to theology. One reason for this was that far more was subsumed under the heading of 'motion' than we would expect today: basically any kind of change, including birth, death, growth and metamorphosis, as well as the more limited changes of place that we think of when we hear the word 'motion'. The *Physics* was the principal work in which Aristotle discussed motion, although he returns to the subject over and over again throughout his scientific writings. Early in the *Physics* Aristotle reminds his readers that art imitates nature.[4] That innocuous little statement – a cliché to us – evoked powerful resonances in medieval grammarians. Right through the Middle Ages, grammarians were desperately anxious to rescue language from its apparent arbitrariness (and this was the driving force behind Speculative grammar, as we shall see). To be told that art – which they took to mean all the Liberal Arts, including grammar – imitates nature implied that language was in some sense natural and non-arbitrary. In what respect? Reading on, they found a clue: 'Nature is the principle of motion, stability and change.'[5] From the middle of the twelfth century on, one scholar after another joined in the quest to identify the principles of motion, stability and change at work in language. Different groups of scholars looked for it in different aspects of language – the masters of Paris in syntax, the masters of Oxford in speech sounds.

Syntax

In the *Physics* Aristotle refers in passing to motion of that which affirms or denies a predicate (V 1), and to the subject and the goal of motion – an open invitation to medieval grammarians to apply these ideas to syntax. In fact medieval syntax was already dynamic, motion-oriented, for Priscian (like Apollonius Dyscolus before him) had described the relation between the elements of a sentence in terms of the 'transition' of the action from one word to another (see box 4.15, p. 90 above, if your memory needs refreshing).

Syntax in the eleventh and twelfth centuries was founded upon two key notions, *regimen* and *congruitas*. (*Concordantia*, 'agreement' or 'concord', was used by some as a synonym of *congruitas*.)

- *regimen* 'government': relations where one word 'governed' another, compelling it to be in a particular case;
- *congruitas* 'agreement': relations involving agreement, i.e. where two words entered into a relationship such that their properties had to be the same.

Regimen had been a part of grammars ever since Hugo of St Victor, who wrote a grammar early in the twelfth century. At the most basic level, teachers like Hugo found their pupils' needs were best met by a simple list of the cases and the ways in which they were governed. Thus, one grammarian uses this sentence to exemplify the use of the accusative with a transitive verb:

lego   librum
I-read   a-book-ACC
'I am reading a book'

8.2 Aristotle's *Physics*

He comments:

Librum is in the accusative case and is governed by the verb *lego* as the second element by virtue of transitivity in accordance with this rule: every transitive verb used transitively governs one or more accusatives to which the action of the verb passes, as in *lego librum* 'I am reading a book', *scribo litteram* 'I am writing a letter.'[6]

As you can see from this explanation, the position of the element in the construction – first (*ex parte ante*) or second (*ex parte post*) – was crucial. Each relation of government was categorised by its semantic or syntactic force: possession, acquisition, transitivity, effect of the material cause and so on.

Relations of government were similarly assembled and catalogued. In this next extract the anonymous teacher describes subject–predicate agreement. The terms used are *suppositum* and *appositum*, the grammarian's equivalent of the logician's *subiectum* and *predicatum* (subject and predicate) respectively (see box 8.5).

The first agreement is of the *suppositum* with the *appositum*, e.g. *homo currit* 'a person is running'. *Homo* 'person' is the *suppositum*, *currit* 'runs' is the *appositum*. The same number and person are required in them both, and the nominative case of the noun signifying substantivally should correspond to a finite mood in the verb.[7]

The principal syntactic features of the Latin sentence, catalogued along these lines, had thus passed into common knowledge by the end of the twelfth century. What the late twelfth- and thirteenth-century grammarians added from their reading of Aristotle's *Physics* was a different way of describing the relationship between the elements in a construction ('constructibles').

Let's take three simple sentences – as nonsensical as any the Generativists have produced – and see how they were analysed in terms of motion by thirteenth-century grammarians.

(1) homo   currit
      a-person   is-running

Motion could be identified in any relationship between *any* two words in a construction. Motion passed from one element, the dependent element (*dependens*), to the element which terminated the dependency (*terminans*). So in *homo currit* one element – *currit* – depends on the other – *homo*. Likewise, in *albus homo*, 'white person', *albus* depends on *homo*. That is, the dependency of both adjective and verb finds its end point, its goal (*terminus*), in *homo*.

(2) percutio   Socratem
      I-hit   Socrates-ACC

In this construction it is again the verb which depends on the noun: the noun *Socratem* terminates the dependency of the first element in the construction, the verb *percutio*.

(3) Socrates   legit   librum
      Socrates-NOM   is-reading   a-book-ACC

> **Box 8.5 Who was the first to talk about subject and predicate?**
>
> Logicians, concerned as they were with truth and falsity, analysed the sentence in a totally different way from grammarians. Instead of taking the word as the unit and charting the types of relationship into which words can enter, they began with the complete meaningful utterance – the proposition – and divided it into its constituents:
>
> - that about which something is said (*hypokeimenon* in Aristotle's Greek, *subiectum* in Boethius's Latin)
> - that which is said about it (*katēgoreumenon* in Greek, *praedicatum* in Latin)
>
> It was only in the twelfth century, however, that grammarians began to consider applying these notions to the analysis of sentences. In the 1160s the terms *suppositum* and *appositum* were adopted by grammarians, who by and large regarded *subiectum* and *praedicatum* as terms proper to logic. Nonetheless, creating equivalent terms did not mean that grammarians took over the logicians' approach to the sentence; they continued to work with a dependency type of syntax. Here and there early modern grammarians such as the Dutch scholar Gerard Vossius (1577–1649) pressed the terms *subiectum* and *praedicatum* into service. But it was not until the late eighteenth century that the logicians' constituency approach – breaking the whole sentence down into ever smaller parts – was really taken up and developed by grammarian-linguists, and only then were the terms *subject* and *predicate* assimilated into the mainstream grammatical tradition.
>
> *Reading*
> A. de Libera and I. Rosier, 'Construction et correction des énoncés', in S. Auroux, ed., *Histoire des idées linguistiques 2* (Liège: Mardaga 1992), pp. 159–78, esp. pp. 169–74.
> R. Pfister, 'Zur Geschichte der Begriffe von Subjekt und Prädikat', *Münchener Studien zur Sprachwissenschaft* 35 (1976), 105–19.
> I. Rosier, 'L'introduction des notions de sujet et prédicat dans la grammaire médiévale', *Archives et Documents de la Société d'Histoire et d'Epistémologie des Sciences du Langage (SHESL)*, 2nd ser., 10 (1994), 81–119.

To analyse a transitive sentence with an expressed subject two dependency relations are necessary: one where *legit* depends on *Socrates*, and another in which *legit* depends on *librum*. In other words, syntactic relations were pictured in terms of dependency relations obtaining amongst pairs of words (always standing for word classes), and not in terms of a constituency model, breaking a complete sentence down into ever smaller units.

Phonetics

Ancient writers had developed the study of speech sounds only to the limited extent that they needed this knowledge for rhetoric. As we saw in chapter 6, medieval teachers regarded the litterae as pointers beyond themselves to a higher meaning and saw no point in studying them in and for themselves. After all, they were utterly arbitrary, differing from one people to another. How could they reveal anything about the world except as signs? And yet speech sounds undeniably existed, a vital element of speech, as did letters, their written representations. If something as apparently arbitrary as the relations between the words in a sentence could be shown to be linked to eternal types of motion, might it not be possible to find the same kind of eternal verity underlying speech sounds? At Oxford, a university which was rapidly gaining a reputation for the study of physics and mathematics, a small group of scholars in the middle of the thirteenth century began to apply Aristotelian ideas to the litterae. Most of their writings are unpublished, and often we do not even know the authors' names. Robert Grosseteste (c.1175–1253), later bishop of Lincoln, was an influential member of this group, but most of his associates are known to us only by modern pseudonyms: 'pseudo-Grosseteste', 'pseudo-Kilwardby', 'the anonymous author of the treatise in Oxford, Bodleian Library, Digby 55' (see box 8.6).

In his brief little treatise on sound production (De generatione sonorum)[8] Grosseteste reminds us that since art (which includes the art of grammar) imitates nature, and nature does everything in the best way possible, the letters of the alphabet necessarily represent the shapes created inwardly when we speak. The seven vowels of Greek correspond to the seven basic types of motion, which are reproduced in the vocal tract when we speak and are represented in the letter forms: I represents motion straight ahead, O represents circular motion around a point, A represents dilation from a point outwards in a cone shape, and so forth. To describe the articulation of the consonants, as some of Grosseteste's associates do, rather more parameters were needed. Pseudo-Grosseteste introduces these terms:

- 'aperture' (apercio)
- three 'points of contact' (clausio), namely:
    - the lips
    - the tip of the tongue against the upper teeth
    - the tip of the tongue against the palate
- three 'dimensions' (dimensio) of the mutae (p, t, c):
    - 'breadth' (latitudo), e.g. ps, ts, cs
    - 'length' (longitudo, profunditas), e.g. b, d, g
    - 'thickness' (spissitudo, aspiracio), e.g. ph, th, ch[9]

As you can see, this author's desire to describe the speech sounds in spatial terms leads him to adapt the names of the dimensions to this unusual use where we would prefer terms more directly descriptive of the phonetic processes involved: 'affrication', 'voicing' and 'aspiration' respectively. (The fact that the author identifies the voiced plosives (b, d, g) as a distinct group, as Priscian did centuries earlier, does not mean that he understood the nature of voicing: this was not grasped by western scholars until the seventeenth century.)

> **Box 8.6 Anonymous, pseudonymous – or female?**
>
> As you'll have noticed, a large number of pre-Renaissance writings on language have come down to us without any indication of their author's name, or with a false one attached. This might happen for several reasons: first, people in the Middle Ages did not feel the same kind of pride and possessiveness about their ideas that we do. (Copyright and patenting were introduced in the early modern period, by which time the notion of the individual personality and the concept of originality had changed dramatically.) Secondly, many writers felt that their name lacked authoritativeness. This applied in particular to woman. We know that some medieval nuns were highly educated, well able to cope with the most complex Latin; yet Hildegard of Bingen stands out as one of the vanishingly few medieval women who both wrote in Latin and signed their works. If you felt you had something to say but felt it inappropriate to put your name on your work, what could you do? You could simply leave your name off and let your text join the vast number of anonymous works already in circulation; but this meant that it would run the risk of attracting no notice, for an early pope had condemned unsigned writings as likely to be purveying dangerous heresies. Alternatively, you could shelter under some more famous name – Augustine, or Grosseteste, or Kilwardby, or whoever it might be. And of course, a librarian anxious to tidy up the catalogue might assign a plausible name to an anonymous work.
>
> As for women grammarians, not a single one is known to us by name from the Middle Ages. Given that women were often teachers, it is highly unlikely that no woman ever wrote a grammar; rather, their writings have probably come down to us anonymously. A couple of female scribes who copied grammars identified themselves – Eugenia, who signed her name in Greek capitals in the grammars that she copied out at a Frankish centre in the latter part of the ninth century (Paris, Bibliothèque Nationale, lat. 7560); and a fifteenth-century nun who added a postscript in German to a collection of grammars, stating that the first two texts had been thoroughly revised and to the best of her knowledge were accurate, but that the third was full of gaps and mistakes, copied as it was from an ancient book. Her confessor has warned her that it is a misleading work, and she now wishes she had never copied it out, and hopes fervently that it will never fall into the hands of a scholar (Karlsruhe, Badische Landesbibliothek, Lichtenthal 88).

As an example of the amount of detail into which these writers went, let's take this description of the *littera* L:

The production of L comes about through contact of the point of the tongue with the hard palate, forcing the air to exit on either side of the tongue ... Because of the curvature of the point of the tongue toward the palate, since the point is its very end, it is represented by a line curving downwards like a hook at the bottom: L.[10]

Similarly, n has two vertical strokes, we are told, because the air shut into the oral cavity is compelled to exit via the nostrils – and so on. The careful articulatory descriptions are presented both as something of value in their own right, and as a means of demonstrating that the letter forms were not as arbitrary as they appeared to be at first sight;

indeed Grosseteste himself had made this point in a cross-linguistic context, arguing that the letter forms in different alphabets – Latin, Hebrew, Greek and even Arabic – mirror the essential gesture of the sound, differing only in accidental features: A basically triangular in all alphabets to represent the conical oral space, R basically curly to represent the rolling of the tongue, and so on.

Although these Oxford scholars carried out a good deal of work on articulatory phonetics – unquestionably the most detailed work in the Christian West until the seventeenth century – their empirical orientation (founded upon a careful study of Aristotle) attracted little attention from their contemporaries. Syntax, semantics and the philosophy of language were more highly prized, not least because of the light that they could shed upon the Scriptures.

8.3 Aristotle's *Metaphysics*: distinguishing the essential from the arbitrary

In Aristotle's *Metaphysics* twelfth-century readers found an important epistemological distinction: that between practical knowledge, leading to action, and theoretical knowledge, leading to truth. Only three disciplines, Aristotle claimed, were truly theoretical: physics, mathematics and theology. Aristotle's readers began to ask themselves whether this was inevitable. Might it be possible to study *any* subject-matter in either a practical or a theoretical manner? How might one go about it? Could language be investigated in a theoretical manner, not merely in the practical, descriptive manner everyone was familiar with?

Since theoretical disciplines dealt with the essential in any phenomenon, leaving the particular, accidental, manifestations to the practical disciplines, the first step was to establish what aspects of language might be truly essential and universal, the same for all languages at all times and places. Clearly, words themselves were not at issue, differing as they did from one language to another. Nor could morphology qualify, nor speech sounds or letters (except in the eyes of the masters of Oxford). Where twelfth- and thirteenth-century scholars did see universal likeness was in syntax and semantics, or, as Magister Jordanus put it some time in the first half of the thirteenth century:

> Although words, insofar as they are simply words, are not the same for all people, nonetheless they are the same for all with respect to their arrangement and the meaning which they convey: meaning is the same for everyone, according to Aristotle, whilst the arrangement of words according to the similarity or dissimilarity of their properties is likewise the same in all languages.[11]

Meaning provided an obvious link with extra-linguistic reality. The properties of the word classes were also universal, according to Magister Jordanus: here was another potential area for study. Ever tempted by the tantalising prospect of demonstrating once and for all a link between language and external reality, medieval philosophers and grammarians set to work, anxious to create a theoretical, or **speculative**, grammar (*grammatica speculativa*) parallel to the existing **practical** grammar (*grammatica practica*). ('Speculative' is the Latin-derived equivalent of the Greek-derived 'theoretical'.)

Naturally the effect of their work was to transform grammar as it had hitherto existed, for in the course of time it had become the custom to combine the discussion of apparently universal features such as number and tense with the specific details of Latin morphology. What form did the new discipline take?

Speculative grammar

In many ways, Speculative grammars look exceedingly traditional – in some respects more so than some of the practical grammars being produced around the same time. Speculative grammars may take the form of a treatise on the eight parts of speech, or of a Priscian commentary (usually, though not invariably, on the last two books of the *Institutiones grammaticae*), or alternatively of *questiones*, 'questions' with elaborate, highly formalised argumentation for and against, on particular points of difficulty. The inherited grammatical categories are taken for granted; indeed, they provide the starting-point. What is new is the ontological framework upon which that traditional doctrine is hung. For whereas the ancient and medieval grammarians had to a large extent taken these categories for granted, Speculative grammarians wanted to establish once and for all how each category related to reality. How did they go about it? The process took place in three stages. Petrus Helias, writing in the 1140s, shortly before the advent of the Speculative movement, took the first step in his widely read *Summa super Priscianum* ('Compendium on Priscian'). One aspect of Priscian's work which many scholars in the later Middle Ages found unsatisfactory was his discussion of the word classes. As the celebrated philosopher William of Conches (†ca 1154) grumbled in a much-quoted passage, 'even though he says quite enough about grammar, Priscian gives unclear definitions without explanation, and he fails to give the *raison d'être* of the word classes and their respective properties'.[12] Petrus pays especial attention to the word classes. Although he retains the substance of Priscian's account, he makes a significant change. In discussing the basis upon which the word classes were identified, Priscian had spoken of what was 'proper' (*proprium*) to each one, as in these examples:

> It is proper to the noun to signify substance and quality.
> It is proper to the verb to signify action or passivity or both with moods and forms and tenses and without case.
> It is proper to the pronoun to be employed in the place of a proper noun and to signify definite persons.
> It is proper to the conjunction to conjoin nouns or any other case-inflected words, or verbs or adverbs.[13]

Petrus realised that Priscian was lumping together criteria of different sorts under the general heading of what is 'proper': semantic, formal, syntactic, distributional, functional. He rewrote this passage in such a way as to distinguish the word classes using a single criterion: the *modus significandi*, 'way of signifying'. He remarks: 'Because there are only seven *modi significandi* or *consignificandi* in discourse ... a word class has been created for each of them.' (Petrus mentions only seven *modi significandi* here, rather than eight, because in this passage Priscian treats the interjection as a kind of adverb, following his Greek sources; later Petrus invents an eighth *modus significandi* to cater for it, in view of the fact that Donatus and the entire Roman tradition had had no doubts about its ontological status!) Petrus's version of the defining features of the four word classes we looked at above is as follows:

> There is one *modus significandi* in discourse to signify substance with quality, and on account of this *modus significandi* the word class *noun* was created, because all nouns signify substance with quality.
> There is another *modus significandi* to signify action or passivity, and on account of this *modus significandi* the verb was created.
> There is another *modus significandi* to signify substance without quality, and on account of this the pronoun was created.
> There is another *modus significandi* to signify the conjoining or disjoining of things, and on account of this the conjunction was created.[14]

Petrus has thus given Priscian's account a high degree of internal coherence by invoking a single criterion, the *modus significandi*, to establish the distinctive identity of each word class. In so doing he provided a basis for the work of the Speculative grammarians.

Petrus's successors continued to explore the notion of *modus significandi*, finding out just how far they could take it. They also began to think more carefully about just what elements need to be taken into account when thinking about meaning and how it is signified. This passage, from an anonymous commentary on Priscian's *Institutiones grammaticae* thought to date from the 1170s, presents three elements as crucial:

In order that the reason for the invention of the letters and of all meaningful word forms should be clear, you should be aware that three things are essential in all dialogue, that is, in the speech of one person to another: the thing under discussion, the concept you have of it, and the word form. The thing is necessary so that dialogue about it may take place, the concept so that we may know the thing through it, and the word form so that we may represent the concept through it.[15]

The emergence of Modistic grammar

By the middle of the thirteenth century grammarians were beginning to link the *modi significandi*, the 'ways of signifying' of words, with the properties of concepts. An early Speculative grammarian known to us as pseudo-Kilwardby writes: 'Note how the properties of the noun are sometimes the ways of comprehending (*modi intelligendi*) the thing signified via some property found in it, and those *modi intelligendi* are recognised from the word form.'[16] The focus is beginning to shift from the word itself to what it signifies, to the *signifié* and its properties. Pseudo-Kilwardby repeatedly tells us that the *modi significandi* correspond to the *modi intelligendi*. He and his contemporaries were beginning to look for an explanation of linguistic categories in terms of the properties of the *signifié*. Via the theories of meaning elaborated in the century since Petrus Helias's lifetime, grammarians were now moving towards an ever more systematic linking of the properties of word classes with the properties of concepts, and then – inevitably for those who held to a Realist ontology, experiencing concepts as a direct reflection of non-sense-perceptible universals – with the properties of universals.

The elaboration of the third stage in the process, the linking of the properties of words (*modi significandi*) with the properties of real-world phenomena via the properties of concepts, was undertaken in the 1260s and 1270s by a number of scholars who are known as Modists (*modistae* pl., *modista* sg.) from their interest in the *modi* (box 8.7).

Box 8.7 The Modists

The Modists were a relatively small group of scholars who studied and in many cases taught in the Faculty of Arts at the university of Paris in the second half of the thirteenth century and the first half of the fourteenth. By no means all of them were French; indeed, some of the most celebrated and influential were from Germany and Denmark (*Dacia* denotes 'Denmark', or sometimes the ecclesiastical province of Scandinavia, at this date), and a few from England. They include:

- Matthew of Bologna (ca 1260), author of *Quaestiones super modos significandi*
- Martin of Dacia (†1304), who studied and taught at Paris; may have been the chancellor to King Erik VI Menved of Denmark; author of *Modi significandi* (1260s or 1270s)
- Simon of Dacia, a Paris teacher and author of *Domus gramatice* (between 1255 and 1270)
- Boethius of Dacia, a Paris teacher, author of *Quaestiones super maius volumen Prisciani* (ca 1270)
- Michel de Marbais, who taught at Paris, author of *Summa de modis significandi* (ca 1270)
- Johannes of Dacia, who studied and taught at Paris, author of *Summa gramatica* (1280)
- pseudo-Albertus Magnus, author of *Quaestiones de modis significandi* (ca 1285)
- Gentile da Cingoli, studied at Paris and Bologna and taught at Bologna, author of *Quaestiones supra Prisciano minori* (ca 1290), and of *Quaestiones in Martinum*

Amongst the better-known figures of the next generation were:

- Thomas of Erfurt, studied at Paris and taught at Erfurt, author of *Novi modi significandi* (ca 1300)
- Radulphus Brito (1270/75–1320 or later), studied and taught at Paris, author of *Quaestiones super Priscianum minorem*
- Johannes Josse de Marvilla, studied and taught at Paris, author of *De modis significandi* (1322)
- Siger de Courtrai (†1341), studied and taught at Paris, author of *Summa modorum significandi*

Reading
Alain de Libera and Irène Rosier, 'La pensée linguistique médiévale 1. Courants, auteurs et disciplines', in Sylvain Auroux, ed., *Histoire des idées linguistiques* 2 (Liège: Mardaga 1992), pp. 115–29.

8.3 Aristotle's *Metaphysics*

Let's follow the account given by the Danish grammarian Martin of Dacia, one of the earliest and best-known Modists:

> Note that the things that exist outside the intellect (*res extra intellectum*) have many properties. They exist, for example, in the modes of condition (*habitus*) and rest (*quies*) and in the modes of acting and undergoing action and in the modes of singular and plural and so forth. Through these properties things are distinguished from one another. All these properties of the thing existing outside the intellect are called its 'modes of being' (*modi essendi*).
>
> The intellect, considering these properties in the thing itself, understands or grasps or apprehends it with these properties, for the intellect understands the thing by co-understanding its properties. The thing itself, understood in this way, is called the 'thing understood, grasped or apprehended' (*res intellecta, concepta, apprehensa*), and its properties, which were previously called the *modi essendi* of the thing outside the understanding, are called the 'modes of understanding' (*modi intellegendi*) of the thing understood.
>
> Next, when the intellect wishes to signify its concept to another [intellect], it imposes a *vox* upon the thing understood in order to express its concept, i.e. the thing understood, through a *vox* as if it were a sign. Just as an innkeeper indicates [the presence of wine] by hanging out a circle, so the intellect expresses or signifies the thing understood by means of a *vox*. After the imposition or conjoining of this *vox* the thing is called the 'thing signified' (*res significata*), and all the properties of the thing which were previously called the *modi essendi* of the thing outside [the understanding] and the *modi intelligendi* of the thing understood are now called 'ways of signifying' (*modi significandi*). And thus the initial issue is now resolved, namely, that the *modi significandi* are derived from the properties of things, which are the *modi essendi*.[17]

In the introduction Martin takes us step by step through the process whereby linguistic categories are derived from real-world categories. He tells us that real-world things have many properties: action, rest, passivity, uniqueness, plurality and so on. These properties help to distinguish one thing from another. All these properties of real-world things are called their 'modes of being', *modi essendi*. When we begin to think about a thing, the mind grasps its nature – what makes it unique – by apprehending its properties. We form a concept of the thing and of its properties, the *modi intelligendi* (literally, 'modes of comprehending'). When we want to signify that concept to someone else, we have to utter a spoken word in order to express it, in just the same way as an innkeeper hangs out a sign to indicate that he has wine for sale. The spoken word is the sign of the concept, and – most importantly – the properties of the sign are derived from the properties of the concept. In other words, the linguistic 'modes of signifying' (*modi significandi*) which, as we shall see, are the grammatical properties of the word classes, are derived ultimately from the real-world properties of the things which words, via concepts, ultimately denote. As Martin says, 'The *modus significandi* is the unique quality of the thing consignified in a spoken word ... The *modus significandi* is the form of a word class in that it gives it existence and distinguishes it from all other word classes.'[18] Schematically:

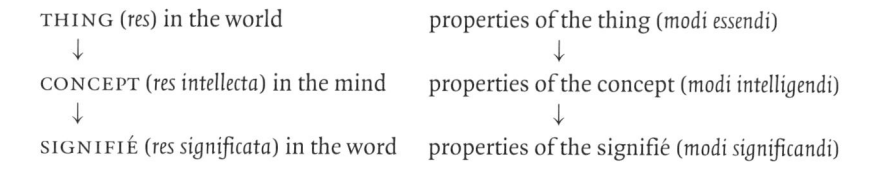

THING (*res*) in the world	properties of the thing (*modi essendi*)
↓	↓
CONCEPT (*res intellecta*) in the mind	properties of the concept (*modi intelligendi*)
↓	↓
SIGNIFIÉ (*res significata*) in the word	properties of the signifié (*modi significandi*)

Let's take an example to make this clear. Supposing you say something which makes everyone burst out laughing. How will you describe this incident? You might choose a word which conveys the change inherent in the event (its 'mode of flux', which defines its semantic nature) and is predicable of something else (its 'mode of being predicated of something else', defining its syntactic function) – a verb, as in 'They all *laughed.*' Or you might prefer to use a word with the mode of permanence and the mode of determinate reference – a noun, as in 'There were shrieks of *laughter.*' Your little brother might tell the story slightly differently, picking a word with the mode of something which affects the soul and the mode of being added to words which signify through the mode of flux – an interjection, as in 'They all went "Ha, ha, ha!"' Each of these word classes has a slightly different relationship to reality through their different *modi significandi* (see box 8.8), yet they all represent different facets of the same phenomenon.

Thus, the properties of the word classes are in principle derived from the real-world properties of the things from which they descend. The noun, for instance, has the properties, or modes, of condition and stability and definite reference. It shares the mode of condition and stability with the pronoun, but is distinguished from it by the mode of definite reference, which the pronoun lacks. On the other hand, it is distinguished from the verb in that the verb has the property of flux and of being predicated of a subject. The Modists work their way through the eight word classes showing how each of them ultimately has some connection, via its properties, with reality. Martin invokes the modes to account for such awkward and at first sight recalcitrant phenomena as the mismatch of grammatical and real-world gender. Why, for example, are there two Latin synonyms for 'stone', one masculine (*lapis*) and one feminine (*petra*)? He looks at the traditional etymology of each word (for etymology was another way of discovering

---

Box 8.8 The modi significandi
Each Modist had his own battery of favourite *modi*, resulting in a plethora of slightly differing terms. In fact most Modists recognised the same basic categories which they varied according to taste. Amongst the fundamental types were these:

- *modi significandi essentiales* 'essential modes of signifying', pertaining to those essential features which define a word class;
- *modi significandi accidentales* 'accidental modes of signifying', pertaining to properties (accidents) of the word classes such as number, gender, person and tense, including:
    - *modi absoluti* 'absolute modes', pertaining to the semantic aspect of the word class or property
    - *modi respectivi* 'respective modes', pertaining to the syntactic function of the word class;
- *modi significandi activi* 'active modes of signifying', by which the word form (*vox*) signifies the properties of the thing;
- *modi significandi passivi* 'passive modes of signifying', by which the properties of the thing are signified by the word form.

the connection of words to real-world phenomena): *lapis* was explained as *laedens pedem*, 'injuring the foot', and *petra* as *pede trita*, 'rubbed away by the foot'.[19] The mode of the (active) agent, associated with the male, was thus appropriately linked with the word of masculine gender, and the mode of the (passive) patient, the recipient of the action, was equally appropriately linked with the word of feminine gender.

As you can see, although the *modi significandi* were thus supposed to reflect pre-existing universal categories, in practice they were derived directly from long-established linguistic categories. In effect, the Modists were justifying grammatical categories elaborated in Antiquity rather than creating a heuristic tool for arriving at new categories. Nonetheless, Parisian teachers and students dedicated themselves to refining this apparatus to ever greater levels of subtlety, and Modistic grammar spread from Paris to other centres. The Modists have received a large amount of attention from modern scholars, in part because their interest in universals strikes a chord with readers trained in the Chomskyan tradition: they were the first to enunciate, explicitly and consciously, the principles of universal grammar. All the same, they constitute only a very small part of the linguistic activity of the Middle Ages. Modistic grammar was one development of the Speculative tradition (and not the only one, as we saw in section 8.3 above), which in its turn emerged only in the later twelfth century and was paralleled by an equally lively and certainly more widely exercised tradition of practical grammar.

Intentionalist grammarians and the speech act

Even as it took shape, some thinkers regarded Modistic grammar as too limited in its fundamental assumptions to explain everything that goes on when we use language. If grammaticality is the only criterion by which an utterance may be judged, what can we do with ill-formed but acceptable, comprehensible and effective utterances such as 'A crowd are rushing' (*turba ruunt*) and 'Water, water!' (*aqua, aqua*)? Toward the middle of the thirteenth century the English scholars Roger Bacon (the Oxford Franciscan reputed to have invented gunpowder) and Robert Kilwardby, along with several others whose names have not come down to us, elaborated a distinction between two levels of sense: the 'initial understanding' (*intellectus primus*), the level on which the *modi significandi* operated, and the 'secondary understanding' (*intellectus secundus*), the level on which the *signifiés* (Saussure's *signifié* corresponds very closely to the Latin *res significata*) came into play. Thus, 'a crowd are rushing' could be accounted for in that the plural verb agrees, not with the singular noun form, but with the plural *signifié*: a crowd consists of many individuals. It is the speaker's intention, *intentio proferentis*, which brings about the infringement of a grammatical rule. This process becomes even more transparent if you see a house on fire and shout, 'Water, water!' Strictly speaking, all you have uttered is a string of two nouns standing in no grammatical relation to one another; there is no verb, no explicit indication of what you want to happen with the water. Yet your meaning comes across more effectively than if you had said, 'Would you be so kind as to fetch some water?', for the ungrammaticality of your utterance conveys not only what is needful, but also makes plain the urgency of the situation by revealing your emotions. The intentionalist grammarians took into account both speaker and hearer, and by incorporating the notion of the speaker's intention into their theory of utterance meaning they arrived at a way of judging the utterance which took into account the function of the *signifiés* as well as grammatical relations. As a result, they were able to deal with ungrammatical as well as grammatical utterances, and to account for the performative nature of the words of the sacraments, of oaths, and even of magic spells. In their view, the Modists stopped too soon. As one anonymous writer noted, 'There are two kinds of grammarians: one kind teaches the structure of common speech . . . and the other kind teaches and investigates the structure of individuals' speech . . . that of literary authors and philosophers, for instance. Although the first kind of grammarian doesn't investigate *signifiés* or things predicated of them, the second kind does investigate them.'[20] Other writers go further, referring to the latter type as 'advanced'. Needless to say, the Modists fought back, not relishing this challenge to their cherished *modi significandi* as the unique measure of grammaticality – for once you start to admit intention and context into your explanations, your pretensions to an absolute, exceptionless, quasi-scientific theory evaporate. Pragmatics (and sociolinguistics, too, one might add) presents a serious challenge to any syntactic or semantic theory which claims total explanatory validity on its own. By 1300 the Modists were scornfully putting down the intentionalist approach, claiming it was out of date. But another challenge was on its way.

The end of Speculative grammar

The Speculative approach to language was founded upon the belief that there is a direct, one-to-one correspondence between linguistic phenomena, mental categories, and universals, an approach, which, as we have seen, was in turn motivated by a deep-seated desire to rescue language from its intrinsic arbitrariness by showing how it was linked with extra-linguistic reality. Given that the ontology of Speculative grammar was founded upon belief in independently existing universals, Speculative grammar stood or fell with the universals. Early in the fourteenth century the proponents of universals – the Realists – met a concerted challenge from another group of philosophers, the Nominalists. The most famous of the Nominalists was the English Franciscan William of Ockham (ca 1285 – ca 1347), who studied at Oxford and cut short a promising career as a theologian to concentrate on political philosophy after getting embroiled in papal controversy. In one of his earlier writings, the extremely influential *Summa logicae* (ca 1323), Ockham attacked the notion of universals. The only universals he would accept were signs – natural signs like smoke and laughter, and conventional signs, i.e. words. These universals were the result of mental activity – a kind of abstraction or mental picturing – that takes place when we think, and exist only in that activity. Otherwise, only individuals could be said to exist. Developing the linguistic consequences of this position, Ockham argued (following Boethius's commentary on Aristotle's *De interpretatione*) that words existed on three distinct levels:

> mental word (*oratio mentalis*)
> spoken word (*oratio vocalis*)
> written word (*oratio scripta*)

Like Aristotle, he claimed that concepts or mental impressions signified naturally, whereas spoken or written forms signified only by convention. Synonyms, after all, may have quite different properties on the level of the word, but stand for one and the same concept. (Not for Ockham any subtle attempts to identify an ontological basis for the gender difference between *lapis* and *petra*!) If there is thus a certain mismatch between the lexicon of spoken language (which admits redundancy, in the form of synonyms, for stylistic purposes), and that of mental language, mightn't the same be true of grammatical classes and properties? Can we really claim, for example, that the verb and the participle reflect different concepts when 'Socrates is running' and 'Socrates runs' are exactly equivalent in terms of their truth value? What about the pronoun and the noun? Mental language, Ockham concludes, has no need of pronouns and participles. The situation is much the same with the properties of individual word classes. Case and number are represented in mental language, as one can see if one tries to vary the case or number of the terms in a proposition: the sense changes. But if one changes the gender or composition of a term, the truth-value of the proposition is unchanged: *homo est albus* 'l'homme est blanc' means exactly the same as *homo est alba* 'l'homme est blanche', even if it looks odd. Likewise, mood, number, tense, voice and person in the verb exist also in mental language – for 'Socrates loves' is very different from 'Socrates is loved' – whereas conjugation and composition are properties of spoken and written language alone.[21]

Although Ockham does not explicitly set out to attack modistic grammar, these arguments strike right at its very core. If there is no one-to-one correspondence between linguistic categories and those of mental language, let alone real-world phenomena, its entire ontological underpinning crumbles away. As Ockham's *Summa logicae* spread across Europe, more and more scholars found themselves agreeing with it; and later in the fourteenth century other scholars launched direct attacks upon modistic grammar. It was for the logician to consider what was common to all languages – Ockham's mental language; the grammarian was told in no uncertain terms to get back to the particulars of Latin, or Greek, or whatever language it might be. And yet the whole idea of a universal grammar, one which embodied the principles common to all languages, remained enormously attractive. In southern and eastern Europe the search for such a grammar continued through the sixteenth and seventeenth centuries, while northern Europeans plunged into a completely new approach to language.

8.4 Practical grammar

Long before the advent of Speculative grammar, grammarians had felt it appropriate to separate discussion of those categories of language which reflected real-world properties, such as number, gender, mood, tense and voice, from the purely arbitrary forms in which they were instantiated. As we saw in chapter 4, the *Schulgrammatik* genre gave logically ordered form to linguistic categories which were taken to be universal, while grammars of *regulae* type imposed an arbitrary order, usually alphabetical, upon the specific data of Latin inflectional morphology. Various attempts were made to combine information of the two types; Priscian, for example, devoted several books of the otherwise logically structured *Institutiones grammaticae* to the Latin declensions and conjugations, and later the Insular elementary grammarians integrated information from grammars of *regulae* type into the basic *Schulgrammatik* structure. From the Carolingian Renaissance on, however, people generally preferred to revert to the ancient plan of keeping theoretical and practical information separate. In the twelfth century Donatus's *Ars minor* was still the basic introduction to grammar, offering as it did a well-organised outline of the fundamental categories of language exemplified through Latin; but the *regulae* grammars were no longer in use. How were teachers to make the more tedious formal aspects of grammatical doctrine memorable? Little by little a tradition was growing up of putting into verse those bits of information – largely lexical and morphological – that could not be organised logically. Thus, Petrus Helias inserted clusters of mnemonic verses into his huge *Summa super Priscianum* to facilitate memorising which fourth-declension nouns were masculine and which feminine, for example. Longer collections of such verses helped pupils to master *differentiae*, words that look similar but need to be distinguished (Serlo of Wilton, writing some time before 1180, was the author of the most famous); or the formation of the perfect stem of verbs, one of the chief bugbears of Latin morphology (Petrus Riga, who lived from about 1140 to 1209, wrote a popular text on this subject). By the end of the twelfth century these collections of mnemonic verses were being assembled into works that come close to being full-scale grammars. The most celebrated was the *Doctrinale* by Alexander of Villa-Dei (Ville-Dieu, near Avranches, Normandy), said to have been completed in 1199. Although the *Doctrinale* is often described as a thorough-going grammar, in fact it isn't really. What it focuses upon are just those awkward bits of information, mostly morphological, which do not sit well in a logically structured work. It totally lacks the hierarchical structure and the discussion of universal properties characteristic of the *Schulgrammatik* genre from Donatus on. What does Alexander include? Here are the contents of the four books:

1. noun declension, outlining the endings of each of the five declensions; heteroclites, or nouns which are of one gender in the singular and another in the plural; the formation of the comparative and superlative; gender; the formation of preterites and supines of verbs; defective and irregular verbs; the four 'forms' of verbs (perfective, inchoative, meditative, frequentative)
2. syntax: government and construction
3. prosody
4. accents and figures of speech

Thus, Alexander makes no attempt to cover all the word classes systematically, nor even all the properties of those he does discuss.

Is it really possible to convey morphological information in verse? Alexander sets out even the paradigms in verse form, as in this description of the singular of the fourth declension:

> Quarta dat us recto; dabit u, sed non nisi neutro.
> u non mutabis, donec plurale tenebis.

8.4 Practical grammar

> us genetivus habet; sed tertius ui tibi praebet.
> um quarto dabitur; quintus recto sociatur.
> u sextus retinet; sed flecte domum sapienter.[22]

The fourth declension assigns -us to the nominative case; it will also assign -u, but only to the neuter. -u you will not alter until you get to the plural. The genitive takes -us, and the dative offers you -ui. -um is assigned to the accusative, and the vocative is similar to the nominative. The ablative retains -u. Be careful how you inflect *domus*.

How much of the declension of the masculine noun *fructus* 'fruit', the neuter noun *genu* 'knee', and the irregular noun *domus* 'house' can you reconstruct from Alexander's account? Here is the solution:

Nom.	fructus	genu	domus
Gen.	fructus	genu	domus *or* domi
Dat.	fructui	genu	domui *or* domo
Acc.	fructum	genu	domum
Voc.	fructus	genu	domus
Abl.	fructu	genu	domo

From what Alexander says in the introduction, it is clear that he envisaged his work being studied at an intermediate level, after pupils had learnt the basic grammatical categories from the *Ars minor*, but before they went on to the *Institutiones grammaticae*. Alexander's work was evidently just what a great many teachers were looking for, for it enjoyed enormous popularity up to the end of the Middle Ages and beyond, being commented on by a number of scholars and running to some 300 printed editions, the last of them in 1588. Around 500 medieval manuscript copies of it still exist. What is more, several popular early modern grammars – Johannes Despauterius's *Commentarii grammatici* (1537), the standard grammar throughout the sixteenth century in the Low Countries, northern France and much of Germany; Emmanuel Alvarus's *De institutione grammatica* (1572), a grammar written for use in Jesuit schools and widely used throughout Catholic Europe in the sixteenth and seventeenth centuries; and even Claude Lancelot's *Nouvelle methode pour apprendre facilement la langue latine* (1644), written for the school of Port-Royal and widely imitated in the seventeenth and eighteenth centuries – adopted its basic structure, even though they were wholly or largely in prose.

In the 1220s and 1230s verse form was extended to the logically structured grammar as well, pioneered by such Anglo-Norman scholars as Henry of Avranches, who versified the *Ars minor* and wrote a couple of versified grammars of his own, and the influential John of Garland, who wrote two extremely long full-scale grammars in verse. Several others followed their example. Here is a snippet from an anonymous verse version of the *Ars minor* found in a thirteenth-century manuscript in the library of Worcester Cathedral:

> Si quis me interroget quot orationis
> Partes sunt, respondeo uerbo rationis
> Octo sunt. Non dubito, plures non habentur.[23]

> If you were to ask of me
> Of speech how many parts there be,
> I'd answer with the voice of reason
> 'Eight': aught else is out of season.

By the fourteenth century even Speculative grammar, filtering down to the school classroom, was being put into verse, as in Jean Josse de Marvilla's *De modis significandi* (1322). The original reason for adopting verse form – to impose order upon material which lacked any logical order of its own – was now completely forgotten.

8.5 A new development: making the invisible visible

At most universities students were obliged to hear the *Institutiones grammaticae* read and expounded once or twice during their course. But it was apparent that they did not find

13   Diagram from the margin of a twelfth-century English copy of Priscian's *Institutiones grammaticae* setting out the implicit structure of Priscian's discussion of pronouns.

8.5 Making the invisible visible

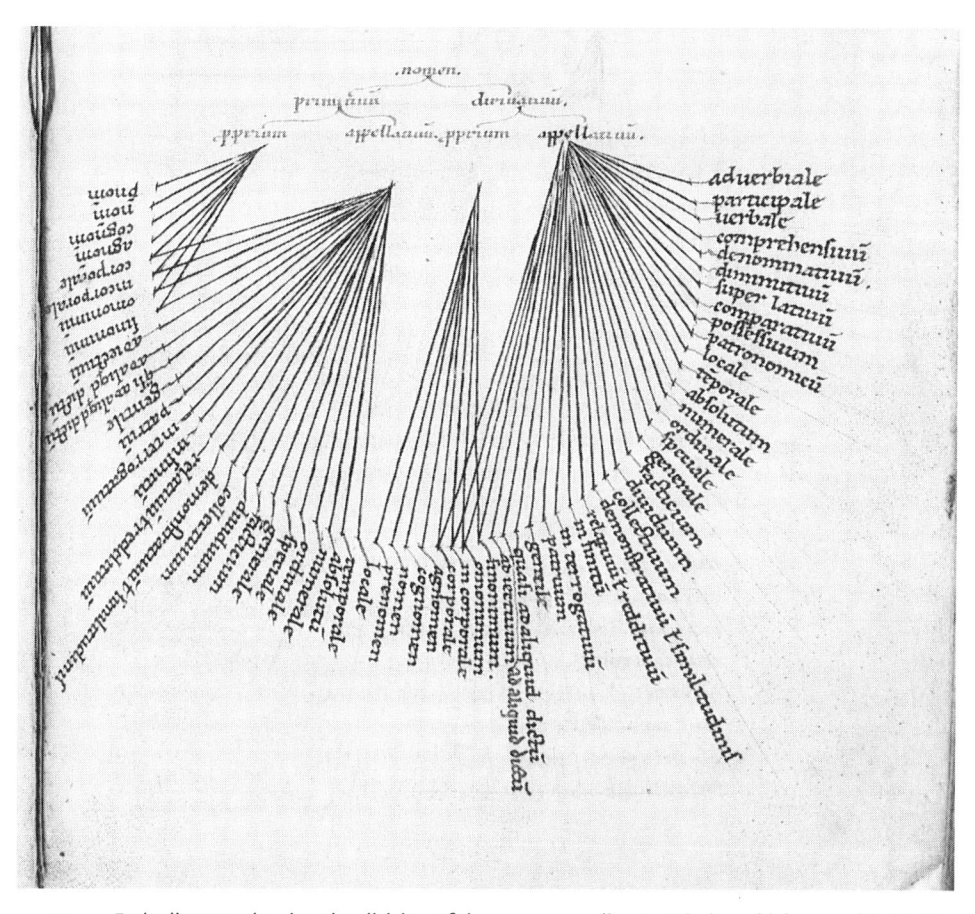

14 Early diagram showing the division of the noun according to Priscian which was added in the twelfth century to a copy of the *Institutiones grammaticae*.

it easy to get to grips with this massive 700-year-old work organised in an unfamiliar manner. Priscian's method of organisation, although carefully worked out, is for the most part implicit rather than explicit, a far cry from the generous signposting to which university students were by now accustomed. Teachers, anxious to give them all the help they could, adopted a new policy. In the earlier Middle Ages, their glosses on the *Institutiones grammaticae* had focused on its doctrine; now they began to spell out its structural articulations. Some teachers did so simply by writing notes like 'Here Priscian gives the etymology of the word "noun"', 'Here he explains the definition of the noun' in the margins. Others wrote paragraphs explaining the structure of each section, as Petrus Helias does in his *Summa super Priscianum*. Some readers inserted marks into the text indicating where Priscian started on a new subject, sometimes devising a complicated numbering system for the sections. A few drew tree diagrams in the margins to make visible the implicit structure of the doctrine. At first a marginal aid (in both senses!), diagrams gradually came to play an important role in the presentation of grammatical doctrine. Practical and Speculative grammarians alike came to depend upon them for showing anything from the divisions of the speech sounds (the anonymous treatise in

15 Paradigm from a deluxe grammar ca 1487. The scribe has used skulls to indicate missing parts of the paradigm, such as the imperative imperfect, perfect and pluperfect.

Digby 55 mentioned above has some extremely elaborate diagrams on the classification of speech sounds) to the structure of a sentence. By the fifteenth century many works produced in northern Europe (England, northern France, the Low Countries and parts of Germany), manuscript and printed, were full of diagrams and tables to make the information visually striking and memorable (see figure 15). And this reflects an incipient change in pedagogy, as we see from the instructions to the teacher in the preface to a late fifteenth-century grammar from the Low Countries, the *Exercitium puerorum grammaticale* ('Grammatical practice for children'):

In order to teach our children this text it is not necessary to read it out to them first, for the contents are represented to the eyes extremely clearly and simply. Masters, instructors and assistants do not need to wear themselves out reading, shouting, bellowing, but can assign a greater or lesser amount to the pupils, depending upon their ability, level and age, and let them read, reread, paraphrase and repeat.[24]

What a contrast with the educational practice of most of the Middle Ages! Yet it was a long time before it could be taken for granted that pupils would own their own textbooks, even with the lowering of prices brought about by the introduction of paper and the invention of printing; indeed, methods of pedagogy in use since Antiquity were still commonplace in much of Europe and the English-speaking world well into the nineteenth century.

Further reading

Background

David Knowles, *The Evolution of Medieval Thought* (London and New York: Longman 1988), chs. 9, 13–15, 27.

Michael Haren, *Medieval Thought: The Western Intellectual Tradition from Antiquity to the 13th Century* (London: Macmillan 1985), pp. 132–59.

Jacques Le Goff, *Intellectual Life in the Middle Ages* (Oxford: Blackwell 1993).

Anders Piltz, *The World of Medieval Learning* (Totowa, NJ: Barnes & Noble 1981).

O. Pedersen, *The First Universities: Studium generale and the Origins of University Education in Europe* (Cambridge: Cambridge University Press 1997).

John Marenbon, *Later Medieval Philosophy (1150–1350)* (London and New York: Routledge 1987), chs. 1, 2, 11.

Jacques Verger, 'The universities and scholasticism', in David Abulafia, ed., *The New Cambridge Medieval History* 5, c. 1198–c.1300 (Cambridge: Cambridge University Press 1999), ch. 10 (pp. 256–76).

S. Ebbesen and I. Rosier-Catach, 'Le trivium à la Faculté des arts', in O. Weijers and L. Holtz, eds., *L'enseignement des disciplines à la Faculté des Arts (Paris et Oxford, XIIIe-XVe siècles)* (Turnhout: Brepols 1997), pp. 97–128.

Grammar in the later Middle Ages: brief surveys

G. L. Bursill-Hall, 'Linguistics in the later Middle Ages', in E. F. K. Koerner and R. E. Asher, eds., *Concise History of the Language Sciences* (Oxford: Pergamon 1995), pp. 130–7.

D. Perler, 'Medieval language philosophy', in ibid. pp. 137–44.

Alfonso Maierù, 'Medieval linguistics: the philosophy of language', in G. Lepschy, ed., *History of Linguistics 2: Classical and Medieval Linguistics* (London and New York: Longman 1994), pp. 272–315.

Michael Covington, 'Grammatical theory in the Middle Ages', in T. Bynon and F. R. Palmer, eds., *Studies in the History of Western Linguistics in Honour of R. H. Robins* (Cambridge: Cambridge University Press 1986), pp. 23–42.

Jan Pinborg, 'Speculative grammar', in N. Kretzmann, A. Kenny, J. Pinborg and E. Stump, eds., *The Cambridge History of Later Medieval Philosophy* (Cambridge: Cambridge University Press 1982), pp. 254–69. [Brief survey of Modistic grammar.]

Irène Rosier, 'La théorie médiévale des Modes de signifier', *Langages* 65 (1982), 117–28. [A succinct outline of Modistic theory.]

K. M. Fredborg, 'Speculative grammar', in P. Dronke, ed., *A History of Twelfth-Century Western Philosophy* (Cambridge: Cambridge University Press 1988), pp. 177–95. [Deals only with the twelfth century.]

I. Rosier-Catach, 'Modisme, pré-modisme, proto-modisme: vers une définition modulaire', in Sten Ebbesen and Russell L. Friedman, eds., *Medieval Analyses in Language and Cognition*, Det Kongelige Danske Videnskabernes Selskab, Historisk-filosofiske Meddelelser 77 (Copenhagen 1999), pp. 45–81. [Important reassessment of the diverse currents of thirteenth-century linguistic thought.]

I. Rosier-Catach, 'La tradition de la grammaire universitaire médiévale', in Mario De Nonno, Paolo De Paolis and Louis Holtz, eds., *Manuscripts and Tradition of Grammatical Texts from Antiquity to the Renaissance 2* (Cassino: Università degli Studi di Cassino 2000), pp. 449–98.

Longer studies

A. de Libera and I. Rosier, 'La pensée linguistique médiévale', in S. Auroux, ed., *Histoire des idées linguistiques 2* (Liège: Mardaga 1992), pp. 115–86. [The most up-to-date survey currently available, by two specialists in the field.]

Irène Rosier, *La grammaire spéculative des Modistes* (Lille: Presses Universitaires de Lille 1983).

Michael A. Covington, *Syntactic Theory in the High Middle Ages: Modistic Models of Sentence Structure* (Cambridge: Cambridge University Press 1984). [Less specialised than its title suggests, this book provides an accessible account of the emergence and decline of Modistic grammar along with a sketch of the syntactic theory.]

G. L. Bursill-Hall, *Speculative Grammars of the Middle Ages: The Doctrine of partes orationis of the Modistae* (Paris: Mouton 1971).

Jan Pinborg, *Die Entwicklung der Sprachtheorie im Mittelalter*, Beiträge zur Geschichte der Philosophie und Theologie des Mittelalters 42 (Münster: Aschendorff and Copenhagen: Frost-Hansen 1967). [Fundamental work on which much recent writing is still based. Includes Latin text of several medieval attacks on the Modists.]

Charles Thurot, *Extraits de divers manuscrits latins pour servir à l'histoire des doctrines grammaticales au Moyen Age* (Paris 1869, repr. Frankfurt am Main: Minerva 1964). [A history of grammar in the Middle Ages based on manuscripts in the collections of Paris and Orléans, amply documented with quotations from the sources. Despite its age it is still useful for some aspects of grammar in the later Middle Ages.]

Specialised studies

The Speculative tradition
The literature on Speculative and more especially Modistic grammar is extensive; for further references see the surveys listed above. A few fundamental works are listed below.

L. G. Kelly, 'La *Physique* d'Aristote et la phrase simple dans les ouvrages de grammaire spéculative', in A. Joly and J. Stéfanini, eds., *La grammaire générale des Modistes aux Idéologues* (Villeneuve d'Ascq: Publications de l'Université de Lille III 1977), pp. 107–24.

I. Rosier, 'Les parties du discours aux confins du XIIe siècle', *Langages* 92 (1988), 37–49.

I. Rosier, 'La notion de partie du discours dans la grammaire spéculative', *Histoire Epistémologie Langage* 3 (1981), pp. 49–62.

I. Rosier, 'Transitivité et ordre des mots chez les grammairiens médiévaux', in S. Auroux et al., eds., *Matériaux pour une histoire des théories linguistiques* (Lille: Presses Universitaires de Lille 1984), pp. 181–90.

J. Biard, *Logique et théorie du signe au XIVe siècle* (Paris: Vrin 1989), esp. chs. 1 and 4. [On Ockham and later attacks on the *modi significandi*.]

Mary Sirridge, 'Robert Kilwardby as "scientific grammarian"', *Histoire Epistémologie Langage* 10.1 (1988), 7–28.

Irène Rosier, 'Mathieu de Bologne et les divers aspects du pré-modisme', in Dino Buzzetti, Maurizio Ferriani and Andrea Tabarroni, eds., *L'insegnamento della logica a Bologna nel XIV secolo*, Studi e memorie per la storia dell'Università di Bologna, n.s. 8 (Bologna: Istituto per la Storia della Università di Bologna 1992), pp. 73–164.

I. Rosier, *La parole comme acte: sur la grammaire et la sémantique au XIIIe siècle* (Paris: Vrin 1994). [Ground-breaking study of intentionalism, including translations of excerpts from a number of important texts.]

Constantino Marmo, *Semiotica e linguaggio nella scolastica: Parigi, Bologna, Erfurt 1270–1330. La semiotica dei modisti* (Rome: Istituto Storico Italiano per il Medio Evo 1994).

I. Rosier, 'Grammaire, logique, sémantique, deux positions opposées au XIIIe siècle: Roger Bacon et les modistes', *Histoire Epistémologie Langage* 6.1 (1984), 21–34.

I. Rosier, 'Roger Bacon and grammar', in Jeremiah Hackett, ed., *Roger Bacon and the Sciences: Commemorative Essays* (Leiden: Brill 1997), pp. 67–102.

Grammatica practica
Margaret Gibson, 'Milestones in the study of Priscian, circa 800–circa 1200', *Viator* 23 (1992), 17–33.

M. Gibson, 'The early scholastic *Glosule* to Priscian, *Institutiones grammaticae*: the text and its influence', *Studi Medievali*, 3rd series, 18 (1977), 248–60.

V. Law, 'Panorama della grammatica normativa nel tredicesimo secolo', in C. Leonardi and G. Orlandi, eds., *Aspetti della letteratura latina nel secolo XIII* (Perugia and Florence 1986), pp. 125–45.

R. W. Hunt, *The History of Grammar in the Middle Ages: Collected Papers*, Studies in the History of Linguistics 5 (Amsterdam: John Benjamins 1980). [Reprints seven articles, mostly on grammars of the eleventh and twelfth centuries.]

Tony Hunt, *Teaching and Learning Latin in Thirteenth-Century England*, 3 vols. (Cambridge: Brewer 1991). [Survey based on wide-ranging first-hand knowledge of manuscript materials; focus is on Anglo-Norman glosses, which are printed in full. Much useful information on grammars by English authors.]

Vivien Law, 'Why write a verse grammar?', *Journal of Medieval Latin* 9 (1999), 46–76. [Examines the origins of the verse grammar and its place in later medieval education, and lists editions and manuscript sources of a large number of works.]

Translations and editions

Although many Speculative grammars have been edited, only a few have been translated:

Thomas of Erfurt, *Grammatica speculativa*, transl. G. L. Bursill-Hall (London: Longman 1972). [Parallel Latin and English text and lengthy introduction.]

I. Rosier, 'Traduction d'un extrait de la syntaxe du traité *De modis significandi* de Martin de Dacie', *Archives et Documents de la Société d'Histoire et d'Epistémologie des Sciences du Langage* 3 (1981), pp. 58–77.

L. G. Kelly, *Quaestiones Alberti de modis significandi*, Studies in the History of Linguistics 15 (Amsterdam: Benjamins 1977). [Latin text, English translation and commentary.]

A. C. Senape McDermott, *Godfrey of Fontaine's Abridgement of Boethius of Dacia's Modi significandi sive Quaestiones super Priscianum maiorem*, Studies in the History of Linguistics 22 (Amsterdam: Benjamins 1980). [Parallel Latin and English text.]

A quite large number of Speculative grammars have been edited, in whole or in part. Useful bibliographical guides to the editions can be found in:

S. Auroux (ed.), *Histoire des idées linguistiques* 2 (Liège: Mardaga 1992), pp. 127–9.

E. F. K. Koerner and R. E. Asher, *Concise History of the Language Sciences* (Oxford: Pergamon 1995), p. 136. [Editors' names and date of publication only.]

An invaluable guide to locating the vast number of unprinted texts, both Speculative and practical, in the manuscript collections of Europe and North America is provided by:

G. L. Bursill-Hall, *A Census of Medieval Latin Grammatical Manuscripts* (Stuttgart–Bad Cannstatt: frommann-holzboog 1981). [Provides a summary of the contents of all manuscripts containing Latin grammatical texts copied between ca 1000 and ca 1500. Details should always be verified.]

Grammatica practica has been less well served by modern editors, although this situation is beginning to change. Amongst the few such grammars that are available in print (Latin text only) are:

Alexander of Villa Dei, *Doctrinale*, ed. D. Reichling (Berlin: Hofmann 1893).
John of Genoa (Balbi), *Catholicon* (1460 edition repr. Farnham 1971).

Petrus Helias, *Summa super Priscianum*, ed. L. Reilly, 2 vols. (Toronto: Pontifical Institute of Mediaeval Studies 1993).

Henry of Avranches, *Libellus Donati metrice compositus*, ed. J. P. Heironimus and J. C. Russell, *Two Types of Thirteenth Century Grammatical Poems*, Colorado College Publication, General Series no. 158, Language Series III, no. 3 (Colorado Springs, Colorado 1929), pp. 10–15.

John of Garland, *Compendium gramatice*, ed. T. Haye (Vienna: Böhlau 1995).

Remigius, Schleswig 1486, ed. Jan Pinborg, Det Kongelige Danske Videnskabernes Selskab, Historisk-filosofiske Meddelelser 50:4 (1982). [A facsimile edition of the first Latin grammars printed in Denmark, consisting of six short school treatises: *Dominus que pars, Regimina, Ordo constructibilium, Regule gramaticales, Metra de constructionibus, De comparatione*.]

Viginti quatuor sunt iuncturae, ed. and transl. András Cser (Piliscsaba: Pázmány Péter Katolikus Egyetem, Bölcsészettudományi Kar 2000). [A short syntactic treatise.]

9 Medieval vernacular grammars

9.1 What is a vernacular grammar?

To many people nowadays the word 'vernacular' means 'colloquial' or 'informal', smacking of street usage, graffiti, perhaps obscenity – certainly not the sort of thing you'd expect to find in a grammar. 'Vernacular' contrasts with 'formal', one's linguistic Sunday best; in contemporary English, the distinction is more a matter of register than anything else. In medieval Europe the situation was more complex. The Italian poet Dante described the vernacular in 1304 as the language which we pick up from those around us without any rules. In the Italy of Dante's day, some dialect of Italian would have been the local vernacular; across the Alps, in Germany, some form of Middle High or Low German would have fulfilled that role, while in France Old French and Occitan, and in England Middle English and Anglo-Norman French were the most widespread vernaculars. Although little by little all these languages were coming to be used in writing, they were still far from offering serious competition to Latin. Latin maintained its status as the language of serious written scholarship and of international communication to the end of the Middle Ages and well beyond. Latin, Greek and Hebrew were regarded as qualitatively very different from any vernacular; as Dante puts it, 'We also have a secondary form of speech called *grammar* by the Romans . . . Few people succeed in mastering it, for we learn its rules and doctrine only by devoting much time and effort to it.'[1] (This is his way of formulating the sociolinguistic distinction between *High*, prestige, standardised, languages and *Low* languages lacking in prestige and the trappings of standardisation, such as dictionaries and grammars.) Given the huge importance of Latin for literate activity throughout the Middle Ages, a vast amount of energy went into studying and transmitting it to subsequent generations. The vernaculars, in contrast, received little scholarly attention, partly due to the low esteem in which they were held as the unfortunate reminder of human wrongdoing at Babel (see chapter 5). What made people begin to take the vernaculars seriously? How did the first vernacular grammars come to be written?

First, what do we mean by a vernacular grammar? The term is loosely used to include any kind of grammar written in a vernacular language – but, as we have seen already, the language in which a grammar is written isn't the only distinctive thing about it. To label a particular text simply 'a Latin grammar' tells us very little about it: is it concerned primarily with conceptual issues such as the properties of the noun or the nature of number or gender or tense, or, like the modistic treatises, with charting the way in which linguistic categories reflect the world? Or does it focus closely upon the specific forms of Latin, like the Insular elementary grammars or the *Doctrinale* of Alexander of Villa Dei? Just as medieval Latin grammars can be divided broadly into two groups – those that focus on universal issues and those that are concerned with the particular features of Latin itself – so too medieval vernacular grammars can be divided into the same two groups.

Universal grammars

Questions such as 'what is a proper noun?', 'what is a verb?', 'how many word classes are there?', 'what are the properties of the conjunction?' are as close to universal as any you are likely to find in a medieval grammar. Such concerns apply equally well to any European language; indeed, they had already been transferred from Greek to Latin. There is no inherent reason why they should not also be asked about Old Irish or Old Icelandic: one can find proper nouns (for instance) just as easily there as in Latin. Gradually – and the circumstances differed from one country to another – European scholars began to realise that they could write grammars of this type in their own vernacular, drawing examples from that language rather than from Latin or Greek. The earliest vernacular grammars in the Greek East are of this type – the Syriac reworking of the *Tekhnē* attributed to Dionysius Thrax, or the seventh-century Armenian scholar David's commentary on the *Tekhnē*, or the anonymous *On the Eight Parts of Speech* in Old Church Slavonic. In the West, the Third and Fourth Grammatical Treatises in Old Icelandic (Old Norse) exemplify the same trend.

Particular grammars

These works aim to describe the features of a specific language, either Latin or the vernacular.

(a) *Vernacular-medium grammars of Latin*. In all the grammars we have so far encountered, Latin was both the medium and the goal of instruction, rather like today's English-medium EFL textbooks. Gradually, as people started to write their own vernaculars, they began to experiment with putting their Latin teaching materials into the vernacular. Ælfric's *Excerptiones de Prisciano* (see section 9.3 below) is one such work, and several of the Middle English and Old French *Donats* of the fourteenth and fifteenth centuries likewise aim to teach the forms of Latin through the vernacular. Although the challenge of explaining the peculiarities of Latin in the vernacular sometimes led teachers to spot significant differences between Latin and their own language, their comments are always designed to help their pupils come to understand the structure of *Latin* better; elucidating the structure of the vernacular was at best a mildly interesting diversion, never the focus.

(b) *Vernacular-medium grammars of the vernacular*. These are grammars of a vernacular presented in that same vernacular. They may be more or less heavily influenced by grammars of the universal type, and often they try to introduce basic grammatical concepts along with the forms of the vernacular, but many of them display a remarkable ability to think about languages which are in some cases quite dissimilar to Latin without attempting to force them into the morphological categories familiar from grammars of Latin. They borrow 'universal' concepts like 'noun', 'active' and 'compound', but recognise that their languages may well have additional features – an article, for instance – or lack some of those found in Latin, such as the five declensions. Only later, during the Renaissance, do people deliberately try to squeeze their own languages into the Latin mould, as we shall see in chapter 10. We'll look at two medieval vernacular grammars, the Old Icelandic *First Grammatical Treatise* and the Occitan *Leys d'Amors*, in sections 9.4 and 9.5 below. Other works which fall into this category are the Old Irish *Auraicept na nÉces* ('Scholars' Primer'), the earliest portions of which date from the seventh century; the *Donatz Proençals*, composed by Uc Faidit in the second quarter of the thirteenth century; and the *Donait françois*, written at the beginning of the fifteenth century to help an Englishman called Johan Barton improve his French.

9.2 Why write a vernacular grammar?

If people were getting on quite well in their diglossic situation, with the respective zones of Latin and the vernacular clearly demarcated, how did they come to start writing grammars in or of the vernacular? The answer depends very much on local circumstances. During the Middle Ages the vernacular entered formal language study only in response to some pressing immediate need. Given the low status of the vernacular, no scholarly distinction could be attained by writing about it; indeed, Ælfric even apologised for using Old English in his grammar, as we'll see below. Nor was there a feeling that describing a language was in itself a meritorious activity: that attitude dates from the middle of the nineteenth century. No, the circumstances vary from one milieu to another, but invariably reflect an immediate need. Let's take three examples which we'll look at in greater detail below:

- Toward the year 1000 in England, the Anglo-Saxon monk Ælfric felt that although the future of Old English vernacular literacy seemed reasonably assured, the number of people who could cope with Latin was declining: it made sense, therefore, to write an introduction to Latin in Old English.
- An anonymous scholar in mid-twelfth-century Iceland, the so-called 'First Grammarian', keenly aware of the inadequacies of the orthography of his own language, decided to outline a revised orthography both of and in Old Icelandic, for he, like Ælfric, knew that not all his literate compatriots necessarily knew Latin.
- In mid-fourteenth-century Provence the standards of verse composition were slipping, or so the older poets thought. They organised an annual poetry

competition and commissioned Guilhem Molinier to write a grammar of Occitan to serve as a point of reference.

All three grammarians were working in settings in which there was an established tradition of writing and reading the vernacular. That is a vital prerequisite for a vernacular grammar – or else it will find no users.

9.3 Vernacular grammar in England

Vernacular literacy was established twice over in medieval England, first in the tenth and eleventh centuries, and then in the fourteenth and fifteenth. Latin had been introduced into England during the conversion to Christianity in the course of the seventh century and studied with the aid of the Latin-medium Insular elementary grammars (see chapter 6 above). By 700 latinity was well established, and there was a flourishing tradition of Latin literature represented by such authors as Aldhelm, Bede, and later Alcuin. In the ninth century, however, the social and political order came under pressure from Viking attacks. Realising the cultural dangers inherent in the impending decline in literacy in Latin, King Alfred encouraged the production of translations of central Christian texts into the vernacular. Gradually a relatively standardised form of Old English emerged, known to philologists as Late West Saxon. The impetus behind this movement faltered during the tenth century, however, and Latin culture again declined. It was revived by the arrival of some members of the Benedictine reform movement from France, giving an impetus to educational as well as institutional reform. The active and extensive use of Old English was again promoted.

One of the most prolific authors to use Old English in the wake of this movement was Ælfric (ca 950 – after 1010). A monastic teacher trained by Æthelwold of Winchester, one of the leading scholars of the day, Ælfric spent much of his life at Cerne Abbas, Dorset, and toward the end of his life became abbot of Eynsham, near Oxford. His ambition was to provide a comprehensive corpus of vernacular reading-matter for monks and nuns, a complete Christian education in Old English. His voluminous œuvre includes numerous sermons and saints' lives, paraphrases of parts of the Bible, a translation of Bede's study of time-reckoning (vital in connection with the calculation of movable feasts such as Easter), and three works designed to help with the study of Latin via the vernacular:

- a Latin grammar, *Excerptiones de arte grammatica anglice* ('Excerpts from/on grammar in English'), in Old English;
- a Latin–Old English glossary classified by subject, from the heavenly hierarchies down to man, the natural world, and human artefacts and activities;
- a Latin colloquy, or dialogue, intended to help his pupils expand their command of everyday spoken Latin by presenting brief accounts of the daily activities of people practising various professions – the baker, the fisherman, the ploughman, the merchant, the monk and so on. (The Old English gloss that was soon added to the colloquy to assist its users is now better known than the Latin original, for it is often used as practice material by students of Old English.)

These three works provide a comprehensive introductory course in Latin – a course specifically designed for people who were already literate in their own language but were not yet able to cope on their own with Latin.

But, far from being proud of his novel enterprise, Ælfric is terribly apologetic: he anticipates criticism. In the introduction to the grammar he says that he knows that many people will think that it was a waste of time, hardly worth the effort, to write a grammar in the vernacular. He asks them to remember that he is writing, not for learned greybeards, but for children. And he goes on to point out that scholarship – even literacy – has twice only narrowly survived in England: before Alfred came to the throne, and in Ælfric's own lifetime. He hopes that his work will help to avert another such decline.[2] His wish was granted – up to a point.

How did Ælfric go about providing an introduction to Latin in Old English, a language that had not previously been used to expound grammatical concepts in writing? As much as he could, he drew upon already existing resources. His starting-point was a tenth-century adaptation and abbreviation of Priscian's *Institutiones grammaticae*, a work called *Excerptiones de Prisciano* ('Excerpts from Priscian'). He shortened the text still further, added a few snippets from other sources along with a lot of paradigms, and translated the result into Old English. Here and there he added a bit of local colour; for instance, he chooses the noun *citharista* 'harpist' as the model for the first-declension paradigm. Harpists might not be part of our everyday life, but in medieval Britain the wandering bard with his harp under his arm was a familiar figure. King Edgar, Bishop Æthelwold and Archbishop Dunstan, all prominent figures in England in the second half of the tenth century, are used to exemplify various grammatical phenomena; even the revered eighth-century Northumbrian writer Bede (*Baeda* in Latin) appears, exemplifying first-declension masculine proper nouns! Phrases and sentences such as 'the nun keeps long hours teaching the girls', 'they are spinning wool', 'our fisherman's net' and 'the tools of your cobbler' bring a glimpse of Anglo-Saxon village life into the pages of the grammar. Grammatical terminology, too, needed to be made comprehensible. Where he could, Ælfric drew upon an existing tradition of oral translation (which we glimpse now and again in the glossing to Latin grammars) of such common terms as 'noun' (OE *nama*), 'verb' (OE *word*), 'part of speech' (OE *dæl*), 'tense' (OE *tīd*), 'gender' (OE *cynn*); where no such widely accepted term existed, he simply translated each element of the Latin term when it first occurred, but then used the Latin term. Thus, 'consonant' was translated as *samod swēgend*, literally 'together-sounding', and 'preposition' was translated as *foresetnys*, literally 'fore-set-ness' ('preposed element', perhaps) but in the subsequent text Ælfric uses the Latin terms *consonans* and *praepositio*.

When it came to finding equivalents for the five tenses recognised by Latin grammarians, Ælfric adopted an interesting strategy. Old English, like other West Germanic languages, has only two morphologically distinct tenses, the present ('I do') and the preterite ('I did'). During the Anglo-Saxon era a number of periphrastic forms emerged, corresponding to our 'I have done', 'I had done', 'I'll do' and so on (and a similar process took place at the same time in Old High German, the ancestor of modern German). In order to create these new tenses both English and German made use of a range of auxiliary verbs – 'to have', 'to be', 'to do', 'to become', 'shall', 'will'. By Ælfric's day Old English was well into this experimental phase, and Ælfric himself used these periphrastic forms heavily in his sermons. And yet when it came to finding English equivalents for the five Latin tenses, he looked elsewhere:

	Latin	Old English	
present	amo	ic lufige	'I love'
imperfect	amabam	ic lufode	'I loved'

Nowadays we'd be more likely to render the Latin imperfect as 'I was loving' or 'I used to love'.

| *perfect* | amavi | ic lufode fulfremedlīce | 'I loved completely' |

We would render the Latin perfect as 'I loved' or 'I have loved'; Ælfric, anxious to follow the sense of the technical term 'perfect' as closely as possible, inserts the adverb *fulfremedlīce* 'completely', 'perfectedly'!

| *pluperfect* | amaveram | ic lufode gefyrn | 'I loved distantly' |

Would you guess that this stood for 'I had loved'? Again, Ælfric's instinct is to find an approximate equivalent for the term 'pluperfect', literally 'more than perfect', rather than to look for the corresponding verb form in his own language.

| *future* | amabo | ic lufige gyt tō dæg oððe | 'I love still today |
| | | tō merien | or tomorrow'[3] |

The equivalent to the modern English 'I shall love', *ic sceal lufian*, carried connotations of obligation in Ælfric's day, but would have been a possible translation.

In short, it appears that Ælfric failed to recognise the functional equivalents for the Latin tenses in his own language; instead, he resorted to adverbs suggested by the Latin tense names to hint at the nuance of meaning they conveyed. He was still very far from being able to identify grammatical phenomena unique to Old English, despite his claim, in the preface, that his grammar could serve as an introduction either to Latin or Old English. Perhaps what he had in mind was simply that, fortified by a knowledge of these concepts and a smattering of Latin, monks and nuns would be in a better position to understand the points he makes in his exegetical writings. In fact he makes very few comparisons between Latin and Old English grammar:

- Old English has eight word classes, like Latin;
- the impersonal mood is seldom used in either Old English or Latin;
- the genders of Latin nouns do not always correspond to those of English ones, e.g. the Latin word *mulier* 'woman' is feminine, whereas its Old English equivalent, *wīf*, is neuter;
- Latin has six words corresponding to the single English conjunction *and*.

Ælfric's grammar achieved almost instantaneous popularity, displacing other grammars aiming at a similar audience to the point where, by 1100, it seemed to have a virtual monopoly in England. Of the twenty-four extant grammatical manuscripts written between Ælfric's own lifetime and 1100, more than half contain a copy of it, and remarkably few other works at the same level are to be found.

But the arrival of the Normans in 1066 changed the linguistic, educational and intellectual life of England out of all recognition. Previously, England had been a diglossic society in which Latin was the medium of intellectual and much religious life, but the Old English vernacular was steadily making inroads into its domains, as Ælfric's work testifies. When Norman French was superimposed upon this situation, Latin retained its position as the language of intellectual and religious life, while Old English reverted to its lowly status as the vehicle of everyday life, Norman French occupying an intermediate position as the language of the royal court, parliament (up until 1362) and the law courts:

Anglo-Saxon England

Church, intellectual life	LATIN
vernacular, court, law courts	OLD ENGLISH

Anglo-Norman England

Church, intellectual life	LATIN
court, parliament, law courts	ANGLO-NORMAN
vernacular	MIDDLE ENGLISH

The move toward using English as the medium of grammar books ceased after about 1100 (indeed, two copies of Ælfric's grammar were glossed in French in the course of the twelfth century), and teachers went back to Latin-medium textbooks. Norman teachers imported the latest textbooks from across the Channel, and would-be scholars from England were as likely to travel to the schools of Paris and northern France as to Salisbury or Oxford. In the fourteenth century education became significantly more widespread than hitherto, disseminated by schools founded in towns to educate the children of the growing middle class. Their needs were relatively modest: the boys needed to be able to read and write their native language so as to correspond with fellow-merchants, and to keep accounts, and also to acquire a veneer of Latin to prove their educated status, while the girls were taught literacy and numeracy in their own language but not usually in Latin. Vernacular literacy was becoming an increasingly routine accomplishment. Wealthy families all over western Europe commissioned copies of their favourite stories in English or French or German, such as the famous Auchinleck manuscript (thirteenth century) which contains many of the most celebrated Middle English romances, or the Große Heidelberger Liederhandschrift (formerly known as the Manessische Handschrift), a collection of Minnesang verse assembled in Zurich around 1320. All this implies a well-established tradition of literacy in the vernacular. Little by little it was becoming possible for a literate person with limited cultural and intellectual aspirations to live his or her whole life through the medium of the vernacular (except, of course, for church services, where only the sermons were normally in the vernacular).

Schools responded only slowly to this need. In the fourteenth and fifteenth centuries, and for a long time thereafter, education meant Latin, and what parents wanted for their fees was a smattering of Latin. But teachers gradually realised that it made sense to use the vernacular as the means of approach to Latin. Sometimes they glossed the Latin text of Donatus (for the *Ars minor*, now somewhat expanded with extra paradigms, was still the standard beginners' grammar) with occasional vernacular terms; sometimes the glossing expanded into a full-scale word-for-word translation, as we see in the opening of this translation of the *Ars minor* into Early New High German dating from 1473:

Partes oracionis *die tail der red* quot *wievil* sunt *syen*?
Octo *ächt*.
Que *welche*?
Nomen *der nam* Pronomen *der fürnam* Verbum *das wort* . . .[4]

Here and there the more adventurous teachers, such as John of Cornwall, a respected grammar teacher in Oxford in the mid-fourteenth century, introduced vernacular examples into the text to make the meaning clearer to their pupils. Early in the fifteenth century an influential teacher, John Leylond, took the next step, composing three grammatical treatises in English:

- *Accedence*, an introduction to the basic concepts of grammar with both English and Latin examples, and paradigms of Latin nouns and pronouns.
- *Informacio*, a set of instructions on how to translate a Latin sentence into English, teaching a large amount of syntax along the way. (Another popular syntactic text, not by Leylond, was the *Formula*, which provided a set of Latin sentences exemplifying the rules of agreement with English explanation.)
- *Comparacio*, a short work on the formation of the comparative of Latin adjectives.

This is how Leylond goes about teaching syntax in the *Informacio* (if this text looks hard, just read it out loud, and you'll find the strange spelling will cease to get in your way):

What schalt thow doo when thow hast an Englysch to make yn Latyn?
I schall reherse myne Englysche onys, ij or iij, and loke owt my principall verbe and loke whether he betoken 'to do' or 'to suffer' or 'to be'; and yf he betokyn 'to do' the doyr schall be the nominatiff case to the verbe and the sufferer schall be suche case as the verbe wyll haue after hym; and [=if] hit betoken 'to suffer' the sufferer schall be the nominatiff case to the verbe and the doer schall be the ablatyff case with a preposicion . . .
A cherch is a place the wheche Cristyn men bethe bounden to loue.
Whyche ys thi pryncipall verbe yn thys reson [=sentence]?
Ys.
Whan a verbe personall ys thy principall verbe, how schall thu know his nominatyff case?

16　The opening of a Middle English syntactic treatise from Trinity College, O.5.4 (s. xv), f. 4v.

By thys questyon 'Who or what?', as 'Who or whatt ys?', 'A cherche ys'.
A *cherche*: what case?
The nominatiff case.
Why so?
For he commyth byfore the verbe, et cetera.⁵

You can see how Leylond adopts very much a vernacular-based approach to teaching Latin: first he helps his pupils understand the structure of an English sentence (always using the concepts of Latin grammar), and then he gets them to move from the English nominative (the term *subject* was not widely used by grammarians until the eighteenth century) to the Latin nominative. He makes a swift transition from English examples to Latin ones, however, for his focus is on the syntactic peculiarities of Latin that are likely to trip up English schoolboys.

　These workmanlike little texts were widely used throughout the fifteenth century, and were repeatedly printed toward the end of the century. Part of the material they contained was incorporated into Lily's *Short Introduction of Grammar*, the standard grammar in England from the 1540s, to its transmutation into Kennedy's *Latin Primer* three hundred years later (see box 10.8, p. 238 below). Their importance is greater than might at first sight appear: as you will have noticed, the terminology they use is very similar to that of our traditional grammars today. By popularising this terminology at so early a date, they created a grammatical metalanguage for English long before other European languages possessed one. Because teachers drew upon Norman French for these terms (which come ultimately from Latin), they were able to create a series of lexical distinctions between the metalinguistic term and the corresponding term in the language of everyday use, something which is possible in few other European languages. A few examples:

time	tense
name	noun
word	verb

9.4 Reforming the orthography: the Old Icelandic *First Grammatical Treatise*

Iceland lay outside the mainstream of European intellectual life until relatively late in the Middle Ages. It had been settled by Vikings, roving sailor-adventurers mostly from Norway, from the end of the ninth century on. The Icelanders formally adopted Christianity as their religion in the year 1000. Iceland differed from most other parts of Europe in possessing a lively tradition of vernacular writing alongside a rather less well developed tradition of intellectual and religious writing in Latin, partly due to the more tolerant attitude of the Icelandic Church toward native traditions. Icelandic (this is the name which modern scholars now use for the language formerly called Old Norse) was used to record the lays and sagas in which their myths, legends and heroic deeds were celebrated; it was used (as was the case with all the German peoples) for their law code, which was read out annually to an assembly of all adult males, the Thing; and it was used for Christian literature, both translations from Latin and original writing. In the twelfth and thirteenth centuries Icelanders went to Paris to study at university and returned to head schools at home, bringing the latest works of continental scholarship with them; all in all, there seems to have been a fair amount of contact between Icelandic intellectuals and their continental counterparts from the twelfth century on.

The first grammatical work in Old Icelandic, a treatise on orthography known as the *First Grammatical Treatise*, dates from the middle third of the twelfth century (see box 9.1). In the preamble the unknown author remarks that each people records its history and laws in its own tongue; since languages have diverged from the original language, different letters are needed in each one. Hence, if one sets out to write one language using the letters of another, some letters will turn out to be unnecessary, but others will be missing. Nonetheless, he adds, the English write their own language with the Latin letters, just adding a few extras where the resources of Latin prove to be inadequate. (This is correct: the Old English alphabet is basically that of Latin but with three letters borrowed from the runic *futhark* to represent sounds which do not figure in the Latin alphabet: þ[θ], called *thorn*; ð[ð], called *eth*; and ƿ [w], called *wen*. In addition, the digraph æ was given a new phonetic value: [æ].) The First Grammarian announces that he has decided to adopt the same policy in devising a more appropriate alphabet for Old Icelandic, using Latin letters where possible, but dropping or adding them as necessary. This results in the loss of a few of the consonant symbols and in the addition

> **Box 9.1 Why 'First' Grammatical Treatise?**
>
> The *First Grammatical Treatise* is known to us from a manuscript copied around 1360 now kept in the Arnamagnæan collection in the Royal Library, Copenhagen, Cod, AM 242, otherwise known as the Codex Wormianus (so-called because it once belonged to the seventeenth-century Danish antiquary Ole Worm). The longest text in the manuscript is the *Prose Edda* by Snorri Sturlason, a sort of handbook for poets. It consists of three parts:
>
> - a collection of Norse myths;
> - definitions of poetic terminology with examples from myths and legends;
> - a long poem containing examples of over a hundred different verse forms.
>
> Although we think of the *Edda* today as an important source of Norse myths, Snorri saw it as a didactic work, and in fact it is accompanied in this manuscript by four other works of grammatical content:
>
> - an introduction pointing out how useful it is to be able to understand the works of earlier writers, and consequently how important the study of orthography is;
> 1. an orthographical treatise;
> 2. a treatise on the letters of the alphabet which attempts to classify them using diagrams of a sort normally found in works on musical theory;
> 3. a work which corresponds roughly to Book I and closely to Book III of Donatus's *Ars maior*, dealing with the *litterae* (including the Old Icelandic runes) and with the figures of speech, replacing Donatus's examples from the Latin poets with ones taken from Icelandic scaldic verse;
> 4. a miscellany based on Book III of the *Ars maior* and a rhetorical treatise covering figures of speech and rhetorical figures, again with many examples, this time from Icelandic Christian poets.
>
> Because these treatises lack titles, scholars nowadays refer to them by the order in which they occur in this manuscript as the *First Grammatical Treatise*, the *Second Grammatical Treatise*, and so on.

of a large number of new vowel symbols to represent the new sounds which arose in Old Icelandic from the various vowel mutations. This is how the First Grammarian explains his reasoning:

To the five vowels that already were in the Latin alphabet – a, e, i, o, u – I have added these four that are here written: ǫ, ę, ø, y. Ǫ gets its loop from *a* and its circle from *o*, since it is a blending of their two sounds, spoken with the mouth less open than for *a*, but more than for *o*. Ę is written with the loop of *a*, but with the full shape of *e*, since it is a blending of the two, spoken with the mouth less open than for *a*, but more than for *e*. Ø is made up from the sounds of *e* and *o*, spoken with the mouth less open than for *e* and more than for *o*, and therefore written with the cross-bar of *e* and the circle of *o*. Y is a single sound made up from the sounds of *i* and *u*, spoken with the mouth less open than for *i* and more than for *u*, so that it shall have the first branch of the capital U ...[6]

The First Grammarian works with a single feature: how open or closed does the mouth appear relative to a set of sounds he takes to be familiar to his readers? Other features – front/back, high/low, tense/lax – are ignored in favour of the one which is most easily checked by looking in a mirror. His descriptions are angled at justifying the *form* of the letter (its *figura*), in very much the same manner as Grosseteste and pseudo-Grosseteste adopted, as we saw in section 8.2 above. Later he goes on to answer an imaginary opponent, justifying the need for his new letters by demonstrating their phonemic status in a series of sentences:

A man inflicted one wound (*sar*) on me; I inflicted many wounds (*sǫr*) on him . . . The priest swore (*sor*) fair (*sør*) oaths only. . . . Sour (*sur*) are the eyes of the sow (*syr*), but better so than if they popped.

Minimal pairs exemplified in sentences where they are clearly distinguished by the semantic context was a technique in widespread use at the time in the teaching of Latin prosody, to exemplify long and short syllables in words that would otherwise be homonyms, as in Serlo of Wilton's *De differentiis*, written at about the same time.[7] The First Grammarian goes on to use the same technique in distinguishing a series of nasalised vowels, and then to make a further distinction between long and short nasal and non-nasal vowels, creating a vast number of vowel phonemes for Old Icelandic. In fact many of the distinctions he makes are believed by modern scholars to be sub-phonemic, although he justifies them by claiming that they change the meaning. When he has to use examples which cross word boundaries (only four times, though) one might well begin to wonder!

9.5 Thinking about the vernacular: the Occitan *Leys d'Amors*

In the central Middle Ages the south of France was a distinct country with its own king and court, its own cultural traditions and its own language, Occitan (sometimes called Provençal). Occitan was a Romance language spoken right along the Mediterranean coast and in Catalonia as well: medieval Catalan was to all intents and purposes the same language. Its literature begins around 1000 with translations from Latin. Soon, travelling minstrels, the troubadors, were making their way from castle to castle singing their love poetry in this beautiful language, introducing the ethos of courtly love into medieval Europe. This poetry was at its height in the eleventh and twelfth centuries. So too were the other branches of Occitan literature, from romances to mystery plays and treatises on every subject from medicine to cosmology. Even outside the Occitan linguistic area, in adjacent parts of France and even in Italy, Occitan literature was appreciated, and foreign poets too attempted to contribute to its riches. But in the twelfth century a catastrophe overtook this region. Many people in Provence had turned to a sect called the *Cathars* and adopted their beliefs. The king of France saw in this an opportunity to break the strength of the count of Toulouse, the most powerful ruler in the area, and launched a crusade against the Cathars in the name of Christianity, the Albigensian Crusade (named after the cathedral city of Albi, a Cathar stronghold). By early in the thirteenth century the power of the count of Toulouse was broken, and Provence was assimilated into the kingdom of France. During this troubled period many troubadors fled to Italy, inspiring an interest in their poetry amongst Italian rulers, some of whom became troubadors composing in Occitan in their own right – Terramagnino de Pisa, Lanfranc Cigala and Bonifacio Calvo of Genoa, and most famous of all, Sordello of Mantua.

One consequence of the adoption of Occitan by a number of Italian troubadors was a need for grammars and dictionaries for these non-native speakers. Several of the early works on Occitan were written in Italy – the *Donats Proençals* of Uc Faidit, a grammar of Occitan in both Occitan and Latin; a versified version of a treatise on poetics by Raimon Vidal, the *Razos de trobar*; and an Occitan–Italian glossary. Italians made a number of manuscript copies of Occitan grammars written in Provence and Catalonia as well.

Provence too came to feel the need for grammars and dictionaries, for in the aftermath of the Albigensian Crusade many people felt that poets weren't what they used to be. In an attempt to keep up standards an organisation by the name of Consistoire du Gai Savoir was founded (in 1323, still in existence) with the object of organising regular poetry contests. The judges soon realised that without rules or guidelines it was difficult to decide which was the best of the works performed, so they entrusted Guilhem Molinier and several colleagues (mostly Toulouse lawyers), with the task of composing a grammar. The result, a huge work called the *Leys d'Amors* ('Law of Love'), appeared in several versions between 1332 and 1356. It became the starting-point for several later grammarians of Occitan, especially in Catalonia. Let's look at the contents of one of the earlier versions:

> **Book I** sets out basic concepts and rules on orthography. Molinier goes right back to first principles. The three things necessary for writing a book, he declares, are the will, the knowledge and the ability. Then he explains the three reasons for writing this work:
>
> - to bring together and organise information that was previously scattered all over the place;
> - to make the art of composing troubador poetry accessible to all, where formerly it had been kept secret, and to reveal the essential rules and doctrines that the troubadors used but never made explicit;
> - to restrain crazy desires and dishonest actions on the part of lovers, and to teach them what sort of love they should practise. This moral motive – not usually made explicit in grammars! – arises out of the fourteenth-century striving to transform the ethos of courtly love into devotion to the Virgin Mary. Molinier then goes on to introduce the *litterae* of Occitan and phonological rules governing their use in verse, and explains the nature of syllables and accents.
>
> **Book II** presents the rules of versification, explaining the structure of lines, stanzas and poetic genres.
>
> **Book III** discusses the eight word classes of Occitan. Molinier clearly knew Priscian's *Institutiones grammaticae* thoroughly, and was also familiar with

the concepts of Speculative grammar, which by the middle of the fourteenth century were known to anyone who had followed the Arts course at university. Here and throughout the work he insists on the independence of Occitan: only the usage of Occitan can be definitive for Occitan, not the usage of Latin or any other language.

Book IV explains various barbarisms and solecisms, taking up not only the list in use ever since Donatus, but adding a number characteristic of troubador poetry, such as false rhyme and repeated rhyme.

Book V addresses the question of how one goes about versifying, taking up a statement – *mays dura anta que sofracha* 'shame lasts longer than suffering' – and showing how one might go about turning it into all kinds of different poetic forms, with helpful tips on traps to avoid.[8] He even gives tips on how to find a rhyme: supposing you want a word ending in -*ori*. You start off with *a_ori* and try out every letter in the blank: *abori, ablori, abrori, acori, aclori, acrori* . . . Out of this list only *acori* (a form of the verb *acorar*, 'to set one's heart upon something') is an Occitan word, so you'd press on with this technique until you arrived at something usable.

How does Molinier cope with features of Occitan which have no Latin equivalent? Let's look at how he handles the article.

Occitan, like other Romance languages, had developed both a definite and an indefinite article, which are lacking in Latin. Modern grammarians generally regard the article as a distinct word class, since it has distributional and inflectional properties which distinguish it from the members of other classes. But since he and his contemporaries *knew* that there were just eight word classes – the idea that one could add any new ones to that list did not occur to people until the sixteenth century – the option of setting up a ninth class was not available. Molinier arrived at his analysis by a different route. He studies Occitan nouns with care to discover whether they can be said to have declensions, like Latin nouns (remember box 4.10?). Concluding that the evidence is too slight – he finds that the sole case distinction of Occitan, +-s, does not occur universally – he argues that Occitan cannot be said to have declensions; but it does show case by means of markers, *habitutz*, placed *before* the word. From the examples he gives it is plain that he means the definite article, sometimes in combination with a preposition.

Realising that the definite article never occurs with proper nouns, Molinier decides to call it the *habitutz comuna*, the 'common article'. Is there a proper article corresponding to it? He points out, 'You can see quite well that when you say "Mr Garnier", "Mrs Gauceranda" (*En Garnier, Na Gauceranda*), this gives a certain degree of honour to the person, according to our way of speaking, which is lacking if we just say "Garnier" or "Gauceranda".' He concludes that *En, Na, An*, the Occitan equivalent of Mr and Mrs, is a kind of proper article, corresponding to the common article *lo/la*. (What word class would you assign Mr and Mrs to?) But a counter-example pops into his mind. What about an expression like this?

Vos, En Figuiers, ades seretz trencatz
You, Mr Fig-tree, are now going to be cut down[9] 'Fig-tree' is a common noun, and yet it here has the proper article En. Molinier's solution is to explain that in such cases the article is being used 'improperly' (*impropriamen*): 'every utterance which one addresses in the second person to an irrational thing, a thing lacking reason, is figurative and not used in its proper sense'. Like very many ancient, medieval and early modern grammarians, Molinier was fully aware of the difference between literal and figurative language use, and was alive to potential transgressions of grammatical rules arising from figurative usage.

The *Leys d'Amors* is of particular interest, not just as an early description of Old Occitan, but as one of the earliest examples of someone using the grammatical framework that had for centuries been applied to Latin to describe a vernacular, and doing so creatively and with a good deal of flexibility. Molinier never claims that the *formal* structure of Latin must be represented in or projected upon Occitan; he states outright, for example, that there are no declensions in Occitan to correspond to those of Latin. What he does take over from Latin grammar are the categories of what later came to be called 'general' or 'universal' or 'philosophical' grammar – the word classes, the functions of the cases, and categories such as mood, tense and voice. This attitude is characteristic of medieval grammarians of the vernacular. They take over only those categories which seem to them to suit their language and jettison the rest, rejoicing in the similarities but perfectly happy to admit that their language has no declensions or whatever it might be. Almost paradoxically, their assumptions about the status of Latin and the vernacular helped enormously. Knowing as they did that Latin, being one of the three sacred languages, was qualitatively different from any vernacular, they did not expect to be able to discover a vernacular analogue for every single phenomenon of Latin grammar. Interested only in arriving at a serviceable framework for describing the vernacular, they had no compunction about dropping what didn't suit them. They were completely free from any patriotic urge to force their language into the Latin mould. In this they could hardly be more different from Renaissance grammarians of the vernacular, as we shall see in chapter 10.

Further reading

Items which include an edition, and where possible a translation as well, of the original texts have been favoured over studies (and are indicated with an asterisk), although you will find some of both under each heading, as well as some background literature. More languages are represented here than it was possible to include in the discussion in chapter 9.

Old English

*Julius Zupitza, ed., *Aelfrics Grammatik und Glossar* (Berlin: Weidmann 1880, reprinted with introduction by H. Gneuss 1966).
*G. N. Garmonsway, *Ælfric's Colloquy* (London: Methuen 1947).

Vivien Law, 'Ælfric's Excerptiones de arte grammatica anglice', in her Grammar and Grammarians in the Early Middle Ages (London: Longman 1997), pp. 200–23, reprinted from Histoire Epistémologie Langage 9 (1987), 47–71.

Edna Rees Williams, 'Ælfric's grammatical terminology', Publications of the Modern Language Association of America 73 (1958), 453–62.

Helmut Gneuss, 'The study of language in Anglo-Saxon England', Bulletin of the John Rylands University Library of Manchester 72 (1990), 3–32, repr. in his Language and History in Early England (Aldershot: Variorum 1996), no. III.

Fabrizio Raschellà and Felicetta Ripa, 'Elfrico grammatico e l'insegnamento linguistico nell'Inghilterra anglosassone', Annali dell'Istituto Universitario Orientale di Napoli, sezione germanica 1, 1–2, n.s. (1991) 7–36.

Middle English

*David Thomson, ed., An Edition of the Middle English Grammatical Texts (New York and London: Garland 1984). [To sample a selection of the many texts printed in a large number of slightly different versions, you could start with the Introduction (pp. xi–xxiii) and then read Accedence Text A (pp. 1–8), Informacio Text U (pp. 93–103) and Formula Text AA (pp. 140–7), along with the commentary.]

*Cynthia R. Bland, The Teaching of Grammar in Late Medieval England: An Edition, with Commentary, of Oxford, Lincoln College MS Lat. 130 (East Lansing, MI: Colleagues Press 1991). [Edition of an version of the Accedence not known to Thomson and of a Regimina treatise.]

Nicholas Orme, English Schools in the Middle Ages (London: Methuen 1973), ch. 3.

Old Icelandic (Old Norse)

*Einar Haugen, ed. and transl., First Grammatical Treatise: The Earliest Germanic Phonology (London: Longman 1972).

*Hreinn Benediktsson, ed. and transl., The First Grammatical Treatise (Reykjavík: Institute of Nordic Linguistics 1972).

*Federico Albano Leoni, ed. and transl., Il primo trattato grammaticale islandese (Bologna: Il Mulino 1975).

*Fabrizio D. Raschellà, ed. and transl., The So-Called Second Grammatical Treatise: An Orthographic Pattern of Late Thirteenth-Century Icelandic (Florence: Le Monnier 1982).

*Björn M. Ólsen, Den tredje og fjærde grammatiske afhandling i Snorres Edda tilligemed de grammatiske afhandlingers prolog og to andre tillæg (Copenhagen: Knudtzon 1884). [Text of the Third and Fourth Grammatical Treatises.]

*Finnur Jónsson, Óláfr Þórðarson, Málhljóða- og Málskrúðsrit: grammatisk-retorisk afhandling, Det Kgl. Danske Videnskabernes Selskab, Historisk-filologiske Meddelelser 13,2 (Copenhagen: Bianco Lunos 1927). [Text of the Third Grammatical Treatise.]

F. D. Raschellà, 'Die altisländische grammatische Literatur: Forschungsstand und Perspektiven zukünftiger Untersuchungen', Göttingische Gelehrte Anzeigen 235 (1983), 271–315. [Includes a useful bibliography.]

Bjarne Ulvestad, 'Greinn sú er máli skiptir: tools and tradition in the *First Grammatical Treatise*', *Historiographia Linguistica* 3 (1976), 203–23. [Unleashed a controversy over whether the First Grammarian could in fact be regarded as 'the world's first phonologist'.]

Old and Middle Irish

*George Calder, ed. and transl., *Auraicept na n-Éces: The Scholars' Primer* (Edinburgh: Grant 1917).

*Anders Ahlqvist, ed. and transl., *The Early Irish Linguist: An Edition of the Canonical Part of the Auraicept na nÉces*, Commentationes Humanarum Litterarum 73 [1982] (Helsinki: Societas Scientiarum Fennica 1983).

*Lambert McKenna, *Bardic Syntactical Tracts* (Dublin: Dublin Institute for Advanced Studies 1944). [Text only.]

*Osborn Bergin, 'Irish grammatical tracts I–V', supplements to *Ériu* 8–10, 14, 17 (1916–55). [Text only.]

Brian Ó Cuív, 'Linguistic terminology in the mediaeval Irish bardic tracts', *Transactions of the Philological Society* (1965), 141–64.

B. Ó. Cuív, 'The linguistic training of the mediaeval Irish poet', *Celtica* 10 (1973), 114–40.

G. B. Adams, 'Grammatical analysis and terminology in the Irish bardic schools', *Folia Linguistica* 4 (1970), 157–66.

Medieval Welsh and Breton

*G. J. Williams and E. J. Jones, eds., *Gramadegau'r Penceirddiad* (Cardiff: Gwasg Prifysgol Cymru 1934).

A. T. E. Matonis, 'The Welsh bardic grammars and the Western grammatical tradition', *Modern Philology* 79 (1981), 121–45.

A. T. E. Matonis, 'Problems relating to the composition of the Welsh bardic grammars', in A. T. E. Matonis and Daniel F. Melia, eds., *Celtic Language, Celtic Culture. A Festschrift for Eric P. Hamp* (Van Nuys, CA: Ford & Bailie 1990), pp. 273–91.

Ceri W. Lewis, 'Einion Offeiriad and the bardic grammar', in A. O. H. Jarman and G. R. Hughes, ed., *A Guide to Welsh Literature 1282–c. 1550*, vol. 2 (Cardiff: University of Wales 1997), ch. 3.

*Gwenaël Le Duc, 'Le Donoet, grammaire latine en moyen-breton', *Etudes Celtiques* 14 (1974–5), 525–65 and 16 (1979), 237–59.

Louis Lemoine, 'Les méthodes d'enseignement dans la Bretagne du haut Moyen Age d'après les manuscrits bretons: l'exemple du Paris, B.N., Lat. 10290', in *Landévennec et le monachisme breton dans le haut Moyen Age* (Landévennec: Association Landévennec 1986), pp. 45–63.

Medieval French

*Thomas Städtler, *Zu den Anfängen der französischen Grammatiksprache* (Beihefte zur Zeitschrift für romanische Philologie 223, Tübingen: Niemeyer 1988). [Includes editions of a number of texts.]

*B. Merrilees, 'Donatus and the teaching of French in medieval England', in Ian Short, ed., *Anglo-Norman Anniversary Essays* (London: Anglo-Norman Text Society 1993), pp. 273–91.

*B. Merrilees and Ann Dalzell, 'L'Art mineur de Vatican, Bibliotheca Apostolica Vaticana Vat. lat. MS 1479', *Archives et Documents*, 2nd ser., 4 (1990), 45–52.

*B. Merrilees and B. Sitarz-Fitzpatrick, *Liber Donati: A Fifteenth-Century Manual of French* (London: Anglo-Norman Text Society 1993).

*Maria Colombo, 'L'Art mineur de Paris, B.N. n.a.f. 4690', *Archives et Documents*, 2nd ser., 4 (1990), 13–26.

*M. Colombo, *Un rifacimento antico-francese dell'Ars minor di Donato: il manoscritto Parigi BN lat. 14095*, Memorie, Classe di Lettere, Scienze Morali e Storiche, Istituto Lombardo 39.1 (Milan: Istituto Lombardo Accademia di Scienze e Lettere 1988).

*Maria Colombo Timelli, 'Il rifacimento dell'Ars minor di Donato del ms. Parigi B.N. n.a.f. 1120. Introduzione ed edizione', *Annali dell'Istituto Universitario Orientale di Napoli, sezione romanza* 22 (1990), 5–27.

*Maria Colombo Timelli, *Traductions françaises de l'Ars minor de Donat au Moyen Age (XIIIe-XVe siècles)* (Florence: La Nuova Italia 1996).

*Pierre Swiggers, 'Le Donait françois: la plus ancienne grammaire du français', *Revue des Langues Romanes* 89 (1985), 235–51.

Serge Lusignan, *Parler vulgairement: les intellectuels et la langue française aux XIIIe et XIVe siècles* (Paris: Vrin 1986). [Socio-cultural background.]

Douglas Kibbee, *For to Speke Frenche Trewely. The French Language in England, 1000–1600: Its Status, Description and Instruction*, Studies in the History of the Language Sciences 60 (Amsterdam: John Benjamins 1991).

Brian Merrilees, 'Teaching Latin in French: adaptations of Donatus' Ars minor', *Fifteenth-Century Studies* 12 (1987), 87–98.

B. Merrilees, 'L'Art mineur français et le curriculum grammatical', *Histoire Epistémologie Langage* 12 (1990), 15–29. [Assigns the eight extant versions to distinct places in the grammatical curriculum.]

Pierre Swiggers, 'La plus ancienne grammaire du français', *Medioevo Romanzo* 9 (1984), 183–8.

William Rothwell, 'The teaching of French in medieval England', *Modern Language Review* 63 (1968), 37–46.

Occitan (Old Provençal) and Catalan

*J. H. Marshall, *The Donatz Proensals of Uc Faidit* (London: Oxford University Press 1969).

*A. F. Gatien-Arnoult, ed. and transl., *Las Flors del Gay Saber, estier dichas Las Leys d'Amors*, 3 vols. (Paris: Silvestre n.d.; Toulouse: Bon et Privat n.d.; Toulouse: Paya 1841–3).

*Joseph Anglade, ed., *Las Leys d'Amors*, 4 vols. (Toulouse: Privat 1919/20).

*José María Casas Homs, ed., 'Torcimany' de Luis de Averçó: Tratado retórico gramatical y diccionario de rimas, siglos XIV–XV, 2 vols. (Barcelona: Consejo Superior de Investigaciones Científicas, Sección de Literatura Catalana 1956).

Brigitte Schlieben-Lange, 'Okzitanisch: Grammatikographie und Lexikographie', in Günter Holtus, Michael Metzeltin, Christian Schmitt, ed., *Lexikon der Romanistischen Linguistik*

(LRL) 5,2 (Tübingen: Niemeyer 1991), pp. 105–26. [Useful description of the eight principal medieval Occitan/Catalan grammatical texts with comprehensive bibliography.]

Pierre Swiggers, 'Les plus anciennes grammaires occitanes: tradition, variation et insertion culturelle', in Gérard Gouiran, ed., *Contacts de langues, de civilisations et intertextualité* 1 (Montpellier: Centre d'Etudes Occitanes de l'Université de Montpellier et la SFAIEO. 1992), pp. 131–48.

Spanish

Emilio Ridruejo, 'Notas romances en gramáticas latino-españolas del siglo XV', *Revista de Filología Española* 59 (1977), 47–80. [Evidence for Spanish vernacular grammatical terminology before Nebrija.]

Hans-Josef Niederehe, 'El castellano y la gramática, objetos de estudio antes de la gramática de Nebrija', in Manuel Alvar, ed., *Estudios Nebrisenses* (Madrid: Ediciones de Cultura Hispánica 1992), pp. 97–110.

Italian

*Giovanni Farris, *Frammenti di grammatica medievale latino-volgare* (Savona: Sabatelli 1975).

For references to older editions of the Italian material, published in Italian journals between 1905 and 1921, see Städtler (French section above) p. 62 n. 35.

Middle and Early New High German

*Johannes Müller, *Quellenschriften und Geschichte des deutschsprachlichen Unterrichtes bis zur Mitte des 16. Jahrhunderts* (Gotha: Thienemann 1882, repr. Hildesheim: Olms 1969). [Includes an edition of the Old High German grammatical glosses and a Middle High German version of the *Ars minor* along with much sixteenth-century material.]

*Erika Ising, *Die Anfänge der volkssprachlichen Grammatik in Deutschland und Böhmen* I. *Quellen.* (Berlin: Akademie-Verlag 1966). [Includes a German version of the *Ars minor* from 1473.]

E. Ising, *Die Herausbildung der Grammatik der Volkssprachen in Mittel- und Osteuropa* (Berlin: Akademie-Verlag 1970), esp. pp. 31–51.

Heinrich Weber, 'Die Ausbildung der deutschen Grammatik (einschliesslich der niederländischen)', *Histoire, Epistémologie, Langage* 9 (1987), 111–33.

Nikolaus Henkel, 'Mittelalterliche Übersetzungen lateinischer Schultexte ins Deutsche. Beobachtungen zum Verhältnis von Formtyp und Leistung', in V. Honemann, K. Ruh, B. Schnell and W. Wegstein, eds., *Poesie und Gebrauchsliteratur im deutschen Mittelalter* (Tübingen: Max Niemeyer 1979), pp. 164–80.

Hansjürgen Kiepe, 'Die älteste deutsche Fibel. Leseunterricht und deutsche Grammatik um 1486', in Bernd Moeller, Hans Patze and Karl Stackmann, eds., *Studien zum städtischen Bildungswesen des späten Mittelalters und der frühen Neuzeit*, Abhandlungen der Akademie der Wissenschaften in Göttingen, philologisch-historische Klasse, 3rd ser., 137 (Göttingen: Vandenhoeck & Ruprecht 1983), pp. 453–61.

Old Church Slavonic and Medieval Russian

*V. Jagić, Codex Slovenicus rerum grammaticarum, Slavische Propyläen 25 (Berlin 1896, repr. Munich: Fink 1968). [Pp. 40–6 contain a short text in Old Church Slavonic, *On the eight parts of speech*. The introduction to the volume is in Russian apart from a brief preface in Latin.]

Dean S. Worth, *The Origins of Russian Grammar. Notes on the State of Russian Philology before the Advent of Printed Grammars* (Columbus, Ohio: Slavica 1983). [Pp. 14–21 discuss the Old Church Slavonic text printed by Jagić.]

10 The Renaissance: discovery of the outer world

10.1 Turning-points in the history of linguistics

There are two turning-points in western intellectual history, two brief periods when people's way of looking at the world changed fundamentally. The first was the Golden Age of ancient Greece, the era of Socrates, Plato and Aristotle, when people for the first time realised that they were free to use and develop the intellect, no longer constrained by the dictates of the gods. For nearly two thousand years – the span of time we know as Classical Antiquity and the Middle Ages – western scholars worked through the fruits of that extraordinarily fertile epoch, recasting Greek and Roman teachings on language and accommodating them to the altered needs of a Christian world and a Latin-based culture. Whenever there was an impetus for change during this lengthy period it came from one of two sources: the rediscovery of Greek ideas or an immediate practical need. No major new ideas came to ancient or medieval western linguistics from any other source.

During the brief period we know as the Renaissance – approximately 1450 to 1600 – all this changed. As in ancient Greece, the driving force was not an external event, but rather an inner one, a shift in people's perception of and response to the world. To understand this we need to think once more about the nature of knowledge. People always try to acquire knowledge which they consider to be both true and worthwhile; that basic urge never changes. What has changed repeatedly in the course of history is the kind of knowledge which satisfies those criteria. During the Middle Ages writers stressed the importance of the universal, transcendental and spiritual; preachers exhorted their congregations to shun earthly things and open their *oculi mentis*, their mind's eye, or their *oculi cordis*, the eyes of the heart, to spiritual truth. And this message came from people who in their time were the leaders of intellectual life – by no means social outcasts or academic misfits. Consequently, medieval scholars devoted much of their energy to universal aspects of language. Where people did concern themselves with a particular language, this arose out of an immediate need, such as the Church's

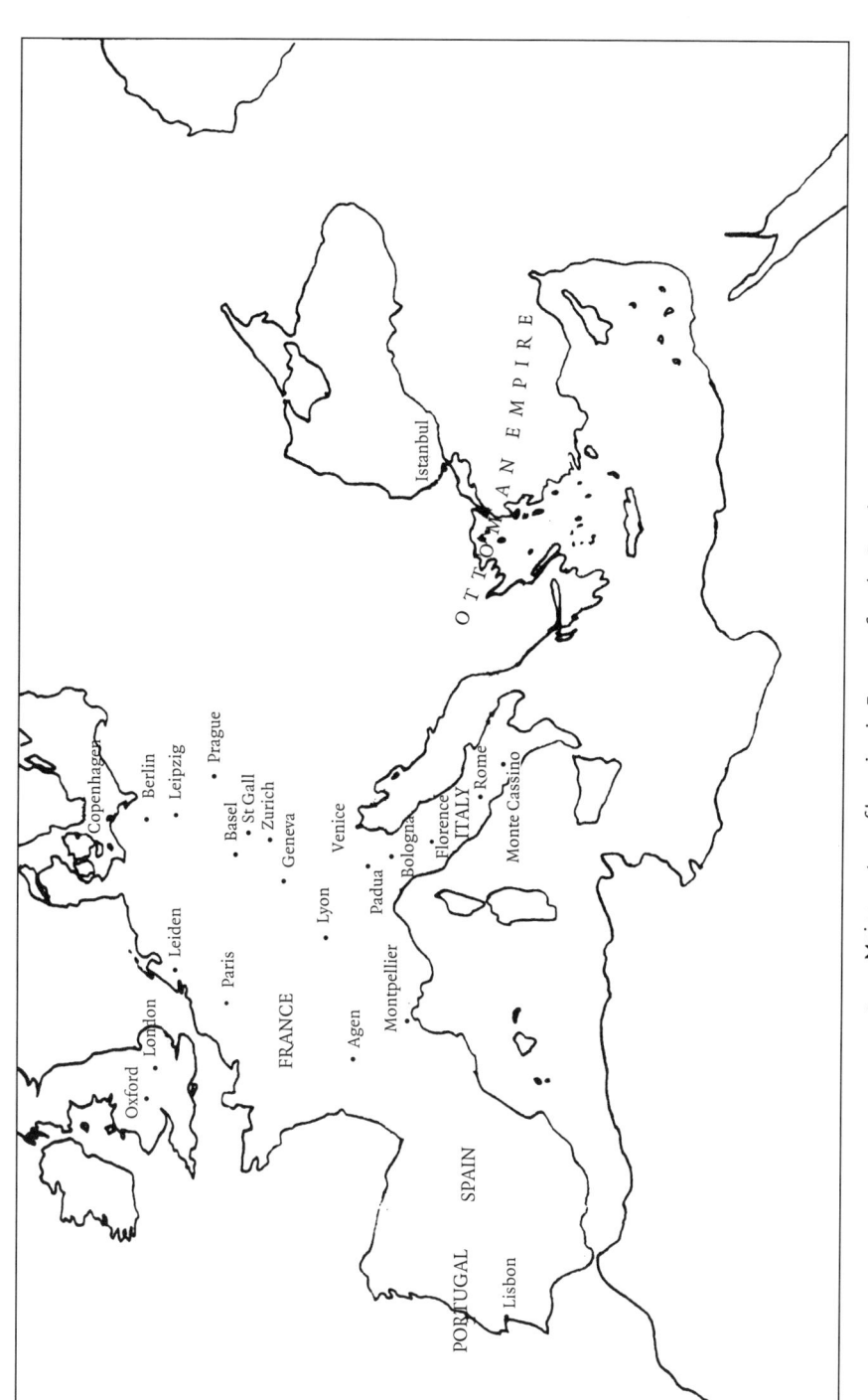

4 Major centres of learning in Europe after the Renaissance

17 Luca della Robbia's portrayal of Grammar, one of the Liberal Arts represented on the bell tower of the Duomo in Florence (1437). This scene of a Humanist with two pupils is a far cry from the allegorical figure of Grammar at Chartres cathedral (fig. 11).

insatiable need for people competent in Latin. Such needs bore much the same relationship to the intellectual mainstream of the day as technology does (or did in the past) to science.

10.2 Focus on the material world: training the faculty of observation

Roughly in the middle of the fifteenth century (although you can see signs of this a good two hundred years earlier) a far-reaching change took place. The western European

10.2 Focus on the material world

18　Artists drawing from life to prepare the illustrations for a book on plants, Leonhard Fuchs's *De historia stirpium* (Basel, 1542).

attitude to the outer world was transformed. Interest shifted from the universal and transcendental to the particular, visible, material phenomena all around us. Whereas the details of the material world had previously seemed ephemeral and unimportant, now they took on the tantalizing allure of the unknown. Previously, convinced that life on Earth was a punishment rather than an opportunity, Europeans had done their best to ignore the most earthly parts of it; but once that attitude changed, they wanted to get to grips with the material in every conceivable way: by sketching and sculpting it, by weighing it and measuring it, by collecting it, by classifying it, by exploiting it and manipulating it to suit their needs and desires. You can see the consequences in every area of intellectual, cultural and economic life.

This shift in inner attitude to the material world was coupled with a growing ability to turn the focus of attention outwards so as to concentrate on observing visible, tangible phenomena. Of course people had been able to observe the outer world long before, but it was not an activity which had struck them as particularly interesting or worthwhile. Pure intellectual activity with the minimum of input from sense-observation was more highly prized. As a representative of the old mentality, the highly developed intellectuality of the medieval philosopher, think of today's stereotypical mathematician, so absorbed in his complex mental edifice of theorems and equations that he fails to notice that the bus he was waiting for has come and gone; and contrast that with the nowadays much commoner mindset of the engineer, photographer, biologist or historian, all of them eager to observe outer phenomena with the same painstaking devotion that the mathematician lavishes upon his inner constructs. That is the essential difference between the medieval relationship to the outward appearance of earthly phenomena, and the Renaissance one: in medieval terms, it is the difference between observing with

> **Box 10.1 Opening windows onto the world**
>
> In art, for example, if you compare the Annunciation by Botticelli (p. 217) with a scene from a French manuscript from around 1300, you will see that in the medieval scene everything is highly stylised. The trees – direct descendants of those in Roman manuscripts of a thousand years earlier – are unlike any existing species; the draperies, postures and expressions of the human figures are conventional; and the backdrop is not a landscape but a pattern suggesting the harmony of the cosmic spheres. In other words, although the scene depicted is an earthly one, it is not a *particular* earthly one. No specific setting is depicted; rather, the stylised figures and trees represent the Tree, the Human Being, as universal types. In the fifteenth century windows start to open, almost literally, on the outer world. In Annunciations a window in the back wall opens onto the world beyond – a winding river, low hills, a solitary poplar – still remote and ethereal, but hinting at a particular earthly landscape. Simultaneously we find the beginnings of portraiture, with painters trying to catch the essence of the character revealed in a particular face. The first dated landscape is a sketch by Leonardo drawn on 15 August 1473. This new-found ability to observe the external world pervades Renaissance art. Artists begin to draw from life rather than from a mental image of the inner nature of the world. Perhaps the most striking case was when Albrecht Dürer placed a chunk of turf on his table and painstakingly represented every last blade of grass, in a work of meticulous craftsmanship.
>
> *Reading*
> M. Baxandall, *Painting and Experience in Fifteenth-Century Italy* (Oxford: Oxford University Press 1972).
> G. Richter, *Art and Human Consciousness* (Edinburgh: Floris Books and Spring Valley, NY: Anthroposophic 1985), ch. 7.

the *oculi mentis*, the mind's eye, and the *oculi carnis*, the ordinary eyes of the body (see box 10.1). Previously the only valid route to knowledge, the cultivation of the *oculi mentis* now seemed far less exciting than training the faculty of observation (see box 10.2). Even the titles of books reflected the new preoccupation: books called *Observationes in . . .*, 'Observations on' this and that, poured from the presses, a title unheard of in the Middle Ages.

Now that material things were regarded as interesting and important in their own right, it made sense to collect them. In the 1530s botanical gardens were founded in Padua and Bologna, and later in Florence, Paris, Montpellier and Leiden; and people began to compile collections of pressed flowers – a very simple process, but no one had seen the point of it before. Travellers brought back specimens of exotic flora and detailed drawings of the animals, flowers and trees of increasingly remote parts of the world. For that same new-found interest in the outer world, seasoned with a strong admixture of desire for economic advantage, led European monarchs to support voyages of exploration: southward along the west coast of Africa, round the Cape of Good Hope,

> **Box 10.2 Observation and the artist: Claude Lorrain (1600–82)**
>
> Nowadays we assume that landscape artists will take their easels outside to the valley they mean to paint, or (less satisfactorily) work from photos; either way, they are working from observation. But even well into the seventeenth century this wasn't taken for granted. The German artist and biographer Joachim von Sandrart describes the working habits of one of the greatest landscape painters ever, Claude Lorrain, like this:
>
> In his earnest striving to master this art he tried to get at Nature in every possible way. He lay stretched out in the fields before daybreak and past nightfall in order to work out how to represent the red sky of dawn, sunrise and sunset, and the twilight hours utterly naturally. When he had observed this thoroughly in the open air, he at once mixed his colours appropriately and then rushed home and applied himself to the painting he was working on with far greater fidelity to Nature than anyone before him had achieved. He practised this arduous and austere mode of study for many years, making the long trek out into the countryside and back every day, until one day he ran into me in Tivoli as I worked by the wild cliffs next to the famous waterfall, paintbrush in hand, and saw that I was painting from life right on the spot, making lots of paintings directly from Nature and not from my imagination or fantasy. This appealed to him so much that he enthusiastically adopted the same working method.
>
> Despite Sandrart's claim, no painting by Claude made directly from nature survives. Claude continued to paint imaginary landscapes peopled with mythological figures, using the landscape as a backdrop to scenes of universal significance, rather than depicting the scenes of everyday life that were so dear to many of his Dutch contemporaries, such as Frans Hals.
>
> *Reading*
>
> Joachim von Sandrart, *Academie der Bau-, Bild- und Mahlerey-Künste von 1675*, ed. A. R. Peltzer (Munich: Hirth 1925).
> Humphrey Wine, *Claude: The Poetic Landscape* (London: National Gallery Publications 1994).
> Helen Langdon, *Claude Lorrain* (Oxford: Phaidon 1989).

up the coast of East Africa and along the southern shores of Arabia, across to India, southeast Asia, and the Far East. Simultaneously they travelled westward across the Atlantic, along the eastern seaboard of North and South America, and gradually venturing inland. Unfamiliar animals crossed the oceans too: the much-travelled rhinoceros of which Dürer made his celebrated engraving was a present from the sultan of Gujarat to King Manuel II of Portugal, who, on discovering that it was as difficult to feed as the celebrated white elephant of Siam, sent it on to the pope. Royal menageries, filled initially with unusual gifts from explorers and potentates, grew gradually into our modern zoos. The artefacts with which explorers tried to impress their royal patrons,

19   Scene from a French manuscript ca 1300.

from narwhal tusks (often thought to be unicorn horns) to wampum pouches, were assembled in cabinets of curiosities, the ancestors of today's museums.

Those same explorers who were returning with sketches of exotic beasts and seeds of unknown plants were also coming into contact with people; and they had the same practical problem every traveller has of trying to communicate with people without a common language. There were various ways of getting around this, and indeed some travellers wrote descriptions of some quite elaborate exchanges that were conducted entirely through sign language (see box 10.3). A number of explorers and traders tried to progress beyond this level, compiling rudimentary phrasebooks and vocabulary lists. Missionaries often went further, learning enough of the language to communicate their spiritual message, sometimes with the aid of a native assistant, sometimes directly and through translations of the Gospels. Often missionary phrasebooks and grammars belong to the 'technology' side of linguistics; they respond to an immediate practical

10.2 Focus on the material world

20 Sandro Botticelli, *Annunciation*.

need and were compiled without much thought for theoretical principles (see box 10.4). But sixteenth-century scholars at home in their studies took a different kind of interest in all these new and 'exotic' languages of which reports were gradually drifting back to Europe. Some of them systematically began to collect specimens of every known language. What constituted a 'specimen' of a language? The answer was easy: the Lord's Prayer (called *Paternoster*, 'Our Father', in Latin). A short text fundamental to Christianity, it was often the very first thing to be translated. One scholar after another published anthologies of the Lord's Prayer in as many languages as possible, enabling

> **Box 10.3 Becoming aware of non-verbal communication: an explorer describes a sign-language encounter**
>
> When Europeans travelled beyond the confines of their own continent they rapidly discovered that the *tres linguae sacrae* did not after all hold sway throughout the world, as they had believed. Equally fast, however, they began to experience the human capacity for coming to an understanding regardless – or equally, for arriving at tragic misunderstandings. This is how the Portuguese explorer Pêro Vaz de Caminha describes an encounter between Captain Pedro Alvares Cabral and some Brazilians in 1500:
>
> When they saw him, the captain was sitting on a throne with a carpet spread out as a dais, well dressed, with a huge gold necklace on his chest . . .
> They lit torches and went in with no hint of politeness, addressing neither the captain nor anyone else. But one of them caught sight of the captain's necklace and began to make gestures, pointing with his hand at the ground and then at the necklace, as if to tell us that there was gold in the ground; and then he saw a silver candlestick, and again gestured toward the earth, as if there was also silver there. . . Then he saw one of a number of white beads from a rosary . . . and he gestured at the ground and then at the beads and at the captain's necklace, as if to indicate that they would give gold in exchange.

us to chart the expansion of European linguistic awareness:

- 1555 Conrad Gesner, *Mithridates*: 22 languages, including Armenian, Ethiopic, Polish, Hungarian, Welsh, Icelandic and two dialects of Sard.
- 1593 Jerome Megiser, *Specimen quadraginta diversarum atque inter se differentium linguarum ac dialectorum*: 40 languages, including Lapp, Turkish, Tatar, Chinese and a language of the Americas.
- 1680 Andreas Muller, *Orationis Dominicae versiones ferme centum*: around 90 languages, including Breton, Basque, Georgian, Malay, Malagasy, 'Angolan', 'Mexican', Poconchi, 'Virginian', and a comparative table of the words for 'father' in all the languages represented.
- 1715 John Chamberlayne, *Oratio Dominica in diversas omnium fere gentium linguas versa et propriis cuiusque linguae characteribus expressa*: ca 150 languages, including Manx, Cornish, Albanian, Guaraní, Tungus, Bengali, Singhalese, Thai, Javanese, and comparative tables of the words for 'father', 'heaven', 'earth' and 'bread' in all the languages represented.
- 1787 Lorenzo Hervás y Panduro, *Saggio pratico delle lingue (Idea dell' Universo, vol. 21)*: 300+ languages, including 'Hottentot', Telugu, Ostiak, Yakut, Permian, Cheremis, Kamchatka, Vietnamese, various dialects of Malay, Tibetan, Kurdish, and 55 languages of the Americas.
- 1806–17 J. Adelung and J. Vater, *Mithridates oder allgemeine Sprachkunde mit dem Vater Unser als Sprachprobe in bey nahe fünfhundert Sprachen und Mundarten* (4 vols.): 500 languages, including Berber, Ossetic, Ingush and a vast range of others. Uses specimens from a wide range of texts, not just the Lord's Prayer.

Box 10.4 Early European grammars of non-European languages

Arabic: 1505, by Pedro de Alcalá, in Granada.
Ge'ez (Ethiopic): 1552, by Mariano Vittorio da Rieti.
Tarascan (spoken on the coast of the Gulf of Mexico): 1558, by Maturino Gilberti, a Franciscan missionary from Toulouse, in Mexico City.
Quechua: 1560, by the Spaniard Domingo de Santo Tomás.
Tupi (the language most widely used along the Brazilian coast): 1595, by the Portuguese Jesuit Joseph de Anchieta, in Coimbra.
Japanese: 1604, by the Portuguese Jesuit interpreter João Rodrigues, in Nagasaki.
Tagalog: 1610, by Francisco de San José.
Malay: 1612, by Albert Corneliszoon Ruyl, in Amsterdam.
Turkish: 1612, by the adventurer and language-collector Jerome Megiser, in Leipzig.
Persian: 1639, by Ludovicus de Dieu, in Leiden.
Guaraní: 1640, by Antonio Ruyz de Montoya, in Madrid.
Vietnamese: 1651, by Alexandre de Rhodes, in Rome.
Kongo: 1659, by Giacinto Brusciotto, in Rome.
Massachusett: 1666, by the English preacher and missionary John Eliot, in Cambridge, Massachusetts.
Georgian: 1670, by the Italian missionary Francisco-Maria Maggio, in Rome.
Chinese: 1703, by the Spanish Dominican missionary Francisco Varo, in Canton (Guangzhou).
Urdu: 1741, by B. Schulzius, in Madras, printed at Halle in 1745.
Inuit (Greenlandic): 1760, by the Danish missionary Paul Egede.
a Creole (Virgin Islands Creole Dutch [Negerhollands]): 1770, by Jochum Magens, in Copenhagen.
Bengali: 1778, by Nathaniel Brassey Halhed, in Hoogly, Bengal.
Kurdish: 1787, by Maurizio Garzoni, an Italian Jesuit missionary, in Rome.
Maori: 1820, by Thomas Kendall, an English missionary, in London.
Cree: 1844, by Joseph Howse, an employee of the Hudson's Bay Company, in London.
Saramaccan: 1844, by A. Helwig van der Vegt, in Amsterdam.

Many of these grammars were written by missionaries, particularly by those belonging to the Society of Jesus (Jesuits). The Congregation for the Propagation of the Faith (Sacra Congregatio de Propaganda Fide), founded in 1622 by Pope Gregory XV, oversaw a college where both Europeans and people from other continents could be trained as Roman Catholic missionaries, and ran a printing press with an unrivalled range of non-European types which printed a large number of brief introductions to various languages in areas where missionaries were active. Grammars published outside Europe tended to have little impact on linguistic thinking in Europe itself, for until the early nineteenth century copies rarely found their way back.

> *Reading*
> Even Hovdhaugen, ed., '... and the word was God': Missionary Linguistics and Missionary Grammar (Münster: Nodus 1996).
> Victor Hanzeli, Missionary Linguistics in New France (The Hague: Mouton 1969).
> Elke Nowak, ed., Languages Different in all their Sounds ... Descriptive Approaches to the Languages of the Americas 1500 to 1850 (Münster: Nodus 1999).
> Rüdiger Schreyer, The European Discovery of Chinese (1550–1615) or The Mystery of Chinese Unveiled, Cahiers voor Taalkunde 5 (Amsterdam: Stichting Neerlandistiek VU 1992). [Describes the experiences of European missionaries trying to learn Chinese and their impressions of the writing system, translating entertaining passages from the sources.]

10.3 The scientific mentality: collectors and dissectors

The faith in observation led not only to all the phenomena we have just considered, but also to the rise of empiricism. The particular kind of knowledge acquired through observation conjoined with experimentation – empirical knowledge – gradually usurped the word which had originally meant knowledge of any kind: *science*. (The Latin word *scientia* meant 'knowledge' as opposed to 'wisdom', *sapientia*; in many European languages the equivalent word – *scienza*, *Wissenschaft*, наука and so on – still means 'knowledge' in general.) From the sixteenth century on, many aspects of language developed in parallel with the corresponding aspects of the sciences. Indeed, during that century, and to some extent later on, the same individuals were involved in developing both linguistics and science. Many men of an empirical turn of mind took up medicine, that being the university discipline which offered the most opportunities to train the faculty of observation. (Natural science did not become a degree subject in its own right until the nineteenth century.) A number of them – several trained at Padua, the foremost centre in Europe for anatomy and surgery in the sixteenth century – went on to write influential works on language:

- Thomas Linacre (1460–1524). Studied medicine at Padua and became royal physician to Henry VIII. Author of *De emendata structura latini sermonis* ('The correct structure of the Latin language', London 1524), a treatise on Latin syntax intended to provide an accurate and detailed account illustrated with a very large number of examples from classical literature.
- Jacques Dubois (Jacobus Sylvius, 1478–1555). Trained in medicine at Paris and Montpellier and taught Andreas Vesalius, later professor of anatomy at Padua and the most famous of all Renaissance anatomists. Author of *In linguam gallicam isagωge* ('Introduction to the French language', Paris 1531), the first grammar of French by a Frenchman, and the first grammar to try to demonstrate the connection between French and Latin.
- Julius Caesar Scaliger (1484–1558). Studied medicine at Padua and practised at Agen, southwestern France. Author of *De causis linguae latinae* ('The principles of the Latin language', Lyon 1540), a vigorous critique of the mistaken analyses

10.3 The scientific mentality

THRESOR DE L'HISTOIRE DES LANGVES DE CEST VNIVERS,

Contenant les Origines, Beautez, Perfections, Decadences, Mutations, Changements, Conuersions, & Ruines des Langues

Hebraique,	Nubienne,	Bohemienne,	Botnienne,
Chananeenne,	Abyssine,	Hongroise,	Biarmienne,
Samaritaine	Grecque,	Polonoise,	Angloise,
Chaldaique,	Armenienne,	Prussienne,	Indiéne Oriëtale,
Syriaque,	Seruiane,	Pomeranienne,	Chinoise,
Egyptienne,	Esclauonne,	Lithuanienne,	Iapanoise
Penique,	Georgiane,	Vualachienne,	Iauienne,
Arabique,	Iacobite,	Liuonienne,	IndienneOcciden-
Sarrasine,	Cophtite,	Rusienne,	tale,
Turquesque,	Hetrurienne,	Moschouitique	Guineanenouuelle
Persane,	Latine,	Gothique,	Indienne des Ter-
Tartaresque,	Italienne,	Nortmande,	res neufues, &c.
Africaine,	Cathalane,	Francique,	Les langues des A-
Moresque,	Hespagnole,	Finnonienne,	nimaux & Oi-
Ethiopienne,	Alemande,	Lapponienne,	seaux.

PAR M. CLAVDE DVRET BOVRBONNOIS, PRESIDENT A MOVLINS.

Nous auons adiousté DEVX INDICES: *L'vn des Chapitres: L'autre des principales matieres de tout ce Thresor.*

SECONDE EDITION.

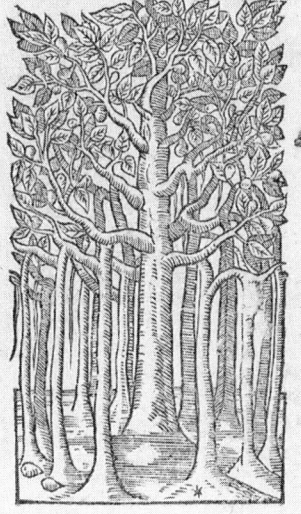

A YVERDON,
De l'Imprimerie de la Societé HELVETIALE CALDORESQVE.
M. DC. XIX.

21 The title page of Claude Duret's *Thresor* gives a vivid idea of the range of languages already known about by 1619, when this edition came out.

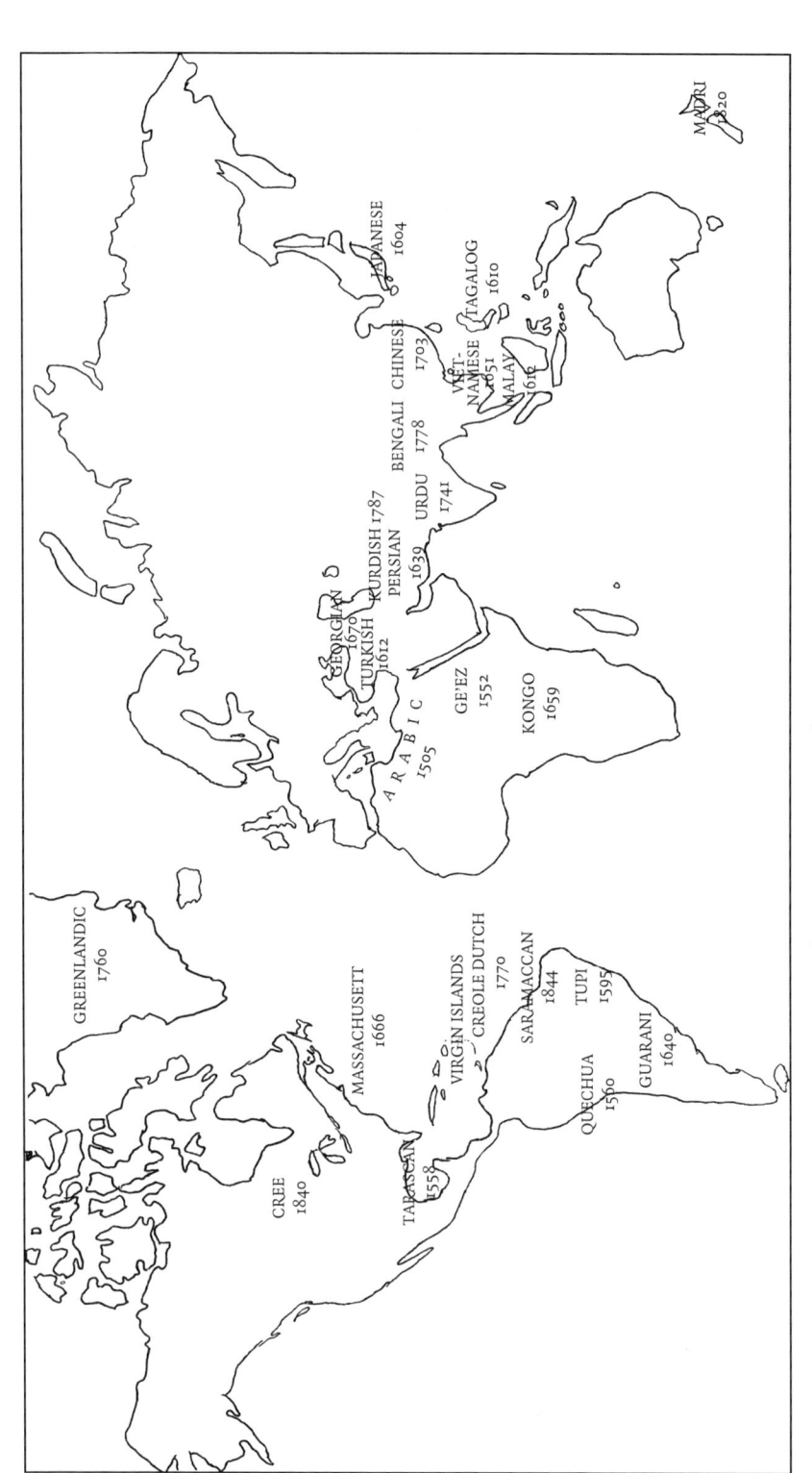

5 Early European grammars of non-European languages

of previous grammarians, with systematic application of the Aristotelian four causes to language in order to show that it is a natural phenomenon governed by natural laws, rightly a branch of philosophy (the study of rule-governed phenomena) rather than an arbitrary art. One of the first works to include a substantial treatment of phonetics.

- Conrad Gesner (1516–65). Trained in medicine at Montpellier and Basel. Author of encyclopedias of animals, plants, fossils, rocks and minerals, and languages. His *Mithridates: de differentiis linguarum tum veterum tum quae hodie apud diversas nationes in toto orbe terrarum in usu sunt* ('Mithridates: the individual characteristics of languages both ancient and modern in use today amongst the various peoples across the globe', Zurich 1555) includes alphabetically organised entries on every language then known, recording who spoke the language and where with (wherever possible) a brief account of its external history or a short word-list. A fold-out table presents the Lord's Prayer in twenty-two languages.

- Hieronymus Fabricius ab Aquapendente (Girolamo Fabrici d'Acquapendente, ca 1533–1619). Professor of anatomy at Padua, building the anatomy theatre that can still be visited there and teaching (amongst others) William Harvey, who later worked out how the blood circulates. Author of three treatises on speech:

    De voce ('The voice', 1600), a detailed anatomical description of the vocal tract and its function;

    De locutione et eius instrumentis ('Speech and the organs of speech', 1603), an account of phonetics based heavily on the writings of Aristotle and other ancient scholars;

    De brutorum loquela ('Animal communication', 1603), an investigation of the nature of animal communication, comparing it with human speech.

Thus, these medically trained writers on language were amongst the first to broach a new series of questions: how can the newly developed empirical methodology best be applied to language? What kind of problems can it help to solve? Just what belongs to the domain of linguistics? What counts as language? To what extent is language a physical phenomenon governed by the laws of nature? Is it a uniquely human phenomenon? How many languages are there, and how do they differ? These questions, matters of urgent concern to Renaissance linguists, are no less important for us today.

10.4 The rediscovery of Classical Latin

When people think of the Italian Renaissance, they usually think first of its backward-looking aspect, the rediscovery of Classical Antiquity. This too is permeated through and through with the ever more disciplined use of observation, this time directed at the past. Scholars, artists, architects, and even popes and statesmen were seized with a desire to recreate the excitement, the creativity, the refinement and perfection which they saw in all aspects of ancient Greek and Roman civilisation. Lawyers re-examined the canonical texts of Roman law to discover their significance at the time they were written; pedagogues sought to reform education along the lines laid down by

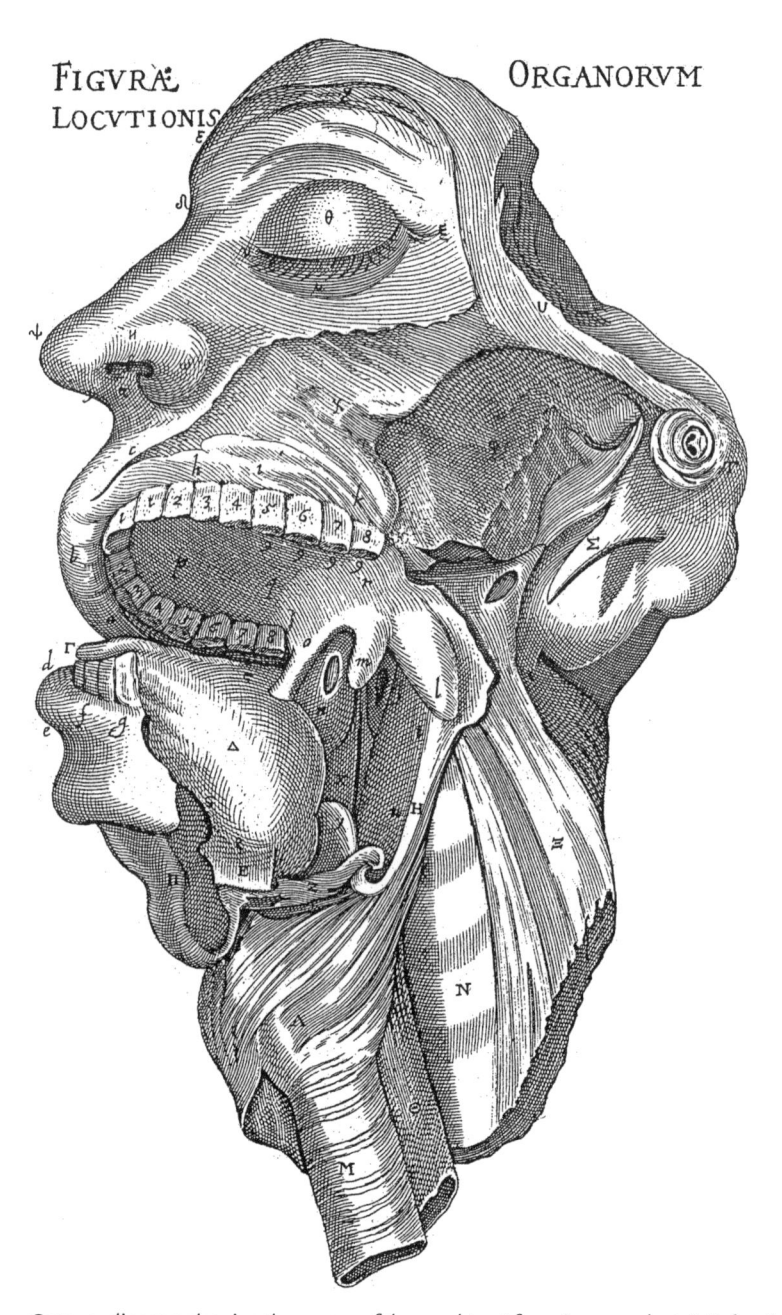

22 Cutaway diagram showing the organs of the vocal tract from Aquapendente's *De locutione* (1603).

Quintilian; architects modelled their palaces and city halls upon a close study of Roman buildings and the architectural treatise by Vitruvius (who lived some time between 100 BC and AD 100); and everyone with any scholarly pretensions whatsoever steeped themselves in ancient literature. In order to construct as accurate a picture of the ancient world as possible, these scholars – known as *Humanists* – went to great lengths to unearth texts which had lain unread for centuries. Boccaccio, Petrarch, Coluccio

10.4 The rediscovery of Classical Latin

Salutati, Poggio Bracciolini and others travelled to one ancient monastery after another hoping to find new treasures: Boccaccio unearthed the sole surviving manuscript of Varro's *De lingua latina* at Monte Cassino in 1355, while Poggio discovered a complete copy of Quintilian's *Institutio oratoria*, hitherto known only in a mutilated version, at St Gall in 1416. Other classical works rediscovered during the Renaissance included the poems of Catullus and Tibullus, a number of Cicero's speeches and letters, and Suetonius's *De grammaticis et rhetoribus*. Simultaneously Greek was becoming more widely known, taught by Byzantine scholars who fled from Constantinople to Italy as the Ottoman Turks drew ever closer to the capital of the Byzantine empire, which fell to them in 1453 (see box 10.5).

Box 10.5 How did the West learn Greek?

Despite the trickle of westerners in the thirteenth and fourteenth centuries who, like Robert Grosseteste and James of Venice, learnt enough Greek to translate into Latin, a knowledge of the language remained confined to a very small number of individuals. In 1326 Petrarch learnt a little (but not enough to be able to understand Homer's poems) from a visiting Greek monk from southern Italy, and some of his Humanist successors tried to teach themselves by comparing Greek and Latin versions of the New Testament. The real breakthrough came with the arrival in Florence in 1397 of Manuel Chrysoloras, the first Byzantine scholar to take up residence in Italy for some seven hundred years. He was followed in the course of the fifteenth century by a host of others fleeing before the Ottoman Turks, who captured Constantinople in 1453 and made it the capital of their huge empire, which by 1600 included the Balkans and Hungary as well as Greece and much of the Middle East. To the delight of their Italian pupils, these Byzantine scholars brought with them copies of nearly the whole range of Ancient Greek literature, most of which had been lost to the West since the end of Antiquity. One by one these texts were translated and printed, making available a vast range of knowledge about Greek thought and culture. Florence became a major centre for the study of these texts, particularly during the lifetime of Marsilio Ficino and Pico della Mirandola, who strove to reconcile Neoplatonism with Christianity. (Ficino even wrote a short commentary on the *Cratylus*.) Several of these scholars from Byzantium – Chrysoloras, Theodore Gaza and Constantine Lascaris were the most notable – wrote grammars for the use of their Italian pupils. Chrysoloras's grammar, the *Erotemata*, was the first book ever to be printed in a Greek font (Milan 1476).

Reading
W. K. Percival, 'Greek pedagogy in the Renaissance', in W. Hüllen and F. Klippel, eds., *Holy and Profane Languages: The Beginnings of Foreign Language Teaching in Western Europe* (Wolfenbüttel 2000).
N. G. Wilson, *From Byzantium to Italy* (London: Duckworth 1992).
R. Weiss, *Medieval and Humanist Greek: Collected Essays* (Padua: Antenore 1977).
M. Cortesi, 'Umanesimo greco', in G. Cavallo, C. Leonardi and E. Menestò, eds., *Lo Spazio Letterario del Medioevo 1. Il Medioevo Latino III. La Ricezione del Testo* (Rome: Salerno 1995), pp. 457–507.

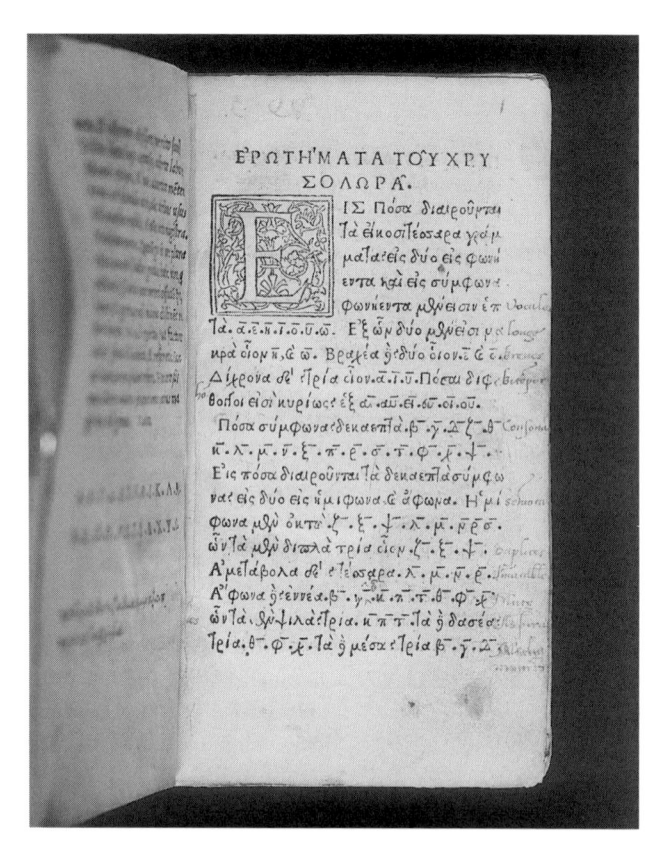

23 The opening of Chrysoloras's *Erotemata*, his beginners' grammar of Greek in question-and-answer form. Because the text is entirely in Greek, although it was intended for foreign learners, an early owner of this volume (printed at Ferrara in 1509) added Latin running headings in the margin as a help in finding his way around. Some publishers brought out editions of this grammar with a Latin translation printed on facing pages.

Renaissance scholars began to think of their own work as inaugurating a new classical age, with all those centuries that separated them from the Romans as merely the intervening time, the 'Middle Ages'. Everything associated with the Middle Ages seemed to be a backward step, a decline from the glories of the ancient world. As they steeped themselves in classical literature, anxious to reconstruct the civilisation of ancient Rome down to the last detail, Renaissance scholars started to notice differences between the way in which authors such as Cicero expressed themselves, and the forms of expression characteristic of their own day. Of course they had always known that Classical Latin and Church Latin differed somewhat, but now they responded in a new way. Their admiration for the lofty sentiments expressed by their favourite philosopher-orator, Cicero, was now transferred to his style, as they marvelled at the elegance of his sentences and the copiousness of his vocabulary. Medieval Latin, the vehicle of the subtle reasoning of Scholastic philosophy, suddenly looked clumsy and hair-splitting, weighed down by the coinages through which its lexicon had been enriched to cope with

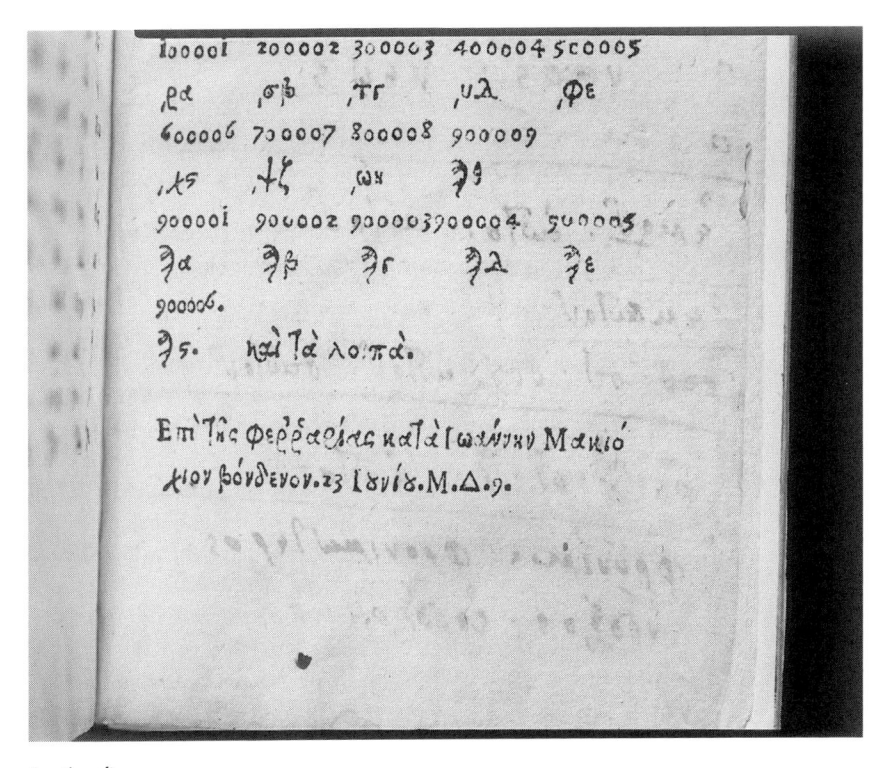

23 (continued)

the demands of intellectual issues which the Romans had never dreamt of. Even the very grammars from which the Humanists had learnt Latin as children were now disparaged: 'Alexander ... Hugutio, Papias, the *Catholicon*, the *Brachylogus*, the *Graecismus*, John of Garland, and other ludicrous names, all of whom taught their homeland barbarous gobbledygook instead of proper Latin', as the Spanish pedagogue Luis Vives put it in 1531.[1] The Modists were if anything worse. The Westfalian scholar Alexander Hegius (†1498), a schoolmaster at Deventer, an important centre of Dutch Humanism, launched an excoriating attack on them in these words:

Those grammarians who wrote on the *modi significandi* – if indeed they can be called grammarians – wrote like barbarians. After all, the ancients, who never breathed a word about the *modi significandi*, spoke perfectly correctly. It is obvious, therefore, that knowledge of the *modi significandi* not only does grammar-teachers no good; it is actually severely detrimental to them. Why do the Italians not teach their children the *modi significandi*? Because they love them too much to stuff them full of such useless noxious rubbish![2]

What could be put in their place? The Humanist instinct was to look to the grammars of Antiquity – Varro, Diomedes, Servius, Sergius, and the *regulae* grammars by Phocas, Eutyches, pseudo-Palaemon and pseudo-Augustine. All were printed, some repeatedly, in the early decades of printing (see box 10.6). Toward 1500, collections of the works of several ancient grammarians were brought out, culminating in the great *Grammaticae latinae auctores antiqui* ('Ancient authorities on Latin grammar') edited by Helias Putsch

> **Box 10.6 Linguists and printing**
>
> In the twelfth century paper arrived in Italy from the East, spreading slowly throughout Europe. By the end of the fourteenth century it was well established as a cheaper and more readily available material for books and other documents alongside parchment (see box 7.1, p. 142 above). Simultaneously, the locus of book production was shifting from monastic scriptoria to commercial stationers' shops in university towns. Both changes meant that books were becoming more numerous and more widely available, although they remained an expensive investment. Once printing with movable type was invented, in the middle of the fifteenth century (by Johannes Gutenberg in Mainz, according to the traditional story), the mass production of many identical copies now became possible for the cost of a single manuscript book. As people of moderate education who would previously never have dreamt of owning a book now became able to buy a few volumes, the demand for books in the vernacular increased. Printers were faced with more than one dilemma: books in Latin appealed to an international audience, whereas using the vernacular restricted their market; and as long as there was no agreement on the orthography of the vernacular, vernacular editions faced an uncertain future. Printers therefore developed a lively interest in language issues. Some, such as Aldus Manutius in Venice or Johannes Amerbach in Basel or Jossius Badius in Lyon and Paris, were noted Humanists in their own right, contributing to the editing and publication of ancient Greek and Latin texts as well as of contemporary literature; others, particularly in France, dedicated themselves to promoting their vernacular through the publication of grammars, dictionaries and treatises on the cultivation of the vernacular. The range of their linguistic interests can be seen from these examples:
>
> - Aldus Manutius (1449/1450–1515), a Venetian Humanist, specialised in printing editions of the Greek classics, including the first edition (*editio princeps*) of Apollonius Dyscolus's *Syntax* (1495) along with the much-used introductory Greek grammar by Theodore Gaza, a Byzantine scholar in Italy. Aldus himself wrote two grammars, one of Latin (1494) and one of Greek (1515).
> - Geoffroy Tory (ca 1480–1533), printer in Paris, author of *Champ Fleury* (1529), a treatise in defence of the French language and an important contribution to typography and (incidentally) to the standardisation of French orthography.
> - Robert Estienne (1503–59) moved to Geneva from his native Paris, where he had been the royal printer, because of his Protestant leanings. Author of an influential grammar of French (1557), of some children's grammars of Latin, and of important French–Latin, Latin–French dictionaries.
> - Henri Estienne (1531–98), Robert's son, and a major printer and editor of Greek texts. Author of the *Traicté de la conformité du language François avec le Grec* ('Treatise on the conformity of French and Greek', 1565), of a French grammar (1582), and of several works defending the French language against the Italianisms flooding in at the time, as well as of a particularly important Greek dictionary and a commentary on Varro's *De lingua latina*.

> Reading
>
> Elizabeth L. Eisenstein, *The Printing Revolution in Early Modern Europe* (Cambridge: Cambridge University Press 1983).
>
> Lucien Febvre and Henri-Jean Martin, *The Coming of the Book: The Impact of Printing 1450–1800* (London: NLB 1976), esp. ch. 8 section 4.
>
> L. D. Reynolds and N. G. Wilson, *Scribes and Scholars: A Guide to the Transmission of Greek and Latin Literature*, 3rd edn (Oxford: Clarendon 1991), ch. 4.

(who died at the age of twenty-five) in 1605. This remained the standard edition of the Late Latin grammarians up until the appearance of Heinrich Keil's *Grammatici Latini* (1855–70): Keil printed the texts in the same order as Putsch had done, in a remarkable display of editorial continuity down the centuries.

That initial delight at discovering that so many of the works of the Late Latin grammarians were still accessible soon faded into disappointment as Renaissance teachers realised that many of their questions remained unanswered. Grammars which had been admirably suited to the needs and expectations of fourth- and fifth-century Romans were out of place in fifteenth- and sixteenth-century Italy and Germany. (Varro's *De lingua latina* was the only Roman work that attracted a continuing stream of readers, and indeed several noted Renaissance philologists, including J. J. Scaliger, the son of J. C. Scaliger, and the printer Henri Estienne, wrote commentaries on it.) No matter how ardently the Humanists longed to recreate the world in which Cicero had lived, there was no escaping the fact that their world was utterly different. One by one, teachers from Guarino Veronese on decided they could do a better job themselves, and tried their hand at composing their own grammars. How much more aware they now were of the pedagogical specificity of the needs of their pupils can be seen in the explanation by the Bavarian Humanist theologian Johannes Cochleus (1479–1552) of why he decided to write his own grammar:

It may well seem superfluous to add a new grammar to the vast number by other people already in existence, with still further variations on the rules of one and the same art. But in fact anyone who gives careful consideration to the lot of German youth will realise that there is nothing available to facilitate and accelerate their studies. It is true that our teenagers are steeped in Alexander [of Villa Dei]'s short little verses from earliest childhood, but they are clumsy, both lacunose and repetitive, and encumbered with mile-long glosses. If you give them Priscian instead, you will find that he is far too verbose and so cannot be had for a reasonable price. And add to that the fact that he is full of Greek, but is nowadays almost always printed without it, mutilated. Diomedes is a good deal more concise, but is quite difficult, and is too advanced. If you opt for Phocas, Caper or Donatus, you will find that they are too short. If you try a modern author – Perottus, Sulpitius or Aldus – well, they are Italians and are far better suited to their young people than to ours, for they omit or assume knowledge of some parts of grammar and digress a great deal, and often refer to the Greeks.[3]

Even allowing for Cochleus's obvious desire to create a niche for his own book, it is apparent that he was voicing the feelings of his generation, a generation that was rapidly becoming aware that its needs, both scholarly and pedagogical, were not in fact completely met by the works of its revered Roman predecessors. As early as 1430 Lorenzo Valla (1407–57), a scholar with a love of historical documentation which foreshadowed that of nineteenth-century scholars, was writing a treatise on Latin grammar, *Elegantiae de latina lingua* (printed repeatedly under various titles from 1471 on), based upon detailed first-hand study of literary authors. Valla scoured the pages of ancient authors to find examples of the grammatical and lexical problems which intersted him, such as the difference between the near-synonyms *estimo/existimo/cogito/excogito* 'think'. Valla's work provided the model for what was to become a three-part process. First, scholars in all fields turned away from their immediate medieval forerunners to go back to the classics: what had Aristotle, or Galen, or Priscian, said? Then they searched for evidence to corroborate the pronouncements of ancient sources, whether by observing the movement of the planets or by dissecting corpses or by collecting examples of classical Latin usage from texts. Little by little, though, it dawned on them that what they read in their revered ancient sources was not always right – that the sun did not in fact revolve around the earth, for instance, or that the structure of the heart was not what textbooks claimed, or that a language might have more than eight parts of speech. The sixteenth century saw this process taking place over and over again in every domain of intellectual activity, from astronomy and botany to anatomy and linguistics.

10.5 Latin: a language like any other?

Renaissance scholars inherited the doctrine of the *tres linguae sacrae* from the Middle Ages. The whole complex of ideas surrounding the respective status of Latin and the vernacular had been outlined by Dante in his *De vulgari eloquentia* ('Eloquence in the vernacular'), a work originally composed in 1304 which was widely read only after it was printed in 1529 (in an Italian translation of Dante's original Latin text). Dante characterises the difference between the vernaculars and the sacred languages as follows:

We call that form of speech which toddlers pick up from those around them when they first start to make out words in the vernacular; or, to put it more concisely, the vernacular is that form of speech which we absorb by imitating our carers, without any rules. We also have a secondary form of speech called *grammar* by the Romans. The Greeks have this secondary form of speech too, and some other nations as well, but not all. Few people succeed in mastering it, for we learn its rules and doctrine only by devoting much time and effort to it. The vernacular is the nobler of the two because it was the first to be used by the human race; because everyone in the world uses it, even if it is divided into different words and accents; and because it is natural to us, whereas the other is created by art.[4]

Dante later explains that *grammar*, 'the unalterable sameness of speech in different times and places', was invented in order to compensate for the constant fluctuation to which the vernaculars were subject.[5] He thus envisages a two-tier system of languages, based upon his own experience, which looks like an account of a typical diglossic situation. Latin is (like Greek and Hebrew):

> shaped by art
> regulated by rules

10.5 Latin: a language like any other?

>   learnt through formal study
>   unchanging through time and space

The vernacular, on the other hand, is:

>   given by nature
>   without rules
>   learnt at one's mother's knee
>   subject to constant random fluctuation.

Medieval scholars were convinced that the vernacular languages of everyday use were inferior to Latin because of their ever-changing nature, devoid of rules. The only escape-route from the linguistic effects of divine wrath that they could see was to cultivate Latin, a truly international language with universally acknowledged rules. If you wrote in Latin, you could be confident that your writings would be understood in countries far from your own, centuries after your lifetime. But as Renaissance scholars pondered the writings of classical authors, they realised that the situation was more complicated. Their beloved Cicero described how when he began to write, Latin had been regarded as a rude uncultivated language severely handicapped by a lack of specialised vocabulary for the discussion of technical subjects. Up until then Roman philosophers had always written in Greek because of the inadequacy (they believed) of their native tongue. As an ardent defender of Latin, Cicero took it upon himself to create a Latin philosophical vocabulary. Near the end of his life he offered this assessment of his native language:

I feel strongly, and have often maintained, that the Latin language is not only not impoverished, as is commonly believed, but is actually richer than Greek. When have our excellent orators and poets ever lacked for any ornament of speech, whether lexical or stylistic, ever since they have had a model to imitate?[6]

As Renaissance scholars were keenly aware, it was Cicero's own work which had provided the model for subsequent Roman philosophers and orators. This realisation led them to two further conclusions: first, Latin had not always been the refined and flexible tool, ideally suited to rhetorical expression and logical argumentation alike, that it was in their own day. If it had once been a rude uncultivated language it had obviously changed its character. Latin was therefore subject to change, just like any present-day vernacular. Secondly, Cicero's part in the story implied that human activity could affect language in a positive as well as a negative way. This lesson was not lost upon Renaissance scholars, who saw in Cicero a clear role model for themselves. The Renaissance rediscovery of Ciceronian Latin thus had an unanticipated effect: intended initially to reinforce and confirm Latin's exalted position as one of the three sacred languages, it revealed upon closer investigation that Latin had a past, like any other language, and was as subject to the vicissitudes of time and human activity as Italian or French or English.

10.6 Ennobling the vernaculars

Now that Latin was no longer unattainably remote, no longer a qualitatively different language but one which differed only in degree and historical circumstance from other languages, it took on a new relationship to the vernaculars: role model. If Cicero's hard work had refined Latin to the point of its present-day perfection, who was to be the Cicero of German or English or Dutch? When a writer was hailed as the 'Cicero of our language' it was not just his eloquence that was signalled, but his role in 'ennobling' the language by making it a suitable vehicle for the discussion of subjects such as theology and philosophy, which had previously been the all-but-exclusive preserve of Latin. Grammarians, lexicographers and literary authors vied for the title. The first battle they had to fight was with their own compatriots, for it was no small task to dislodge the inherited picture of language relationships from its commanding position – scarcely a lesser task than that faced by Copernicus and Galileo as they sought to persuade their contemporaries that the earth was not the centre of the solar system. Some scholars tried to do so by writing treatises on linguistic issues, like the *Prose della volgar lingua* (begun ca 1512, published in 1525) by Pietro Bembo in Italy, or the *Diálogo de la lengua* (1535–6) by Juan de Valdés in Spain; or in short tracts called 'Defence and Ennobling of the Language', such as Joachim du Bellay's *Deffence et illustration de la langue françoyse* (1549); or in orthographical treatises. Certain themes come up over and over again:

1. The language needs cultivation in order to become a fit medium of literary and scholarly expression. If even Latin needed this cultivation, we need not feel ashamed to undertake the same task on behalf of our own language. As the French Humanist printer Geoffroy Tory wrote in 1529:

If it be true that all things have had a beginning, certain it is that the Greek language, and the Latin as well, were for long unpolished and without rules of grammar, as our own is today; but virtuous and studious writers took pains and diligently strove to reduce them to fixed rules, the better to put them to worthy use in writing and committing to memory the useful branches of knowledge, to the profit and honour of the public weal.[7]

2. Great writers such as Cicero and Quintilian play a vitally important part in ennobling the language. The Italians could point to their own 'classics', Dante, Boccaccio and Petrarch; but the French, the Spaniards and the rest agonised over which, if any, of their writers might qualify.

3. *Copia verborum*, 'copiousness of vocabulary, wealth of lexical resources', had to be created. Renaissance scholars threw themselves into the task of expanding the lexicon through neologisms and borrowings with such energy that Gesner reported in 1555 that literary English had in just one generation become incomprehensible to the man in the street, studded all over with borrowings from French and Latin.[8] (And that was before Shakespeare was even born!)

4. The language needs to be 'fixed' or 'regulated' with rules. Rules served, it was held, to rescue the language from its barbarousness and its paradoxical imprisonment in the stream of change. Once the language could be shown to have rules – to be a lingua

regolata, as the Italians said – then it was demonstrably equal to Latin. A language with rules was a fit medium in which to celebrate the glorious deeds of illustrious monarchs, as Antonio de Nebrija pointed out to Queen Isabella of Spain in the first grammar of Spanish (1492; see box 10.7 below):

I decided to reduce our Spanish language to art above all so that everything written in it now and henceforth would remain unchanged and be understood for all time to come, as we see has been done in Greek and Latin, which, although they are many centuries old, have nonetheless remained unchanged because they were subjected to the rules of the art. If we do not do likewise in our language, in vain will your chroniclers and historians record and immortalise the memory of your glorious deeds, and in vain do we attempt to translate foreign works – a task which takes years – into Spanish. One of two things will have to happen: either the memory of your doings will perish with the language, or else it will be kept alive in exile, amongst foreign nations, for it has no home of its own in which to live.[9]

The Italians were the first to take up the question. The publication of Dante's *De vulgari eloquentia* in 1529 sparked off a great debate, the *questione della lingua*, 'language question'. Humanists such as Pietro Bembo debated the respective merits of Latin and Italian, and – once that issue was resolved in favour of the vernacular – of the various Italian dialects. The Tuscan of the great writers of the thirteenth and fourteenth centuries commanded widespread support, but the question was still very much alive even in the mid-nineteenth century.

From about 1525 the issue was taken up by writers in Spain, Portugal and France. Because Italy was the leader in cultural affairs, scholars elsewhere avidly studied everything that the Italians produced, and took up their current controversies and tried them out in their own circumstances. While Juan de Valdés in Spain, João de Barros in Portugal, Joachim du Bellay in France and Richard Carew in England, and their compatriots, were arguing a case for the potential of their respective languages, others were taking practical steps to develop them. After all, in order to demonstrate that the vernacular was a *lingua regolata* someone had to undertake the laborious work of creating rules for it: in short, who was going to be the first grammarian of the vernacular (box 10.7)?

Leon Battista Alberti: Grammatica della lingua toscana (between 1437 and 1441)

While standing around waiting for an audience with Pope Eugene IV one day early in 1435, a group of Humanists started arguing about the status of Latin in ancient Rome. Had it been the language of everyday use, known to everyone – women, children, slaves, as well as highly educated men – or had it been a 'high' language, accessible only to the educated, as it was in Renaissance Italy, with some other language functioning alongside it as the vernacular? Are we really to believe, asked Leonardo Bruni, that preteens, childminders and the unlettered mob really had at their fingertips all the subtleties of Latin grammar which we educated men can barely get right after years of study? Many of the leading scholars of the day – the architect and artist Leon Battista Alberti (1404–72), the pedagogue Guarino Veronese, the indefatigable unearther of

Box 10.7 The first grammars of the vernacular
The medieval grammars of the vernacular described in chapter 9 bear only a slight relation to the Renaissance grammars we are about to consider. The medieval grammars correspond to the technology of the day, responding to an immediate practical need and teaching it with any tools which came to hand, whether or not they were legitimised by Latin grammars, as we saw in chapter 9. With the first Renaissance grammars we enter into a completely different conceptual world, one in which the goal was not to capture relevant peculiarities of the vernacular as accurately as possible, but rather to show in what respects the vernacular conformed to those aspects of (Latin) grammar which were considered universal. Thus, in the eyes of this first generation of Renaissance vernacular grammarians, the more closely their grammars resembled Latin grammars, the more successful they were. Only later, when the rule-governed nature of the vernacular was widely accepted (for the major western European languages, at least), did a new generation of grammarians begin to pose the question in different terms: what new categories do we need to introduce in order to describe the vernacular as fully as possible? It is because of this lack of ideological continuity between the vernacular grammars of the late Middle Ages and those of the Renaissance that it makes sense to ask who the first Renaissance grammarians of the vernacular were.

> Italian: Leon Battista Alberti, *Grammatica della lingua toscana* (1437–41, first printed in 1908)
> Spanish: Antonio de Nebrija, *Gramatica de la lengua castellana* (1492)
> French: John Palsgrave, *Lesclarcissement de la langue françoyse* (1530)
> Czech: Beneš Optát, Petr Gzel, Václav Philomates, *Grammatyka Czeská* (1533)
> Portuguese: Fernão de Oliveira, *Grammática da lingoagem portuguesa* (1536)
> Welsh: Gruffydd Robert, *Gramadeg Cymraeg* (1567)
> Polish: Petrus Statorius (Piotr Stojeński), *Polonicæ grammatices institutio* (1568)
> German: Laurentius Albertus, *Teutsch Grammatick oder Sprach-Kunst* (1573)
> Dutch: Hendrick Spieghel, *Twe-spraack vande Nederduitsche Letterkunst* (1584)
> Slovene: Adam Bohorič, *Arcticae horulae successivae, de latinocarniolana literatura* (1584)
> English: William Bullokar, *Pamphlet for Grammar* (1586)
> Croatian: Bartol Kašić (Bartholomaeus Cassius), *Institutiones linguae illyricae* (1604)
> Hungarian: Albert Molnár, *Nova grammatica ungarica* (1610)
> Estonian: Henricus Stahl, *Anführung zu der Esthnischen Sprach* (1637)
> Modern Greek: Simon Portius, Γραμματικὴ τῆς Ρωμαϊκῆς γλώσσας / *Grammatica linguæ graecæ vulgaris* (1638)
> Basque: A. Oihenart, *Notitia utriusque Vasconiae, tum Ibericae, quam Aquitanicae* (1638)
> Ukrainian: J. Uževyč, *Gramatyka slovenskaja* (1643, printed in 1970)
> Latvian: J. G. Rehehausen (Reichhusen), *Manuductio ad linguam letticam facilis et certa* (1644)
> Finnish: Eskil Petraeus, *Linguae finnicae brevis institutio* (1649)

> Icelandic: Runólfur Jónsson (Runolphus Jonas), *Recentissima antiquissimae linguae septentrionalis incunabula, id est, Grammaticae Islandicae rudimenta* (1651, reprinted in 1688 in England by the antiquary George Hickes)
> Lithuanian: Daniel Klein, *Grammatica lituanica* (1653)
> Breton: Julien Maunoir, *Le sacré collège de Jésus* (1659)
> Danish: Erik Pontoppidan, *Grammatica danica* (1668)
> Irish: Bonaventure Hussey, *Rudimenta grammaticae hibernicae* (1659, first printed 1968?)
> Lusatian/Wendish/Sorbian: Jacub Xaver Ticin (Jacobus Xaverius Ticinus), *Principia linguæ wendicæ quam aliqui wandalicam vocant* (1679)
> Frisian: authorship uncertain (possibly S. A. Gabbema or G. Japix), *Friesche grammatica* (1681)
> Swedish: Ericus O. Aurivillius, *Grammaticae svecanae specimen* (1684, first printed in 1884)
> Russian: Heinrich Wilhelm Ludolf, *Grammatica russica* (1696)
> Cornish: Edward Lhuyd, 'A Cornish Grammar', in his *Archæologia Britannica* (1707)
> Albanian: Francesco Maria da Lecce (Aletius), *Osservazioni grammaticali nella lingua albanese* (1716)
> Rumantsch: Fl. da Sale, *Fundamenti principali della lingua retica griggiona* (1729)
> Sami (Lapp): Petrus Fiellström, *Grammatica lapponica* (1738)
> Catalan: Josep Ullastra, *Gramatica cathalána* (1743, first printed in 1980)
> Rumanian: Dimitrie Eustatievici, *Gramatica rumânească* (1757)
> Scottish Gaelic: William Shaw, *An Analysis of the Galic Language* (1778)
> Norwegian: Niels Svenungsen, *Det norske fieldsprog* (1821, first printed 1985)

classical texts Poggio Bracciolini, the philologist Lorenzo Valla, and the translator Francesco Filelfo – got involved, writing letters and treatises to prove their point. At first they delved into classical literature for examples of erudite women or Latinless slaves to support their case; but soon it dawned upon Alberti that there was another possible approach. If today's vernaculars, as spoken by the least literate members of society, could be shown to possess rules, then the question would be answered. So in or around 1440 he decided to write a grammar of Italian. In the introduction he sets out his position forthrightly:

Those who maintain that the Latin language was not common to all the people of Rome, but was reserved to a few learned scholars, as we see it is today, will, I believe, abandon that error when they see this little work of mine, in which I have assembled the usage of our language in concise notes. Great scholars, first amongst the Greeks and later among the Romans, did likewise, and called guidelines similar to these, meant to teach writing and speaking without mistakes, by the name of grammar. Read and assimilate this art as it is in our language.[10]

Alberti was well aware of how very different the rules of Italian are in many particulars from those of Latin. He points out, for instance, that there are no distinct morphological exponents for the cases except in the personal pronouns *io, tu, esso*, case function being indicated by the article (plus a preposition). Likewise, there are no morphologically distinct passive verb forms; rather, the passive is expressed with the aid of the verb *sono* 'I am' plus the past participle passive. On the other hand, he was writing for people many of whom believed that *grammatica* meant Latin. Consequently, in order to prove that the vernacular too possessed grammar, Alberti needed to demonstrate that it conformed to the long-established rules of Latin grammar. His way of handling the Italian tenses shows this particularly clearly. Italian, like the other Romance languages, has a number of compound tenses composed of an auxiliary verb plus a participle, and these tenses are fully integrated into the mood-tense-aspect system of the language, like the *passé composé* in French. But Alberti lists just five tenses: *sono* 'I am', *ero* 'I used to be', *fui* 'I was', *ero stato* 'I had been', *saró* 'I shall be'. Why just these five? Because they correspond to the five tenses traditionally recognised for Latin: present, imperfect, perfect, pluperfect, future. Having listed them, Alberti realises that he has omitted *sono stato* 'I have been', and adds a note to cover it:

The Tuscans have a past-tense form indicating something that has happened just now: *sono, sei, è stato*; plural *siamo, siete, sono stati*. One says: 'Yesterday I was (*fui*) at Ostia, today I have been (*sono stato*) at Tivoli.'[11]

In other words, he is sensitive to this peculiarity of the vernacular, but does not want to modify the inherited framework to the extent of saying that there are six tenses (or more) in Italian: the point was, after all, to show that Italian *conformed* to the rules of *grammatica*, i.e. Latin.

Antonio de Nebrija, *Gramatica castellana* (1492)

Antonio de Nebrija (1444–1522), a noted Spanish Humanist, was for centuries best known for his grammar of Latin, *Introducciones Latinae* (1481), a long and detailed work with a marginal commentary in the medieval tradition which was still being reprinted in Spain (somewhat revised) as late as 1855. Far less famous in its own time was his grammar of Spanish, *Gramatica castellana*, published in the year of Columbus's discovery of the New World. It was dedicated to Queen Isabella, and we have already seen the passage from its preface where Nebrija explains to his royal patron the importance of vernacular grammars in regulating the language and so combating the effects of language change. The grammar is divided into two unequal halves which at first glance seem to cover the same material; in fact, however, they are intended for different readers. The division is based upon Quintilian's distinction between a 'methodical' or theoretical discipline, and a 'historical' or descriptive one (*Inst. or.* I ix 1). The first, 'methodical', part (Books I–IV) contains 'the precepts and rules of the art' *siguiendo la orden natural de la gramatica* ('following the natural organisation of grammar'). It is intended for native speakers who wish to become aware of the rules of their language, and also for those who want to approach Latin via a knowledge of Spanish grammar. The second, 'historical' (=descriptive), part (Book V) is headed: 'Introduction to Spanish for speakers of a foreign language who wish to learn it', *siguiendo la orden de la doctrina* ('organised according to pedagogical considerations'). Although the material covered in the two halves is similar, the way in which it is treated is quite different. To take the chapter on the verb as an example, that in the first section (III x) is organised like any ancient work in the *Schulgrammatik* tradition: definition, list of properties (the same ones as in Priscian's *Institutiones grammaticae*, although in a different order), brief account of each property in turn, with examples. The whole discussion is not much more than two pages long. What of phenomena not found in Latin, such as the periphrastic tenses? Like Alberti, Nebrija simply lists the five traditional tenses recognised by Latin grammar and gives vernacular examples. The periphrastic forms are relegated to a separate chapter (III xi) headed *De los circunloquios del verbo* ('Verbal periphrastic forms'). In other words, Nebrija acknowledges their existence and their importance, but integrating them into the Latin framework at this point would vitiate the purpose of this section of the work: to show in what respects Spanish conforms to the rules of *grammatica*, i.e. Latin. In fact Nebrija is well aware, as Alberti was before him, of the extent to which Spanish and Latin diverge, reminding us that Spanish sometimes has more forms than Latin, sometimes fewer (III xi). He gives us no paradigms in this part of the work: it is assumed that the native-speaker users are already able to conjugate the verbs of their own language. In the second, 'historical', part intended for foreigners the discussion of verb conjugation takes up far more space: six chapters (V iv–ix), some fifteen pages. Conjugation is the first thing introduced, and paradigms are set out at length, with the periphrastic tenses fully integrated into the system. You really could learn Spanish from this work!

It is unusual to find one and the same individual writing a grammar in which the two approaches are so clearly demarcated. Nonetheless, even in the 'methodical' section Nebrija departs here and there from tradition, abandoning the time-honoured figure of eight parts of speech (he is one of the first grammarians to do so) by adding the article and the gerund. In practice, those Renaissance grammarians who set out to demonstrate that the rules of *grammatica* (Latin) are also to be found in the vernacular often realised as they went along that they were neglecting important aspects of the vernacular, and adopted various compromises. But Nebrija realises that the two approaches are in fact incompatible: either one attempts to show how closely Spanish conforms to the rules of a quasi-universal *grammatica*, as in his 'methodical' portion, or one writes a grammar which takes full account of all the peculiarities of Spanish, structured in whatever way seems most appropriate, as in his 'historical' section. Although the *Gramatica castellana* itself was never as widely read as his Latin grammar (it was not reprinted until 1744), it is a forerunner of the distinction between *universal* and *particular* grammar which was to provide a framework for grammatical discourse down to the present day.

William Bullokar (ca 1520–ca 1590): *Pamphlet for Grammar* (1586)

The English were slow to take to writing grammars of their vernacular. Aware as they were of its 'mongrel' pedigree, and of their continental colleagues' mocking nickname for it – *spuma linguarum*, 'scum of languages' – they knew there was no hope of tracing its ancestry back to one of the three sacred languages. However, the strong tradition of vernacular-medium instruction in England (see chapter 9 above) little by little helped to awaken teachers to an awareness of the peculiarities of their own language. Vernacular-medium grammars of Latin such as the *Formula* and the *informacio* (*Latinitas*) signalled various contrastive points. The standard grammar of Latin from the mid-sixteenth century to the early nineteenth, *A Shorte Introduction of Grammar* by William Lily and John Colet (see box 10.8) continued this tradition, cannibalising substantial portions of fourteenth- and fifteenth-century works lightly modified. Nonetheless the basic work of thinking through the changes needed to convert the inherited grammatical framework into something appropriate for English still remained to be done. William

---

Box 10.8 From Donatus's *Ars minor* to Kennedy's *Shorter Latin Primer*: the *Shorte Introduction of Grammar* by Lily and Colet

As new grammar schools were founded in one town after another, each teacher compiled his own teaching materials from those already in existence. Since pupils were expected to memorise the textbook wholesale, this meant that if the child changed school, or if a new teacher took over, they had to go right back to the beginning and start again – clearly a huge waste of time and effort. In a bid to put an end to this situation, Edward VI granted a royal monopoly in 1547 to the *Shorte Introduction of Grammar*, a work compiled by two English Humanists, John Colet (1467–1519) and William Lily (ca 1468–1522), who had taught at St Paul's School in London in the early decades of the century. The fact that they used English as the medium of instruction in this introductory work (the more advanced companion volume, *Brevissima Institutio*, was in Latin) meant that its circulation was limited to England. Comparable works on the Continent – Despauterius's *Commentarii grammatici* (1509–19) and Alvarus's *De institutione grammatica* (1572) – attained widespread international circulation through being entirely in Latin. The first serious rival of the *Shorte Introduction* was the Eton Latin grammar (1758), an updated version of it produced for use at Eton College, the famous public (= private) school. The Eton Latin grammar gained ground in the latter part of the eighteenth century at the expense of the *Shorte Introduction*, which by now was looking very dated. The first half of the nineteenth century saw the proliferation of various grammars composed for use at one or another of the great public schools, culminating in the appearance of Benjamin Hall Kennedy's various primers, the first of which appeared in 1844 with the Eton Latin grammar as its starting-point. Kennedy's *Shorter Latin Primer* (1888), still in use today, thus has a pedigree which stretches back via the Eton Latin grammar, the *Shorte Introduction of Grammar*, the Middle English *Accedence* and related texts, to Donatus's *Ars minor*.

Reading

N. Orme, *English Schools in the Middle Ages* (London: Methuen 1973), pp. 87–115.

V. J. Flynn, 'The grammatical writings of William Lily, ?1468–?1523', *Papers of the Bibliographical Society of America* 37 (1943), 85–113.

C. G. Allen, 'The sources of "Lily's Latin Grammar": a review of the facts and some further suggestions', *The Library*, 5th ser., 9 (1954), 85–100.

C. Stray, 'Primers, publishing, and politics: the classical textbooks of Benjamin Hall Kennedy', *The Papers of the Bibliographical Society of America* 90 (1996), 451–74.

10.6 Ennobling the vernaculars

Bullokar, a retired soldier, was the first to try. His *Pamphlet for Grammar* (1586), published in the reformed orthography which was so dear to his heart, bears a distinct family resemblance to Lily and Colet's Latin grammar. In those sections where the discussion focuses on semantic categories which are arguably universal, as in the chapters on the adverb, conjunction and interjection, this is particularly true: Bullokar lists the same classes in the same order with little deviation except in the names given to the classes. But in the chapters on the inflecting word classes Bullokar keeps his distance from his model, arguing:

Note further, that some significations expressed in some language, or languages, by one or by diverse parts of speech, are in another language expressed by another part or parts of speech: yet all may yield perfect sense or meaning in the language so used.[12]

He is sensitive to the typological differences, both phonological and morphosyntactic, between his own analytical language and the highly synthetic Latin:

The speech being also as greatly aided (for the distinction of voice, and perfect signification or meaning of words) by the diverse divisions or parts in the voice, for which we have now seven and thirty diverse and distinct letters, and seven diphthongs: as the Latin and some other languages (being driven thereunto through lack of so many divisions in voice as English hath) are aided by their diverse and many syllables in most words: our English words (not being formative [i.e. lacking derivational affixes]) are commonly but of one syllable, yet capable of anything, that any other language may bear or utter ... yet our language [is] as sensible as theirs, and sooner conceived in sense to the ear by the reasons aforesaid, though (hitherto) utterly defaced of the credit due unto it, for lack of true orthography and Grammar, now performed to the great credit and perpetual stay of the best use of the same speech forever ... (pp. 54f.)

What changes does Bullokar make?

- Lily and Colet, like their late medieval predecessors, had divided the eight word classes into two equal groups based on the presence (noun, pronoun, verb, participle) or absence (adverb, conjunction, preposition, interjection) of inflection. Bullokar departs from this symmetrical schema to place the English participle (-ing, -ed) in the uninflected category.
- Bullokar's English noun paradigms show only two morphologically distinct forms, one for the nominative/accusative/gainative[=dative]/vocative, and the other for the genitive.
- Although Bullokar speaks of the 'nominative case' and so forth, he normally uses these terms to denote syntactic function (as do Nebrija and Alberti), and only occasionally to denote morphological inflection.
- He recognises the auxiliary role of 'have' and the special status of modal verbs.

Bullokar represents an early stage in the lengthy process of creating a grammatical analysis of English, that of measuring the vernacular against Latin; but at the same time he is sensitive to its peculiarities and ready to defend them. Unlike his successors, he is unwilling to make major changes to the inherited framework, for that would negate

A verb is declined with mood, tence, number, and person : either activ hauing a participle passiue: or a verb substantiue, or neuter.	A Verb iz a part of spe'ch declyned with mood, tenc, number, and persn.

It iz caled a Verb-Activ when it signifieth too doo : az, I lov, I te'ch, and hath a Participl of the Passiu-voic deryued of it : az loued, tauht : which participl being ioined with the verb-substantiu, too be, taketh hiz mood or maner of suffering, and hiz tenc also, of the verb-substantiu, and hiz cás, gender, number, and persn, of hiz ruling substantiu: az, I am loued, be'thy loued : O-that he'wær loued: would-God we'had ben loued: if they hau ben loued : when we'shal be'loued, &c. and hauing no participl-passiu iz caled a verb-neuter, whooz participial iz ioyned with the verb substantiu in being only : az, I being runn too the town, my father cám hóm. Mor iz sayed of a participl in the týtl thær-of. |
| To haue, a possessiue : to haue-leiuer, a choice-atiue. | Too Hau, may be'caled a Verb-possesiu, and hiz compound, Too Hau-leuer, a verb-choicatiu. Al other verbz ar caled Verbz-Neuterz-Un-perfect, bicauz they reqýr the Infinitiu-mood of an other verb too expres their signification or mæning perfectly: and be'thæz, may, can, miht or mouht, could, would, should, must ouht, and som týim, wil : shal, being a mer sýn of the futur tenc. |

24   The beginning of William Bullokar's discussion of the verb, including his list of modal auxiliaries, reproduced in his reformed orthography from the facsimile of his *Pamphlet for Grammar* (1586) Leeds.

the grammar's purpose: to demonstrate the rule-governed character of English. His seventeenth-century successors had fewer inhibitions.

Conclusion

All three grammarians found themselves snared in a paradox: they wanted to demonstrate that their respective vernaculars were rule-governed, 'had grammar'. But as long as grammar was popularly identified with Latin, the only way to do so was to show that the vernaculars had the *same* rules as Latin. Proving the conformity of the vernacular to Latin thus became an urgent task. Areas of non-conformity needed to be clearly delineated, a demand which had the effect of waking grammarians and their readers up to points where the vernacular diverged from Latin. It was left to the next generation to integrate both aspects of the grammar of the vernacular – places where it resembled Latin and places where it differed – into a single description. Meanwhile, however, that elusive notion 'different *and* equal', which has challenged the western world ever since the Renaissance, makes its first tantalising appearance in the history of linguistics. Paradoxically, the medieval certainty that the vernaculars were different from (and therefore inferior to) the *tres linguae sacrae* meant that medieval grammarians like Guilhem Molinier or the author of the *First Grammatical Treatise* were free to describe them in whatever terms they chose. In the deliberately latinate grammars of the Renaissance we glimpse the first hints of the breaking down of the old hierarchical way of picturing the world.

10.7 New ways of thinking about linguistic form: Christians meet Hebrew

For much of the Middle Ages Jews living in Europe had been confronting the same linguistic challenge as their Christian neighbours: how were they to maintain a knowledge of Hebrew, the language of their sacred and scholarly texts and ritual, when their language of everyday use was the local vernacular? A large part of their pedagogical energy went into teaching boys enough Hebrew to enable them to read the Torah and recite the prayers in Hebrew. The first grammars of Hebrew appeared in the tenth century. Modelled initially upon grammars of Arabic (see box 10.9), these works were far more form-conscious than contemporary works by Christian Europeans. Phonetics played a large part: most medieval Hebrew grammars included a lengthy description of the consonants, and sometimes of the vowels as well. (The Hebrew alphabet included symbols for the consonants only; vowels could be added optionally in the form of diacritics placed above and below the symbols for the consonants.) The most popular system of classification of the consonants, disseminated through a kabbalistic text, the *Sēpher Yetsīrāh* ('Book of Creation'), set them out in five groups according to their areas of articulation:

> gutturals
> palatals
> linguals
> dentals
> labials[13]

> **Box 10.9 Grammar in the Arab world**
>
> Islam, a religion which originated in revelations to Muhammad gathered in the Qur'an (Koran), dates its foundation to the year 622, the date of Muhammad's flight (Hejira) from Mecca to Medina, the site of the first mosque. After Muhammad's death in 632 his successors, the caliphs, led their followers across the Middle East and the north of India, ultimately reaching the farthest point of southeast Asia; and westwards across North Africa to Spain. They made thousands of converts whose native language was not Arabic – Syriac, Persian, Turkish, Uzbek, Urdu, Bengali, Malay, Berber; yet they continued to require that the Qur'ān be read in Arabic. This created an educational need for descriptive grammars of Arabic for the use of non-native speakers very similar to that of the contemporary western Church for grammars of Latin. The first grammarian of Arabic whose work survives is Sībawayhi, a Persian who died around 793. His grammar, called simply al-Kitāb 'the book', is a huge and minutely detailed description of Arabic syntax, morphology and phonetics. Linguistic form is at its very core, and was to remain at the heart of the Arabic grammatical tradition. Centuries later, the centrality of form is obvious even in a beginners' grammar, the Ājurrūmiyya by Ibn Ājurrūm (1273–1323), from Fez (Morocco). Ibn Ājurrūm defines the three word classes recognised by the Arabs like this:
>
> The sentence has three constituents: the noun, e.g. 'Said', 'man'; the verb, e.g. 'he hit', 'he will hit', 'hit!'; and the letter (or particle) that contributes to the meaning, e.g. the interrogative particle hal, 'in', 'not'.
>   How does one recognise the noun and distinguish it from the verb and the particle?
>   The noun is recognised by the i-ending and by the n-ending and by taking the letters alif and lam [= al, the definite article, which is always joined to the word it modifies] and the particles which are followed by the i-ending. . .
>   How does one recognise the verb?
>   The verb is recognised by qad [a modal particle], by s- and sawf [particles that express futurity], and by the vowelless -t of the feminine.
> How does one recognise the particle?
>   The particle is that with which neither the marks of the noun nor those of the verb are valid.
>
> Even someone who knew little more of Arabic than the alphabet could identify which words belonged to which word class from these definitions.
>   When Arab philosophers and grammarians began to study Aristotelian logic, in the tenth century, they started to take a greater interest in meaning and in the philosophy of language.
>   Other important grammarians of Arabic include:
>
> - al-Mubarrad (825–898), editor and populariser of Sībawaihi's Kitāb.
> - az-Zajjājī (860/870–949), author of the Kitāb al-jumal, a pedagogical grammar still in use at Islamic universities, and of the Kitāb al-Īḍāḥ, the first grammar to present a formal theory of linguistic argumentation.

- Ibn Jinnī (932/942–1002), a prolific grammarian with wide-ranging interests and author of the Kitāb al-lumaʿ.
- al-Fārābī (870–950) adopted a critical stance towards traditional grammar based partly upon his knowledge of logic, partly on his acquaintance with a wide range of languages.
- al-Jurjānī (†1078), a rhetorician with a keen interest in semantics.
- Ibn Mālik (1203–1274), author of the 'Alfiyya, a popular beginners' grammar in verse.
- Ibn Ājurrūm (1273–1323), author of the Ājurrūmiyya, a popular beginners' grammar still in use in the twentieth century.

Reading

1. Brief surveys

Yasir Suleiman, 'Arabic linguistic tradition', in E. F. K. Koerner and R. E. Asher, eds., *Concise History of the Language Sciences from the Sumerians to the Cognitivists* (Oxford: Pergamon 1995), pp. 28–38.

Cornelis H. M. Versteegh, 'Die arabische Sprachwissenschaft', in Helmut Gätje, ed., *Grundriss der arabischen Philologie 2. Literaturwissenschaft* (Wiesbaden: Reichert 1987), pp. 148–76.

Georges Bohas, J.-P. Guillaume and Djemal Kouloughli, 'L'analyse linguistique dans la tradition arabe', in S. Auroux, ed., *Histoire des idées linguistiques* 1 (Liège: Mardaga 1989), pp. 260–82.

2. Longer accounts

Kees Versteegh, *Landmarks in Linguistic Thought 3. The Arabic Linguistic Tradition* (London and New York: Routledge 1997).

G. Bohas, J.-P. Guillaume and D. E. Kouloughli, *The Arabic Linguistic Tradition* (London and New York: Routledge 1990).

Jonathan Owens, *The Foundations of Grammar: An Introduction to Medieval Arabic Grammatical Theory*, Studies in the History of the Language Sciences 45 (Amsterdam and Philadelphia: John Benjamins 1988). [Explains the basic concepts of medieval Arabic grammar with reference to contemporary linguistic theory.]

Kees Versteegh, *The Explanation of Linguistic Causes: Az-Zaǧǧāǧī's Theory of Grammar. Introduction, Translation, Commentary*, Studies in the History of the Language Sciences 75 (Amsterdam and Philadelphia: John Benjamins 1995). [Presents the text of one of the theoretically most interesting of the Arab thinkers about language in an approachable way.]

The descriptions of morphology are essentially based on the *littera*, working through the alphabet and examining the functions of each *littera* – as inflectional ending, as derivational affix, as monosyllabic preposition, pronoun or article. One such was such the widely read work by Elias Levita (1469–1549), a German Jew who lived in Italy for most of his life, teaching many Christians both in person and through his textbooks.

¶ Diuisio duarum & viginti hebraicarum
literarum in quinq; plationes.

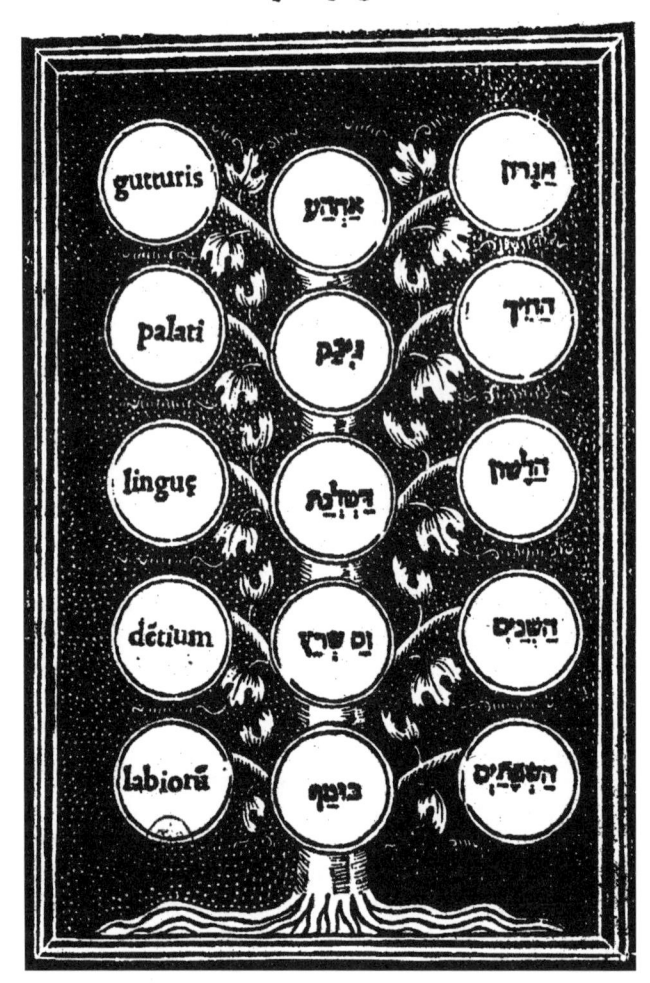

25   Diagram from Agathius Guidacerius's *Grammatica hebraicae linguae* (Rome, 1514?), setting out the classifications of the Hebrew consonants, giving the name of the place of articulation in Latin on the left and in Hebrew on the right, and in the centre, on the trunk of the tree, listing the sounds belonging to that category.

Here is an example from his grammar:

Mem [the letter מ] at the start of a word forms a verbal noun, e.g. *merhab* 'breadth'. Secondly, it forms the participle in all conjugations except the first, e.g. in the second [conjugation] *m dabber* 'speaking', *mə-shubbar* 'broken' ... Thirdly, it has the same force as *min* 'from, out of, down from', e.g. *mē'eretz* 'from earth'. The Hebrews can also use it to paraphrase the comparative... In final position it means 'their', 'them', e.g. *hikkītīm* 'I struck them', *tzəbā'ām* 'their army', *nos'ēm* 'take them'.[14]

10.7 New ways of thinking about linguistic form

One could in principle write a grammar of any language in similar terms: try writing an entry along these lines for s in English or French or Spanish, or m in Latin, or n in German, or i in Italian, or y in Russian. What a contrast with the traditional Greco-Roman way of organising a grammar by the mostly semantically defined word classes! Likewise, semantic classifications within the word classes played a relatively small part in most grammars of Hebrew; far more important was the analysis of the root.

Arriving at an accurate analysis of the **root** occupied the energy of grammarians of both Arabic and Hebrew for several centuries, and the results of their analysis likewise take up the lion's share of their grammars (see box 10.10). As the grammarians eventually concluded (notably Yehudah Hayyūj, working in Spain around 1000), the vast majority of words in both languages are built around a root of three (rarely four or five) consonants which remains constant through the inflectional and derivational paradigm (except that certain consonants may undergo phonological changes). Thus, from the root Š-M-R (שמר 'guard') come:

ŠāMaRtī 'I guarded'	שמרתי
niŠəMoR 'we shall guard'	נשמר
ŠōMēR 'a guard'	שמר
miŠəMeReth 'keeping watch'	משמרת
hammiŠMeReth 'the (act of) keeping watch'	המשמרת
mēhammiŠMeReth 'from the (act of) keeping watch'	מהמשמרת

Š-M-R is the root and citation form (vowels are generally not indicated in Hebrew texts). However, that form, when vocalised (supplied with vowels) in the conventional manner, was identical to the third person singular of the perfective form of the verb – ŠāMaR (שמר) – the normal citation form and the starting-point of the paradigm. This, as we shall see, led to a misunderstanding on the part of the first Christian Hebraists.

Throughout the Middle Ages, European Christians had dreamt of learning Hebrew, the most venerable and remote of the *tres linguae sacrae* and the language spoken by Adam and Eve in Paradise (or so they believed). In practice their knowledge was extremely limited: the alphabet was quite widely known, and a certain amount of vocabulary was known from St Jerome's glossary of the Hebrew proper names in the Bible and from his Bible commentaries. Only in the thirteenth century did a few Christians learn enough Hebrew to start to go beyond this, and to venture upon the first attempts at writing grammars: Roger Bacon in Oxford, Robert Grosseteste in Oxford or Lincoln, and Gerard of Huy in what is now Belgium, and in the fourteenth century Henry of Hessen in Germany, among others. The decree of the Council of Vienna (1311–12) that chairs of Arabic, Hebrew, Greek and Syriac should be established at five universities

Box 10.10 Medieval grammarians of Hebrew

- The Masoretes, a group of scholars in Palestine active from the eighth to the tenth centuries who devised the system of vowel symbols used to indicate vowels in the Torah and in pedagogical literature to this day.
- Sa'adyah Gaon (892–942), a religious leader in present-day Iraq, author of the first grammar and dictionary of Hebrew to survive.
- Yehudah ben David Hayyūj (ca 945-ca 1000), from Fez, working in Cordoba, Spain, the first grammarian to introduce the notion of the triliteral root.
- Abūal-Walīd Marwān ibn Janāh, from Cordoba, working in Saragossa, Spain, author in the 1040s of the first full description of Hebrew morphology (in Arabic, translated into Hebrew ca 1171).
- Abraham Ibn Ezra (1089/1092–1164/1167), from Toledo, Spain, working in Italy and elsewhere, author of numerous influential grammatical treatises.
- David Qimhi (1160–1235), based at Narbonne, France, and author of the most popular of all medieval grammars, the Sēpher Mikhlōl, which was widely studied in the sixteenth century and repeatedly reprinted (and translated into English by William Chomsky, Noam Chomsky's father).
- Prophiat Duran (Isaaq ben Moses, †ca 1414), from Perpignan, France, working in Catalonia, author of the first grammar of Hebrew to apply Aristotelian doctrine to the language in a thoroughgoing way (Maᶜaseh Efod, 1403).
- Elias Levita (1469–1549), from Neustadt, near Nuremberg, Germany, spending most of his life in Italy, where he became an important teacher of early Christian Hebraists. His Sēpher ha-Diqdūq (1518), published with parallel Latin translation by Sebastian Münster (1529), became another important textbook for sixteenth-century Christians.
- Abraham ben Meir de Balmes (ca 1440–1523), teaching at Naples and Padua, author of Miqneh Abram/Peculium Abrae (1523), a lengthy grammar in and of Hebrew with parallel translation into Latin by the author applying both Platonic and Aristotelian doctrine to Hebrew, and conversant with and critical of a wide range of grammarians in both the Hebrew and the Latin traditions.

Reading

David Téné, 'Hebrew linguistic tradition', in E. F. K. Koerner and R. E. Asher, eds., *Concise History of the Language Sciences from the Sumerians to the Cognitivists* (Oxford: Pergamon 1995), pp. 21–8. [A concise survey.]

David Téné, 'Linguistic literature, Hebrew', in *Encyclopaedia Judaica* (English) vol. 16 (Jerusalem: Encyclopaedia Judaica 1971), cols. 1352–90. [Includes list of grammarians with dates and principal works.]

Wilhelm Bacher, *Die Anfänge der hebräischen Grammatik* and *Die hebräische Sprachwissenschaft vom 10. bis zum 16. Jahrhundert*, Studies in the History of the Language Sciences 4 (Amsterdam: Benjamins 1975).

Hartwig Hirschfeld, *A Literary History of Hebrew Grammarians and Lexicographers* (Oxford: Oxford University Press 1926).

10.7 New ways of thinking about linguistic form

(including Paris and Oxford) remained a pious hope for many years in the absence of the necessary expertise.

In the course of the fifteenth century a new motivation lent urgency to the desire to learn Hebrew. The theologians leading the religious reform movements which culminated in the breaking away of the various Protestant churches from the Church of Rome realised that the Humanist fashion for getting back to the original sources might provide useful historical legitimation of their doctrinal position: Hebrew became a vital adjunct to Christian religious debate. But how were Christians to learn it? If they swallowed their prejudices and plucked up their courage to enter the Jewish quarter, they were likely to be met with suspicion (hardly surprisingly in view of the tense relations between Jews and Christians in many medieval cities). If they succeeded in finding a cooperative rabbi, there was no guarantee that he would be a specialist in Hebrew grammar; he might turn out to be a theologian of the first order, but perhaps with little interest in the grammatical scholarship of his day. Even when they were lucky enough to locate a suitable teacher, they found that the grammars used by Jews were in Hebrew, which rendered them quite inaccessible to Christians. One eager Humanist, the Swiss scholar Konrad Pellikan, looked back with wry amusement upon his desperate efforts to learn Hebrew around the year 1500. He had got hold of the Hebrew text of part of the Bible – the Prophets and the Psalter – and tried to work out the grammar by comparing each word with its Latin equivalent. But he ran into a problem: 'I worked my way through the first psalm and found it was easy enough as regards nouns and adverbs, but to my great frustration I could hardly find any instances of the first person of the present indicative, the base form [of the paradigm] in Latin: *amo, lego, audio* . . .' Six months later he learnt that the German Hebraist Johannes Reuchlin (1455–1522) was visiting. Pellikan reports: 'As far as I was concerned, still stuck on those verbs, nothing could be better news. . . So I anxiously put my question to him. Then the truly humane Dr Reuchlin replied, with just a hint of a smile, that the base form in Hebrew wasn't the first person, either indicative or imperative, but the third person singular of the perfect. I was delighted, for I knew that the Bible was full of such forms from the very first line of Psalm 1: *abiit, stetit, sedit* etc.'[15]

Perhaps it was partly as a consequence of this meeting that Reuchlin decided to write a grammar of Hebrew in Latin, the language all western Christian scholars could read. He published his *De rudimentis hebraicis* in 1506 to satisfy this need. Printed from right to left, like Hebrew books (although it is in Latin!), it made both the Hebrew language and Hebrew grammatical concepts accessible to western Christians for the first time. It was from Reuchlin and his successors over the next few decades (such as the hugely popular *Tabula in grammaticen hebraeam* (1529) by Nicolas Clenard) that Humanists learnt their Hebrew, and learnt to classify sounds according to their place of articulation and to identify roots. The five articulatory classes were soon applied to the description of the sounds of the vernaculars. (They didn't make their way into grammars of Latin and Greek until the nineteenth century, so strong was the force of tradition.) As for the notion of root, however, that underwent something of a transformation. Here is how Reuchlin introduces it:

Every word is either primitive or derivative. Strip a derivative noun of its various garments until it is naked and the primitive form appears. I'll run through a Latin example with you first. For instance, if you want to reduce the plural noun hae inhonorificabilitudines to its primitive state, what will you do? You'll strip away all the layers until the primitive form appears without any additions, like this:	Reuchlin uses the traditional Latin term primitivum, meaning a word form without any derivational affixes, as the equivalent of the Hebrew šōrēš 'root'. His successors translated šōrēš with the Latin word for 'root', radix.
	Inhonorificabilitudines is the Latin equivalent of antidisestablishmentarianism, a plausible but in pratice never used word, a grammarians' (and children's) plaything. It has a long history: the very similar honorificabilitudinitas appears in the grammar of Peter of Pisa toward the end of the eighth century.
1. Drop the article, hae. 2. Drop the first compositional element, the preposition in.	Reuchlin includes the article partly because it was conventionally often given along with the noun in Latin paradigms to identify the cases more clearly, partly because in Hebrew it is written joined to the noun.
3. Drop the compositional element ifica from facio.	We would segment honori-fica.
4. Drop the verbal termination of ability bilis. 5. Drop the termination of abstraction tudo. 6. Drop the genitive case inflection din. 7. Drop the termination of number es.	
Thus, once you have removed hae - in - ifica - bili - tudin - es, what's left? Just that bare element honor. That is the primitive. Now do the same with Hebrew words.[16]	Reuchlin seems to have experienced some difficulty in working out where to divide the tudo and the din portions of the word, and opts for the safest course: not to segment at all!

The consequence was that Reuchlin's readers assumed that the root was identical both with the semantic core of the word, and with an existing lexeme (see box 10.11 for Elias Levita's version of the same process in Hebrew). In short, they identified it with the thema, the starting-point of the paradigm as conventionally set out – the nominative singular for nouns and the first person singular, present indicative active, for verbs in western European languages. The idea that the root might be an abstraction without an independent existence as a meaningful lexeme escaped them: this concept did not arrive in the West until the nineteenth century. However, with the advent of the notion even in this watered-down form, the morphology of the vernaculars could be described

Box 10.11 How did Jewish scholars explain the notion of root?

It was through the writings of late medieval Jewish popularising grammarians, rather than from direct study of the treatises by the Arab and Jewish scholars of the central Middle Ages who had elaborated the notion, that Renaissance Christians derived their notion of *root*. One such account was to be found in the *Compendium hebraicae grammaticae* (1525), a Latin translation by the German Humanist Sebastian Münster (1489–1552) of a grammar by Elias Levita, a work from which many Christian Hebraists learnt their Hebrew. In this passage Levita explains how to distinguish between *radical* letters, those which occur only as part of a root and never have any grammatical function, and *servile* letters, those which might occur as part of a root or have grammatical function:

The division of letters into radical and servile letters.

In Hebrew almost all nouns and verbs consist of three essential (*substantiales*) letters. The others, found at the beginning and end of the word, are called auxiliary (*adminiculativae*). There are eleven letters which are always radical (= essential) and never servile (= auxiliary), namely ק, ר, צ, ג, ד, פ, ח, ... The remaining eleven letters, i. e. ל, א, ו, מ, ש, ב, ת, are sometimes radical and sometimes servile. That is, when they are servile, they form the persons, numbers and voice of verbs, and the cases and numbers of nouns; in the pronouns they form relations and other functions, as we shall soon explain. Thus, when you are presented with a word, you must remove all the accidental letters if you want to find its root and theme (*radix et thema*: by 'theme' they meant the traditional starting-point of the paradigm, e.g. the first person singular, present indicative active, in Latin and Greek). For example, וישמר (*veyšišmōr* 'I shall guard'): in this word *v* (ו), *y* (י), and *v* (ו) are servile, while the root is שמר (š-m-r).

Had Levita gone on to analyse this example in detail, he would have explained that the root š-m-r 'guard' forms its first person singular of the future tense by prefixing yi- and infixing -ō-; the initial *ve-* is the conjunction 'and', which is always written together with the following word in Hebrew.

The subsequent history of the notion in the western tradition was not altogether straightforward. An account of it which takes the Arab presentation of it as its starting-point is to be found in:

Jean Rousseau, 'La racine arabe et son traitement par les grammairiens européens (1505–1831)', *Bulletin de la Société de Linguistique de Paris* 79 (1984), 285–321.

---

more explicitly than the old terminology permitted (see box 6.7 if your memory needs refreshing). By early in the seventeenth century, terms were available for each separate component of the word depending on its position:

>   *radix* 'root'
>   *affixum* 'affix'
>   *praefixum* 'prefix'
>   *suffixum* 'suffix'

> **Box 10.12 Terminology 3: root and affix**
>
> Christians learnt to look at word structure in a new way when they began to study Hebrew. Although grammars of Hebrew by Jews also used 'letter' and 'syllable' as morphological units, they possessed a repertoire of terms which involved various bits being added to the root:
>
> | PRAEFIXUM | | RADIX | | SUFFIXUM |
> |---|---|---|---|---|
> | prefix | + | root | + | suffix |
>
> AFFIXUM
> affix
>
> In complete contrast to the organic way of picturing word structure characteristic of medieval Christian linguistic discourse, Hebrew grammarians provided Christians with a means of articulating a mechanistic way of conceptualising the word. Using the new terminology, the word was pictured as made up of a series of building-blocks. Each unit was given a name determined by its position: *prefix* before the root, *suffix* following it, or *affix* for anything added to it anywhere. Some grammarians, such as the German scholar Christophorus Crinesius, who uses the new terminology particularly freely in his grammar of Syriac (1611), distinguishes between *free form* (*vox separabilis*) and *bound form* (*vox inseparabilis*). Note the change in the metaphor: whereas previously in the Greco-Roman tradition a free form had been called a *nomen integrum* 'whole word', and a bound form had been called a *nomen corruptum* 'a truncated word', preserving the picture of an entity in different states, Crinesius's terms continue the new building-blocks image.

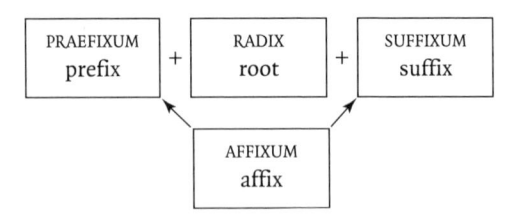

These terms rapidly made their way into modern languages via the new grammars of the vernaculars (see box 10.12).

Quite apart from the linguistic broadening of horizons brought by Hebrew – the first non-Indo-European language to become accessible in western Europe – the new grammatical concepts and terminology assimilated through studying the language provided vital tools for the development of phonology and morphology (particularly as applied to the vernaculars) in the early modern period. Now that Europeans were at last alive to the potential interest of linguistic form, they were quick to appreciate the new ideas.

Further reading

Primary sources are indicated with an asterisk.

Bibliographical resources

Mirko Tavoni et al., eds., *Renaissance Linguistics Archive 1350–1700: A First/Second/Third Print-Out from the Secondary-Sources Data-Base* (Ferrara: Istituto di Studi Rinascimentali 1987, 1988, 1990). [Bibliography of secondary literature relating to linguistics in the Renaissance.]

Bernard Colombat and Elisabeth Lazcano, eds., *Corpus représentatif des grammaires et des traditions linguistiques*, 2 vols., *Histoire, Epistémologie, Langage*, hors-série 2 and 3 (Paris: Société d'histoire et d'epistémologie des sciences du langage 1998, 2000). [Systematic descriptions of a wide range of grammars of Greek, Latin, French, Spanish, Italian, Portuguese, Church Slavonic and Russian (vol. 1), and of German and English (vol. 2), with bibliography for each text.]

See also references to specialised bibliographies for vernacular traditions below.

Background

Anthony Goodman and Angus MacKay, *The Impact of Humanism on Western Europe* (London and New York: Longman 1990). [Collection of articles on Humanism in various countries with attention to language issues.]

Charles G. Nauert, Jr, *Humanism and the Culture of Renaissance Europe* (Cambridge: Cambridge University Press 1995).

Jill Kraye, ed., *The Cambridge Companion to Renaissance Humanism* (Cambridge: Cambridge University Press 1996).

Lisa Jardine, *Worldly Goods: A New History of the Renaissance* (London: Macmillan 1996).

Allen G. Debus, *Man and Nature in the Renaissance* (Cambridge: Cambridge University Press 1978), chs. 1, 3, 4.

A. Rupert Hall, *The Revolution in Science 1500–1750* (London and New York: Longman 1983), chs. 1 and 2.

Alfred W. Crosby, *The Measure of Reality: Quantification and Western Society, 1250–1600* (Cambridge: Cambridge University Press 1997).

Brian P. Copenhaver and Charles B. Schmitt, *Renaissance Philosophy* (Oxford and New York: Oxford University Press 1992).

L. D. Reynolds and N. G. Wilson, *Scribes and Scholars: A Guide to the Transmission of Greek and Latin Literature*, 3rd edn (Oxford: Clarendon 1991), ch. 4.

William Boyd and Edmund J. King, *The History of Western Education* (Totowa, NJ: Barnes and Noble 1975), chs. 6–8.

Renaissance linguistics: surveys

W. Keith Percival, 'Renaissance linguistics: the old and the new', in Theodora Bynon and F. R. Palmer, eds., *Studies in the History of Western Linguistics in Honour of R. H. Robins* (Cambridge: Cambridge University Press 1986), pp. 56–68.

Mirko Tavoni, 'Renaissance linguistics: western Europe', in G. Lepschy, ed., *History of Linguistics 3* (London and New York: Longman 1998), pp. 1–108.

Discovery of non-European languages

J. R. Firth, *The Tongues of Men* (London: Watts 1937, repr. London: Oxford University Press 1970), ch. 5. [Very brief survey of the 'discovery of Babel'].

W. Keith Percival, 'La connaissance des langues du monde', in S. Auroux, ed., *Histoire des idées linguistiques* 2 (Liège: Mardaga 1992), pp. 226–38.

Even Hovdhaugen, ed., *'and the word was God'* . . . : *Missionary Linguistics and Missionary Grammar* (Münster: Nodus 1996).

Elke Nowak, ed., *Languages Different in all their Sounds. . . Descriptive Approaches to the Languages of the Americas 1500 to 1850* (Münster: Nodus 1999).

Maria Leonor Carvalhão Buescu, *O estudo das línguas exóticas no século XVI* (Lisbon: Instituto de Cultura e Língua Portuguesa 1983), chs. 4 and 5. [Account of European encounters with 'exotic' languages.]

Maria Leonor Carvalhão Buescu, 'Le paradigme grammatical medievo-latin dans la grammaire portugaise de la Renaissance', in Irène Rosier, ed., *L'héritage des grammairiens latins de l'Antiquité aux Lumières* (Paris: Société pour l'Information Grammaticale 1988), pp. 271–82. [Surveys achievements of Portuguese linguistics during the Renaissance with particular attention to grammars of non-European languages.]

Michel Adnès, 'Parler un Nouveau Monde: le cas du Pérou', in S. Auroux, ed., *Histoire des idées linguistiques* 2 (Liège: Mardaga 1992), pp. 271–98.

Manfred Peters, 'Conrad Geßner als Linguist und Germanist', *Gesnerus* 28 (1971), 115–46.

*Conrad Gesner, *Mithridates*, repr. with introduction by Manfred Peters (Aalen: Scientia 1974; also repr. Hildesheim: Olms 1999).

Humanist linguistics

Pierre Lardet, 'Travail du texte et savoirs des langues: la philologie', in S. Auroux, ed., *Histoire des idées linguistiques* 2 (Liège: Mardaga 1992), pp. 187–205.

W. Keith Percival, 'Renaissance grammar: rebellion or evolution?', in Giovannangiola Secchi Tarugi, ed., *Interrogativi dell'Umanesimo* 2 (Florence: Olschki 1976), 73–90.

George A. Padley, *Grammatical Theory in Western Europe 1500–1700: The Latin Tradition* (Cambridge: Cambridge University Press 1976), ch. 1.

Louis Kukenheim, *Contributions à l'histoire de la grammaire grecque, latine et hébraïque à l'époque de la Renaissance* (Leiden: Brill 1951). [Greek: pp. 7–45; Latin: pp. 46–87.]

Fidel Rädle, 'Kampf der Grammatik. Zur Bewertung mittelalterlicher Latinität im 16. Jahrhundert', in Udo Kindermann, Wolfgang Maaz and Fritz Wagner, eds., *Festschrift für Paul Klopsch* (Göppinger Arbeiten zur Germanistik 492, Göppingen: Kümmerle 1988), 424–44. [Attitudes to medieval grammar held by German Humanists.]

Francisco Rico, *Nebrija frente a los bárbaros: el canon de gramáticos nefastos en las polémicas del humanismo* (Salamanca: Universidad de Salamanca 1978). [Attitudes to medieval grammar held by southern European Humanists.]

Peter Lebrecht Schmidt, 'Die Wiederentdeckung der spätantiken Grammatik im italienischen Humanismus', *Studi Italiani di Filologia Classica*, 3rd ser., 10 (1992), 861–70.

Jean Stéfanini, 'Aristotélisme et grammaire: le *De causis latinae linguae* (1540) de J. C. Scaliger', *Histoire Epistémologie Langage* 4.2 (1982), 41–54.

David Marsh, 'Grammar, method, and polemic in Lorenzo Valla's *Elegantiae*', *Rinascimento*, 2nd ser., 19 (1979), 91–116.

Grammars of the Renaissance vernaculars

Luce Giard, 'L'entrée en lice des vernaculaires', in S. Auroux, ed., *Histoire des idées linguistiques* 2 (Liège: Mardaga 1992), pp. 206–25.

George A. Padley, *Grammatical Theory in Western Europe 1500–1700: Trends in Vernacular Grammar*, 2 vols. (Cambridge: Cambridge University Press 1985 and 1988).

W. Keith Percival, 'The grammatical tradition and the rise of the vernaculars', in Thomas A. Sebeok, ed., *Current Trends in Linguistics* 13.1 (The Hague: Mouton 1975), pp. 231–75.

Louis Kukenheim, *Contributions à l'histoire de la grammaire italienne, espagnole et française à l'époque de la Renaissance* (Amsterdam: N. V. Noord-Hollandsche Uitgevers-Maatschappij 1932).

Italian

Paul Grendler, *Schooling in Renaissance Italy: Literacy and Learning, 1300–1600* (Baltimore: Johns Hopkins University Press 1989).

Ciro Trabalza, *Storia della grammatica italiana* (Milan: Hoepli 1908, repr. Bologna: Forni 1963).

Robert A. Hall, Jr, *The Italian Questione della lingua: An Interpretative Essay*, University of North Carolina Studies in the Romance Languages and Literature 4 (Chapel Hill, NC 1942).

Maurizio Vitale, *La questione della lingua* (Palermo: Palumbo 1984).

P. Swiggers and S. Vanvolsem, 'Les premières grammaires vernaculaires de l'italien, de l'espagnol et du portugais', *Histoire, Epistémologie, Langage* 9.1 (1987), 157–81.

*Dante, *De vulgari eloquentia*, ed. and transl. Steven Botterill (Cambridge: Cambridge University Press 1996).

*Leon Battista Alberti, *Grammatica della lingua toscana*, ed. Giuseppe Patota, L. B. Alberti, *Grammatichetta e altri scritti sul volgare* (Rome: Salerno 1996). Also ed. C. Grayson (1964 and 1973).

Cecil Grayson, 'Leon Battista Alberti and the beginnings of Italian grammar', *Proceedings of the British Academy* 49 (1963), 291–311.

*Pietro Bembo, *Prose della volgar lingua* (1525), ed. C. Dionisotti, (Turin: Unione Tipografico-Editrice Torinese 1966), pp. 73–309.

*Mario Pozzi, *Discussioni Linguistiche del Cinquecento* (Torino: Unione Tipografico-Editrice Torinese 1988). [Includes tracts on the vernacular by a number of minor sixteenth-century writers.]

*Mirko Tavoni, *Latino, grammatica, volgare: storia di una questione umanistica* (Padua: Antenore 1984). [Includes Latin text of the original sources, and detailed discussion of each one.]

Mirko Tavoni, 'The 15th-century controversy on the language spoken by the ancient Romans: an inquiry into Italian Humanist concepts of "Latin", "grammar", and "vernacular"', *Historiographia Linguistica* 9 (1982), 237–64. [Summarises the argument of his book.]

French

Edmund Stengel, *Chronologisches Verzeichnis französischer Grammatiken vom Ende des 14. bis zum Ausgange des 18. Jahrhunderts nebst Angabe der bisher ermittelten Fundorte derselben*, ed. and updated by Hans-Josef Niederehe, Studies in the History of Linguistics 8 (Amsterdam: Benjamins 1976).

Michèle Goyens and Pierre Swiggers, 'La grammaire française au XVIe siècle: bibliographie raisonnée', in Pierre Swiggers and Willy Van Hoecke, ed., *La langue française au XVIe siècle: usage, enseignement et approches descriptives* (Louvain: Peeters 1989), pp. 157–73.

Jean-Claude Chevalier, *Histoire de la grammaire française*, Que sais-je? 2904 (Paris: Presses Universitaires de France 1994). [Succinct but useful introductory survey.]

Colette Demaizière, *La grammaire française au XVIe siècle: les grammairiens picards*, 2 vols. (Paris: Didier 1983). [Sylvius and Ramus are amongst the grammarians discussed.]

Douglas A. Kibbee, *For to Speke Frenche Trewely: The French Language in England, 1000–1600: Its Status, Description and Instruction*, Studies in the History of the Language Sciences 60 (Amsterdam and Philadelphia: Benjamins 1991).

Jean-Claude Chevalier, *Histoire de la syntaxe: naissance de la notion de complément dans la grammaire française (1530–1750)* (Geneva: Droz 1968). [Much useful general information on individual French grammars of the period.]

Jacques Julien, 'La terminologie française des parties du discours et de leurs sous-classes au XVIe siècle', *Langages* 92 (1988), 65–78.

*Joachim du Bellay, *La deffence et illustration de la langue françoyse*, ed. Louis Terreaux (Paris: Bordas 1972).

John Palsgrave, *Lesclaircissement de la langue françoyse* (1530, repr. Paris: Slatkine 1972).

D. A. Kibbee, 'John Palsgrave's *Lesclaircissement de la langue françoyse* (1530)', *Historiographia Linguistica* 12 (1985), 27–62.

*Jacobus Sylvius (Jacques Dubois), *In linguam gallicam Isagωge* (1536).

Michel Glatigny, 'A l'aube de la grammaire française: Sylvius et Meigret', *Histoire, Epistémologie, Langage* 9.1 (1987), 135–55.

*Louis Meigret, *Le Traité de la grammaire française* (1550), ed. Franz Josef Hausmann (Tübingen: Narr 1980). [In modern orthography.]

Franz-Josef Hausmann, 'Louis Meigret, Humaniste et linguiste', *Historiographia Linguistica* 7 (1980), 335–50.

Franz Josef Hausmann, *Louis Meigret, Humaniste et linguiste* (Tübingen: Narr 1980).

*Robert Estienne, *Traicté de la grammaire françoise* (1557, repr. Geneva: Slatkine 1971).

Elizabeth Armstrong, *Robert Estienne, Royal Printer* (Cambridge: Cambridge University Press 1954; repr. [Abingdon:] Sutton Courtenay 1986).

*Petrus Ramus (Pierre de la Ramée), *Gramere* 1562 (repr. Menston: Scolar 1969 and Geneva: Slatkine 1971) and *Grammaire* (1572, repr. Geneva: Slatkine 1971 and Hildesheim: Olms 1999).

Pierre Swiggers, 'Les grammaires françaises (1562, 1572) de Ramus: vers une méthode descriptive', in Pierre Swiggers and Willy Van Hoecke, eds., *La langue française au XVIe siècle: usage, enseignement et approches descriptives* (Louvain: Peeters 1989), pp. 116–35.

German

Claudine Moulin-Fankhänel, *Bibliographie der deutschen Grammatiken und Orthographielehren I. Von den Anfängen der Überlieferung bis zum Ende des 16. Jahrhunderts* (Heidelberg: Winter 1994).

*Johannes Müller, *Quellenschriften und Geschichte des deutschsprachlichen Unterrichtes bis zur Mitte des 16. Jahrhunderts* (Gotha: Thienemann 1882, repr. Hildesheim: Olms 1969). [Contains editions of primary sources, notably Ickelsamer.]

Max H. Jellinek, *Geschichte der neuhochdeutschen Grammatik von den Anfängen bis auf Adelung*, 2 vols. (Heidelberg: Winter 1913–14).

Andreas Gardt, *Geschichte der Sprachwissenschaft in Deutschland vom Mittelalter bis ins 20. Jahrhundert* (Berlin and New York: de Gruyter 1999).

*Erika Ising, *Die Anfänge der volkssprachlichen Grammatik in Deutschland und Böhmen 1. Quellen* (Berlin: Akademie-Verlag 1966).

E. Ising, *Die Herausbildung der Grammatik der Volkssprachen in Mittel- und Osteuropa* (Berlin: Akademie-Verlag 1970).

Heinrich Weber, 'Die Ausbildung der deutschen Grammatik (einschliesslich der niederländischen)', *Histoire, Epistémologie, Langage* 9.1 (1987), 111–33.

Günther Hampel, *Die deutsche Sprache als Gegenstand und Aufgabe des Schulwesens vom Spätmittelalter bis ins 17. Jahrhundert* (Giessen: Schmitz 1980).

Monika Rössing-Hager, 'Konzeption und Ausführung der ersten deutschen Grammatik. Valentin Ickelsamer: "Ein Teütsche Grammatica"', in Ludger Grenzmann and Karl Stackmann, eds., *Literatur und Laienbildung im Spätmittelalter und in der Reformationszeit* (Stuttgart: Metzler 1984), pp. 534–56.

*Laurentius Albertus, *Teutsch Grammatick oder Sprach-Kunst* (1573, repr. C. Müller-Fraureuth, Strassburg: Trübner 1895). [In Latin.]

*Albert Ölinger, *Vnderricht der Hoch Teutschen Spraach* (Strasbourg 1574, repr. Hildesheim: Olms 1975). [In Latin.]

* Johannes Clajus, *Grammatica germanicae linguae . . . ex Bibliis Lutheri germanicis et aliis eius libris collecta* (1578, repr. Hildesheim: Olms 1973). [In Latin.]

Spanish

Hans-Josef Niederehe, *Bibliografía cronológica de la lingüística, la gramática y la lexicografía del español (BICRES) desde los comienzos hasta el año 1600*, Studies in the History of the Language Sciences 76 (Amsterdam and Philadelphia: Benjamins 1994).

Antonio Ramajo Caño, *Las gramáticas de la lengua castellana desde Nebrija a Correas* (Salamanca: Universidad de Salamanca 1987).

Werner Bahner, *La lingüística española del siglo de oro* (Madrid: Ciencia Nueva 1966), transl. from German, *Beitrag zum Sprachbewusstsein in der spanischen Literatur des 16. und 17. Jahrhunderts* (Berlin: Rütten & Loening 1956).

*Antonio de Nebrija, *Gramatica castellana* (1492). Several modern reprints and editions, e. g. by M. Á. Esparza and R. Sarmiento (Madrid: Fundación Antonio de Nebrija 1992), with facsimile and transcription as well as introduction and bibliography.

Eugenio de Bustos Tovar, 'Nebrija, primer lingüista español', in Víctor García de la Concha, ed., *Nebrija y la Introducción del Renacimiento en España* (Salamanca: Academia Literaria Renacentista 1983), pp. 205–22.

Miguel-Ángel Esparza Torres, *Las ideas lingüísticas de Antonio Nebrija* (Münster: Nodus 1995).

Julio Casares, 'Nebrija y la Gramática castellana', *Boletín de la Real Academia Española* 26 (1947), 335–67.

Juan M. Lope Blanch, *Nebrija cinco siglos después* (Mexico, DF: Universidad Nacional Autónoma de México 1994).

W. Keith Percival, 'Antonio de Nebrija and the dawn of modern phonetics', *Res Publica Litterarum* 5.1 (1982), 221–32.

*Juan de Valdés, *Diálogo de la lengua* (1541–2), ed. Cristina Barbolani (Madrid: Cátedra 1982).

Portuguese

Telmo Verdelho, *As origens da gramatografia e da lexicografia latino-portuguesas* (Aveiro: Instituto Nacional de Investigação Científica 1995).

Maria Leonor Carvalhão Buescu, *Gramaticos portugueses do século XVI* (Lisbon: Instituto de Cultura Portuguesa 1978).

Maria Leonor Carvalhão Buescu, *Historiografia linguística portuguesa: século XVI* (Lisbon: Sá da Costa).

*Fernão Oliveira, *Grammatica da linguagem portuguesa* (1536), ed. M. L. Carvalhão Buescu (Lisbon: Biblioteca Nacional 1974).

*João de Barros, *Gramatica da lingua portuguesa* (1540), partial repr. ed. M. L. Carvalhão Buescu (Lisbon: Faculdade de Letras da Universidade de Lisboa 1971).

English

Robin C. Alston, *A Bibliography of the English Language from the Invention of Printing to the Year 1800*, 11 vols. (Menston: Scolar 1965–77, repr. in part with corrections Ilkley: Janus 1974). [Volumes 1–3 cover grammars of English.]

Ian Michael, *Early Textbooks of English* (Reading: Colloquium on Textbooks, Schools and Society 1993).

Emma Vorlat, *The Development of English Grammatical Theory 1586–1737 with Special Reference to the Theory of Parts of Speech* (Leuven: University Press 1975).

Ian Michael, *English Grammatical Categories and the Tradition to 1800* (Cambridge: Cambridge University Press 1970).

Helmut Gneuss, 'Die Wissenschaft von der englischen Sprache: Ihre Entwicklung bis zum Ausgang des 19. Jahrhunderts', *Sitzungsberichte der bayerischen Akademie der Wissenschaften, philosophisch-historische Klasse*, 1990.1, pp. 1–129. [Brief sketch of most aspects of the subject with select bibliography.]

Otto Funke, *Die Frühzeit der englischen Grammatik* (Berne: H. Lang 1941).

Ivan Poldauf, *On the History of Some Problems of English Grammar before 1800* (Prague: Nákladem Filosofické Fakulty University Karlovy 1948).

*J. L. Moore, *Tudor-Stuart Views on the Growth, Status and Destiny of the English Language* (Halle: Niemeyer 1910, repr. College Park, MD: McGrath 1970).

John Algeo, 'The earliest English grammars', in Mary-Jo Arn and Hanneke Wirtjes, eds., *Historical and Editorial Studies in Medieval and Early Modern English for Johan Gerritsen* (Groningen: Wolters-Noordhoff 1985), pp. 191–207.

Nils Erik Enkvist, 'English in Latin guise: a note on some Renaissance textbooks', *Historiographia Linguistica* 2 (1975), 283–98.

*William Bullokar, *Pamphlet for Grammar 1586*, ed. J. R. Turner, *The Works of William Bullokar* 2 (Leeds: University of Leeds School of English 1980). Also repr. by D. Bornstein (Gainesville: Scholars Facsimiles and Reprints 1977).

R. H. Robins, 'William Bullokar's *Bref Grammar for English*: text and context', in his *Texts and Contexts: Selected Papers on the History of Linguistics*, ed. V. Law (Münster: Nodus 1998), pp. 169–84, repr. from G. Blaicher and B. Glaser, eds., *Anglistentag 1993 Eichstätt. Proceedings XV* (Tübingen: Niemeyer 1994), pp. 19–31.

Otto Funke, 'William Bullokars *Bref Grammar for English* (1586): Ein Beitrag zur Geschichte der frühneuenglischen Grammatik', *Anglia* 62 (1938), 116–37.

The Renaissance discovery of Hebrew

The Hebrew grammatical tradition

Wilhelm Bacher, *Die Anfänge der hebräischen Grammatik and Die hebräische Sprachwissenschaft vom 10. bis zum 16. Jahrhundert*, Studies in the History of the Language Sciences 4 (Amsterdam: Benjamins 1975).

James Barr, 'Linguistic literature, Hebrew', *Encyclopaedia Judaica* 16 (Jerusalem: Keter 1971), 1352–1401. [Includes section on medieval and Renaissance grammarians by David Tené.]

The study of Hebrew and Arabic by Christians during the Middle Ages

Gilbert Dahan, Irène Rosier, Luisa Valente, 'L'arabe, le grec, l'hébreu et les vernaculaires', in Sten Ebbesen, ed., *Geschichte der Sprachtheorie 3: Sprachtheorien in Spätantike und Mittelalter* (Tübingen: Narr 1995), pp. 265–321.

The study of Hebrew by Christians during the Renaissance

Sophie Kessler-Mesguich, 'Les grammaires occidentales de l'hébreu', in S. Auroux, *Histoire des idées linguistiques* 2 (Liège: Mardaga 1992), pp. 251–70.

W. Keith Percival, 'The reception of Hebrew in sixteenth-century Europe: the impact of the Cabbala', *Historiographia Linguistica* 11 (1984), 21–38; repr. in Antonio Quilis and Hans-J. Niederehe, eds., *The History of Linguistics in Spain*, Studies in the History of the Language Sciences 34 (Amsterdam: Benjamins 1986), 21–38.

Christoph Dröge, ' "Quia morem Hieronymi in transferendo cognovi . . ." – Les débuts des études hébraïques chez les humanistes italiens', in *L'hébreu au temps de la Renaissance*, ed. Ilana Zinguer (Leiden: Brill 1992), pp. 65–88.

Marie-Luce Demonet-Launay, 'La désacralisation de l'hébreu au XVIe siècle', in *L'hébreu au temps de la Renaissance*, ed. Ilana Zinguer (Leiden: Brill 1992), pp. 154–71.

Cecil Roth, *The Jews in the Renaissance* (Philadelphia: Jewish Publication Society of America 1959), ch. 7.

*Ludwig Geiger, 'Zur Geschichte des Studiums der hebräischen Sprache in Deutschland', *Zeitschrift für deutsche Theologie* 21 (1876), 190–223. [Pellikan's experiences in learning Hebrew are described on pp. 203–12.]

Ludwig Geiger, *Das Studium der hebräischen Sprache in Deutschland vom Ende des XV. bis zur Mitte des XVI. Jahrhunderts* (Breslau: Schletter 1870).

L. Kukenheim, *Contributions à l'histoire de la grammaire grecque, latine et hébraïque à l'époque de la Renaissance* (Leiden: Brill 1951).

11 A brief overview of linguistics since 1600

11.1 Introduction

From the very first pages of this book we've seen how closely the history of thinking about language and the history of thinking itself are connected. We've followed people's priorities and preferences in linguistic research, and found echoes in their epistemology, education, philosophy, science – in every area of their life touched by thinking. The period of time covered, the fifth century BC to the sixteenth century AD, is bounded by two major moments of change in the history of thinking generally, and so in the history of linguistics too; and, as we've seen, there were various lesser turning-points along the way. Even in the much shorter span of time since 1600 – a mere four hundred years – further changes have taken place in thinking and outlook, reflected just as clearly in linguistics as anywhere else. In this chapter we'll recapitulate by surveying the broad trends in linguistics in the two millennia covered in this book; and then we'll glance ahead at the four hundred years that take us up to the present day. That's not to say that what happened in that relatively brief period has not been significant in its own way; of course it has, and you've probably come across writers and lecturers who have dismissed everything that happened before the Neogrammarians, or Saussure, or even Chomsky, as not worth a glance. Some of the attitudes held by these scornful contemporary practitioners – such as the tendency to despise the old because it's old – took shape during this intervening period, while others go right back to the Greeks. From this point on each discipline needs its own separate treatment, and so, ideally, does each national tradition. So for details you'll have to go to a larger handbook, or to more specialised works. But to give you at least a quick glimpse of how the attitudes, assumptions and research priorities that inform much of present-day linguistics came into being, we'll survey linguistics between 1600 and 1900 after the recapitulation, and glance at what is really new in twentieth-century linguistics.

11.2 Looking back: main themes

Two turning-points stand at the beginning and end of the period we have covered: first, the transition to a way of experiencing the world in which reasoning replaced direct spiritual perception, which seems to have been taking place a little before Socrates, Plato and Aristotle spurred logical thinking into existence in the decades around 400 BC; and secondly, the Renaissance realisation that the sense-perceptible world could be every bit as interesting as mental constructs, a change of attitude which led directly to the cultivation of observation and the rise of empiricism, and with it the scientific way of thinking which so deeply pervades every academic discipline today, including linguistics.

The Greeks of the fifth and fourth centuries threw themselves into the task of understanding what thinking could achieve. Was it a reliable tool for gaining knowledge? Could it be improved? Plato showed how thinking might be taken beyond itself, to knowledge of the Forms; his pupil Aristotle (not a believer in the Forms) spelt out the laws implicit in the thinking Plato himself had used, founding the discipline of logic. These laws underpinned the grammars written by the Greeks and their cultural heirs in the Roman world. Their hierarchical structure, carefully formulated definitions, meticulous categorisation of linguistic phenomena, but also their tendency to favour phenomena with obvious semantic content over those that were purely formal, and a corresponding tendency not to perceive any intrinsic order in formal phenomena – all these are a legacy of that basis in logic which is so apparent in ancient grammatical texts.

Roughly halfway between the two turning-points came a powerful impulse directing attention to the formal side of language. The adoption of Roman Christianity in western Europe had the effect of compelling educated people to engage with linguistic form. The life of the Church, and intellectual activity generally, were in the West dependent upon the Latin language, which in non-Latin-speaking countries entailed a huge pedagogical investment: one generation after another had to spend years grappling with linguistic form at the most basic level, in learning Latin. To some extent the way for this kind of work, analysing Latin from the outside, as a foreign language, had been prepared in the later Roman empire, when teachers had compiled the information about inflectional morphology that was missing from the logically based *Schulgrammatik* type of work in *regulae* grammars. The fact that the order imposed upon the forms was always artificial – alphabetical or numerical – testifies to the difficulties these people experienced in seeing any rationale behind the formal aspects of language. The history of descriptive grammar in the Middle Ages is peppered with attempts to get to grips with form, either by integrating it into the hierarchically ordered *Schulgrammatik* structure, as in the Insular elementary grammars, or by imposing a further kind of artificial ordering principle upon it, as was done in the verse grammars of the late medieval period.

At the same time, though, that major enterprise begun by the Greeks, the study of the relationship between language, thought and reality, occupied the best minds of the millennium, from Augustine to Alcuin, Eriugena, and the Scholastic philosophers. The *modistae* went so far as to construct a thoroughgoing theory of grammar based upon their realist view of this relationship, though they confidently took the long-established linguistic categories as their starting-point. Of course, they made no attempt to deal with form; however, by the end of the thirteenth century some of their contemporaries were beginning to find it easier to do their visualising on the page than in their minds.

Little tree diagrams representing the underlying logical structure of the text began to appear in the margins, and then, at first hesitantly and sparsely, and later with gathering enthusiasm, writers experimented with getting tables and diagrams to take over the work of representing the formal data. This major mental shift culminated in the sixteenth century, when the leading scholars of the Northern Renaissance set about dedicating themselves to the study of everything that could be observed by the senses. The consequent shift to empiricism as the preferred epistemology (backed up, of course, by reasoning) colours the whole of intellectual life since the Renaissance. Without that shift, contemporary natural science would be unthinkable. So too would be anthropology, sociology and the visual arts as we know them today, to name just a few areas – and very many branches of linguistics: descriptive linguistics, typology, historical and comparative linguistics, anthropological linguistics, sociolinguistics, phonetics and many others. Not that the transition was either easy or instantaneous, let alone universal. Initially, observation was used to corroborate doctrines that had been passed down for centuries; then, when contradictions were observed, people attempted to squeeze them into the existing structures of knowledge somehow or other; and only after a great deal of counter-evidence had accumulated did some individual find the courage to propose a quite new explanation.

11.3 The process continues: observation and linguistics after 1600

Nationalism and religious controversy, themselves born of the new-found awareness of the Other – one of the many consequences of waking up to what was out there in the world – helped to focus attention on the early stages of the European languages. Thus in England different sects, anxious to prove how much closer they were to the original purity of the Anglo-Saxon Church than their rivals, ferreted out and published Old English texts which shed light upon the beliefs and practices of the early days of the Church in England. They plunged into detailed study of the language with the help of Ælfric's grammar and glossary (first published in 1659 by William Somner), and later with the assistance of new grammars of Old English by scholars such as Elizabeth Elstob, one of the first known woman grammarians. The seventeenth-century fashion for patriotic antiquarian research inspired the compilation of vast compendia on the antiquities of, for example, the northern and Celtic inhabitants of the British Isles, including grammars of their languages, by scholars such as George Hickes and Edward Lhuyd.

As these scholars assembled their collections of data, their grammars and dictionaries and editions of texts in medieval languages, they came up against phenomena which seemed to imply language change. That raised a major conceptual problem: hadn't all present-day language come into being when the Tower of Babel was destroyed? Then how could they be changing, and worse still, how could new languages be appearing? One scholar after another grappled with this issue. One of the more systematic was the Swedish antiquary Georg Stiernhielm. He published an edition of the Gospels in Gothic, the oldest Germanic language of which substantial records remain.[1] He printed the Gothic text facing the text in Icelandic, Swedish and Latin set out in parallel columns, providing invaluable comparative data for the linguist. As he worked on the text and reflected upon the relationship of Gothic to the many Germanic languages and dialects with which he was acquainted, Stiernhielm began to elaborate many of the principles which are now central to the historical study of language. For instance, all languages, he said, even Hebrew, are subject to change, whether or not catastrophic precipitating events – invasions, deportations, wars and so forth – have taken place. In the course of time a language, particularly if spread over a wide geographical area, will split into dialects, and the dialects will in turn mature into languages. He attempted to distinguish language from dialect partly in terms of mutual intelligibility, partly by arguing that a distinct language will have its own lexical stock shared to a large degree by all its dialects, but that dialects diverge in their inflections, pronunciation and word formation. He concluded his introduction by summarising the conclusions already reached a generation earlier by Claude Saumaise (Salmasius) in his *De hellenistica* (1643)[2] as to a major language family which had once covered vast tracts of Europe and Asia, the *Scythian* or *Japhetic* family. From the ancient Scythian language are descended, Stiernhielm says, such languages as Persian, Gothic, German, Latin, Greek, Slavonic, Phrygian and Celtic – most of the major members of the family now known as *Indo-European*. On the other hand, he says, Hungarian and Finnish, which show many lexical similarities, and Estonian and Lapp (dialects of Finnish, he thinks), are not connected with Slavonic nor with any other language of his acquaintance. Although he doesn't give this family a name, it is clearly the *Finno-Ugrian* family, well over a century before it was put on a sound philological footing by the Hungarian scholar Gyarmathi (1799).[3] Everything was thus now in place for the development of a thoroughgoing historical and comparative linguistics – yet it didn't happen for nearly 150 years. Why not?

The Renaissance change of direction did not go unchallenged. Whenever you find yourself heading towards an extreme, you'll find that the opposite extreme will soon present itself. Intellectual history obeys the same laws as life in general. Since the Renaissance we can see a clear alternation between two opposing orientations in linguistics: the particular, born of the new observational epistemology, and the universal, a continuation of the old rationally based approach to knowledge. Of course, to speak of an 'alternation' between the two makes it sound far too neat. For one thing, each approach takes on elements of the other, so that rationalists learn to use observational data to back up their claims, and empiricists draw upon the tools of logical reasoning in which they are trained at school and university. In practice, there are always adherents of both outlooks around at any given moment, but one of the two will tend to predominate, both in prestige and in the choice of research questions and methods favoured by the majority of scholars. One will be regarded as the mainstream, the other the preserve of those considered old-fashioned, marginal, or fringe.

Even as the language-collectors, the phoneticians, the descriptive grammarians and the rest were revelling in the newly recognised wealth of data, others were waking up to the disadvantages of the new knowledge and the new outlook upon the world. Once you became aware of the diversity in the world, you also had to realise that the former apparent unity of the world was an illusion. No longer was it possible to say, as

26   Lucas van Valckenborch, `The Tower of Babel' (1594)

it was in Dante's day, that the entire world was dominated by Latin, Greek and Hebrew; whole continents were now known where these languages had never been heard of. The biblical story of the division of languages at the building of the Tower of Babel now became a deeply felt experience, and for many people a very painful one. Between roughly 1550 and the early years of the seventeenth century some 140 pictures of the Tower of Babel were printed,[4] bringing home visually the new awareness of linguistic separateness and dispersal. On the day-to-day level, the rise of the vernaculars, so important to national pride, meant that as Latin was gradually displaced as the medium of scholarly communication, whole countries found themselves cut off from the intellectual life of their neighbours. The consequences are still with us: on the positive side, once you are literate in English, you have access to literature from the English-speaking world on any subject imaginable, from horticulture to globalisation to child-rearing, but in order to gain access to what French or Bulgarian or Thai or Kazakh thinkers have to say on the same subjects, you'll have to learn their languages (or read them in translation – if translations exist). Precisely the same problem confronted western Europeans as they woke up to the consequences of the discovery of Babel during the first half of the seventeenth century.

Reactions took many forms. Even before the end of the sixteenth century, the Spanish Humanist Francisco Sánchez de las Brozas (1523–1600), generally known as Sanctius, was attacking the mindless empiricism that he associated with Lorenzo Valla's still very popular but unstructured work on Classical Latin usage, *Elegantiae de latina lingua* (see p. 230 above). The very title of Sanctius's work – *Minerva, sive de causis linguae latinae* ('Minerva, or the Underlying Principles of the Latin Language', 1587) – makes his position clear, and he goes on to articulate it in his characteristic forthright manner:

A perverse opinion, or rather a piece of unbelievable stupidity has taken over the minds of many people, namely, that there are no underlying principles in the Greek and Latin languages, and no reason for looking into the matter in depth. I have never seen anything more idiotic than this figment of the imagination, and it would be hard to dream up anything fouler. Does a human being, who is after all a rational being, really act, speak and plan without understanding and reason?[5]

His own working method is 'to set out the underlying principles first and then to give examples (if possible) in order to make the matter clear'. Sanctius's *Minerva* was the first in a series of widely read philosophical grammars which prepared the way for the more celebrated *Grammaire générale et raisonnée* (1660) – Tommaso Campanella's *Philosophia rationalis* (1618), Christoph Helwig's *Libri didactici grammaticae universalis* (1619), and Juan Caramuel y Lobkowitz's *Grammatica audax* (1654). In complete contrast, the Silesian mystic Jacob Böhme (1575–1624) tried to circumvent language altogether, urging people to learn to read the 'signatures' of things (*signaturae rerum*), inbuilt clues as to the hidden nature and potential of everything on Earth. Yet another remedy for Babel was propounded by others such as the French scholar Marin Mersenne and the Englishmen Francis Lodwick and Cave Beck, who urged the construction of a *universal character*, a system of signs that could be read off in any language. Soon, however, such schemes came up against the uniqueness of each language. If an Englishman wrote out the signs for 'butter' and 'cup' to represent 'buttercup', a German would be none the wiser, for the corresponding term in his language, *Hahnenfuß*, contains a different buried metaphor, 'hen's foot'. George Dalgarno and John Wilkins, working in Oxford in the 1660s, realised that if a universal character scheme were to have any chance of success, it must be founded upon a comprehensive classification of reality. Once everything had been assigned to its proper place in the scheme, it could then be labelled in any convenient way – with spoken sounds, written symbols, even musical notation – and then communication, and indeed thought itself, could proceed on a completely rational basis. Wilkins's monumental *Essay Towards a Real Character and a Philosophical Language* (1668) begins with just such a classification of reality, with God and the angels, the celestial bodies, topographical features, rocks and minerals, plants, animals and much, much more drawn up in neat dichotomies – or as neat as he could make them. The system was not without its problems. As his reluctant assistant, the botanist John Ray, grumbled,

I was constrained in arranging the Tables not to follow the lead of nature, but to accommodate the plants to the author's prescribed system. This demanded that I should divide herbs into three squadrons or kinds as nearly equal as possible; then that I should split up each squadron into nine 'differences', as he called them, that is subordinate kinds, in such wise that the plants ordered under each 'difference' should not exceed a fixed number; finally that I should join pairs of plants together or arrange them in couples. What possible hope was there that a method of that sort would be satisfactory, and not manifestly imperfect and ridiculous?[6]

Wilkins was working on the pre-Renaissance assumption that reality must be perfectly rational (or at any rate, that it must conform to his Aristotelian notion of rationality).

Ray, far more the empiricist than Wilkins, knew from experience that reality was messy, irregular and apparently irrational.

In France the rationalists pressed on nothing daunted with the search for the rational order underpinning language. At the school of Port-Royal, a monastic community outside Paris, an empiricist grammarian, Claude Lancelot, collaborated with a philosopher, Antoine Arnauld, in a work which bore the title *Grammaire générale et raisonnée* ('General and Rational Grammar', 1660). Language, they declared, reflected the three fundamental mental operations: forming a concept such as 'circle'; forming a judgement, such as 'the Earth is round'; and reasoning, as in 'all virtues are praiseworthy, and patience is a virtue, therefore patience is praiseworthy'. Ultimately, all linguistic categories in all languages could be traced back to mental categories, although many anomalies could now be observed – the purely arbitrary assignment of nouns in Latin and Greek to the neuter gender when it could have been done rationally, for instance. For the next century and a half scholars explored the possibilities they read between the lines of the *Grammaire générale et raisonneé*. They recognised two fundamentally different approaches to the study of language, neatly characterised by the French scholar Nicolas Beauzée in Diderot and d'Alembert's famous *Encyclopédie* (1757):

General grammar is the rationally ordered science of the immutable general principles of spoken or written language in any language. *Particular grammar* is the art of applying to the immutable general principles of written or spoken language the arbitrary conventions in common use of a particular language.[7]

Similarly, the first edition of the *Encyclopædia Britannica* (1771) contrasts 'grammar considered as an Art', its aim being language teaching, and 'grammar considered as a *Science*, [which] views language in itself'.[8] Neither the study of language 'in and for itself' nor the search for 'immutable general principles' common to all languages is a twentieth-century innovation; they rest upon a tradition which goes back via the general grammar movement of the eighteenth century to the sixteenth- and seventeenth-century philosophical grammars of Sanctius, Campanella, C. Helwig and Caramuel, which in turn look back to the Modists (*modistae*).

But even as these ideas were spreading across Europe, and general/universal/ philosophical grammars modelled on the *Grammaire générale et raisonnée* were pouring off the presses, more empirically minded scholars were assembling evidence that seemed to conflict with the basic premises of the general grammar movement. Attacks came from several sides. The English philosopher John Locke, in his *Essay concerning Human Understanding* (1689), argued that it was exceedingly difficult, if not impossible, to be certain that what *you* mean by a complex notion such as *wisdom* is the same as what *I* mean. Only if we systematically break all such complex notions down into their constituent simple notions will we have any hope of reaching a mutual understanding. Still worse problems lie in wait if you move to another language. Locke writes:

A moderate skill in different Languages, will easily satisfie one of the truth of this, it being so obvious to observe great store of Words in one Language, which have not any that answer them in another. Which plainly shews, that those of one Country, by their customs and manner of Life, have found occasion to make several complex Ideas, and give names to them, which others never collected into specifick Ideas.[9]

Locke's *Essay*, translated during the eighteenth century into French, Latin, German, Italian and Modern Greek, spread swiftly across Europe, instilling doubt in the hitherto unchallenged universality of the signified by the words we use. That doubt opened the way to the linguistic relativity which plays so large a part in our experience of language today, particularly in cross-cultural encounters.

An explicit statement of linguistic relativity was still several generations off, however. It required not only a firm philosophical foundation such as Locke had provided, but also a large body of comparative linguistic data. While the universalists were eagerly demonstrating how the universals of thought could be found in English, or German, or Dutch, or Russian, or even Persian, those of a more empirical turn of mind were assembling and working through information about an ever-expanding body of languages. Those universalists who took an interest in the peculiarities of specific languages were fired by the search for the genius (*génie*) of the language, a central theme of the eighteenth century. What is it that gives the language (and so the people that speaks it) its essence? The English Aristotelian James Harris set out a rhetorical typology of languages in his *Hermes: or a Philosophical Inquiry Concerning Language and Universal Grammar* (1751), working uncompromisingly from his image of the character of the nation to its modes of thought, and from there to the language and the way it is used. Thus, of the speakers of the languages of the autocratic states of the Middle East he says: 'Their Ideas became consonant to their servile State, and their Words became consonant to their servile Ideas.' As for the Romans, 'a Nation engaged in wars and commotions, ... their language became, like their Ideas, copious in all Terms expressive of things political, and well adapted to the purposes both of History and popular Eloquence.' Finally, the Greeks: 'the Language of these Greeks was truly like themselves; 'twas conformable to their transcendent and universal Genius . . . thus [it] is . . . made for all that is great, and all that is beautiful, in every Subject, and under every Form of writing.'[10] But that was by no means the only approach to typology at the time: Abbé Gabriel Girard, writing in Paris five years earlier, looked not at style and vocabulary to establish his typology but at syntax. In his grammar of French, *Les vrais principes de la langue françoise: ou la parole réduite en méthode, conformément aux loix de l'usage* ('True Principles of the French Language, or Speech Reduced to Method in Accordance with the Laws of Usage', 1747) he divided the European languages known to him into three classes based on word order, presence or absence of an article, and presence or absence of case inflection.[11] Characteristically, those universalists who took an interest in linguistic diversity sought order in their data by elaborating a typological classification. This permitted them to focus on the question which interested them most of all – how do languages reflect reality and the concepts we form of it? – without getting caught up in the details of precisely when a given form or construction might be attested, what its origin might be, whether it might be borrowed from or affected by some other language – in short, without taking into account historical considerations.

That preoccupation with the genius of the language so characteristic of the French Enlightenment was taken up with enthusiasm by the Germans (and not only by them) in the years around 1800, becoming one of the most striking features of early Romanticism. Johann Gottfried Herder (1744–1803) urged his contemporaries in his influential *Ideen zur Philosophie der Geschichte der Menschheit* ('Outlines of a Philosophy of the History of Man', 1784–5) to study the *Volksgeist*, the genius or spirit of the people, in all its manifestations: in the folksongs and fairytales, in the costumes, the customs, and in the language. It was in 'the physiognomy of their language', he said, that the genius of a people revealed itself most clearly. He called for a philosphical comparison of languages.[12] Comparison, too, was at the heart of the call by Friedrich von Schlegel (1772–1829) a generation later for the study of 'the inner structure of languages, or comparative grammar, which will give us quite new insights into the genealogy of languages in the same way as comparative anatomy has shed light on higher natural history.'[13] By the time Schlegel was writing, in 1808, the possibilities of comparison as an epistemological tool were being explored with great energy in every possible domain. Comparison involves a particularly active combination of observation and of reasoning. There are differences here, comparativists say to themselves: how are we to explain them? Explanations can be sought on various levels, from the purely external, largely descriptive type to the teleological – 'the zebra has developed stripes in order to be better camouflaged' – to a kind which seeks to enter into the phenomenon and come to understand how it developed as it did from within, as it were, attempting to grasp its essence and its individual laws of development. The prototypical comparative discipline, and unquestionably the most prestigious one at the start of the nineteenth century, was comparative anatomy. In 1805 the French scholar Georges Cuvier brought out his lectures on the subject, *Leçons d'anatomie comparée*, which took people's breath away. Instead of describing the anatomy of each animal species one after another, as most previous writers had done, he took up one system at a time – first the bones and muscles, then the sense organs, and so on. In the process he traced a whole series of correlations: slow-moving animals with hooves will have flat teeth and be herbivorous, whereas animals build to run fast will have sharp claws, pointed teeth, and be carnivorous, for example. These correlations he later drew upon in order to reconstruct whole skeletons from a few fossil bones. The key elements of comparativism as manifested in Cuvier's *Leçons* were taken up by the first generation of linguists in the nineteenth century. Each of them tried out one major facet of comparativism, whether inspired by Cuvier directly or by the image of his working methods that had passed into popular consciousness.

Only one of these early nineteenth-century writers on language had actually studied anatomy, the scholar-diplomat Wilhelm von Humboldt (1767–1835). Humboldt's ideas about language were complex and far-reaching; indeed, he articulated several themes that were only to catch on generations later: the importance of studying language for its own sake; the study of language for its own sake being like the study of any other natural phenomenon;[14] the autonomy of linguistics;[15] the importance of the human language capacity;[16] the centrality of relationships rather than of things to thought.[17] Humboldt, like Cuvier and also like Goethe the scientist, lived for comparativism. That same year he drew up a *Plan einer vergleichenden Anthropologie* ('Plan for a Comparative Anthropology') in which he pointed out that just as in comparative anatomy one goes about explaining the structure of the human body by investigating the structure of animals, so one should have a parallel discipline to investigate the characteristics of the moral or mental organisation of the human beings. By studying all aspects of human diversity – clothing, occupations, entertainment, gesture, gait, colour, physique, language and psychology – we can 'learn to know the human being exactly as he is and assess in freedom what he can develop into'.[18] On the basis of a knowledge of languages rivalled by few linguists before or since, he gradually elaborated his ideas in greater detail. His experience as a diplomat involved in the redrawing of the map of Europe after the Napoleonic wars had given him immediate personal experience of how one's way of thinking could be affected by one's language, and how language was in turn shaped by thought. Language was the point of transition from subjectivity to objectivity and a tool with which to discover what one didn't know.[19] Languages differ not just in sounds and signs, but in their speakers' world-view: 'This is the basis and the ultimate goal of all linguistic research,' he wrote.[20] In his last work he summed this up in a celebrated sentence: 'Language is, as it were, the outer appearance of the spirit of the peoples; their language is their spirit and their spirit their language.'[21] Elsewhere: 'Ideas and language, almost always go the same way, bound up tightly with one another, and exert a reciprocal influence upon one another.'[22] In many of his writings, particularly towards the end of his life, Humboldt strove to grasp the relationship between the language of a particular people and their mentality; this was a subject which was to fascinate many of his successors.

Not, however, his young protégé Franz Bopp (1791–1867). It was Bopp who in many respects set the tone of mainstream linguistic research during the nineteenth century, not least because he occupied a chair at Berlin University through Humboldt's good offices for over forty years. Although Bopp was encouraged by his teacher, K. J. Windischmann, to study Sanskrit, the religious and literary language of ancient India which dominated the imagination of early nineteenth-century Europe, in order to help translate the central texts of Indian philosophy and religion, he soon dropped all pretence of an interest in these areas, writing to Windischmann:

Of everything that pertains to India, the language is the most important to me, and only in the dissection of its organism and in investigations into its relationship to cognate dialects and its significance in the general sphere of languages do I take up my pen with real pleasure and inner confidence.[23]

The study of languages in and for themselves was what really interested him, and morphological analysis lay at the heart of his work. His first book was a detailed comparison of the verb forms of the Indo-European languages (1816). Here is an example of his method:

The [Latin] imperfect is indicated in transitive verbs by *ba-m, s, t* and the future by *bo, is, it*. *Bam* and *bo* I derive (like *fuvi*) from the Indian root *Bhū*. The Indian aspirated *b*, which changes to an aspirated *p* in *fuvi*, has become a plain *b* in *bam* and *bo*. In the same way *Tibi* comes from *Tubhya*, and the dative plural in *bus* from the Indian one in *bhyah*.[24]

Bopp's early carefree habit of deriving Latin forms (and forms in other languages) from Sanskrit is toned down in his later writings. Throughout his work, even in his great *Comparative Grammar of the Sanscrit, Zend, Greek, Latin, Lithuanian, Gothic, German, and Sclavonic Languages*, there is a timelessness about the way in which he handles linguistic forms, nonchalantly comparing forms from languages two millennia apart without mentioning the date of attestation.[25] His goal was not to arrive at an appreciation of the essence of the individual languages, as it was with Humboldt and (as we shall see) with Jacob Grimm, but to arrive at the point where the differences become insignificant and the underlying unity of all languages shines out instead. In his letters he exclaims triumphantly that he has demonstrated that Greek grammar is no different from that of Sanskrit.[26] Later in his career he attempted to demonstrate that both Georgian and the Malayo-Polynesian group of languages are connected with Indo-European – a position which might find favour today, given the fashion for mega-families, but which did not appeal to the linguists of his own day.

Jacob Grimm (1785–1863), the third of the scholars who played a decisive part in shaping the goals and methodology of nineteenth-century linguistics, adapted still another facet of Cuvier's methodology while bringing a new element into linguistic studies: historicism. In response to Herder's call, and in tune with the spirit of Romanticism, Jacob and his brother Wilhelm dedicated their lives to collecting materials to help illumine the essence of the German people – myths, sagas and legends, medieval legal texts, the famous fairy tales, a huge etymological dictionary of German (begun in 1854, before the *Oxford English Dictionary*, but not finished until 1960, long after it), and of course the grammar. Jacob's first major linguistic project was a comparative grammar of the Germanic languages, the *Deutsche Grammatik* (1819, second edition 1822–65). Instead of describing one language at a time in its entirety, he proceeds in a manner reminiscent of Cuvier, taking one word class at a time and working his way through its forms in each of the early Germanic languages – Gothic, Old High German, Old Saxon, Old English, Old Frisian, Old Norse – and then through the corresponding later medieval stages – Middle High German, Middle Low German, Middle English, medieval Dutch – and finally through the modern equivalents, wherever possible choosing the same word to illustrate the declension pattern across all the languages. Unlike Bopp, for whom languages seem to exist outside time and space, Grimm cares deeply about the historical setting of his data. Not only does he give lengthy lists of similarly inflected words – sometimes over 200! – he also directs you to examples of the less common forms in the early texts which are his sources, with precise page references. Already in the plan of the work an appreciation of the historical sequence of development is apparent; and he spells out his views in the prefaces, pointing out how astonishingly unhistorically the modern languages have been dealt with, and stating uncompromisingly: 'I am against the concepts of general logic in grammar; they bring with them seeming rigour and definitiveness of the rules, but get in the way of observation, which I regard as the soul of linguistic research.'[27] Grimm's respect for the data enabled him to make very many statements about the patterns that he perceived in his vast mass of carefully ordered forms, and these generalisations stand at the start of the great nineteenth-century tradition of linguistic laws. That patient fidelity to the forms before him, abandoning all *a priori* notions about what ought to be there, was Grimm's legacy to his successors.

11.3 Observation and linguistics after 1600

All these manifestations of comparativism – Grimm's dedication to historical accuracy and painstaking observation, Bopp's carefully worked-out linguistic dissection, and Humboldt's desire to find a way of investigating the reciprocal influence of language and thought – were taken up by the next generation of scholars, both in Germany and outside. Let's look at two figures who stood out in their own time.

First, Humboldt's interest in language and thought was given a foundation in the newly developed discipline of psychology by the Berlin-based Jewish scholar Heymann Steinthal (1823–99). Interested in Humboldt's ideas since his student days, Steinthal, together with his friend, the psychologist Moritz Lazarus, created a new discipline, Völkerpsychologie, 'ethnopsychology', and founded an influential journal, Zeitschrift für Völkerpsychologie und Sprachwissenschaft ('Journal of Ethnopsychology and Linguistics'), to further its investigation. In the introduction to the first issue (scholars often present their reflections on where their subject is going and where they would like it to go in the introduction to a new journal) Steinthal and Lazarus contrasted the activity of nature – inexorable, law-governed, mechanical, repetitive – and of Geist, the human mind or spirit, which is to be found in our free creative activity. Since language is a process which comes into existence every time anyone speaks, created freely in the moment, it belongs to the domain of Geist rather than to nature, and consequently, they conclude, linguistics is a human (or as they and their contemporaries preferred to say, a historical) discipline.[28] In keeping with his insistence on the centrality of Geist as the truly living element in language Steinthal particularly encouraged work on semantic change; one of his followers, Ludwig Tobler, outlined the basic principles of historical semantics.[29]

Steinthal directed some of his most vehement comments on the state of contemporary linguistics at the work of a scholar who in many ways was the intellectual heir of Franz Bopp: August Schleicher (1821–68). Schleicher was a comparativist very much in the Boppian mould: his major work was a Compendium of the Comparative Grammar of the Indo-European, Sanskrit, Greek and Latin Languages (1861–2),[30] a direct successor to Bopp's Comparative Grammar. He refined and developed the techniques of morphological analysis, applying them to a wider range of Indo-European languages, modern as well as ancient. Where Schleicher went much further than Bopp was in his development of the metaphor of language as an organism. He had developed this notion to some extent in his second book, Die Sprachen Europas in systematischer Übersicht (1850),[31] but the publication in 1860 of a German translation of Charles Darwin's Origin of Species (1859) spurred him to take his thinking further. In an essay called (in its English translation) Darwinism Tested by the Science of Language (1863) he maintained that language was not like an organism, it *was* an organism:

Languages are organisms of nature; they have never been directed by the will of man; they rose, and developed themselves according to definite laws; they grew old, and died out. They, too, are subject to that series of phenomena which we embrace under the name of 'life'. The science of language is consequently a natural science; its method is generally altogether the same as that of any other natural science.[32]

He goes on to point out that the idea of gradual variation – slow evolutionary change over long periods of time – which was so shocking to the scientific community was something he had always taken for granted. Indeed, as we saw on p. 261 above, the notion of gradual change had been familiar to linguists ever since Stiernhielm's day, whereas many biologists and geologists in the mid-nineteenth century were still wedded to the notion of catastrophism, the idea that change requires some huge and drastic external stimulus – floods, earthquakes, volcanic eruptions and so forth, the geologist's equivalent of the seventeenth-century linguist's wars and deportations. Schleicher further demonstrated that others of the evolutionary notions that looked so revolutionary in Darwin's work were well-known among linguists, from the struggle for existence – witness the impending extinction of Basque, threatened on all sides by Indo-European – to the survival of the fittest: 'certain peoples, such as the Indians of North America, are unfitted for historical life on account of their endlessly complicated languages, bristling with overabundant forms, ... [and] can only undergo retrogression, even extinction.'[33] The evolutionary sequence in the life of languages he linked with internal characteristics of the languages themselves (like Steinthal he was a keen typologist), paying minimal attention to their speakers. Hence Steinthal's comment on Schleicher and his followers that they took into account 'only the organism – the lifeless body of language – and not its life; they dissect its corpse'.

The idea of language as an organism, neatly encapsulated in the title of a famous popularising work about linguistics by the American scholar William Dwight Whitney, *The Life and Growth of Language* (1875), caught the imagination of scholars and public alike. But while this image of language was in its heyday, another was quietly taking shape. Wilhelm Scherer (1841–86), a Germanic philologist, published a history of the German language, *Zur Geschichte der deutschen Sprache* (1868), in which he rejected Schleicher's claim that language is an organism and linguistics a natural science. Instead, he preferred to speak in terms of a 'mechanics of society', or even, borrowing Steinthal's term, of ethnopsychology (*Völkerpsychologie*).[34] He was convinced of the importance of psychological factors in language, although he went into them less deeply than Steinthal. His major contribution was to transfer several further notions across from the evolutionary sciences, applying them where he could to language in society rather than to language as an independently evolving organism: the importance of uniformitarianism – the idea that the same principles have been at work ever since language originated – which implied that ancient languages such as Hebrew, Sanskrit, Greek and Latin, which were still felt by many scholars (not to mention members of the public) to be qualitatively different from modern languages, had been governed by exactly the same principles as any modern dialect, even the messy irregularity-inducing force of analogy; determinism, summed up in the catchphrase *gleiche Ursachen, gleiche Wirkungen* 'same causes, same effects'; and the vital importance of a sound knowledge of articulatory phonetics as a basis for statements about sound change. Scherer thus looks in two directions at once: in his insistence on the centrality of psychology for understanding linguistic processes he looked back consciously to Steinthal and Humboldt; but in his application of the increasingly rigorous and mechanical principles of evolutionary science he almost belied his own statements about the social nature of language.

That same ambivalence is apparent in the work of a group of scholars sometimes regarded as the founders of modern linguistics (who you select from amongst the rival contenders depends on your view of what 'modern' implies). Known as the *Neogrammarians* (*Junggrammatiker*), they were a group of young men who were together at Leipzig University in the 1870s: Karl Brugman(n), Hermann Osthoff, Eduard Sievers, Wilhelm Braune, Hermann Paul and others. Most of them studied with the classical philologist Georg Curtius, a man who was deeply interested in the direction linguistic research was taking. He pointed out in 1870 that there were two fundamental notions which were of the highest importance for linguistic research: analogy and phonological laws.[35] His pupils had no problems with that. What deeply annoyed them was his scepticism about the extent to which phonological laws really were laws in the same sense as a natural law like gravity or the Second Law of Thermodynamics. After a dramatic break with him, Brugman and Osthoff went independent, bringing out their articles in a series of volumes called *Morphologische Untersuchungen auf dem Gebiete der indogermanischen Sprachen* ('Morphological Investigations in the Domain of the Indo-European Languages'). It was the preface to the first volume, known to us today as the *Neogrammarian Manifesto* (1878), that caught people's attention. In it the two authors announce that since the appearance of Scherer's *Zur Geschichte der deutschen Sprache* the methodology of linguistics has been transformed. They (or rather Brugman, the actual writer of the preface) point out:

Language is not a thing which leads a life of its own outside and above human beings; it has its true existence only in the individual. Hence all changes in the life of a language can only proceed from the individual speaker.[36]

Linguists should therefore keep the speaker in view. Sound changes, innovations and analogical formations are incomprehensible unless approached with a knowledge of the psychological factors at work, as Steinthal had pointed out back in 1860, they remark. The two principles they enunciate as the central tenets of the Neogrammarian movement also have a familiar look about them:

First, every sound change, insofar as it proceeds mechanically, takes place in accordance with laws that admit of no exception . . . Secondly, given that analogy plays a very important part in the life of modern languages, this type of linguistic innovation is to be acknowledged without hesitation for older periods, even the most ancient too.[37]

These were the two aspects of contemporary linguistic research which Curtius had singled out as the most significant (though he wouldn't have agreed with the Neogrammarians' insistence on the exceptionlessness of the sound laws), and, as the Neogrammarians themselves recognised, the way for them had been prepared by Wilhelm Scherer.

The Neogrammarians themselves (with the exception of Hermann Paul) did little to develop the study of psychological side of language and language change, preferring to focus on the discovery of yet more sound laws, the collection of ever more data, and, increasingly, on the elaboration of ever more scientifically based ways of studying sounds: articulatory phonetics found eager proponents amongst them. But from around 1880 one scholar after another began to explore the new possibilities. Hermann Paul's textbook *Prinzipien der Sprachgeschichte* ('Principles of the History of Language',

1880, still in print), the canonical work of its era, gave meaning and psychological considerations an important place. Georg von der Gabelentz, a pupil of Steinthal's, took up psychological factors and the role of the speaker in his *Die Sprachwissenschaft: Ihre Aufgaben, Methoden und bisherigen Ergebnisse* ('Linguistics: Its Tasks, Methods and Results to Date', 1891), and outlined two methods of carrying out research into language change in progress that we would now describe as apparent-time and real-time studies.[38] Jacobus van Ginneken (1877–1945) went deeply into many of the concerns that pertain to psycholinguistics in his *Principes de linguistique psychologique* ('Principles of Psychological Linguistics', 1907), as did the psychologist Wilhelm Wundt, who in his monumental *Völkerpsychologie: Eine Untersuchung der Entwicklungsgesetze von Sprache, Mythus und Sitte* ('Ethnopsychology: An Investigation of the Developmental Laws of Language, Myth and Custom', 10 volumes, 1900–20) took up such topics as expression through gesture and facial expression as well as in speech; child language acquisition; the evidence from amnesia and other pathologies for perception of the word and word formation; the psychological mechanisms of sound change; and psychological issues in sentence structure. Thus, by the time the Swiss linguist Ferdinand de Saussure (1857–1913), who had in his youth studied with the Neogrammarians in Leipzig, was giving lectures in general linguistics between 1906 and 1911, the speaker had entered linguistics to an extent which would have been inconceivable when the Neogrammarians were young.

What Saussure added, as we can see from his posthumously published *Cours de linguistique générale* (1916), was a focus upon relationships. Even though the scholars active in the last decades of the nineteenth century were gradually abandoning the previous focus upon language as an organism independent of human volition, their initial reaction, in most cases, was to trace the way in which language lived in the mind and speech; how a particular individual interacted with other speakers in the act of speaking was a new concern, one for which the way was prepared by the intense interest at the end of the nineteenth century in society and in the hidden laws of social interaction. Saussure also recognised that relationships were at work in other domains of language, and that it was this which gave individual linguistic phenomena their significance. After all, an individual speech sound does not truly belong to speech unless it enters into a relationship with other sounds, any more than an isolated word or sentence will carry much meaning unless it is uttered as part of an act of discourse.

11.4 Linguistics in the twentieth century

And what of the endlessly complex twentieth century? Its story has already been written numerous times, yet almost exclusively, at any rate in one-volume treatments, from an Anglo-American point of view, and angled at the history of the study of the language system, primarily grammar. Thus, after Saussure we usually jump across the Atlantic to Bloomfield and the distributionalists of mid-century, culminating in Zellig Harris, and finally Chomsky (and no one has dared to speculate where the story goes next). To write in this way conveys the impression, no matter how carefully you try to cover yourself, that America is where the action is, and that little significant work has taken place outside the American current in grammatical theory. Historians of Structuralist linguistics cast their net somewhat wider, taking in the Prague and Copenhagen schools before hopping across the Atlantic. No doubt it helped that the Prague School had Roman Jakobson as its exponent in the US from 1941, and that Louis Hjemslev's doctrine was made available by an English translation (1953) of the Danish original (1943) of his *Prolegomena to a Theory of Language*, published in a widely circulating series. Other European Structuralist movements have been less visible outside their country of origin: Bartoli's Neolinguistics, Bally's stylistics, Firth's prosodic analysis, Trier's work on semantic fields and semantic change, Guillaume's psychomechanics of language. Tesnière's valency theory has been developed actively in Germany and to some extent in Britain, where Martinet's Functional Grammar also has a foothold.

All these movements focus on language structure, working on language as a system 'où tout se tient', in the words of the French scholar Antoine Meillet.[39] All of them are touched, more or less profoundly, by the characteristically twentieth-century focus on relationships articulated so carefully by Saussure. But relationships exist not just language-internally, between the abstract elements which make up the system, but between language and its speakers and amongst the speakers as well. The study of linguistic relationships between speakers is if anything a more radical departure from the past than the many movements which have focused on language as a self-contained system. Symptomatic of the novelty of this approach is the fact that it is the branches of linguistics which arise from this work which most closely reflect contemporary popular concerns and ways of thinking, and indeed help to shape them, whereas the concerns of phonologists, syntacticians, theoretical semanticists and the like tend to go unnoticed by the world at large. If we were to chart their emergence – and since their story does not often find its way into textbooks, it is worth doing so briefly here – we would need to trace two parallel lines of development.

One, leading to sociolinguistics, begins with the European dialectologists of the decades after 1880, whose desire to understand language change led them to carry out microstudies of the speech of individual communities, even, as in the case of Louis Gauchat, writing in 1905, carrying out an apparent-time study, differentiating carefully between the phonetic features of three generations of speakers in a remote Alpine village.[40] Across the Atlantic, dialectologists working in the USA in the 1930s quickly realised that for historical and social reasons regional dialects were less important there than social ones. Sociologists too began to take an interest in social differences in speech, and after a major conference on the sociology of language in 1964 several universities instituted courses in it. It was William Labov who set out a methodology that was in tune with the acute desire of the time for a 'scientific', i.e. quantitative rather than qualitative, way of working. He began his *Social Stratification of English in New York City* (1966) by articulating the assumptions that he saw as restricting the linguistics of his time: rigid separation of synchronic and diachronic investigation, the assumption that sound change cannot be directly observed, the purported inaccessibility of feelings about language, and the inadmissibility of non-linguistic data to explain language change.[41] The study that he then described challenged all four assumptions, and did so using the methodological rigour that had come to characterise American linguistics. That rigour was essential to Labov's purpose, enabling him to demonstrate that one could genuinely arrive at generalisations about the language system from investigations of the speech of individuals – in Saussure's terminology, that one could move from observation of *parole* to a better understanding of *langue*. That approach was tried out in many contexts in the ensuing decades. In the 1990s a new concern began to make itself felt in sociolinguistics. Benedict Anderson's influential *Imagined Communities* (1983) had shown how, far from being constrained by the categories into which they are born, individuals actively engage in the construction of their national and ethnic identity. To some extent (though Anderson did not go into this, being more interested in the use of history and myth) one's use of language is an element in that process. But speakers construct other aspects of their identity through language too – class identity (think of those countless British people in the 1950s and 1960s who modelled their speech on 'BBC English', which brought them a much-desired escape route from the limitations imposed by a marked regional or class accent), gender identity, professional identity and so on – the stuff of sociolinguistic research in the last quarter of the twentieth century. With this new awareness of the linguistic tools for the construction of identity come urgent questions for every speaker: now that I know what the linguistic devices are for sounding authoritative, or conciliatory, or tough, or capable, or helpless, should I use them to shape my behaviour and the way others see me? Consciousness-raising always brings ethical issues with it. The immediacy for our own lives of the questions opened up by recent work on the linguistic construction of aspects of our identity is why works such as Deborah Tannen's *You Just Don't Understand: Women and Men in Conversation* (1990) have caught the imagination of the public and of students alike. What empowers us, what gives us the possibility of taking charge of our own lives a little bit more, naturally strikes us as important; in contrast, research which is hedged about with abstruse formalisms and proudly advertises itself as being relevant only to 'language considered in and for itself' comes across as irrelevant to the pressing business of living.

The second major current in the study of linguistic relationships among speakers leads from anthropology and anthropological linguistics to the ethnography of speaking and pragmatics. As soon as anthropologists start to work with informants of a different language from their own, they become aware of all kinds of mismatches between the linguistically encoded conceptual categories of the foreign language and their own. Whereas those working in the confidently judgemental atmosphere of the mid-to-late nineteenth century tended to interpret such mismatches as deficiencies – lexical gaps or redundancies – in the language of the Other, the new generation of anthropologists working after 1900 saw them in another light. One in particular, Franz Boas (1858–1942), had a very considerable impact upon linguistics in the United States. Significantly, his training at home in Germany was in physics and geography; he was largely self-taught in linguistics, which enabled him to bypass many of the unquestioned assumptions and priorities of his day. His insistence upon describing each language in terms of its own structural categories led to a focus upon painstaking descriptive work, paralleling the careful work being carried out by European dialectologists. That fidelity to the data, characterised by the search not only for the distinctive phonemic inventory and grammatical categories but also for the fundamental lexical categories of the languages under study, prepared the way both for the emphasis on discovery procedures in mid-twentieth-century American linguistics and for what is known as the Sapir–Whorf hypothesis. Perhaps the clearest formulation of this is this sentence by Edward Sapir (1884–1939), himself an anthropologist of distinction: 'We see and hear and otherwise experience very largely as we do because the language habits of our community predispose certain choices of interpretation.'[42] Further developed by Benjamin Lee Whorf, the concept of linguistic relativity harks back unconsciously to Locke and Humboldt. In its strong form (not advocated by its chief proponents) the Sapir–Whorf hypothesis appears to support a kind of linguistic determinism which matches the determinism inherent in both sides of the nature/nurture debate, an increasingly urgent subject in the mid-to-late twentieth century. Even without accepting the strong form of the hypothesis, that glimpse into different ways of thinking – which could only be researched by entering into the thought patterns of your informant, a direct challenge to the externalising and reification demanded by those who modelled their way of working upon the methods of the natural sciences – caught people's imagination. What could one *do* with this knowledge, though? The study of cross-cultural communication pioneered in Joshua A. Fishman's *ethnography of speaking* and latterly (with reference also to communication within a single language community) in *pragmatics* enables people to enter more fully into how others construct their universe – not just in terms of their cognitive categories, but also in the connections they make and their most basic assumptions about how life works. Such investigations would have been impossible without the techniques of *discourse analysis* introduced by Harvey Sacks and since greatly developed. As with sociolinguistic research into the linguistic encoding of gender, ethnicity and other markers of identity, the significance of this form of research comes from the fact that it offers us the chance to enter into discourse with the Other more consciously, and so to contribute constructively to the shaping not only of our own identity but of the Other's as well. The likelihood is that these areas of research will expand enormously in coming decades, with the emphasis increasingly falling upon the linguistic construction of identity and its relationship to the construction of reality, internal and external, through language. And with the development of these concerns will come an increasing interest in ethics, already apparent in those branches of linguistics which use experimental subjects. The ethics of researching using subjects and making that knowledge available – or withholding it – needs to be thought through carefully for every project. What are the possible consequences of our research? The comment of Enrico Fermi, a physicist working on the atom bomb in the 1940s, speaks for itself: 'Don't bother me with your conscientious scruples! After all, the thing's superb physics!'[43] Linguists do not design weapons of mass destruction, but they are potentially in a position of equal responsibility. Once we become aware of the power of what is encoded in the way we speak to alter our perception of identity – our own, our group's and that of others as well – and to manipulate those identities constructively or destructively, we are unleashing a tool which has just as much force as the Bomb, with one big difference: language can be used for good or for ill. We have the choice.

12 Becoming a historian of linguistics

12.1 Going further

So you want to go further in the history of linguistics? Good! You'll need to do a lot more reading, of course: longer surveys of the period from 1600 to the present, more detailed studies of the topics of your choice, and (last but not least) the source texts themselves. Nothing, but nothing, can replace firsthand knowledge of the original sources. You'll need to master the research techniques appropriate to the period or the topic which you wish to pursue further: paleography and textual criticism to facilitate your work with as yet unprinted medieval texts, for instance, or the bibliographical research tools that will help you to find your way through the vast literature of primary and secondary sources for any period. You'll find a guide to some of the research resources in the history of linguistics at the end of this chapter. You may need to attend specialised courses or find suitable books from which to teach yourself the necessary skills. Equally importantly, you'll need to cultivate the inner faculties a historian of linguistics needs, and think about ethics in relation to the impact of your work on others and your research methods.

12.2 Cultivating the faculties a historian needs

Right at the start of this book we thought about empathy as the fundamental attitude of mind that you need to adopt when you approach the texts of a past era. By now it will have become a habit of mind (I hope). With empathy as your fundamental attitude you can now move to cultivating the faculties which every historian of linguistics needs.

First, and most important, you need to be able to read the text before you with absolute fidelity to what it says. Easy? Just try it. How often have you opened a book without any expectations or assumptions? Just to know that what you have before you is a detective story, a cookbook, a linguistics monograph, a modistic grammar, means that you have all sorts of unconscious assumptions about the contents. That prior knowledge immediately colours the way in which we read the text. To a large extent (as Einstein said) it determines what we actually see: think of those generations of subversives who realised they could conceal their explosive message in a text ostensibly about something quite innocent. If instead they wrote a pamphlet called *Heretical Theology* or *Overthrow the State!* even the stupidest functionary would recognise it. Most of the time your prior knowledge – knowing at the outset that what you have before you is an Insular elementary grammar or a *défense et illustration* tract – serves as a shortcut and a point of orientation. Every now and then, though, it is as well to stop and ask yourself: 'How do I know that this text is what they say it is? What do I actually *see*?' You can do that at many levels. For instance, you could take half an hour to look, very carefully and precisely, at your text. Take its outer appearance first. What form does it take – hardback, paperback, book, journal, typescript, manuscript? How is it bound? What substances is it made of? How big is it? How is the text set out on the page? What visual devices are used – space, colour, different sizes of type, different typefaces? Then move to the structure of the text. What units is it divided into? How are they organised – hierarchically, alphabetically, linearly, or in some other way? Are there any clues as to why that mode of organisation has been adopted? Does the author say anything about the structure and organisation? You can do the same with the doctrine: what is the actual theme of the work? What is said about it? What concepts are used and named? How is the exposition developed? Once you have established what is actually there, you are ready for the next step: can you identify some underlying pattern, some unstated and perhaps unconscious motivation behind the phenomena you have observed? Why is it the way it is? Now, what do you base this conclusion on? You'll probably find that you are constantly comparing what you have observed in the text with your prior knowledge. The more consciously you can carry out this process, recognising when you are basing your verdict upon an observation and when you are invoking prior knowledge, or combining the two, the better founded your judgements are likely to be. The very best scholars are those who strip away the largest number of their own assumptions. (Box 12.1 will introduce you to a different way of practising this exercise.)

Observation is one vital skill that the historian needs to practise (and believe me, it doesn't come without a great deal of practice). The second vital quality, certainly for any intellectual historian, is a sensitivity to *metamorphosis*, to processes of change

---

Box 12.1 What do you see?

Here is a simple exercise – or at any rate, it looks simple. Its purpose is to help you to experience how hard it is to observe what's in front of you. Find a plant and put it on the table in front of you and a few friends. Then ask yourselves what you see. 'A plant', you'll probably all say, or 'a flower'. How do you know? Probably because of what you were told when you were very little. Try again: what do you *see*? Now it becomes more interesting. How many learnt concepts do you have to strip away to get down to the level of pure observation, to the basic data provided by your senses? And then how long can you keep going, each of you naming something new, until you run dry? Is there a point at which you find it necessary to reintroduce some of the learnt concepts? The exercise takes on new dimensions if you carry it out several times in the course of a week.

through time. We know that change is taking place constantly all around us; as Dante put it, one day you realise that the boy next door has grown up without your ever having caught him in the act of growing. Our senses provide us with a series of split-second snapshots of the present moment, snapshots that we connect using our memory and our thinking. Take the bulb that you plant in a pot: months later a green shoot appears, and after a while a leaf, and after another month, perhaps, a flower. You can't actually see the changes taking place, yet you are confident that the later stages are in some way connected with the earlier ones. Your ability to recall what the earlier stages were like, together with your ability to link them in a sequence, to identify a temporal and a causal sequence – in short, your ability to combine observation and memory with thinking – is what allows you to speak of processes occurring through time. In researching the transformation of ideas through time, or the metamorphosis of grammatical genres, you confront just such a series of snapshots, of glimpses of a point in time. It is up to you to reconstruct the process which led from one stage to the next. What needs to be in place before the later state can come about? Try taking something which belongs near the start of a series, like Donatus's *Ars minor*, and something from near the end of the series, such as one of your own school grammars. Observe the differences between them in every domain – visual presentation and layout on the page, source and target language, organisation, examples, content, metalanguage. What needs to have changed since Donatus's day to make the modern grammar possible? Is there a particular sequence in which these changes must have come about? In this example you can check your results by studying the intermediate stages (and very numerous they are too). In other cases we have far less to go on. If you need a breather from texts, you could try this exercise with almost anything: the farming practices of today compared with those of the ancient world, or the development of a musical instrument, or means of transportation and so on. If you practise this exercise from time to time you will gradually build up the sensitivity to the really important changes, of attitude and of outer circumstance, that are the precondition for the specific changes that you observe.

In practising this exercise you may also start to develop the third vital quality that the historian of linguistics needs: *a sense for when something new has arrived*. In studying metamorphosis you focus upon continuity; by looking out for possible interruptions to the natural development you cultivate an awareness of what is truly new. Take some really new idea – the very latest phonological theory, say, or the newest ideas in syntax or typology or historical linguistics – and try a thought experiment. Ask yourself what needed to be in place for that idea to be possible. What was it that made it thinkable now rather than ten years earlier, or ten years later, or a century ago? You'll probably find with practice that you cast your net more widely each time, ranging outwards from the immediate intellectual antecedents of the idea itself to the ways of thinking which underlie it and to more general cultural preconditions. You could also try it with ideas which appeared longer ago: the concept of the phoneme, for example, or social networks, or systematic phonological correspondences, or the notion of root. Ideas from other spheres are just as good for sharpening this faculty: try out globalisation, or environmental consciousness, or feminism, or Mutually Assured Destruction, or progress, or profit, or copyright, or sin, or heaven, or anything else that occurs to you. After a while you'll find that you will develop a sense for what emerges organically out of what came before and what represents something new breaking through.

12.3 Ethics and the historian of linguistics: the impact of your work

Only recently have linguists begun to realise that their work has consequences for others, and therefore that they have a responsibility to think carefully about how and why they choose their research topics and go about carrying out their research. Would you know what to do if someone you'd asked to describe their most exciting experience (in order to elicit rapid speech processes) broke down while describing an assault, clearly deeply upset and unable to cope with the resurging traumatic memories? Or if a group of young people you were interviewing started to describe a robbery they'd committed? Or if you became aware of deliberate, violent, attempts to stamp out a language variety in your research area? What would you say if you found yourself in the same position as the anthropologist Robert Chenciner was once in a village in Daghestan? When he reported his findings to his informants, telling them that their language appeared to be unrelated to any other, they said to him: 'Does that mean we should declare independence?'

Although sociolinguists have been the first to wake up to the ethical implications of their research, others are not far behind – psycholinguists, language acquisition researchers, language planners, even forensic phoneticians. Clearly, when your activities could result in changes to the education of thousands of people, or in a new set of laws that will affect people's lives on the level of day-to-day interaction, or in helping to put someone in prison, the ethical aspect is obvious. Historians of linguistics do not think of themselves as involved with the here and now in quite the same way. Only if we are researching very recent history, and some of the people we are writing about are still alive, does ethics impinge in an obvious way upon what we do. But there is another area in which our research and writing have consequences: in our readers' response.

First of all, for people in many parts of the world, history is a living part of their identity. This is so to an extent that English-speaking people often find difficult to understand, with their rather loose grasp of history and an outlook on life pervaded by the feeling that scientific and technological concerns are central and human activities and attitudes somehow less significant, arbitrary, subjective. If you, as a historian, were to suggest that someone from some other country – a minor grammarian or lexicographer, say, never mind the standardising grammarian or author of the definitive dictionary of the national language – might have been influenced by foreign ideas, you might well find that you have deeply offended your readers in that country. Perhaps, you may argue, they needed to be woken up to the truth. Perhaps so; but if they have not been properly prepared for it, how valuable an experience is it? They are unlikely to be convinced; rather, they are likely to assume that your offensive statement means that you are no longer a friend of their country. Similarly, people almost anywhere are quick to interpret a comparison, explicit or implicit, as a value judgement. If you can first persuade your readers to stand back from their own history and that of their neighbours and observe it from a distance, then you will be able to work constructively and helpfully. But that is a big task, bigger than it sounds. It involves nothing less than a transformation of consciousness, a painful process wherever and whenever it takes place. You need to bring to bear all the powers of empathy and sensitivity you can muster to write for people with a different relationship to their past.

What of people not so far from home? The dangers in national or ethnic historiography of any kind are becoming increasingly obvious, what with studies of differences – huge differences – in the way in which German, French, British, Russian and Japanese school textbooks represent the Second World War, for instance; or in traditional accounts of British activity in India versus the revisionist accounts of a new generation of both British and Indian historians; or in recent attempts to prove the Holocaust never happened. Would you expect to find the same point of view, or even the same facts, in histories of Ireland since 1968 by Protestant and by Catholic historians? Or in histories of the Middle East by a right-wing Israeli and by a left-wing Israeli or a Palestinian? Bringing people up on one version of history rather than another shapes their outlook, their perception of events (even at the basic level of what actually happened) and their significance, and the way they perceive themselves and members of other groups and interact with them. As growing numbers of people study linguistics and its history, these considerations are becoming issues for us too. Let's consider a few of the many questions that are coming to the surface.

- How are you going to portray non-European linguistic traditions? As an appendage to European and American work, something peripheral or marginal to be invoked when they impinge upon the development of western linguistics? Or are you going to try to give your readers something of a sense of their lengthy independent development and achievements? If so, do you possess the knowledge that would enable you to do so reliably, or had you better leave the task to an expert?
- How are you going to handle issues such as the role of linguists under totalitarian regimes? Language planning and educational policy are areas which have in the last 150 years given scope for increasing involvement on the part of linguists, and their work has sometimes been controversial. On the other side, linguists living under deplorable regimes may do their best to awaken their contemporaries to what is going on, or, if they do not possess the strength to take an active stand – not everyone is cut of the cloth of which heroes are made – to distance themselves inwardly from those regimes. Can you help your readers to become alive to such ethical dilemmas – dilemmas which may some day confront us?
- Even within the western tradition, similar issues of coverage are becoming more and more important. Do you have any right to gloss over pre-modern developments (and what do you mean by 'modern', exactly?), dismissing them as insignificant, if you have never looked into them? Is it right to publish a work ostensibly on the history of linguistics from the beginning when in fact you have little to say about pre-modern developments, and what little you do say is taken from secondary accounts?

12.4 Ethics in working methods

Issues for the historian of linguistics in the actual process of research come up both in the choice of topic and in the process of carrying out the research. First, choice of topic.

- Why am I choosing this topic for research?
  If your answer is 'because I've been asked to do it', think again. There are consequences on two levels: to yourself personally, and to your readers. Everything, but everything, that you put into the world has consequences. A superficial encyclopedia article that you're not ready to write, as well as overstretching you, is unlikely to bring forth any new insights and could seriously mislead your readers. A damning book review, even if it is perfectly justified, could destroy the person's career or be the last straw that leads to depression or suicide. A really boring book or article or conference paper – and there is hardly a scholar in the world who hasn't been guilty of these – can put a student or aspiring scholar off for life, drawing a dark veil of facts without insight over what should be a subject full of significance for ourselves, for what is more engrossing than reading about ourselves?

  If your answer is 'because it's there', perhaps you'd better sit down and have a think. Early on in our careers most of us snatch eagerly at any topic of research that looks available, i.e. isn't already being researched by someone else. But it shouldn't take long before you can tell the difference between some really worthwhile project which genuinely advances our understanding of human evolution, and some makework project which is neither here nor there. Supposing you decide to give a paper on some work on language you have recently come across, outlining its content and structure in considerable detail. Very well, that's the stage of observation. We all have to start with that. But if you don't go beyond that stage, giving thought to *why* this work might be significant, then your audience has every right to wonder why you are inflicting this tedious stuff upon them. And in the longer term, you will start to ask yourself that question. Very few people can go on slogging away decade after decade at something which didn't have much meaning even when they first took it up, full of beginner's enthusiasm.
- What is the wider significance of this topic?
  Does it have implications beyond its narrow confines? Almost every problem does (and if yours doesn't, why are you working on it?). What are those implications? Even if you only hint at them here and there, you'll still wake your readers up and get them thinking. You may even inspire them to go off and do a little research themselves.
- Can I write in such a way as to inspire others? Can I give others a glimpse of where we might go next, and enthuse them to work for this in their own sphere? The alternative is to aim to have the last word, killing the subject stone-dead.
- What feelings will I unleash amongst my readers?

Are they feelings that will be constructive and helpful, or are they more likely to lead to destructive thoughts and actions? If the latter, can I find a way of writing that will help people to think more constructively about this issue? If not, do I have any right to write about it? What is my motivation in doing so?
- Can I write about this topic in such a way as to help people to grasp something of the significance of human evolution on the level of thought, hopefully firing them with enthusiasm to contribute to this evolution in a positive way?

Secondly, the research process, for ethical issues come up here too.

- Have you checked to make sure no one else is working on your chosen topic? This is particularly important if it is the kind of project where it doesn't make sense to duplicate effort, such as a bibliography or an edition.
- Do you have first-hand knowledge of the sources for the developments you are writing about?
  If not, how do you know that the secondary sources you rely upon aren't distorting the reports of other secondary sources? All of us have our own horror stories of how textbook writer X took over a mistake from textbook writer Y: do you want to copy someone else's errors? Obviously there are limits to what you can verify for yourself, but the further you go before you draw the line, the more firmly based your conclusions will be.
- Have you taken other scholars' work into account and given them due credit? Prefaces and footnotes are the usual place for this. People who've helped you with statistics or bibliographical work merit a mention as much as those famous scholars with whom you had stimulating conversations. Indeed, if you've spent much time in libraries, particularly in special collections, the staff might appreciate a word of thanks. One librarian once told me that whenever a new book arrived by someone they knew, the staff turned eagerly to the acknowledgements to see whether their help had been mentioned. You'll probably be able to think of other individuals and organisations who merit a mention.
- Does your data really support the story you want to tell?
  If you are having to squeeze it and twist it to make it fit, that story may not be the right one. And if you find yourself generalising from one instance, think again. No era is ever perfectly homogeneous, and you will always find scattered instances of throwbacks to an earlier epoch, and of forerunners of what is to come.
- Is your work really ready to be published?
  You'll know when it is. Until then, you'll have a niggling feeling that it's not quite ready, that some new insight might occur to you or some book or article come your way that will change your thinking. Trust that feeling! Most scholars have a bottom drawer where they keep works that need maturing. Deadlines often – not always – have a detrimental effect upon scholarship.

To sum up, you have a responsibility, as a historian of linguistics, both to the material from the past that you work with, and to the people whose lives will be affected, however slightly, by what you write. Of course, no one can foresee all the consequences of their actions, but at least we can try! The more conscious you can become of what you are doing and its possible – and actual – effects in the world, the more responsible and the more insightful you will become, both as a historian and as a human being.

Research resources for the history of linguistics

1   **Bibliographical resources**

Annual bibliographies

These come out once a year and list articles published in a great range of journals, as well as books and monographs. To use them effectively, jot down the authors/subjects you want to look up, scan the table of contents to see how the bibliography is organised, and look your queries up in each volume, working backwards from the most recent.

- *Bibliographie Linguistique*. Covers all aspects of linguistics. The history of linguistics section is subdivided by period in the more recent volumes.
- *L'Année Philologique*. Secondary literature and new editions of Classical Greek and Latin texts, as well as sections organised by subject.
- *Medioevo Latino*. Medieval Latin material from 500 to 1300 (since 1995 goes up to 1500). Look under 'Discipline: Grammatica' and 'Filologia e letteratura: Linguistica' in the table of contents, and under the names of individual authors. The *Fortleben* ('Survival') section includes studies of the transmission and medieval use of ancient grammarians, listed by ancient author's name.
- *MLA Bibliography*. Heavily literary in orientation.

Various countries publish bibliographies devoted to their own literature which are more or less helpful on linguistic literature. In general, those linguists who played an important part in the general intellectual life of their people are likely to be well covered, whereas humble grammarians seldom get a look in.

Bibliographies in book/article form

These can be located via the annual bibliographies listed above. Since they are not regularly updated, you will need to supplement their listings by using the relevant annual bibliographies. A number of books and articles on various topics in the history of linguistics also have useful bibliographies, such as G. Lepschy, ed., *History of Linguistics*,

4 vols. in English to date (London: Longman 1994–), and S. Auroux, ed., *Histoire des idées linguistiques*, 2 vols. to date (Liège: Mardaga 1989–). A few of the various specialist bibliographies are listed below:

- B. Colombat, ed., *Corpus représentatif des grammaires et des traditions linguistiques*, 2 vols. (*Histoire Epistémologie Langage* hors-série no. 2, 1998, and no. 3, 2000). Includes brief characterisation of work and biographical data of author, details of editions, select bibliography. Invaluable starting-point! Vol. 1 contains entries on grammars of Greek, Latin, French, Spanish, Italian, Portuguese (including Brazilian grammars), Old Church Slavonic and Russian; vol. 2 covers grammars of German, English, Arabic, Hebrew, Yiddish, Sanskrit, Pali and Prakrit, Tamil, Chinese, Japanese, and major works in the history of historical and comparative philology, general linguistics, and phonetics and phonology.
- J. J. Murphy, *Medieval Rhetoric: A Select Bibliography*, 2nd edn (Toronto: University of Toronto 1989).
- V. Law, 'Grammar in the early Middle Ages: a bibliography', in her *Grammar and Grammarians in the Early Middle Ages* (London: Longman 1997), pp. 273–97, an updated version of the bibliography first published in her, ed., *History of Linguistic Thought in the Early Middle Ages*, Studies in the History of the Language Sciences 71 (Amsterdam: John Benjamins 1993), pp. 25–47.
- K. Koerner, 'Medieval linguistic thought: a comprehensive bibliography', *Historiographia Linguistica* 7 (1980), 265–99, repr. in his, ed., *Studies in Medieval Linguistic Thought Dedicated to Geoffrey L. Bursill-Hall*, Studies in the History of the Language Sciences 26 (Amsterdam: Benjamins 1980), pp. 265–99.
- M. Tavoni et al. (eds.) *Renaissance Linguistics Archive*. Lists secondary literature only, i.e. no editions (yet). Useful indices. Three volumes have appeared; rumour has it that the project has come to a halt.
- K. Koerner, 'History and historiography of phonetics: a state-of-the-art account', in his *Professing Linguistic Historiography*, Studies in the History of the Language Sciences 79 (Amsterdam: Benjamins 1995), pp. 171–202.
- V. Law, 'The writings of R. H. Robins: a bibliography 1951–1996', in V. Law and W. Hüllen (eds.), *Linguists and Their Diversions: A Festschrift for R. H. Robins on his 75th Birthday* (Münster: Nodus 1996), pp. 27–42. [An easy way to locate Robins's many historiographical writings.]

Many historians of linguistics are compulsive bibliographers, and almost any of their articles or books will provide you with copious bibliographical leads. E. F. K. Koerner and P. Swiggers stand out in this regard.

2 Catalogues of primary sources

How do you locate the works of past linguists? If you're working on a topic which involves looking at grammars, you probably won't be dealing with famous authors, so you'll find reference works like these invaluable:

- M. Passalacqua, *I codici di Prisciano* (Rome: Storia e Letteratura 1978). [Lists and describes all the extant manuscript copies of Priscian's *Institutiones grammaticae*.]
- G. L. Bursill-Hall, *A Census of Medieval Latin Grammatical Manuscripts* (Stuttgart–Bad Cannstadt: frommann-holzboog 1981). [Lists all late medieval manuscripts, from ca 1100, containing grammars and gives a summary description of their contents. Should always be checked against full manuscript catalogues or against the MSS themselves.]
- H. Gwosdek, *A Checklist of English Grammatical Manuscripts and Early Printed Grammars, c. 1400–1540* (Münster: Nodus 2000).
- R. Alston, *A Bibliography of the English Language*, 11 vols. (Leeds 1965–73).
- I. Michael, *Early Textbooks of English: A Guide* (Reading: Colloquium on Textbooks 1993).
- C. Moulin-Fankhänel, *Bibliographie der deutschen Grammatiken und Orthographielehren I. Von den Anfängen der Überlieferung bis zum Ende des 16. Jahrhunderts; II. Das 17. Jahrhundert* (Heidelberg: Winter 1994–).
- E. Stengel, *Chronologisches Verzeichnis französischer Grammatiken vom Ende des 14. Jahrhunderts bis zum Ausgange des 18. Jhs.* (Oppeln 1890, repr. Studies in the History of the Language Sciences 8, Amsterdam: Benjamins 1976).
- H.-J. Niederehe, *Bibliografía cronológica de la lingüística, la gramática y la lexicografía del español desde los comienzos hasta el año 1600* (BICRES), Studies in the History of the Language Sciences 76 (Amsterdam: Benjamins 1994).
- B. Colombat, ed., *Corpus représentatif des grammaires et des traditions linguistiques*: see section 1.

Additionally, if you're working on grammars, you may find that your university library has separate listings under the name of the language – an invaluable resource where they exist, although they tend not to be complete.

3 **Collections of texts of primary sources**

Many of the editions in the older collections have been superseded by more recent editions: use the bibliographies above and be alert to scholars' comments and bibliographical references.

- H. Keil, ed., *Grammatici Latini*, 8 vols. (Leipzig: Teubner 1855–80, repr. 1961 and 1981 by Georg Olms, Heidelberg).
  A concordance to the *Grammatici Latini* has been published by V. Lomanto and N. Marinone, *Index grammaticorum: An Index to Latin Grammatical Texts* (Hildesheim: Olms 1990): useful for terminological studies of the Late Latin grammarians.
- G. Uhlig et al., ed., *Grammatici Graeci*, 4 parts in 6 vols. (Leipzig: Teubner 1868–1910, repr. Hildesheim: Olms 1979).
- *Corpus Christianorum Series Latina* (Turnhout: Brepols): editions of patristic Latin texts, including some grammars, up to 800. To locate editions of early medieval grammatical texts, use the bibliography by Law (section 1 above).

- *Corpus Christianorum Continuatio Mediaevalis* (Turnhout: Brepols): editions of medieval Latin texts from 800 on. To locate editions of later medieval grammatical texts, use the bibliography by I. Rosier in S. Auroux, *Histoire des idées linguistiques* 2 (1991), pp. 127–9.
- Many early modern German grammars have been reprinted by Olms of Hildesheim.
- Scolar Press has brought out a series of facsimile reprints of English texts on language under the editorship of Robin Alston.

Publishers are increasingly resorting to cheaper means of reproduction than the facsimile reprint: microform (microfiche or microfilm) and CD-ROM.

- *Harmonia linguarum*: a microfiche edition of a large number of texts on the origin, history and comparison of languages, 1500–1800.
- The publishers Chadwyck-Healey have recently brought out a collection of nineteenth-century works on language in microform.

4 Biobibliographical resources

- H. Stammerjohann, *Lexicon grammaticorum* (Tübingen: Niemeyer 1996). [A biographical dictionary of linguists with brief bibliographical listings. Another useful starting-point.]
- Another biobibliographical dictionary of linguists, from the Renaissance on, is in progress under the editorship of Pierre Swiggers.
- National biographical dictionaries such as the *Dictionary of National Biography* for England can be a useful starting-point for the lives and professional contacts of post-medieval linguists, and sometimes for medieval ones as well; often they give references to other biographical sources such as obituaries which can be exceedingly difficult to track down.

5 Specialist publishers

Their catalogues, which you can access via the Internet, are a useful bibliographical resource.

- John Benjamins, Amsterdam/Philadelphia (http://www.benjamins.nl)
    Historiographia Linguistica (journal mainly in English, two issues a year).
    Studies in the History of the Language Sciences (SiHoLS) (monograph series).
- Nodus Publikationen, Münster
    (http://www.t-online.de/home/dutz.nodus/katalog.htm)
    Beiträge zur Geschichte der Sprachwissenschaft (journal, two issues a year: articles in various languages including English).
    Henry Sweet Society Studies in the History of Linguistics (monograph series).

6 Specialist journals

Articles on aspects of the history of linguistic thought are published in a *vast* range of journals on every conceivable subject (and some you wouldn't guess as well), which is why it is absolutely vital to use the annual bibliographies listed in section 1 to trace the latest publications in your area. There are, however, four journals which specialise in the history of linguistics:

- Historiographia Linguistica (predominantly in English, two issues a year).
- Histoire Epistémologie Langage (predominantly in French, two issues a year). Indices and abstracts to the years 1979–1995 are to be found in a special volume (hors-série no. 1, 1996).
- Beiträge zur Geschichte der Sprachwissenschaft (various languages, two issues a year).
- Beijing Studies in the History of Linguistics.

7 Book reviews

Reviews of books on aspects of the history of linguistics appear in *Historiographia Linguistica* and *Histoire Epistémologie Langage*, as well as in the newsletters of the national societies (section 8 below) and in countless journals dedicated to literature, linguistics, education, philosophy etc. etc.

8 Societies for the promotion of the study of the history of linguistics

It's worth joining one of the societies for the promotion of the history of linguistics, for they provide an easy way of finding out who's doing what. Unfortunately, the societies have grown up in a somewhat piecemeal way. There is no single umbrella organisation, although the three oldest national societies, listed below, have a very international, often overlapping, membership list. Apart from those listed here, there are societies in Spain, Italy, the Netherlands, Georgia and North America, and an international society devoted to the study of Hebrew linguistics. Details can be found in the various newsletters listed below.

- The Henry Sweet Society for the History of Linguistic Ideas
  This is an international society based in Britain with members working in every area of the history of linguistics, from ancient India and Graeco-Roman Antiquity to the present. Activities:
    Bulletin published twice yearly, with articles, reviews, bibliography (free to members).
    Henry Sweet Society Studies in the History of Linguistics, monograph series.
    annual conference, usually but not invariably in Britain.
    specialist library of books and offprints.
    one-third off the purchase price of all books published by Nodus Publikationen.

membership secretary/treasurer: Professor J. L. Flood, Institute of Germanic Studies, University of London, 29 Russell Square, London WC1B 5DP, e-mail: <jflood@sas.ac.uk>.
http://www.gla.ac.uk/Acad/FacSoc/hsweet.htm
http://www.henrysweet.org
- Studienkreis Geschichte der Sprachwissenschaft
An international society which caters largely for historians of linguistics in German-speaking countries and neighbouring regions. Much English is spoken!
  on-line *Rundbrief* published four times a year, with announcements of conferences and bibliography.
  at least two conferences a year, often on a designated theme, in German-speaking countries, Scandinavia, Holland.
  membership free. Contact Dr K. Dutz, Nodus Publikationen, Postfach 5725, D-48031 Münster, Germany.
  http://t-online.de/home/dutz.nodus
- Société pour l'Histoire et Epistémologie des Sciences du Langage
International membership drawn largely (but by no means exclusively) from French- and other Romance-speaking countries.
  Bulletin published twice a year, with announcements of conferences and numerous book reviews.
  Histoire Epistémologie Langage free to members.
  one-day seminars in Paris.
  e-mail notification of relevant conferences.
  contact: S. Archaimpault, SHESL – UFRL – 8e étage – Bureau 818, Case 7034, 2 place Jussieu, F-75251 Paris Cedex 05, France.
  http://www.htl.linguist.jussieu.fr

9 Conferences

Apart from the meetings organised by the societies listed above, and by the smaller national societies, there are occasional specialist conferences dedicated to a particular theme which are usually advertised through the newsletters of the various societies. Students are always welcome at any history of linguistics conference, and often there is a reduced registration fee for them. The big event in the history of linguistics calendar is the triennial International Conference on the History of Linguistics/the Language Sciences (ICHoLs), usually alternating between the Americas and the rest of the world.

The Henry Sweet Society holds a three-day meeting, usually in southern England, every September except in ICHoLs years, when it holds a one-day meeting in London at Easter.

Notes

Preface

1 P. Schmitter, 'Zurück zum Historismus? Bemerkungen und Daten zu einigen gegenwärtigen Tendenzen in der Historiographie der Linguistik', in E. Feldbusch et al., eds., *Neue Fragen der Linguistik. Akten des 25. Linguistischen Kolloquiums, Paderborn 1990 I. Bestand und Entwicklung* (Tübingen: Niemeyer 1991), pp. 23–9.

1   Getting ready to study the history of linguistics

1 Yakov Malkiel and Margaret Langdon, 'History and histories of linguistics', *Romance Philology* 22 (1969), 530–74, at pp. 532f.
2 *The Rigveda: An Anthology*, transl. Wendy D. O'Flaherty (Harmondsworth: Penguin 1981), p. 80 (I.164.45).
3 'The Theology of Memphis' (Egyptian Creation myth), in James B. Pritchard, transl., *Ancient Near Eastern Texts Relating to the Old Testament*, 3rd edn (Princeton, NJ: Princeton University Press 1969), pp. 4–6, at p. 5.

2   Greek philosophy and the origins of western linguistics

1 *Iliad* I 207–8.
2 Plato, *Meno* 86C (translated following W. K. C. Guthrie, transl., *Plato, Protagoras and Meno* (Harmondsworth: Penguin 1956)).
3 Aristotle, *Nicomachean Ethics* 1109b, transl. J. A. K. Thomson (Harmondsworth: Penguin 1976), p. 110.
4 Astyanax: *Cratylus* 392DE; Atreus: *Cratylus* 395B; *anthrōpos*: *Cratylus* 399C; *sōma*: *Cratylus* 400C; foreign words: *Cratylus* 409D–410A; language change, e.g. *Cratylus* 418B–D; sound symbolism: *Cratylus* 426C–427C; *sklērotēs*: *Cratylus* 434CD–E.
5 Aristotle, *Nicomachean Ethics* 1094b, transl. J. A. K. Thomson, p. 65.
6 The four causes are discussed repeatedly by Aristotle, e.g. at *Physics* II 3.
7 Aristotle, *De interpretatione* I 1.
8 Aristotle, *De interpretatione* I 2.
9 Aristotle, *De interpretatione* I 3.
10 Aristotle, *Categories* c. 4.
11 Aristotle, *Poetics* c. 21–2; *Rhetoric* 1410a; Gorgias: *Rhetoric* 1406b, transl. W. Rhys Roberts, repr. in Jonathan Barnes, ed., *The Complete Works of Aristotle* II (Princeton, NJ: Princeton University Press 1984), p. 2250.
12 Aristotle, *Poetics* 20.

Box Source

Box 2.5 Plato, *Sophist* 261E–262C, transl. H. N. Fowler (Cambridge, MA: Harvard University Press 1921).

3 Towards a discipline of grammar: the transition from philosophy

1 Diogenes Laertius, *Lives of Eminent Philosophers*, transl. R. D. Hicks, 2 vols. (Cambridge, MA: Harvard University Press 1925), VII 55–6. I have used my own renderings of the three terms discussed.
2 Augustine on Varro: *De civitate Dei* VI ii.
3 Varro, *De lingua latina*, transl. Roland G. Kent, 2 vols. (Cambridge, MA: Harvard University Press 1938), V 12–13. I use my own translation here.
4 Varro on the four causes of linguistic change: *De lingua latina* V 6.
5 *oppidum*: Varro, *De lingua latina* V 141.
6 Varro, *De lingua latina* V 7–8, translated following Kent; Wilhelm Pfaffel, *Quartus gradus etymologiae: Untersuchungen zur Etymologie Varros in De lingua latina*, Beiträge zur klassischen Philologie 131 (Königstein/Ts: Hain 1981); see also his article 'Wie modern war die varronische Etymologie?', in Daniel J. Taylor, ed., *The History of Linguistics in the Classical Period*, Studies in the History of the Language Sciences 46 (Amsterdam: Benjamins 1987), pp. 207–28; and in Historiographia Linguistica 13 (1986), 381–402.
7 Varro, *De lingua latina* X 60.
8 Varro, *De lingua latina* VIII 9–12 and X 17, following Kent.
9 Artemidorus: Varro, *De lingua latina* VIII 21.
10 Varro, *De lingua latina* X 43–4.

Box Source

Box 3.2 Diogenes Laertius, *Lives of Eminent Philosophers* VII 48, transl. R. D. Hickes (Cambridge, MA: Harvard University Press 1925), p. 159.

4 From literacy to grammar: describing language structure in the ancient world

1 Plato, *Cratylus* 424C.
2 *Tekhnē grammatikē* c. 1.
3 P. Yale 1.25, ed. Alfons Wouters, *The Grammatical Papyri from Graeco-Roman Egypt. Contributions to the Study of the 'Ars grammatica' in Antiquity*, Verhandelingen van de Koninklijke Academie voor Wetenschappen, Letteren en Schone Kunsten van België, Klasse der Letteren 41, no. 92 (Brussels: Paleis der Academiën 1979), pp. 49–52.
4 Horace, *Epistolae* II i 156.
5 Karl Barwick, *Remmius Palaemon und die römische ars grammatica*, Philologus Supplementband 15.2 (Leipzig: Dieterich 1922), repr. Hildesheim: Olms 1967), p. 11.
6 Sergius, *De littera*, GL IV 475, 7–9.
7 Varro, *De lingua latina* VIII 1.
8 Donatus, *Ars minor*, ed. Louis Holtz, *Donat et la tradition de l'enseignement grammatical* (Paris: CNRS 1981), pp. 585,7–587,29.
9 Nicodemus Frischlin, *Poppysmus Grammaticus* (Prague: Michael Peterle 1587), pp. 40f.
10 Winston S. Churchill, *My Early Life: A Roving Commission* (London: Collins 1930), ch. 1.
11 Donatus, *Ars maior*, ed. L. Holtz (see above), 615,1–617,7.
12 Pompeius, *Commentum artis Donati*, GL V 137,2–10.
13 Servius, *Commentarius in artem Donati*, GL IV 406,22–33.
14 Consentius, *Ars*, GL V 353, 27–8.
15 Priscian, *Partitiones*, ed. Marina Passalacqua, *Prisciani Caesariensis Opuscula* (Roma: Storia e Letteratura 1999), 103,20–104,2, replacing GL III 497, 11–19.
16 Priscian, *Institutio de nomine*, ed. M. Passalacqua, as above, 5,3–6,6, replacing GL III 443,2–14.

Box Source

Box 4.15 Priscian on transitive and reflexive sentences: GL 3.15,9–16; on intransitive sentences: GL 3.32,23–7.

5 Christianity and language

1 Genesis 2:19–20: Scriptures quoted from the Youth Bible, New Century Version (Anglicised Edition) copyright © 1993 by Nelson Word Ltd, 9 Holdom Ave., Bletchley, Milton Keynes MK1 1QR, UK.
2 Genesis 11:1–9: Scriptures quoted from the Youth Bible, as above.
3 *Commentaire d'Išoʿdad de Merv sur l'ancien testament* 1. *Genèse*, transl. C. Van den Eynde, Corpus Scriptorum Christianorum Orientalium 156, Scriptores Syri 75 (Louvain: Durbecq 1955), p. 150 [on Gen. 11: 8–9].
4 Acts of the Apostles 2:1–11: Scriptures quoted from the Youth Bible, as above.
5 Augustine, *Tractatus in Iohannis evangelium* VI 10; sermon 271.
6 John 1:1–2 and 23: King James Bible, slightly modified.
7 Augustine, *De Trinitate* XV x–xi.
8 Augustine, sermon 288. A complete translation of this sermon, updating references to languages, is to be found in *The Works of Saint Augustine* III/8 (273–305A) on the Saints, transl. Edmund Hill (Hyde Park, NY: New City 1994), pp. 110–16.
9 Augustine, *De quantitate animae* XXXI 66.
10 Isidore, *Etymologiae* XI i 14.

Box Source

Box 5.7 Augustine, *De dialectica*, ed. Jan Pinborg and transl. B. Darrell Jackson (Dordrecht and Boston: Reidel 1975). c. 5 (pp. 86–91).

6 The early Middle Ages

1 Unprinted Latin text in St Gall, Stiftsbibliothek, 230, p. 550, with emendations from London, British Library, Cotton Nero A II, ff. 33v–34v.
2 Qiriath-sepher: Joshua 15:15, Judges 1:11.
3 Sergius, *De littera*, GL IV 475, 5–9.
4 Hermann Hagen, *Anecdota Helvetica* (Leipzig: Teubner 1870, repr. Hildesheim: Olms 1961, 1981 [=Grammatici Latini 8]), 302, 1–11.
5 *Magnus quae uox*, unprinted text in Munich, Bayerische Staatsbibliothek, Clm 14737, ff. 159v–160r.
6 *Scholia Vaticana*, ed. A. Hilgard, *Grammatici Graeci* 1.3 (Leipzig: Teubner 1901, repr. Hildesheim: Olms 1979), 197,33–198,6.
7 Smaragdus, *Liber in partibus Donati*, ed. B. Löfstedt, L. Holtz and A. Kibre, *Corpus Christianorum Continuatio Mediaevalis* 68 (Turnhout: Brepols 1986), 6,18–7,27.
8 Quoted from René Guerdan, *Byzantium: Its Triumphs and Tragedy* (New York: Capricorn 1957), p. 49.
9 *Declinationes nominum*, unprinted text quoted from Munich, Bayerische Staatsbibliothek, Clm 6281, f. 108v.
10 The Christian *Ars minor*: V. Law, 'Erchanbert and the interpolator: a Christian *Ars minor* at Freising (Clm 6414)', in V. Law, ed., *History of Linguistic Thought in the Early Middle Ages*, Studies in the History of the Language Sciences 71 (Amsterdam: Benjamins 1993), pp. 223–43.
11 Asporius: *Ars Asperi grammatici*, ed. H. Hagen, *Anecdota Helvetica*, as above, pp. 39–61.
12 Tatwine: *Ars Tatuini*, ed. Maria De Marco, Corpus Christianorum Series Latina 133 (Turnhout: Brepols 1968), 1–93.

13 Boniface, *Ars grammatica*, ed. G. J. Gebauer and B. Löfstedt, *Corpus Christianorum Series Latina* 133B (Turnhout: Brepols 1980), 13–99.
14 Naples, Biblioteca Nazionale, lat. 1, f. 28vb.
15 Paris, Bibliothèque Nationale, lat. 13025, f. 41vb and f. 41va.

Box Sources

Box 6.2 Boniface, Letter 91; cf. also Letters 75 and 76; Bede, *Libri II De Arte Metrica et De Schematibus et Tropis; The Art of Poetry and Rhetoric*, Latin text and English translation by Calvin B. Kendall (Saarbrücken: AQ 1991), pp. 169, 199; I Kings 18:27: Scriptures quoted from the Youth Bible, as above.
Box 6.3 *Virgilio Marone grammatico, Epitomi ed Epistole*, ed. and transl. Giovanni Polara and L. Caruso (Naples: Liguori 1979), Epistola III 1, 7–9 (p. 228); Sergilius: unprinted text quoted from Leiden, Bibliotheek der Rijksuniversiteit, BPL 135, ff. 71v and 73r.
Box 6.4 Translation of Virgilius Maro Grammaticus, *Epitoma* IV 280–96, quoted with a minor modification from V. Law, *Wisdom, Authority and Grammar in the Seventh Century: Decoding Virgilius Maro Grammaticus* (Cambridge: Cambridge University Press 1995), p. 70.
Box 6.5 *Anglo-Saxon Conversations: The Colloquies of Ælfric Bata*, ed. Scott Gwara and transl. David W. Porter (Woodbridge: Boydell 1997), p. 85f.
Box 6.6 *Ars Iuliani Toletani episcopi*, ed. M. A. H. Maestre Yenes (Toledo: Instituto Provincial de Investigaciones y Estudios Toledanos 1973); text quoted by kind permission of the Master and Fellows from Trinity College, Cambridge, R.9.11 (815), f. 151v.

7 The Carolingian Renaissance

1 *Cunabula grammaticae artis Donati*, MPL 40, 613C.
2 defectiveness: Priscian, *Institutiones grammaticae*, GL II 369,18–373,8; time and tense: ibid. 404,24–406,11.
3 Donatus, *Ars maior*, ed. L. Holtz, as above, 614, 2–3.
4 Priscian, *Institutiones grammaticae*, GL II 56,29–57,1.
5 Porphyry, *Isagoge* c. II; cf. also c. VII.
6 Leiden, Bibliotheek der Rijksuniversiteit, Voss. lat. O.88 (Fleury, s. ix^2), f. 7v.
7 Donatus, *Ars maior*, ed. L. Holtz, as above, 632, 5–6.
8 Peter of Pisa, *Ars*, transl. quoted with minor modifications from V. Law, *Grammar and Grammarians in the Early Middle Ages* (London: Longman 1997), p. 139.
9 Marius Victorinus, *De definitione*, MPL 64, 891–910.
10 Sedulius Scottus, *In Donati artem maiorem*, ed. Bengt Löfstedt, Corpus Christianorum Continuatio Mediaevalis 40B (Turnhout: Brepols 1977), 64, 16–23.
11 Alcuin, *Dialogus Franconis et Saxonis de octo partibus orationis*, MPL 101, 854–902, at 874 AB.
12 Priscian, *Institutiones grammaticae*, GL II 56,29–57,1.
13 Eriugena, *Septem periochae*, ed. Anneli Luhtala, 'Early medieval commentary on Priscian's *Institutiones grammaticae*', *Cahiers de l'Institut du Moyen Age Grec et Latin* 71 (2000), 115–88, at pp. 158–9.
14 *Distributio omnium specierum nominum inter cathegorias Aristotilis*, ed. James C. King and Petrus W. Tax, *Notker der Deutsche: Die Werke. 7. Die kleinere Schriften* (Tübingen: Niemeyer 1996).

Box Source

Box 7.6 Alcuin, *Dialogus Franconis et Saxonis*, PL 101, 854CD; Remigius, *Commentum in Donati artem maiorem*, ed. H. Hagen, *Anecdota Helvetica* (=GL 8, Leipzig: Teubner 1880), pp. 219–74, at p. 221; Thierry of Chartres, *Lectiones in Boethii librum De Trinitate* IV 19, ed. Nikolaus

M. Häring, *Commentaries on Boethius by Thierry of Chartres and His School* (Toronto: Pontifical Institute of Mediaeval Studies 1971), p. 192.

8 Scholasticism: linking language and reality

1 Porphyry, *Isagoge* c. 1.
2 Priscian, *Institutiones grammaticae*, GL III 135, 7–9.
3 Abelard, *Theologia scolarium*, PL 178, 1307A.
4 Aristotle, *Physics* II 2.
5 Aristotle, *Physics* III 1.
6 *Regimina*, ed. Jan Pinborg, *Remigius, Schleswig 1486: A Latin Grammar in Facsimile Edition with a Postscript*, Det Kongelige Danske Videnskabernes Selskab, Historisk-filosofiske Meddelelser 50.4 (Copenhagen: Munksgaard 1982), pp. 29–32, at p. 30.
7 *Viginti quatuor sunt iuncturae: A Medieval Latin Grammatical Text with Translation and a Critical Study*, ed. András Cser (Pázmány Péter Katolikus Egyetem, Bölcsészettudományi Kar: Piliscsaba 2000), p. 9. (I have used my own translation.)
8 Robert Grosseteste, *De generatione sonorum*, ed. Ludwig Baur, *Die philosophischen Werke des Robert Grosseteste, Bischofs von Lincoln* (Münster: Aschendorff 1912), pp. 7–10.
9 '*Tractatus de grammatica*': *Eine fälschlich Robert Grosseteste zugeschriebene spekulative Grammatik*, ed. Karl Reichl (Munich: Schöningh 1976), c. 4.
10 The articulation of l: Oxford, Bodleian Library, Digby 55 (s. xiii), f. 127ra.
11 Magister Jordanus, ed. Mary Sirridge, 'Notulae super Priscianum minorem Magistri Jordani, partial edition and introduction', *Cahiers de l'Institut du moyen âge grec et latin* 36 (1980), p. 5.
12 William of Conches: *Wilhelm von Conches, Philosophia*, ed. Gregor Maurach (Pretoria: University of South Africa 1980), IV 59 (p. 116).
13 Priscian, *Institutiones grammaticae*, GL II 55,6–56,17.
14 Petrus Helias, *Summa super Priscianum*, ed. Leo Reilly, Studies and Texts 113 (Toronto: Pontifical Institute of Mediaeval Studies 1993), 2, p. 881,60–2; p. 881,62–7 and 71–2 and 882,92–4.
15 *Promisimus*, ed. K. M. Fredborg, *Cahiers de l'Institut du moyen âge grec et latin* 70 (1999), 111.
16 'The commentary on "Priscianus Maior" ascribed to Robert Kilwardby', ed. K. M. Fredborg, N. J. Green-Pedersen, L. Nielsen and J. Pinborg, *Cahiers de l'Institut du moyen âge grec et latin* 15 (1975), at p. 120.
17 Martin of Dacia, *Modi significandi*, ed. Heinrich Roos, *Martini de Dacia Opera* (Copenhagen: Gad 1961), pp. 1–118, at I i 4–6.
18 Martin of Dacia, *Modi significandi* I iv 11–1.
19 Martin of Dacia, *Modi significandi* I xxiv.
20 Pseudo-Kilwardby, *Super Priscianum maiorem* 99, quoted by Irène Rosier, ' "O magister...": grammaticalité et intelligibilité selon un sophisme du XIIIe siècle', *Cahiers de l'Institut du moyen âge grec et latin* 56 (1988), 1–102, at p. 26 n. 70.
21 William of Ockham, *Summa logicae*, ed. Philotheus Boehner, Gedeon Gál, Stephen Brown (St Bonaventure, NY: Institutum Franciscanum Universitatis S. Bonaventurae 1974), I iii.
22 Alexander of Villa Dei, *Doctrinale*, ed. D. Reichling, *Das Doctrinale des Alexander de Villa-Dei: Kritisch-exegetische Ausgabe* (Berlin: A. Hofmann 1893), lines 295–99.
23 *Ridmus Donati*, Worcester, Cathedral Library, Q.50 (s. xiii), f.46v.
24 *Exercitium puerorum grammaticale per dietas distributum* (1485; Cambridge University Library Inc. 4.A.4.24 (4185) [Cologne: Quentell 1499]), f. a.iij.v.

Box Sources

Box 8.1 Leiden, Bibliotheek der Rijksuniversiteit, BPL 91 (s. xii^1), f. 177r (this portion is in a hand of the thirteenth or fourteenth century); Hans Walther, *Carmina medii aevi posterioris latina II/4. Proverbia sententiaeque latinitatis medii aevi* (Göttingen: Vandenhoeck & Ruprecht 1966), no. 24333 (p. 213).

Box 8.3 Avendeuth: S. van Riet, ed., *Avicenna Latinus, Liber de anima seu Sextus De naturalibus I–II–III* (Louvain: Peeters and Leiden: Brill 1972), p. 95*.
Box 8.4 Brugge, Stadsbibliotheek, MS 536 (s. xii–xiii), f.1ra.

9 Medieval vernacular grammars

1 Dante, *De vulgari eloquentia* I i.
2 Ælfric, ed. J. Zupitza, *Aelfrics Grammatik und Glossar* (Berlin: Weidmann 1880, repr. 1969), pp. 1 and 3.
3 Excerpts reproduced from the translations in V. Law, *Grammar and Grammarians in the Early Middle Ages* (London: Longman 1997), pp. 206–13.
4 Erika Ising, *Die Anfänge der volkssprachlichen Grammatik in Deutschland und Böhmen I. Quellen* (Berlin: Akademie-Verlag 1966), p. 24.
5 *Informacio*, Text X, ed. David Thomson, *An Edition of the Middle English Grammatical Texts* (New York and London: Garland 1984), p. 111.
6 *First Grammatical Treatise: The Earliest Germanic Phonology*, ed. and transl. Einar Haugen (London: Longman 1972), p. 15; p. 17.
7 Serlo of Wilton, *De differentiis*, ed. Jan Öberg, *Serlon de Wilton, Poèmes latins*, Studia Latina Stockholmiensia 15 (Stockholm: Almqvist & Wiksell 1965), pp. 79–88.
8 *Las Flors del Gay Saber estier dichas Las Leys d'Amors*, Monumens de la Littérature Romane, ed. Adolphe Felix Gatien-Arnoult, 3 vols. (Toulouse: Paya 1841–3), vol. 3, p. 382.
9 *Leys d'Amors*, ed. Gatien-Arnoult, vol. 2, p. 126; cf. *Las Leys d'Amors*, ed. Joseph Anglade, 4 vols. (Toulouse: Privat 1919–20), vol. 3, p. 60.

10 The Renaissance: discovery of the outer world

1 Juan Luis Vives, *De causis corruptarum artium (De disciplinis)* II ii, ed. Gregorio Mayáns, *Joannis Ludovici Vivis Valentini Opera omnia* (Valencia: Monfort 1782–90, repr. London: Gregg 1964), VI 88.
2 Alexander Hegius, *Invectiva in modos significandi*, ed. J. Sewin, 'Alexander Hegius († 1498) Invectiva in modos significandi: text, introduction and notes', *Forum for Modern Language Studies* 7 (1971), 299–318, at p. 306, 14–20.
3 Cochleus, *Grammatica Io. Cochlei Norici Rudimenta ad usum latinę linguę necessaria continens* (Strasbourg: Beck 1514), Prologue.
4 Dante, *De vulgari eloquentia*, I i.
5 Dante, *De vulgari eloquentia*, I ix.
6 Cicero, *De finibus bonorum et malorum* I 3 [10].
7 Geoffroy Tory, *Champ Fleury*, transl. George B. Ives (New York: Grolier Club 1927), p. 11.
8 Conrad Gesner, *Mithridates* (Zurich: Froschouer 1555), f. 8v.
9 Antonio de Nebrija, *Gramatica castellana* (Salamanca: s.i. 1492), ff. a.iii v–a.iiii r.
10 Leon Battista Alberti, *Regole della lingua fiorentina*, ed. Giuseppe Patota, *Leon Battista Alberti, Grammatichetta e altri scritti sul volgare* (Rome: Salerno 1996), p. 15 (§1).
11 Alberti, *Regole della lingua fiorentina* (as above), pp. 17 (§6); 25 (§47); 26 (§48); 28 (§49).
12 *The Works of William Bullokar II. Pamphlet for Grammar 1586*, ed. J. R. Turner (The University of Leeds, School of English 1980), p. 44. (I have modernised Bullokar's individualistic orthography.)
13 Sēpher Yetsīrāh II 3.
14 Elias Levita, *Grammatica Hebraica absolutissima (Sēpher ha-diqdūq, 1518)*, in the Latin translation by Sebastian Münster (Basel: Frobenius 1525).
15 Pellikan: Ludwig Geiger, 'Zur Geschichte des Studiums der hebräischen Sprache in Deutschland', *Jahrbücher für deutsche Theologie* 21 (1876), 190–223, at pp. 203–12; this passage is to be found at pp. 208f.
16 Johannes Reuchlin, *De rudimentis hebraicis* (Pforzheim: Anshelm 1506), pp. 582f.

Box Sources

Box 10.2 Joachim von Sandrarts Academie der Bau-, Bild- und Mahlerey-Künste von 1675, ed. A. R. Peltzer (Munich: Hirth 1925), p. 209.
Box 10.3 Quoted by Maria Leonor Carvalhão Buescu, *O estudo das línguas exóticas no século XVI* (Instituto de Cultura e Língua Portuguesa 1983), pp. 39f.
Box 10.9 *Ājurrūmiyya: Einleitung in das Studium der arabischen Grammatiker. Die Ajrūmiyyah des Muhᶜammad bin Daūd*, ed. and (German) transl. Ernst Trumpp (Munich: K. Akademie 1876), pp. 2–6.
Box 10.11 Levita transl. Münster, *Compendium hebraicae grammaticae ex Eliae Iudaei uarijs & optimis libris per Sebastianum Munsterum concinnatum: & iam denuo auctum & recognitum* (Basel: Froben 1529), f. b2rv.

11 A brief overview of linguistics since 1600

1 Georgius Stiernhielm, *D. N. Jesu Christi SS. Evangelia ab Ulfila . . . translata* (Stockholm: Wankif 1671).
2 Claudius Salmasius, *De hellenistica commentarius* (Leiden: Elsevier 1643).
3 Sámuel Gyarmathi, *Affinitas linguae hungaricae cum linguis fennicae originis grammatice demonstrata* (Göttingen: Dieterich 1799), transl. V. E. Hanzeli, *Grammatical Proof of the Affinity of the Hungarian Language with Languages of Fennic Origin*, Amsterdam Classics in Linguistics 15 (Amsterdam: John Benjamins 1983).
4 The figure of 140 paintings of Babel is taken from Sten Karling, *The Stockholm University Collection of Paintings* (University of Stockholm 1978), p. 74, reporting the work of Helmut Minkowski, *Aus dem Nebel der Vergangenheit steigt der Turm zu Babel* (Berlin, 1960).
5 Sanctius, *Minerva* (Salamanca: J. et A. Renaut 1587), I i.
6 John Ray, letter of 7 May 1669, translated by Charles E. Raven, *John Ray, Naturalist: His Life and Works* (Cambridge University Press 1950), p. 182, from the Latin original in Edwin Lankester, ed., *The Correspondence of John Ray* (London: The Ray Society 1848), p. 41.
7 [Nicolas Beauzée,] 'Grammaire', in Diderot and d'Alembert, ed., *Encyclopédie, ou Dictionnaire raisonnée des sciences, des arts et des métiers* (Paris: Briasson, David, Le Breton, Durand 1765), 7:841–7, at p. 842.
8 A Society of Gentlemen in Scotland, 'Grammar', *Encyclopædia Britannica; or, a Dictionary of Arts and Sciences, Compiled upon a New Plan* (Edinburgh: Bell and Macfarquhar 1771), 2:728–45, at p. 728.
9 John Locke, *An Essay concerning Human Understanding* (London: Holt 1689/90), repr. (of 4th edn) P. H. Nidditch (Oxford: Clarendon 1975), III v 8 (pp. 432f.).
10 James Harris, *Hermes: or a Philosophical Inquiry Concerning Language and Universal Grammar* (London: Bolas 1751), III v.
11 Gabriel Girard, *Les vrais principes de la langue françoise: ou la parole réduite en méthode, conformément aux loix de l'usage* (Paris: Le Breton 1747), repr. ed. P. Swiggers (Geneva: Droz 1982), pp. 23f.
12 Johann Gottfried Herder, *Ideen zur Philosophie der Geschichte der Menschheit* (Riga and Leipzig: Hartknoch 1784–91), transl. T. Churchill, *Outlines of a Philosophy of the History of Man* (London: J. Johnson 1800), IX ii.
13 Friedrich von Schlegel, *Über die Sprache und Weisheit der Indier: Ein Beitrag zur Begründung der Alterthumskunde* (Heidelberg: Mohr & Zimmer 1808), transl. by Ellen J. Millington (London: Bohn 1849), both repr. by E. F. K. Koerner and S. Timpanaro, Amsterdam Classics in Linguistics 1 (Amsterdam: Benjamins 1977), p. 28.
14 Wilhelm von Humboldt, 'Über den Nationalcharakter der Sprachen' (fragment of ca 1822), in Albert Leitzmann, ed., *Wilhelm von Humboldt, Werke IV* (Berlin: B. Behr 1905), pp. 420–35, at p. 430.
15 'Über das vergleichende Sprachstudium in Beziehung auf die verschiedenen Epochen der Sprachentwicklung' (1820), *Werke* IV, pp. 1–34, §1.
16 'Versuch einer Analyse der Mexikanischen Sprache' (not later than 1821), *Werke* IV 233–84, at p. 242.

17 'Latium und Hellas oder Betrachtungen über das classische Alterthum', Werke III (1904), pp. 136–70, at p. 170.
18 Humboldt, *Plan einer vergleichenden Anthropologie* (1795), Werke I (1903), pp. 377–410, §§1, 7, 2.
19 'Über das vergleichende Sprachstudium in Beziehung auf die verschiedenen Epochen der Sprachentwicklung' (1820), Werke IV, pp. 1–34, §§19 and 20.
20 Ibid. §20.
21 *Über die Verschiedenheit des menschlichen Sprachbaues und ihren Einfluß auf die geistige Entwickelung des Menschengeschlechts* (Berlin: F. Dümmler 1836, repr. in Werke VII.1 [1907], at p. 42), at p. liii; transl. Peter Heath, *On Language: The Diversity of Human Language-Structure and its Influence on the Mental Development of Mankind* (Cambridge University Press 1988), at p. 46.
22 'Versuch einer Analyse der Mexicanischen Sprache' (not later than 1821), Werke IV, pp. 233–84, at p. 246.
23 Franz Bopp, letter to K. J. Windischmann of 21 November 1829, in S. Lefmann, *Franz Bopp, sein Leben und seine Wissenschaft*, 3 vols. (Berlin: Georg Reimer 1891), vol. 1, p. 81*.
24 Bopp, *Über das Conjugationssystem der Sanskritsprache in Vergleichung mit jenem der griechischen, lateinischen, persischen und germanischen Sprache* (Frankfurt am Main: Andreas 1816, repr. Foundations of Indo-European Comparative Philology 1 [London and New York: Routledge 1999]), p. 96. In the English translation (*Analytical Comparison of the Sanskrit, Greek, Latin and Teutonic Languages, Showing the Original Identity of their Grammatical Structure* [1820], repr. Amsterdam Classics in Linguistics 3 (Amsterdam: John Benjamins 1974)) this passage is substantially recast.
25 Bopp, *Vergleichende Grammatik des Sanskrit, Zend, Griechischen, Lateinischen, Litthauischen, Gothischen und Deutschen* (Berlin: Dümmler 1833–52, repr. Foundations of Indo-European Comparative Philology 10–11 [London and New York: Routledge 1999]), transl. by Lieutenant Eastwick, *A Comparative Grammar of the Sanscrit, Zend, Greek, Latin, Lithuanian, Gothic, German, and Sclavonic Languages*, 3 vols. (London: Madden and Malcolm 1845–50).
26 Bopp, letter to K. J. Windischmann of 14 September 1815, ibid., I p. 29*.
27 Jacob Grimm, *Deutsche Grammatik* (Göttingen: Dieterich 1819, repr. Foundations of Indo-European Comparative Philology 4 [London and New York: Routledge 1999]), p. xvi, 2nd edn, 4 vols. (Göttingen: Dieterich 1822–65, repr. Foundations of Indo-European Comparative Philology 6 [London and New York: Routledge 1999]), vol. 1, p. vi.
28 Heymann Steinthal and Moritz Lazarus, 'Einleitende Gedanken über Völkerpsychologie, als Einladung zu einer Zeitschrift für Völkerpsychologie und Sprachwissenschaft', *Zeitschrift für Völkerpsychologie und Sprachwissenschaft* 1 (1860), 1–73, at p. 15, repr. in W. Bumann, *Heymann Steinthal: Kleine sprachtheoretische Schriften* (Hildesheim and New York: Olms 1970), pp. 307–79, at p. 321.
29 Ludwig Tobler, 'Versuch eines Systems der Etymologie mit besonderer Rücksicht auf Völkerpsychologie', *Zeitschrift für Völkerpsychologie und Sprachwissenschaft* 1 (1860), 349–87, esp. pp. 363–81.
30 August Schleicher, *Compendium der vergleichenden Grammatik der indogermanischen Sprachen*, 2 vols. (Weimar: Böhlau 1861-2); transl. by Herbert Bendall, *A Compendium of the Comparative Grammar of the Indo-European, Sanskrit, Greek and Latin Languages* (London: Trübner 1874–7).
31 Schleicher, *Die Sprachen Europas in systematischer Übersicht* (Bonn: König 1850), Amsterdam Classics in Linguistics 4 (Amsterdam: John Benjamins 1983), esp. ch. IV.
32 Schleicher, *Die Darwinsche Theorie und die Sprachwissenschaft* (Weimar: Böhlau 1863), transl. A. V. M. Bikkers, *Darwinism Tested by the Science of Language* (London: Hotten 1869), Amsterdam Classics in Linguistics 6 (Amsterdam: John Benjamins 1983), p. 27; French transl. by de Pommayrol (1868) repr. by Patrick Tort, *Evolutionnisme et linguistique suivi de August Schleicher, La théorie de Darwin et la science du langage; De l'importance du langage pour l'histoire naturelle de l'homme* (Paris: Vrin 1980).
33 Schleicher, *Über die Bedeutung der Sprache für die Naturgeschichte des Menschen* (Weimar: Böhlau 1865), p. 28. A short excerpt, which includes this sentence, is repr. in H. Junker, *Sprachphilosophisches Lesebuch* (Heidelberg: Winter 1948), pp. 186–91, at p. 191. See previous note for a French translation.

34 Wilhelm Scherer, *Zur Geschichte der deutschen Sprache* (Berlin: Duncker 1868), repr. Amsterdam Classics in Linguistics 16 (Amsterdam: John Benjamins 1995).
35 Georg Curtius, 'Bemerkungen über die Tragweite der Lautgesetze, insbesondere im Griechischen und Lateinischen', *Berichte über die Verhandlungen der Königlich Sächsischen Gesellschaft der Wissenschaften zu Leipzig*, philologisch-historische Classe, 22 (1870), 1–39, at p. 2, repr. in his *Kleine Schriften* 2, ed. E. Windisch (Leipzig: Hirzel 1886), pp. 50–94, at p. 52.
36 Karl Brugman, 'Vorwort', in Hermann Osthoff and Karl Brugman, *Morphologische Untersuchungen auf dem Gebiete der indogermanischen Sprachen* 1 (Leipzig: Hirzel 1878), iii–xx, at p. xii, transl. by Winfred P. Lehmann, *A Reader in Nineteenth-Century Historical Indo-European Linguistics* (Bloomington and London: Indiana University Press 1967), pp. 197–209, at p. 204, quoted here with modifications.
37 Brugman, 'Vorwort' p. xiii, transl. Lehmann, p. 204 (I have used my own translation for this passage).
38 Georg von der Gabelentz, *Die Sprachwissenschaft: Ihre Aufgaben, Methoden und bisherigen Ergebnisse* (Leipzig: Weigel Nachfolger 1891, repr. Tübingen: Narr 1969, 1972, 1984).
39 Antoine Meillet, *Linguistique historique et linguistique générale* (Paris: Champion 1921), p. 16.
40 Louis Gauchat, 'L'unité phonétique dans le patois d'une commune', in *Aus romanischen Sprachen und Literaturen: Festschrift Heinrich Morf . . . dargebracht* (Halle a.d. Saale: Niemeyer 1905), pp. 175–232.
41 William Labov, *The Social Stratification of English in New York City* (Washington, DC: Center for Applied Linguistics 1966), pp. 8–13.
42 Edward Sapir, 'The status of linguistics as a science', *Language* 5 (1929), 207–14, at p. 210, repr. in David G. Mandelbaum, ed., *Edward Sapir: Selected Writings in Language, Culture, and Personality* (Berkeley and Los Angeles: University of California Press 1949), pp. 160–6, at p. 162.
43 Fermi is quoted by Robert Jungk, *Brighter Than a Thousand Suns: A Personal History of the Atomic Scientists* (Harmondsworth: Penguin 1960), p. 184.

Index

Aachen 140
Abelard 163, 165
Abraham ben Meir de Balmes 246
Abraham Ibn Ezra 246
Abu al-Walīd Marwān ibn Janāh 246
Academy, The, of Plato, 18
Adamnán of Iona 141
Ælfric of Eynsham 127, 145, 192, 193–5, 260; Latin grammar of, 193–5, 260; use of *Excerptiones de Prisciano* in, 145, 191, 194; glossary of, 193, 260; colloquy of, 193
Ælfric Bata 127
Aeschylus 15, 16, 21, 54
Aesop 63
Æthelwold, bishop of Winchester 193, 194
affix, concept of the, 249–50
Agen 220
Akkadians 13, 14
al-Fārābī 243
al-Jurjānī 243
al-Mubarrad 242
Albania, Albanian language of, 218, 235
Alberti, Leon Battista 233, 234, 235–6, 237, 239
Albertus, Laurentius 234
Albi 201; Albigensian Crusade of, 201, 202
Alcuin of York 140, 141, 145, 146, 147, 148, 151, 193, 259; *Dialogus Franconis et Saxonis* of, 145, 146, 151–2, 153–4
Aldhelm 145, 193
Aletius (Francesco Maria da Lecce) 235
Alexander the Great 23, 53
Alexander of Ville-Dieu 229; *Doctrinale* of, 180–1, 191, 227
Alexandria, school of, 52–5, 60
Alfred, king of England, 193, 194

Alvarus, Emmanuel, *De institutione grammatica* of, 181, 238
Ambrose, St, 96, 98, 126
Amerbach, Johannes 228
Amerindian languages 218, 270; Tarascan, 219; Quechua, 219; Tupi, 219; Massachusett, 219; Cree, 219
Anderson, Benedict 274
Anonymus Bobiensis 66
Anselm of Bec 163
Apollonius Dyscolos 89, 166, 228
Arabia 105, 214; Arab peoples, 10, 52, 53, 149, 164, 242; Arabic language, 149, 219, 241, 242, 245
Aramaic language 95, 124
Arator 82
Aristarchus 54, 55, 58
Aristophanes of Byzantium 54, 55
Aristotle 20, 21, 23–6, 28–9, 31–2, 38, 42, 52, 91, 112, 115, 143, 147, 149, 150, 154, 155, 158, 161, 162, 165, 168, 171, 179, 210, 223, 230, 242, 259, 263; *Categories* of, 31, 112, 147, 149, 155, 162, 164; *De interpretatione* of, 28, 32, 59, 112, 147, 149, 151, 154, 155, 162, 164; *Organon* of, 27, 149; Ethics of, 20, 24; Physics of, 162, 165–7; Metaphysics of, 24, 112, 162, 171; Rhetoric of, 31–2, 64; Poetics of, 32–3, 59
Arivillius, E. O. 235
Armenia 53; Armenian language, 124, 218; Armenian commentary on the *Tekne*, 191
Arnaud, Antoine 264
Asporius (Asperius, Asper) 130; *Ars* of, 66
Assyrians 13, 14
Athanasius 98
Athens 17, 18, 31, 38–9, 43, 58, 62
Audax 62, 143; *Excerpta* of, 66

Augustine, St, 41, 43, 62, 96, 98, 100, 101–2, 104, 105–7, 109, 140, 259; *De magistro* of, 100, 107; *De doctrina Christiana* of, 99; *Ars breviata* of, 66, 143; pseudo-Augustine *Regulae*, 85, 143, 227
Auraceipt na nÉces (Old Irish grammatical treatise) 192
Austria 124
Avendeuth 164
Avicenna 164
az-Zajjajai, author of *Kitāb al-jumal*, 242

Babel, Tower of: *see under* Bible
Babylonia 104; Babylonian peoples, 13, 14
Bacon, Roger 177, 245
Badius, Jossius 228
Baghdad 14, 149
Barcelona 128
Barros, João de 233
Barton, Johan 192; use of the *Donait françois*, 192
Basel 223, 228
Basil the Great 98
Basque language 218, 234, 270
Beauzée, Nicolas 264
Beck, Cave 263
Bede 94, 115, 116–17, 141, 193, 194; *De schematibus et tropis* of, 116
Beduin, language of, 52
Beijing 108
Bellay, Joachim du 233; *Deffence et illustration de la langue françoyse*, 232
Bembo, Pietro 232, 233
Benedictine Rule 140, 141
Bengali language 218, 219, 242
Berber language 218, 242
Bible 82, 94, 95, 97, 99, 101, 115, 116, 121, 124, 128, 140, 141, 146, 193, 245; Vulgate (Latin) translation of, 82, 95; King James (English) translation of, 95; biblical exegesis, 99–101, 115; myth of Adam and language, 101–2; myth of the Tower of Babel, 101–2, 104, 105, 190, 260, 262
Boas, Franz 274
Bobbio 135
Boccaccio 49, 224, 225, 232
Boethius 147, 149, 161, 168, 178; *De trinitate* of, 151; *De consolatione Philosophiae* of, 149; Latin translations of Aristotle, 149, 162
Boethius of Dacia 174
Bohemia 1, 125; Czech language of, 125, 234
Böhme, Jacob 263
Bohorič, Adam 234
Bologna 214
Boniface, St, 116, 131

Bonifacio Calvo of Genoa 202
Bopp, Franz 267–8, 269
Botticelli, Sandro 214, 217
Braune, Wilhelm 271
Breedon-on-the-Hill 131
Breton language 218, 235
Brugman, Karl 271
Bruni, Leonardo 233
Bulgarian language 262
Bullokar, William 234, 237–8, 239–41
Burgundy 130

Caelius Sedulius 82
Cairo 149
Calcidius 162
Cambridge 158, 160
Campanella, Tommaso 263, 264
Canterbury 158
Caramuel y Lobkowitz, Juan 263, 264
Carew, Richard 233
Carthage 42, 82, 98, 106; *see also* Punic language
Cassiodorus 149
Catalonia 202; Catalan language, 201, 235
Cathars 201
cathedral schools 158
Catholicon 227
Catullus 225
Caucasian languages 14
Caxton, William 128
Celtic languages 261
Cerne Abbas (Dorset) 193
Chamberlayne, John 218
Charisius 62, 86; *Ars grammatica* of, 66
Charlemagne 140, 141, 146, 150
Chartres 158
Cheremis language 218
China 1, 142; Chinese language 77, 218, 219
Chomsky, Noam 3, 39, 108, 177, 246, 258, 272
Christianity 94–111, 124, 164, 259; as a religion of the book, 95; and language teaching, 100–1; and orthodoxy, 96; and ecclesiastical hierarchy, 97
Chrysippus 40
Chrysoloras, Manuel 225
Churchill, Winston 73
Cicero 43, 58, 63, 64, 79, 81, 82, 161, 225, 226, 229, 231, 232; *Rhetorica ad Herennium* attributed to, 64
Cledonius 81
Clement of Alexandria 96
Clenard, Nicolas, *Tabula in grammaticen hebraeam* of, 247
Cochleus, Johannes 229
Colet, John 238, 239

Coluccio Salutati 224–5
Consentius 83; *Ars de nomine et verbo* of, 66
Constantine the Great 96
Constantinople 53, 83, 86, 96, 124, 125, 143, 225
Coptic language 124
Corbie 135, 158
Cordoba 149, 246
Cornish language 218, 235
Crates of Mallos 60
Crinesius, Christophorus 250
Croatian language 234
Curtius, Georg 271
Cuvier, Georges 266, 268
Czech language: *see* Bohemia

Dalgarno, George 263
Dante 3, 190, 232, 262, 278; *De vulgari eloquentia* of, 230, 233
David Qimhi, author of *Sepher Mikhlol*, 246
Declinationes nominum 126, 128–9, 130, 135
Denmark, Danish language of, 235
Despauterius, Johannes, *Commentarii grammatici* of, 181, 238
Deventer 227
dialectic 26–8, 32, 38, 41, 64, 91, 101, 125, 147, 148, 150, 153, 155, 160; *see also* logic
Diocles the Magnesian 40
Diogenes Laertius 38, 39
Diomedes 62, 71, 86, 227, 229; *Ars grammatica* of, 66
Dionysius Thrax 54–6, 121; *see also Tekhnē grammatikē*
Dionysius, the pseudo- 27, 154
Donatus, Aelius 56, 59, 65–80, 83, 86, 87, 90, 112, 116, 121, 126, 130, 143, 145, 153, 161, 203, 229; *Ars minor* of, 65, 66–8, 70–5, 80, 83, 85, 126, 127, 128, 129, 141, 148, 180, 181, 197, 238; *Ars maior* of, 65, 66, 67, 68–70, 79, 90, 100, 118, 151, 153, 200, 278; commentary on Terence of, 66; commentary on Vergil of, 66; vernacular versions of, 191, 200; Old French *Donats*, 191; Icelandic version, 200; commentators on, 127; *and see* Servius, Sergius, Pompeius, Cledonius
Dositheus 143; *Ars grammatica* of, 66
Dubois, Jacques (Jacobus Sylvius) 220
Dunstan, archbishop of Canterbury, 194
Dürer, Albrecht 214, 215
Dutch language 234, 265; Medieval Dutch, 268

Edgar, king of England 194
Edward VI, king of England 238

Egypt, ancient, 9–10, 13, 15, 53, 55, 56, 89; papyrus finds from, 55–6; Great Pyramid at Gizeh, 15; *and see also* Coptic language, Ethiopic language
Einstein, Albert 5, 276
Elamites 13, 14
Elias Levita 243–4, 246, 249; *Sēpher ha-Diqdūq* of, 246
Elstob, Elizabeth 260
England 1, 83, 125, 185, 190, 233, 238; English language of, 3, 59, 77, 231, 232, 234, 237–8, 245, 265; Old English, 3, 125, 132, 145, 192, 193–5, 196, 260, 268; Middle English, 190, 191, 196, 268; Anglo-Norman French of, 190
Estienne, Henri 228, 229
Estienne, Robert 228
Estonia, Estonian language of, 234, 261
Ethiopic language 218, 219
Eton College 238
etymology 44–5, 46, 55, 83, 102, 176–7
Euclid 161
Euripides 15, 20, 54
Europe 1, 3, 212, 214, 217, 219; Renaissance in, 1, 24, 25, 32, 49, 94, 101, 109, 144, 210–57, 260; Reformation in, 100, 247
Eustatievici, Dimitrie 235
Eutyches 143, 227; *Ars de verbo* of, 85
Exercitium puerorum grammaticale 185
Eynsham 193

Fabricius, Hieronymus de Aquapendente (Girolamo Fabrici d'Acquapendente) 223
Fiellström, Petrus 235
Filelfo, Francesco 235
Finnish language 234, 261
Finno-Ugrian languages 261
Fleury 158
Florence 27, 214, 225
Fragmentum Bobiense 85
France 1, 124, 158, 181, 185, 190, 201, 228, 233; French language of, 3, 59, 77, 220, 228, 231, 234, 236, 245, 262; Old French, 190, 191
Freising 158
Frischlin, Nicodemus 73
Frisian language 235; Old Frisian, 268

Gabelentz, Georg von der 272
Galen 230
Gauchat, Louis 273
Geneva 228
Gentile da Cingoli 174
Georgia 53; Georgian language of, 124, 218, 219, 268

Gerard of Huy 245
Germany 1, 124, 125, 181, 185, 190, 229, 268; Germanic languages, 125, 260, 261, 268; German language, 3, 59, 234, 245, 261, 265, 270; Old High German, 125, 155, 194, 268; Middle High German, 190, 268; Early New High German, 197; Old Saxon, 268; *see also* Gothic
Gesner, Conrad 218, 223, 232
Ginneken, Jacobus von 272
Girard, Abbé Gabriel 265
Glosulae in Priscianum 163
Gothic language 124, 260, 261, 268; *see also* Germany
grammar, as intellectual discipline, 29, 38, 40, 41, 52, 54, 62, 81, 100, 101, 109, 125, 146, 150, 162, 235–6; grammar books, 3, 59, 63, 126; of *Schulgrammatik* type, 65, 68, 70, 83, 86, 88, 143, 179; of *regulae* type, 83–6, 87, 88, 143, 179, 227, 259; parsing grammars, 87, 114, 145, 148; elementary grammars (Insular type), 114, 130–1, 141, 143, 145, 180, 191, 193, 259, 277; verse grammars, 180–2, 259; vernacular grammars, 190–209, 232–7; grammar faculties, at Oxford and Cambridge, 160; *and see also* Speculative grammar; Modistic grammar
Greece, ancient 3, 10, 13–33, 83, 96, 148, 210, 265; medieval, 225; Greek colonies in southern Italy, 43; ancient Greek language, 3, 29, 30, 52, 53, 54, 59, 71, 73, 89, 98, 124, 190, 245, 261, 268, 270; modern Greek language, 234, 265; learning of Greek in the Latin West, 225
Gregory the Great 98
Gregory of Nazianzus 98
Gregory of Nyssa 96, 125
Grimm, Jacob 268, 269
Grimm, Wilhelm 268
Grosseteste, Robert 164, 169, 170, 171, 201, 225, 245; *De generatione sonorum* of, 169
Guaraní language 218, 219
Gutenberg, Johannes 128, 228
Gyarmathi, Sámuel 261

Hadrian's Wall 83
Harris, James 265
Harris, Zellig 272
Harvey, William 223
Hebrew language 3, 95, 104, 106, 128, 149, 190, 241, 243–50, 261, 270; medieval Hebrew grammars, 241
Hegius, Alexander 225

Helwig, Christoph 263, 264
Henry of Avranches 181
Henry of Hessen 245
Heraclitus 17, 19, 20, 22
Herder, Johann Gottfried 266, 268
Hermagoras 64
Hermogenes 64
Herodian 88
Herodotus 15, 20
Hervás y Panduro, Lorenzo 218
Hesiod 54; *Theogony* of, 16
Hickes, George 260
Hildegard of Bingen 170
Hittites 13
Hjemslev, Louis 273
Hockett, Charles 108
Homer 9, 15, 53, 54, 65, 225; *Iliad* of, 15, 53; *Odyssey* of, 15, 53
Horace 58, 63, 141
Hugo of Saint-Victor 166
Hugutio 227
Humanists 224, 227, 229, 233, 247; and printing, 228, 232; in Italy, 225; in Holland, 227; in England, 238; in Spain, 236–7; *and see also* Europe, Renaissance in
Humboldt, Wilhelm von 226–7, 268, 269
Hungary 83, 124, 125, 225; Hungarian language of, 125, 128, 234, 261
Hurrians 13
Hussey, Bonaventure 235

Ibn Ājurrūm 242, 243; *Ājurrūmiyya* of, 243
Ibn Mālik 243
Ibn Jinni 243
Iceland 199; Icelandic language of, 218, 235, 260; Old Icelandic (Old Norse), 3, 191, 199–200, 268; *First Grammatical Treatise* in, 192, 199–201, 241; *Third Grammatical Treatise* in, 191; *Fourth Grammatical Treatise* in, 191
India 1, 9, 52, 53, 72, 214, 267, 280; *and see also* Benghali language, Sanskrit
Indo-European languages 14, 77, 250, 261, 267, 268, 269, 270, 271
Ingush language 218
International Phonetic Alphabet 39
Inuit language 29, 219
Iona 141, 144
Iraq 14, 53, 246
Ireland 125, 130, 136, 140, 141, 154, 280; Irish language, 235; Old Irish, 125, 191
Isabella, queen of Spain, 233, 236
Isidore of Seville 101, 108, 149
Islam 52, 53, 95, 242

Isoʿdad of Merv 104
Italy 1, 17, 42, 94, 96, 128, 135, 140, 146, 149, 158, 190, 201, 225, 229, 233, 243; Italian language of, 3, 230–1, 234, 235, 245; Tuscan dialect of, 233, 236

Jakobson, Roman 273
James of Venice 164, 225
Japan, Japanese language of, 219
Javanese language 218
Jerome, St, 66, 82, 95, 96, 98, 140; Vulgate (Latin) translation of Bible of, 82; glossary of Hebrew proper names, 245
Jerusalem 104, 124
Jesuits: *see* Society of Jesus
Jews 10, 104, 128, 164, 243, 247, 250; *and see* Hebrew language, Judaism
Johannes of Dacia 174
Johannes (Jean) Josse de Marvilla 174, 182
John the Baptist 105–6, 107
John Chrysostom 96, 98
John of Cornwall 197
John of Garland 181, 227
John Scottus Eriugena 27, 154–5, 259; *Periphyseon* of, 154; commentary on Priscian of, 154–5
Jónsson, Runólfr 235
Jordanus, Magister 171
Judaism 95, 96
Julian of Toledo 128
Juvenal 63, 141
Juvencus 82

Kamchatka, language of 218
Kašić, Bartol 234
Kazakh language 262
Keil, Heinrich 229
Kennedy, Benjamin Hall 238
Kievan Rus': *see* Russia
Kilwardby, Robert 170, 177
Klein, Daniel 235
Koran: *see* Qur'ān
Kurdish language 218, 219

Labov, William 273–4
Lancelot, Claude 264; *Nouvelle méthode pour apprendre facilement la langue latine* of, 181
Lanfranc Cigala 202
language in relation to the external world 17–18, 158–85, 210, 212–13, 220–3, 258–9; and empiricism, 220–3, 259, 261; and universals, 158, 178
Laon 158
Lapp (Sami) language 218, 235, 261

Lascaris, Constantine 225
Latin language 3, 43–9, 59, 69, 70–5, 77–8, 87–8, 120, 121, 124, 125, 130, 143, 145, 160, 162, 190, 230–1, 233, 245, 259, 260, 261, 262–3, 270; Church Latin, 226; Vulgar Latin, 82; Medieval Latin 226; as a foreign language 125–6, 259
Latvian language 234
Lazarus, Moritz 269
Leibniz, Gottfried Wilhelm 28
Leiden 214
Leipzig, university of, 271
Leo III, pope, 140
Leonardo da Vinci 214
Lelond, John 197–8
Leys d'Amors (Occitan treatise) 192, 201–4
Lhuyd, Edward 235, 260
Liberal Arts (Seven) 3, 64, 100, 101, 149, 161, 166
libraries, medieval, 112, 114, 129, 144
Lily, William 238, 239
Linacre, Thomas 220
Lindisfarne 144
linguistics, historical, as a scholarly discipline, 1–10, 272–5, 276–9; ethical implications of, 279–83; sociolinguistics, 273–4; anthropological linguistics, 274–5; pragmatics, 275; discourse analysis, 275
Lisbon 158
literacy 52, 196–7
Lithuanian language 235
Livy 141
Locke, John 264–5; *Essay concerning Human Understanding* of, 264, 265
Lodwick, Francis 263
logic 26–7, 28–9, 31, 38, 109, 147, 149, 155, 161, 162, 168, 242; *logica vetus*, 162, 164; *logica nova*, 162, 163; *see also* dialectic
Lorrain, Claude 215
Low Countries 1, 140, 181, 185; *see also* Dutch language, Frisian
Lucan 63
Ludolf, Heinrich Wilhelm 235
Lyceum, school of Aristotle, 24
Lyon 228

Macedonia 23, 53
Magyars 144
Malagasy language 218
Malay language 218, 219, 242; Malayo-Polynesian group of languages, 268
Malkiel, Yakov 4
Manx language 218
Manutius, Aldus 228

Maori language 219
Marcus Aurelius 38
Marsilio Ficino 27, 225
Martial 114
Martianus Capella 85, 101, 103, 149; De nuptiis Philologiae et Mercurii of, 85, 101
Martin of Dacia 174, 175–6
Masoretes 246
Matthew of Bologna 174
Maunoir, Julien 235
Mauretania 86
Megiser, Jerome 218
Meillet, Antoine 273
Mercia 131
Mersenne, Marin 263
metalanguage, grammatical 10, 58, 80, 86, 99, 131–2, 136, 145, 198–9; metalinguistic discourse, 30, 54, 79, 83, 107, 153, 154
metaphor, Aristotle's definition of, 32
Michel de Marbais 174
Mithraism 95
modi significandi 172–7, 227
Modists (modistae) 174, 259, 264; Modistic grammar, 173–7
Molinier, Guilhem 193, 202–4, 241
Molnár, Albert 234
monasteries (monasticism) 114, 140, 144, 158; dissolution of monasteries in England, 144
Monte Cassino 43, 225
Montpellier 214, 223
morphology, inflectional 86, 88, 109, 129, 132, 134, 136, 143, 179, 180, 248–9, 250, 259, 267, 271; root, concept of the, 245, 247–8, 249–50; morpheme, concept of the, 68, 80, 131; affix, concept of the, 249–50
Muhammad 242
Muller, Andreas 218
Münster, Sebastian 249
Murethach 154
Muslims 164

Naples 158, 246
Nebrija, Antonio de 233, 234, 236–7, 239; Introducciones Latinae, 236; Gramatica castellana, 236
'Neogrammarians' 258, 271, 272
Neoplatonism 27, 100, 154, 162, 225
Nominalists 162, 178
Northumbria 146
Norway, Norwegian language of, 235
Notker the German 155
Nursling (Hants) 131

Occitan language 3, 190, 201, 202–4; see also Provence
Oihenart, A. 234
Oliveira, Fernão de 234
Optát, Beneš 234
Origen 96
Orléans 158
Ossetic language 218
Osthoff, Hermann 271
Ostiak language 218
Ovid 114, 141
Oxford 196, 245, 247, 263; university of, 158, 160, 166, 169, 170, 178

Padua 214, 220, 223, 246
Palaemon, Remmius 60, 67, 143; pseudo-Palaemon, Regulae 85, 143, 227
Palestine 83, 246
Palsgrave, John 234
paper, use of in printing, 142, 185, 228
Papias 227
papyrus 55–6, 67, 148
parchment 142, 144, 228
Paris 177, 196, 199, 214, 228, 247; Notre-Dame de Paris, 158; university of, 158, 166, 174, 220
Parma 146
Paternoster 217–18
Paul, Hermann 271–2
Paulus Diaconus 140
Pellikan, Konrad 247
Permian language 218
Persia 53; Persian peoples 13, 15; Persian language, 219, 242, 261, 265
Peter Lombard 161
Peter of Pisa 140, 148, 150–2, 248
Petraeus, Eskil 234
Petrarch 224, 225, 232
Petrus Helias 173, 180; Summa super Priscianum of, 172–3, 180, 183
Petrus Riga 180
Phocas 143, 227, 229; Ars de nomine et verbo of, 85
phoneme 278; phonemic writing systems, 9, 201
phonetics 9, 109, 166, 168–71, 200–1, 223, 270; phonology, 9, 109, 250, 271
Phrygian language 261
Pico della Mirandola 225
Pindar 54
Plato 17–23, 24, 26, 30, 33, 38, 42, 43, 44, 45, 46, 100, 101, 147, 161, 162, 210, 259; Meno of, 18; Theaetetus of, 19, 30; Cratylus of, 19–23, 44, 52, 55, 147, 225; Phaedo of, 19; Timaeus of, 162
Plotinus 27, 162

Poconchi language 218
Poggio Bracciolini 225, 235
Poland, Polish language of, 125, 218, 234
Pompeius 81–2, 100, 120
Pontoppidan, Erik 235
Porphyry 27, 162; Isagoge of, 27, 147, 149, 150, 154, 160, 164
Port-Royal, school of, 264
Portius, Simon 234
Portugal 124, 215, 233
pre-Socratic philosophers 17; see also Heraclitus; Pythagoras
predication 29–31, 167–8
Priscian 45, 59, 71, 86–8, 100, 129, 143, 153, 161, 163, 165, 166, 182, 229, 230; Institutio de nomine et pronomine et verbo of, 85, 87–8, 112, 130; Institutiones grammaticae of, 59, 66, 69, 86, 88–91, 112, 128, 145–7, 153, 154, 158, 162, 163, 172, 173, 174–80, 182, 183, 194, 202, 237; Partitiones of, 86–7, 112, 148; Priscianus minor, 165
Proba 82
Probus 86; Instituta artium of, 66, 134; Catholica of, 85
Prometheus, myth of, 16
Prophiat Duran (Isaaq ben Moses) 246
Protagoras 19, 20
Provence 192–3, 201–2; see also Occitan
Ptolemy 161
Punic language 106
Putsch, Helias 227, 229
Pythagoras 3, 15, 17, 42, 43, 44, 46, 48, 161

Quintilian 60, 62, 64, 224, 232, 236; Institutio oratoria of, 60, 64, 225
Qur'ān 52, 242

Radulphus Brito 174
Raphael, painter of The School of Athens, 23
Realists 162, 173, 178
Reichenau 145, 158
Rehehausen (Reichhusen), J. G. 234
Reims 158
Reisch, Gregorius, Margarita philosophica nova of, 161
Remigius of Auxerre 143, 151
Renaissance: see under Europe
Reuchlin, Johannes 247–8; De rudimentis hebraicis of, 247
rhetoric 31–2, 38, 41, 58, 60, 62, 64, 100, 101–2, 116, 125, 161, 168
Rhodes 58, 62
Rig Veda 9
Robert, Gruffydd 234
Romance languages 3, 4

Rome 3, 42, 47, 53, 58, 60, 82, 96, 104, 125, 140, 141; Roman empire, 83, 94, 96, 140, 265
root, concept of the: see morphology
Rumanian language 235
Russia, Russian language of, 235, 245, 265; Kievan Rus', 53; see also Slavonic, Old Church

Sa'adyah Gaon 246
Sacerdos 78, 86; Artes grammaticae of, 66
Sacks, Harvey 275
Salisbury 158, 196
Sallust 63
Sanctius (Francisco Sánchez de las Brozas) 262, 264; Minerva of, 262–3
Sandart, Joachim von 215
Sanskrit 52, 267, 268, 270; see also India
Sapir, Edward 275
Sappho 54
Saragossa 246
Sard language 218
Saumaise (Salmasius), Claude 261
Saussure, Ferdinand de 151, 152, 177, 258, 272, 273, 274
Scaliger, Joseph Justus 229
Scaliger, Julius Caesar 220, 223
Scandinavia 125; Old Norse language of, 125
Scaurus 143; Ars grammatica of, 66
Scherer, Wilhelm 270, 271
Schlegel, Friedrich von 266
Schleicher, August 269, 270
Scholasticism 158–85, 259
Scotland 83; Scots Gaelic language, 235
'Scythian' language: see Indo-European languages
Sedulius Scottus 143, 152–3, 154; commentary on Donatus Ars maior of, 152
Semitic languages 14
Seneca 161
Senisfredo, Raymundo 128
Sēpher Yetsīrāh 241
Sergilius 120
Sergius 81, 227; De littera of, 118
Serlo of Wilton 180, 201; De differentiis of, 180, 201
Servius 82, 227; commentary on Vergil of, 81; commentary on Donatus, Ars maior of, 81
Seville 82
Shaw, William 235
Sibawayhi, al-Kitāb of, 242
Sicily 164
Sievers, Eduard 271
Siger of Courtrai 174

sign, theories of, 151, 163, 169, 177, 178, 265; *and see also modi significandi*
Simon of Dacia 174
Singhalese language 218
Slavonic, Old Church 124, 261; treatise *On the Eight Parts of Speech* in, 191
Slovene language 234
Smaragdus of Saint-Mihiel 115, 121; *Liber in partibus Donati* of, 121
Society of Jesus (Jesuits) 219
Socrates 17, 18, 19, 20, 22, 44, 52, 64, 148, 210, 259
Somner, William 260
Sophists 17, 19, 64
Sophocles 15, 20
Sordello of Mantua 202
Spain 1, 60, 124, 140, 164, 232, 246; Spanish language of, 3, 233, 234, 236–7
Speculative grammar 151, 166, 171, 172–3, 177, 178, 183, 203
Spieghel, Hendrick 234
St Gall 144, 155, 158, 225
Stahl, Henricus 234
Statius 63
Statorius, Petrus (Piotr Stojeński) 234
Steinthal, Heymann 269, 270, 271
Stiernhielm, Georg 260–1, 270
Stoics 38–42, 43, 54, 57–8, 60, 69, 89, 151
Sturlason, Snorri 200; *Prose Edda* of, 200
Suetonius 60, 141; *De grammaticis et rhetoribus* of, 60, 225
Sumerians 13; language of, 14
Sweden 1; Swedish language of, 235, 260
Switzerland 124
syntax 89–91, 109, 145, 166–8, 171, 220, 265
Syracuse (Sicily) 17
Syriac language 124, 149, 191, 242, 245, 250

Tagalog language 219
Tannen, Deborah 274
Tatar language 218
Tatwine 131
Tekhnē grammatikē 55–7, 59, 65, 121; Byzantine commentaries on, 121; Syriac version of, 191; Armenian commentary on, 191
Telugu language 218
Terence 63, 66, 114
Terramagnino of Pisa 202
Tertullian 96, 98, 126
textual criticism 53–4
Thai language 218, 262

Theodore Gaza 225, 228
Theodoric, Ostrogothic king of Italy, 149
Theodulf of Orléans 140
Thierry of Chartres 151–2
Thomas Aquinas 94
Thomas of Erfurt 174
Tobler, Ludwig 269
Tibetan language 218
Tibullus 225
Toledo 149, 164, 246
Torah 10, 241, 245
Tory, Geoffroy 228, 232
Toulouse 158, 201, 202
Tours 145, 146
Tungus language 218
Turkey 53, 83; Ottoman Turks, 225; Turkish language of, 218, 219, 242

Uc Faidit 192, 202; *Donatz Proençals* of, 192, 202
Ukrainian language 234
Ullastra, Josep 235
universities 94–5, 115, 158, 164, 182, 203
Urdu language 219, 242
Ursus of Benevento 145
Uzbek language 242
Uževyč, J. 234

Valdés, Juan de 233; *Diálogo de la lengua* of, 232
Valla, Lorenzo 230, 235, 262; *Elegantiae de lingua latina* of, 230
Varro, M. Terentius 42, 43–9, 60, 65, 69, 77, 227, 228, 229; *De lingua latina* of, 43–9, 70, 89, 112, 225
Venice 228
Vergil 43, 63, 66, 79, 83, 141; *Aeneid* of, 81, 86, 148
Veronese, Guarino 229, 233
Vesalius, Andreas 220
Victorinus, Marius 62, 66, 150, 152
Victorinus, [Maximus] 66
Vidal, Raimon 202; *Razos de trobar* of, 202
Vietnamese language 218, 219
Vikings 144, 193, 199
Virgilius Maro Grammaticus 120, 122, 145
Vitruvius 224
Vives, Luis 227
Vossius, Gerard 168

Walahfrid Strabo 145
Wales, Welsh language of, 218, 234
Wearmouth-Jarrow 116, 141, 144
Wend language 235

Whewell, William 17
Whitney, William Dwight 270
Whorf, Benjamin Lee 275
Wilkins, John 263–4
William of Conches 163, 172
William of Moerbeke 164
William of Ockham 178; *Summa logicae* of, 178–9

Windischmann, K. J. 267
Wundt, Wilhelm 272

Yakut language 218
Yehudah ben David Hayyūj 246
York 146

Zeno of Citium 38